Ransoming, Captivity & Piracy in Africa and the Mediterranean

The Harriet Tubman Series on the African Diaspora

Paul E. Lovejoy and Toyin Falola, eds., *Pawnship, Slavery and Colonialism in Africa*, 2003.

Donald G. Simpson, *Under the North Star: Black Communities in Upper Canada before Confederation (1867)*, 2005.

Paul E. Lovejoy, *Slavery, Commerce and Production in West Africa: Slave Society in the Sokoto Caliphate*, 2005.

José C. Curto and Renée Soulodre-La France, eds., *Africa and the Americas: Interconnections during the Slave Trade*, 2005.

Paul E. Lovejoy, *Ecology and Ethnography of Muslim Trade in West Africa*, 2005.

Naana Opoku-Agyemang, Paul E. Lovejoy and David Trotman, eds., *Africa and Trans-Atlantic Memories: Literary and Aesthetic Manifestations of Diaspora and History*, 2008.

Boubacar Barry, Livio Sansone, and Elisée Soumonni, eds., *Africa, Brazil, and the Construction of Trans-Atlantic Black Identities*, 2008.

Behnaz Asl Mirzai, Ismael Musah Montana, and Paul E. Lovejoy, eds., *Slavery, Islam and Diaspora*, 2009.

Carolyn Brown and Paul E. Lovejoy, eds., *Repercussions of the Atlantic Slave Trade: The Interior of the Bight of Biafra and the African Diaspora*, 2010.

Ute Röschenthaler, *Purchasing Culture in the Cross River Region of Cameroon and Nigeria*, 2011.

Ana Lucia Araujo, Mariana P. Candido and Paul E. Lovejoy, eds., *Crossing Memories: Slavery and African Diaspora*, 2011.

Edmund Abaka, *House of Slaves and "Door of No Return": Gold Coast Castles and Forts of the Atlantic Slave Trade*, 2012.

Christopher Innes, Annabel Rutherford, and Brigitte Bogar, eds. *Carnival: Theory and Practice*, 2012.

Paul E. Lovejoy and Benjamin P. Bowser, *The Transatlantic Slave Trade and Slavery*, 2012.

Joel Quirk and Darshan Vigneswaran, eds., *Slavery, Migration and Contemporary Bondage in Africa*, 2013.

Hakim Adi, *Pan-Africanism and Communism: The Communist International, Africa and the Diaspora, 1919-1939*, 2013.

Bruce L. Mouser, *American Colony on the Rio Pongo: The War of 1812, the Slave Trade, and the Proposed Settlement of African Americans, 1810-1830*, 2013.

Paul E. Lovejoy and Suzanne Schwarz. *Slavery, Abolition and the Transition to Colonialism in Sierra Leone*, 2015.

Dario Euraque and Yesenia Martinez. *The African Diaspora in the Educational Programs of Central America*, 2016.

Paul E. Lovejoy and Vanessa S. Oliveira, eds. *Slavery, Memory, Citizenship*, 2016.

Harriet Tubman Series

Ransoming, Captivity & Piracy in Africa and the Mediterranean

Edited by
Jennifer Lofkrantz and Olatunji Ojo

AFRICA WORLD PRESS
TRENTON | LONDON | CAPE TOWN | NAIROBI | ADDIS ABABA | ASMARA | IBADAN | NEW DELHI

AFRICA WORLD PRESS
541 West Ingham Avenue | Suite B
Trenton, New Jersey 08638

Book design: Dawid Kahts
Cover Design: Ashraful Haque

Library of Congress Cataloging-in-Publication Data
Names: Perspectives on Historical and Contemporary Ransoming Practices (2014: York University (Toronto, Ont.)) | Lofkrantz, Jennifer, 1975- editor. Ojo, Olatunji, editor.
Title: Ransoming, captivity & piracy in Africa and the Mediterranean / edited by Jennifer Lofkrantz and Olatunji Ojo.
Other titles: Ransoming, captivity and piracy in Africa and the Mediterranean
Description: Trenton, New Jersey : Africa World Press, 2016. | "This volume arises from a conference, "Perspectives on Historical and Contemporary Ransoming Practices," that was held at the Harriet Tubman Institute for Research on Africa and its Diasporas at York University on April 25-26, 2014."--Preface. | Includes bibliographical references and index.
Identifiers: LCCN 2016020335| ISBN 9781569024911 (hb : alk. paper) | ISBN 9781569024928 (pb : alk. paper)
Subjects: LCSH: Ransom--Africa, North--History--Congresses. | Ransom--Africa, West--History--Congresses. | Ransom--Mediterranean Region--History--Congresses. | Piracy--Africa, North--History--Congresses. | Piracy--Africa, West--History--Congresses. | Piracy--Mediterranean Region--History--Congresses.
Classification: LCC HV6604.A355 P47 2014 | DDC 364.1540961--dc23
LC record available at https://lccn.loc.gov/2016020335

Table of Contents

Preface

Paul E. Lovejoy

This volume arises from a conference, "Perspectives on Historical and Contemporary Ransoming Practices," that was held at the Harriet Tubman Institute for Research on Africa and its Diasporas at York University on April 25-26, 2014. As such, it is part of the ongoing activities of the Tubman Institute in examining issues relating to the global African diaspora. The conference focused on historical and contemporary ransoming practices in Africa, Europe, and Asia, and in particular, the time period from the sixteenth through the twenty-first centuries. The goal was to promote research dissemination and knowledge exchange across regional and disciplinary divides among scholars working on different aspects of ransoming. A key objective was to achieve a better understanding of the practices of ransoming and the role of ransoming in the economics of captivity and enslavement; the formation, exploitation, and alteration of social, ethnic, and religious identity; and the interactions of individuals across physical, social, ethnic, and religious boundaries. Before this conference, most work on ransoming had been done on Europeans captives in North Africa, while research on ransoming Muslim captives in Europe and ransoming in sub-Saharan Africa was in its infancy. The conference brought together people working on diverse geographical regions to discuss commonalities and differences and to examine historical and contemporary practices for purposes of exploring continuities and differences. Examining the friction between Christian Europe and the Islamic countries of Africa and Middle East is in accordance with the mandate of the UNESCO Slave Route Project to establish a Research Network for the study of slavery in the Mediterranean, Middle East and Indian Ocean.

As the editors of this volume make clear, ransoming is the practice of paying for the release of someone who is being held in captivity as a means of obtaining a financial and sometimes a political compensation. The hostage or hostages are in effect pawns in a power struggle that has dire consequences for the victims should some agreement not be reached that would allow the return of the hostages in return for material and sometimes other recognition. The conference centered on what can be labeled a ransoming frontier between the worlds of Christianity and Islam, Europe and Afro-Asia. The resulting book considers both historical contexts of ransoming in the Mediterranean and West Africa, on the one hand, and more recent examples of kidnapping and holding hostages in the context of radical Islam and *jihād* in contemporary days in the Red Sea and western Indian Ocean, on the other. The focus on practices that require the study of Islamic societies and the friction between Islamic fundamentalism and European and western global hegemony highlights long standing issues of perspective on historical issues that have ignored the Islamic world.

If slavery was officially abolished in Europe in the early nineteenth century and in Africa nearly a century later political fragmentation and economic crisis in parts of Africa and Euro-Asia have produced a new element to the study of ransoming. From Mali to Algeria and Nigeria to Somalia and from the Balkans to Pakistan the incidence of kidnapping for the purpose of ransoming is on the increase. While in previous centuries, ransom was paid to prevent enslavement, today the payment of ransom is more often intended to prevent the torture and murder of victims of kidnapping. Nonetheless, there are discernible continuities between old and modern ransoming practices. The quest for financial reward and diplomatic edge in the struggle for power between European and Muslim countries in the Mediterranean basin and between various African societies remain crucial to understanding kidnapping and ransom negotiations in modern Nigeria, Mali, Somalia (where ransom payment accounts for a large part of national GDP), Palestine and the Middle East, and between criminal organisations in Europe and Latin America with governments seeking to contain or eliminate their activities, which are not examined here. Hence, those who have perpetuated capture for purposes of ransoming, unless afraid of losing captives to flight, usually held their victims near the point of captivity where families or governments could easily and quickly arrange ransom.

The study of ransoming, therefore, offers insights into unequal relationships and the efforts to use human beings as pawns in power struggles that sometimes have been based on ideology and religion and sometimes used as mechanisms for the crass accumulation of wealth and scarce resources. The effectiveness of ransoming relies on a sense of community, including bonds of kinship and loyalty to shared national and secular appeals to inclusion. Ransoming threatens the sense of common identity and the mechanisms of security in protecting communities. Ransoming is a weapon of warfare and armed struggle that challenges moral and legal rights of individuals to their freedom and well being. This volume, therefore, highlights important historical and contemporary tensions that separate nations, communities and kin groups from the enemies that try to undermine and even destroy their existence.

Acknowledgments

This edited volume derives from papers presented at a conference on historical and contemporary ransoming held at the Harriet Tubman Institute for Research on Africa and its Diasporas, York University, Toronto in April 2014. In preparing for the conference and edited volume, we were fortunate to have great support from many individuals and institutions. Without their help, the conference and this book might never have become a reality. The conference on which the collection is based was supported in several ways. The central funding was provided by the Social Science and Humanities Research Council of Canada (SSHRC) Connection Grant. We are most grateful for that support; without it the conference would have impossible. The grant funded a considerable part of the conference including the travel and housing costs of the presenters, each of whom presented essays on topics and regions for which they already had considerable knowledge, refocused on the theme of ransoming.

We extend our appreciation to our hosts, first the Harriet Tubman Institute, especially, Paul E. Lovejoy, who was then Director and who also has written the preface to this book, and the Associate Director, Annie Bunting; the Faculty of Liberal Arts and Professional Studies, Office of the Vice-President Research & Innovation, and the Department of History at York University.

To the panel chairs and discussants, Nielson Bezerra, Annie Bunting, José C. Curto, Martin Klein, Abdi Kursow, Joel Quirk, Stacey Sommerdyk, and Constanze Weise, we are deeply grateful for their excellent comments and tips. We also extend our warm thanks to the conference participants whose papers are not included in the edited collection, Marie Rodet, Ariel Salzmann, Nathan Carpenter, Katrina Keefer, and Christine Sears, whose participation and commentary were valuable to the success of the conference. Last but not the least, we would like to thank our publisher, Kassahun Checole of Africa World Press, who also assisted and was part of the grant application, and Vanessa Oliveira, who unreservedly served as unofficial coordinator of the conference and as an enterprising research assistant.

Introduction

Ransoming Practices in Historical and Contemporary Perspective

Jennifer Lofkrantz and Olatunji Ojo

On a sunny afternoon in August 2003, a special envoy from the German Foreign Office arrived in Bamako, Mali, for a meeting with some Malian administrators. The envoy carried three suitcases filled with cash estimated to be five million euros. Officially, the money was a humanitarian assistance to help the poor in the landlocked country. In reality the German envoy was in Mali to pay the ransom for the release of some of the 32 European captives held by Islamists in the Sahara since March of that year. Press reports revealed that the Malian officials including the President brokered the negotiation.[1]

Holding captives for ransom as a political and economic act has long historical precedents. For example, in the Mediterranean world until the nineteenth century, it was an act of commercial rivalry and "hardball" politics between Christian and Muslim polities where religious identity was entwined with conceptions of citizenship, nationality, ethnicity, religion, class, and race. Likewise, ransoming also took place between African states, and between Africans and Europeans south of the Sahara. In more recent times, kidnapping and piracy for the purpose of ransom payment is big business across the globe. In 1970s and 1980s Europe, Italy was widely known for incidents of kidnapping for ransom.[2] Currently, worldwide, especially in Africa, Latin America, and the Middle East, ransoming is also prevalent. It includes the kidnapping of European and American tourists, soldiers and journalists in the Middle East and Africa, the seizure of family members of human and drug smugglers, debtors, politicians and businessmen in the Caribbean, South America and Nigeria and of commercial vessels and their crew in Somalia and Nigeria. Individuals are held for political as well as economic reasons such as western captives held by the Islamic State of Iraq and Levant (Daesh/ISIS/ISIL) or al-Qaeda in the Maghrib (AQIM). It appears that the "ransom business" has grown over the last two decades. While most countries and individuals refuse to acknowledge paying ransoms, data from the *New York Times* and the United States Treasury Department estimate that al-Qaeda and its direct affiliates collected $125 to165 million in ransom payment between 2008 and 2014, of which $66 million was paid in 2013. Larger amounts have accrued to Somali pirates operating in the Indian Ocean and the Gulf of Aden. According to a 2013 report issued by the International Criminal Police Organization, United Nations Office on Drugs and Crime and the World Bank, ransom payment to Somali pirates between 2005 and 2012 is estimated at between $339 million and $413 million or about $42-52 million a year.[3] People paid ransom to free allies in captivity because the alternative was often worse. Historically, captives who failed to be ransomed were killed or enslaved. In the contemporary period, death is a likely outcome for captives who are not ransomed though with the rise of ISIS in the Middle East and Boko Haram in Nigeria enslavement has also become the fate for many women and children who are not ransomed.[4]

This volume investigates historical and contemporary ransoming policies and practices in the Mediterranean Basin and Africa. The contributors to this volume scrutinize the formation, exploitation and alteration of social, ethnic, and religious identities in ransoming and the interactions of individuals across cultural boundaries since the sixteenth century. The subjects covered in this volume range from ransom and prisoner exchange between Muslims and Christians in the Mediterranean world; the treatment of Muslim captives in seventeenth century France; the ransoming of British captives in eighteenth century Morocco; the Muslim West African discourse on ransoming; case studies on the ransoming of European captives in Asante and Nigeria during the 1860s and 1960s respectively, the West African fight against illegal enslavement and failed ransom negotiations; and contemporary ransoming practices in Nigeria, the Sahara/Sahel, and Somalia.

Conceptualizing Captivity and Ransoming

This volume includes studies of ransoming during the legal slave era and also the contemporary era when slavery is illegal in all internationally recognized political jurisdictions. In terms of the historical period, the study of ransoming as an institution as well as a process offers glimpses into debates about the rationalization and morality of captivity and slavery. Enslavement involves the rupturing of ties between captives and their homelands and their insertion into new societies as slaves. Claude Meillassoux recognized that both ransoming and enslavement were possible fates for captives in his study of slavery in the western Sudan even though he sometimes conflated redemption with ransoming and captives with hostages. He argues that initially, war prisoners removed from their communities were not slaves but captives. Slavery involved "denial of kinship" and "de-socialization" and the insertion of individuals into new societies as slaves.[5] In contrast, the ransoming of prisoners involves relying on and cementing the bonds between captives and their families, friends and allies and the re-integration of the captive into their home society. Membership in a "community" whether that be based on notions of residential, religious or ethnic identity conferred certain benefits such as access to ransoming when taken captive.

Establishing an inclusive definition of ransoming for the historical period is complicated by the frequent conflation of ransoming with related but different practices like the redemption of slaves, the release of hostages, and of piracy/corsairing involving the seizure of goods as well as people. It is important to differentiate between a "captive" and a "slave" and between the redemption of slaves and the ransoming of captives in systems where the practices of both prisoners not yet enslaved and that of enslaved individuals buying or have others purchase their freedom co-existed. In his study of the abolition of slavery in early colonial Tanzania, Thadeus Sunseri described the process by which slaves regained their freedom as "ransoming."[6] Similarly some of the works on captivity and ransoming in North Africa and Europe use "redemption" as a synonym for ransoming.[7] In his study of slavery in Yorubaland, Emmanuel Oroge attributes the low quota of Yoruba-speaking slaves in the Americas before 1800 to their release prior to embarkation. Although Oroge did not specify when the release occurred or the means to determining if reference was to slaves or captives, to the extent this obviated enslavement suggested this was ransoming. Sylviane Diouf distinguishes between purchasing the freedom of enslaved individuals and purchasing the freedom of captives at risk of enslavement and their return to their old homes. She calls the latter "captive redemption," which like Oroge, was the ability to "to buy the freedom of people slated for deportation."[8] Similarly, Géza Dávid and Pál Fodor use the term "ransom slavery" to differentiate between captives taken along the Ottoman border who were released upon payment and permitted to return home with their social position intact and slaves who were freed upon purchase of their freedom.[9]

Michel Fontenay differentiates between what he calls a long-term captive and a short-term slave in the Mediterranean system by distinguishing between "use-value" and "exchange-value" of a prisoner. For Fontenay, a "slave" was a person whose owner's purpose in holding him was to extract labor whereas a "captive" was an investment to be treated primarily as a medium of exchange.[10] In this volume, Daniel Hershenzon challenges Fontenay's focus on "use-value" and "exchange-value." As Hershenzon points out labor power ("use-value") and profit ("exchange-value") were not the only motivations for obtaining prisoners and that often times it was required to locate specific individual captives in order to exchange them for the freedom of specific other captives. Hence the categories of "use-value" (slaves) and "exchange-value" (captives) were fluid. In her chapter in this volume Gillian Weiss complicates the captive/slave divide by raising the question of what was theoretically possible versus what was realistically possible. Theoretically it was possible for "esclaves turcs" laboring on French royal galleys to be freed in exchange for ransom payment. However, since the French Crown was unwilling to part with them they were, in effect, slaves. We could add to Hershenzon and Weiss' views that Fontenay's classification also ignores the fact that many captives and slaves had the same master, lived side by side and performed similar tasks. Captives worked for their captors to cover their subsistence, food, clothing and housing, pending their ransom.

Observations from other parts of Africa support Hershenzon and Weiss. Travellers in nineteenth century Yorubaland distinguished between slaves and captives and between the redemption of slaves and the ransoming of captives. In the mid-1850s, American Baptist Missionary Thomas J. Bowen remarked that "all prisoners taken in war are slaves; and if not redeemed by their countrymen, are set to work by the captors, or sold to dealers."[11] Anna Hinderer, another contemporary with reference to the Ibadan-Ijaye war of 1860-62 noted that soldiers were "capturing prisoners for slaves."[12] Reverend Samuel Crowther, a child slave turned Anglican Bishop, also drew attention to ransoming in a letter to British Consul Thomas Hutchinson of Fernando Po on 10 September 1856

> It is very often the case that after war has destroyed a town, not only all the property is lost, but a large portion of a family is also taken captive to be sold into foreign slavery. Those who fortunately escape being caught, have no other resource *to ransom their captured relatives*, but it is expedient, to pawn a certain number of the family for as many cowries as they need to ransom

> their captured relatives from going into foreign slavery. Thus thousands have been kept from being removed out of the country.[13] (Our italics).

Note carefully Bowen's conception of slavery as the exploitation and sale or the antithesis of "redemption" (more appropriately ransoming) and Hinder-er's separation of prisoners from slaves. The significance of these observations is that one was first a captive/prisoner then a slave, that enslavement allowed exploitation and sale whereas pre-enslavement release guaranteed return to freedom. Ransoming was more than a means of preventing the embarkation of slaves for the Americas since many slaves in Africa were enslaved not far from their original communities and were sold and exploited. It was about preventing enslavement of captives rather than the regulation of market operations or the treatment of slaves.

Further, some African cultures use the words "captive" and "slave" interchangeably while others separate them. In Hausa the term, *fansa* means ransom and redemption but the language separates *kamamme* (prisoner) and *sabon bawa* (new slave) from other categories of slaves: *bawan gandu* (plantation slave), *bawan gona* (farm slave), *bawan gida* (domestic/house slave), and *bawan murgu* (slaves who are allowed to work on their own account giving a set payment in cash to their owners). The *sabon bawa* were acquired purposely for exchange or ransom, and were approximate to captives.[14] In Mandinka, slaves and captives were called *jongo* and *boyinkang* (someone that has been physically overpowered) while the Yoruba used the terms *ẹrú* and *ìgbèkùn* respectively.[15] In Arabic the terms were slave (*'abd*), and captive (*asīr*).

In dealing with the distinction between the institutions of ransoming captives and slave redemption in African and Mediterranean societies we focus on the fate and status of the captive and slave. In this volume, ransoming is defined as "the practice of paying for the release of a captive at the time of capture or soon afterwards."[16] We consider someone to be a ransomed captive if that individual is able to return to their own society with their previous social identity intact. Whereas a ransomed captive returns home and suffers no social liability, redeemed slaves usually remain in their former owner's society in a subservient position or they had been long separated from their society and in their absence had undergone culturally-sanctioned rites of enslavement.

Ransoming was the opposite of Suzanne Miers and Igor Kopytoff's continuum of the assimilation of slaves and their descendants into their owner's society where over time and generations slaves and their descendants became more integrated into free society and their social status improved. Based on the analysis by Miers and Kopytoff's "captives," "hostages," and "slaves" occupied separate stages along the "freeborn to slave continuum." As they envision, slaves and their descendants moved up the continuum. Applying this same continuum to what happens to captives when they are not ransomed, we can say that captives gradually became more marginalized and closer to being slaves the longer they remained in captivity and were separated from their families.[17] Just as with slavery, there was movement along the "continuum" with ransoming. A captive initially seized to extract ransom payment or someone panyarred to enforce debt payment (both economic activities) could at another time be held up as a hostage to secure political concessions such as forestalling an attack, raising a siege, or securing release of a prisoner or forcing return of a fugitive debtor. While traveling in the Senegambian region between 1795 and 1797, an agent of the British African Association, Mungo Park noted the fluidity between being a free person and becoming a hostage or slave. In his words when an African

> takes up goods on credit from any of the Europeans on the coast, and does not make payment at the time appointed, the European is authorised by the laws of the country to seize upon the debtor..., if he can find him, or, if he cannot be found, on any person of his family; or, in the last resort, on any native of the same kingdom. The person thus seized on is detained, while his friends are sent in quest of the debtor. When he is found, a meeting is called of the chief people of the place, and the debtor is compelled to ransom his friend by fulfilling his engagements. If he is unable to do this, his person is immediately secured and sent down to the coast, and the other released. If the debtor cannot be found, the person seized on is obliged to pay double the amount of the debt, or is himself sold into slavery.[18]

It is easier to define ransoming in the contemporary era where slavery is legally outlawed in most societies.[19] In their chapters in this volume, Akachi Odoemene, on Nigeria, and Awet Weldemichael and Abdi Kusow on Somalia, offer similar definitions of ransoming. Odoemene defines ransoming as "the demand of some payment of sort, either in cash or kind, in exchange for an abductee, either a person or some thing often held in a disadvantage position." Weldemichael, on what he calls "ransom piracy," offers a straightforward definition of ransoming as "the paying for the freedom of captives." Kusow, borrowing from Rodanthi Tzanelli, sees kidnapping for ransom as "a rational system of value exchange" whereby "captors hold someone of political/economic significance (i.e. persons who have the ability to negotiate their way back to freedom)."[20] For Kusow, however, what is considered valuable, in the case of piracy, includes a ship's crew and cargo.

Identity and Expectations of Captives and Captors

An important factor in assessing whether a captive was a good candidate to be ransomed by both the captor and the potential payer of ransom was the perceived identity of the captive. White captives in North Africa were labeled as "Christians" (*naṣara*) and their African captors were called "Barbary," "Moors," "Muslims," 'Blacks," or "Arabs" by Europeans. As Suzanne Schwarz and Mohamed H. Mohamed, both in this volume demonstrate, British traders believed that their identity as Christians and as Britons should have protected them from enslavement. Europeans viewed their captivity, forced labor, and potential enslavement by Maghribis as a "reversal of the natural social order" as they viewed themselves racially and religiously superior to their captors. Indeed, in the case of British ship captain James Irving, as discussed by Schwarz, it was precisely Irving's identity as a Briton which eventually encouraged one of his captors to permit his ransom and for British diplomats at al-Sawīra (Essaouira) to raise the ransom fees. A similar logic existed in the case of the Basel missionary captives in late nineteenth century Asante as discussed in this volume by Olatunji Ojo. Even though the missionaries were not British, Asante rulers regarded them as such since they were white, European, and Christian, and were seized from British controlled territory. British colonial officials on the Gold Coast had obviously reached a similar conclusion that they were responsible for the missionaries since they took the lead in the ransom negotiations. Likewise, as Roy Doron argues that during the Nigerian civil war (1967-1970) in the ransom case of some 40 AGIP (*Azienda Generale Italiana Petroli*) oil workers, the Biafran commandos deliberately targeted the Italian workers of the oil firm because their Italian identity made them valuable as both a source of potential revenue and as a means to put the war back onto the international agenda. Moreover, it was their Italian citizenship that encouraged the Italian government to negotiate the captives' ransom.

Identity was manipulated by both captors and captives. As Weiss explains the "esclaves turcs" who labored on the galleys of France's seventeenth century royal fleet were supposed to be captured Muslims who theoretically could be freed upon payment or exchange. The vast majority of "esclaves turcs" were Ottoman and Moroccan Muslims. However, due to the high demand for slave galley labor, many Hungarian and Ottoman Christian and Jewish prisoners, who should not have faced the prospect of captivity and slavery in France by virtue of their European, Christian, and Jewish identities, were also frequently classified as "esclaves turcs." Likewise, as

Jennifer Lofkrantz points out in her chapter on Muslim West African discourses on slavery and ransoming, racial and religious identities were manipulated by elites in the debate of who was and who was not a freeborn Muslim and therefore who could and could not be legally enslaved.

Captives also manipulated identity and were not passive in the construction of their identity. Often captives forged or lied about who they were, where they came from, and who they worked for or associated with as long as this could shorten time in captivity. According to Mohamed's chapter, the French captive, Pierre Raymond de Brisson, presented himself as rich, thereby tempting his captor to transport him to the French outpost in St Louis, Senegal, in exchange for ransom. Also the American Robert Adams described himself as British so he could be taken to the British consulate since the Americans had no formal ransom pact with Morocco. The danger for captives is that tempting captors into demanding ransom could also raise the cost of freedom or make ransom payment impossible. A captor could demand for more than the market/social value of the captive or more than a captive's associate could afford to pay in ransom.

Ransom Negotiation as a Process

Ransoming was underpinned by cross-cultural pacts whereby laws transcended cultural and political boundaries. Meillassoux argues that ransoming was more likely to succeed when opposing cultures/states had mechanisms for exchanging captives.[21] Examples of such mechanisms included inter-state pacts such as the series of Anglo-Moroccan treaties by which Britain and Morocco agreed to free/rescue each other's captives/sailors in exchange for good trade and prisoner exchange. For instance, Captain George Delaval of Britain was sent on two missions to the Sultan of Morocco, Ismail b. al-Sharif. First in 1700, he negotiated a treaty for the ransom of British captives held by the Moroccans and in 1708, another agreement for both countries not to attack each other's ships and sailors. In 1760 and 1790, additional treaties were signed allowing Moroccans access to trade in Gibraltar and for Morocco to transfer all matters including criminal prosecution of British subjects in Morocco to the resident British consul rather than a Moroccan judge.[22]

In this volume the contributors emphasize the necessary cooperation between captors, captives, and those involved in the ransom negotiations either as payers of ransom or as mediators in ransom negotiations. For captors, ransoming captives was a worthwhile endeavor in order to secure a high payment or other forms of reward for the return of a specific captive. While captives and their families, employers or governments often viewed the demand for ransom as an economic crime, especially in the contemporary period, designed to enrich the perpetrators (captors) it was nonetheless worthwhile to pay ransom in order to protect the freedom and life of the captive and secure their release.

Successful ransom negotiations require communication between the captor and the payers of ransom. Whether it was in Europe or Africa, captivity narratives and other related sources show that it was normal for the captives to reveal as much information as possible to the captor such as their names, place of origin and possible contacts such as family members, employers or governments to help with ransom negotiations. The captive de Brisson, as described by Mohamed, was informed by his captor of the impending arrival of a Jewish merchant from whom he (de Brisson) could ask "for some paper" to write to "those from whom you expect assistance." The captor volunteered this information after he had asked de Brisson if there was anyone in al-Sawīra who could pay good ransom on him and his associates.[23] In eighteenth-century Europe, published captivity narratives like de Brisson's circulated widely; so sailors heading to North Africa were familiar with the possibility of captivity, survival tactics during captivity and ransoming procedures.

The captives, based on the information that they volunteered, and with the permission of their captors, were allowed to contact their family, employers or government representatives in order to start ransom negotiations. They wrote letters containing identities of the captor/s, place of captivity and cost of ransom, to be sent (in non-literate societies they sent verbal messages and symbols), through merchants, ransomed captives and returning ransoming missions. How long it took for this information to reach a captive's home and for the latter to come back with ransom payment depended on the distance between the point of captivity, the location of the addressee, mode of transportation and how long it took to mobilize resources for ransom payment. In Europe and West Africa messages often went to designated centers such as commercial and consular posts. Hershenzon, Schwarz, and Mohamed allude to the presence of European diplomats in North Africa whose jobs were to facilitate ransom negotiations and release of European captives. In Spain, the cities of Alicante, Cartagena, Valencia, Madrid and Seville were renowned clearing houses for ransoming operations for captives held in North Africa. In West Africa during times of war, the sending of messages could be hampered, affecting the possibility of ransoming captives, yet the Sokoto Caliphate facilitated the exchange of information on captives at certain markets. In the Bight of Benin, messages and ransoming missions passed through major market towns such as Ouidah, Porto Novo, Badagry and Lagos along the coast and Ketu, Oko, Ijaye and Ilorin in the hinterland. In recent times technology has made communication easier. Captives provided their family names, telephone numbers and or emails with which they or the captors could contact them. Other times the crew of commercial ships contacted their employers or nearby military patrols boats as a kidnapping or piracy operation unfolds thereby giving ample time to start ransom negotiations or military rescue missions.

Once the initial contact was made, ransom mediators/brokers were often employed in order to help negotiate the ransom, facilitate the payment and the return of captives. Mediators were often individuals who were connected to both sides of the negotiation and were able to travel freely and broker relations across political and cultural borders. In early modern Europe and the Maghrib ransom brokers included individuals who occupied spaces "in-between" such as traders, politicians, diplomats, renegades, pirates and *moriscos*.[24] The Trinitarian and Mercedarian religious orders were well known for regularly fundraising for the ransoming of Christians held in the Maghrib.[25] In the eighteenth and nineteenth centuries, the Iron Mongers Company of London and a few philanthropists and investors set aside fund for the ransoming of captured British sailors in Morocco. Other operators were money lenders who, in the case of British captives in Morocco, charged a monthly interest of six per cent on funds spent on ransoming British captives.[26] In West Africa heads of European trade firms drew on company treasuries to ransom their employees from captivity.[27] In coastal West Africa ransom brokers included senior politicians and merchants, such as officials of the Ekpe society and representatives of the Aro in the Bight of Biafra, members of the Poro society in Sierra Leone, and European sailors, Christian Missionaries, and diplomats. In 1851, Egba authorities in Yorubaland variously approached a leading female merchant, Christian Missionaries, British naval officers and diplomats to broker the ransom of one of their subjects held captive in Abomey (Dahomey).[28]

The role of government in ransoming was and continues to be important. Captivity and ransoming are transnational activities that flourish under conditions of both strong and weak states/economic systems. Where government is functional it prevents banditry. As discussed by many of the contributors, when a person is captured, the government could either facilitate or hamper negotiations. In this volume, Mohamed sees the holding of captives in southern Morocco as a reflection of a strong state protecting its territory and resources. The Moroccan state expected Europeans operating in its territorial waters to seek its approval. Failure to do so was met with Moroccans attacking and seizing shipwrecked European sailors and demanding ransom for their release. Such payments served as fines imposed on those violating Moroccan territorial integrity.[29] While most modern states dissuade kidnapping and ransoming, historically state officials funded kidnapping raids, piracy, and brokered ransom negotiations. States only condemned the kidnapping of their citizens or attacks on their vessels. Until the eighteenth century European and North African states sponsored expeditions against trade vessels of rival states. European government officials were also willing to pay ransoms whereas their North African counterparts, like Sokoto officials, preferred for families to make private arrangements or to include the release of Muslim captives as a precondition for peace treaties. Only in the late eighteenth and early nineteenth century did Europe and America adopt the most effective policies to suppress piracy and ransom demand. In addition to refusing to pay demand, first in 1801-1805 and later in 1815-1816, the United States attacked Tripoli and Algiers to stop piratical activities. Britain adopted the same tactical approach by attacking Algiers in 1824. Finally, using piracy as a reason, even though piracy and *corsairing* in the Mediterranean had decreased substantially by then, France sacked and occupied Algiers in 1830 and Tunis in 1881 placing them under colonial rule.[30] Lofkrantz and Ojo in this volume contend that some of the violence associated with slavery in precolonial West Africa resulted from failed ransom negotiations.

Nonetheless kidnapping for ransom is more associated with politically swollen and socially and economically fragile states where the government lacks the means of protecting public resources or maintaining law and order or where people see brigandage as a legitimate or necessary economic weapon. There are contemporary media reports partly blaming senior state officials in Africa, South America and Asia for incentivizing piracy.[31] More than four decades ago Philip Curtin described the socio-economic underpinnings of Muslim revolutions in sixteenth century West Africa. He divided the early Muslim population of the Senegambian region into Arabs and Berbers. The Berbers were devout Muslims, clerics and farmers while the Arabs originated from a Bedouin tradition of nomadic pastoralism, raiding and tribute collection. By the late sixteenth century, the Arabs had reduced the Berbers "to a status of respectable subordination" and forced them "to pay the *ghardma* [ghadīma], a form of protection money."[32] Curtin concluded that the relationship between the two groups mirrored an existing division in the region whereby a group was "peaceful, commercial, and religious, the other military, political, and secular."[33] Similarly, James Webb links human activities in the southern Sahara region in the period of the seventeenth to nineteenth centuries to ecological changes, especially desertification. Specifically he shows how the system of political and economic exploitation adapted to environmental changes. Horses imported from the north gave nomads military superiority over sedentary farmers while the latter offered their grains as tribute (tax) and protection fee to their martial overlords.[34] By highlighting the ecological underpinning of banditry in the Sahel, Curtin and Webb foreshadowed Amy Niang's, in this volume, understanding of kidnapping and ransoming in contemporary Sahelian Africa. The emergence of modern nation-states demarcated by relatively fixed colonial boundaries and frontiers ran counter to the pre-existing social and economic organizations of the Sahelian people. Desertification continues to undermine their agricultural life yet the boundaries limited the possibilities of population migration. Also the trans-Saharan trade on which many once depended has fallen well below its precolonial volume. For Niang, as she states in her chapter, "raiding and ransoming strategies have thus been used as acts of defiance, as a form of adaptation to, and a response to various social strains heightened by capitalism, the disruption of traditional trading and economic circuits, and ultimately as a political weapon." She views the contemporary kidnapping and ransoming of western captives in the Sahel as a continuation of past practices of raiding, *razzia*, and ransoming as a form of resource redistribution and part of an attempt to resurrect fading modes of governance in a society undergoing fundamental and disruptive economic change. Kusow, in this volume, and Mohammed Ingriis also sees historical precedents in Somali piracy which they argue draws on the activities of deprived pastoralists resorting to banditry (Somali: *burcad*) as a means of coping with socio-economic and ecological challenges.[35] Kusow identifies two types of *burcad*—land-based operations (robbery/cattle rustling) or *burcad berry*, and sea piracy or *burcad badeed*. Both types involved payment of ransom. Both old and modern pirates seek material reward.

There are significant parallels in the historical evolution of ransoming in the West African Sahel and in Somalia. Like Niang, chapters by Mohammed and Ojo explore the realities of power between Europeans and African in the age of European expansion. African authorities in Morocco and Asante used captivity and demand for ransom as real and symbolic expressions of power with which they affirmed their autonomy and rejected European encroachment on their territories. Thus ransom payment was a means of redressing political and economic injustices—a fine or fee paid by political subordinates. Accusations of foreigners not respecting territorial boundaries are also crucial to understanding captivity and ransoming in the Nigerian Delta, the Sahel and Somalia as discussed by Odoemene, Kusow, Weldemichael and Niang. If the concern in the Niger delta owed to excessive material accumulation and aggrandizement by foreign-owned oil companies at the expense of the local population's environmental and economic needs, it is about foreign fishing trawlers depleting the fishing potentials of the Somali waters.

Yet, there are certain distinctions between old and modern piracy. Kusow, Weldemichael and Odoemene highlight how modern pirates use sophisticated weapons like fast moving boats, tug boats, "mother ships," satellite and cellular phones, and Global Positioning Systems (GPS) that enabled them to range ever further from the coast. Also rather than a return to an ancient activity contemporary ransoming is a reflection of ongoing socio-economic malaise such as a weak (and some would say failed) state, lack of effective governmental system to protect public and private resources, and lack of economic opportunity, especially for the youth. From Somalia to the Sahel and Nigeria modern piracy began in the late 1990s as a popular response to foreign plundering of marine and land resources through illegal fishing activities, dumping of toxic waste, maladaptation to western-style political and economic systems, marginalization in the global system, regional wars, and natural disasters.[36] Non-state actors, or in Eric Hobsbawm's conception, "social bandits," seeking social justice and an end to mass poverty filled the vacuum created by the absence of a functioning central state.[37] This "Robin Hood" mentality/motivation, what John Anderson calls the "expropriation of the expropriators," was later overtaken by criminal elements interested in the profits of ransoming than safeguarding public resources.[38] Weldemichael notes that contemporary Somali pirates might have begun their operations like many other "social bandits" but they gradually devolved into full time criminal enterprises: huge amount of earnings made by the pirates never stayed within the Somali economy. Piracy also has serious social and economic costs for the country. It has further destroyed the local fishing industry, raised the cost of living in coastal towns and increased alcohol and drug use among the youth. In Nigeria, Odoemene differentiates between kidnapping-for-ransom in the Niger Delta motivated by politics; that is, communities seeking compensation for oil pollution and destruction of land and water resources and demanding fair distribution of oil wealth (i.e. diplomacy by another name) and the Nigerian hinterland kidnappers (mostly unemployed youths), who unlike their Somali counterparts are inspired largely by the desire for quick wealth.[39]

Asymmetry in Ransom Negotiations

The primary goal of a captor is to maximize social and economic payment while the payer of ransom wants to reduce it. Ransom negotiations involve hard bargaining. The question remains: who has the upper edge during ransoming negotiations? What cost and benefit analysis underpin ransom payment and the exchange of captives? Also, how much money or numbers of captives is an appropriate exchange for a captive to be ransomed?[40] While it often appears that those holding captives for ransom hold the stronger position, it is often the captors who believe that they are the ones in the less powerful position. This was dependent on time and place and can be seen in the asymmetry in ransom negotiations. For example, both Hershenzon and Weiss note the asymmetry in the Mediterranean ransoming environment with Christians held in North Africa more likely to be ransomed than Muslims held in Europe. Hershenzon attributes this disparity to formal institutions such as the religious orders involved in ransoming Christian captives, the willingness of Maghribis to permit the ransom of captive Christians and the unwillingness of Europeans to free captive Muslims for money despite Muslim attempts to ransom their fellow Muslims. In both the contemporary Niger delta and the Somali coast, captors often view themselves as the weak and oppressed fighting against a more powerful economic elite. Odoemene views ransoming in the contemporary Niger delta as resulting from official corruption and the mismanagement of human and natural resources, Kusow and Weldemichael note that many Somalis see piracy as the only effective recourse they had against local, regional, and global injustice.

During the legal slave trade era in Africa ransom prices were usually set higher than the price of the captive would fetch on the slave market because freedom is valued higher than captivity and slavery. In this volume, Lofkrantz and Ojo show that in West Africa members of the upper class and their allies more than commoners, Europeans more than Africans, men more than women and adults more than children attracted higher ransom payment. Yet they also had a higher chance of been ransomed because of their high social and economic status. Rich families, states and companies could speed up the ransoming process by paying captors out of their surplus wealth. For instance, in 1787, Barbier Borro, a Sierra Leonean man, secured his own ransom by selling twenty-two of his slaves. His other slaves became so fearful that they might also be sold that they ran away.[41] In other words, the freedom of a notable citizen was priced higher than the liberty of more than 22 slaves.

There are parallels between historical and contemporary ransoming practices whereby citizens of certain countries or senior government officials and business executives and other rich citizens and their families are more prone to seizure. At the same time, though the ransom price for these elite captives is set very high they have better chances of regaining their freedom than had they come from poor countries or families. In May 2014, the United States government traded five senior Taliban prisoners detained for twelve years at Guantanamo Bay, Cuba, for Army Sergeant Bowe Bergdahl, held by the Afghan Taliban since 2010. Opponents of the deal, while not wholly condemning Bergdahl's release, rejected the process. They argued that prisoner exchange, especially of five senior Taliban operatives for one soldier, was so lopsided it could encourage seizure of more Americans by other violent groups to extract future concessions.[42] Israel is also known to have engaged in what seems to be an unequal prisoner exchange especially when this involved relations with its Arab neighbors. In 1983, Israel swapped 4,765 Lebanese prisoners for six soldiers, and two years later it released 1,150 Arabs for three of its soldiers. One of the recent cases was the release in 2011 of 1027 Hamas detainees in exchange for an Israeli tank gunner, Gilad Shalit. Israel has also freed Palestinian prisoners in order to recover its dead soldiers. In 2004, it released over 400 Palestinian and 30 Hezbollah prisoners, and the remains of 59 Lebanese killed by the Israeli Defense Force (IDF) in exchange for the bodies of three IDF soldiers captured by Hezbollah in 2000.[43] These exchanges contrast with recent kidnapping cases in Nigeria whereby the poor are hardly ever seized by kidnappers. Indeed a popular joke in Nigeria is that the kidnapping of poor people produces nothing except a "double shortage" or "double loss" to the kidnappers. The kidnappers would receive no ransom payment and would have to feed and house the captives from their own resources. These cases, especially those with a numerical disparity in the exchange of prisoners, and the scholarship on ransoming highlight the asymmetry in captivity and ransom negotiations and payment.

More than the exchange of prisoners, kidnappers, pirates, and ransomers for profit operating in contemporary Africa and the Middle East are more interested in financial payments and they usually demand up to several million dollars in ransom. In a recent survey of 23 European and American captives seized by ISIS between November 2012 and December 2013, fifteen were freed upon ransom payment while eight (one Russian, four Americans, and three Britons) were killed because their governments refused to pay ransom. When the militants killed the Russian captive, Sergey Gorbunov, they showed the other hostages a video of his body.[44] While some states refused to pay ransom others paid but never made public the amount. What is incontrovertible is that these were huge amounts depending on the nationality and socio-economic class of the captive. A French official once declared: "France does not break its principles … the non-payment of ransoms." Reports challenge this claim. The *Guardian* of London reported that France paid up to 43 million euro between 2008 and 2014 to rescue its citizens. This amount included $18 million paid for the release of four journalists abducted in Syria.[45] In Nigeria recent cases of kidnapping for ransom have targeted elite citizens or their associates like the former president of the Nigerian Bar Association, Okey Wali, the mother of the Finance Minister, Kamene Okonjo, and a sister of the Petroleum minister, Osigo Agama.[46] If Chief Wali was seized in his own right as a successful lawyer, the two women were kidnapped and held for ransom because they were related to elite female politicians. In contemporary ransoming operations the risk of enslavement, in some areas, is mitigated by the collapse of the slave trade but captives face other challenges. Captors often threaten to kill their captives to extract huge payments from the captives' supporters. They have also starved and subjected captives to other forms of hardships and humiliation such as showing families videos of malnourished captives surrounded by gun-totting captors and of sobbing captives or telling them they would prepare "orange suits" for the captives – a reference to the costume ISIS militants force their captives to wear before executing them.[47] The tactic is chosen to inflict psychological pain on the captive and allies. The more ill a captive the more pressure is put on payers of ransom and the greater the desire to pay ransom and prevent the death of the captive. When Madam Okonjo, the mother of the Nigerian Finance Minister, was abducted from her house by a gang of kidnappers in December 2012 her captors demanded ransom to the tune of 200 million naira (c.$1.3m) which the family negotiated down to thirteen million naira c.($80,000). Yet Okonjo was lucky to be alive because another captive, 72-year old Mrs Reginat Obi Daity, kidnapped by the same gang of kidnappers was killed because her family paid only two million (c.$12,000) of the ten million naira (c.$60,000) demanded in ransom.[48]

Conclusion

Drawing on historical and anthropological perspectives the chapters in this volume demonstrate the ethnic, national, religious, and institutional underpinnings of ransoming operations and the conflicting interests of different actors involved in ransoming whether they were captives, captors, kin, government officials, or mediators. The contributors demonstrate the different motivations for holding captives and willingness to ransom which were affected by time, place, and economic and political conditions. Through the use of specific case examples they illustrate the emotional impact that captivity had on captives and the people who cared about them. The volume also opens up discussion on kidnapping and piracy for ransom in other parts of the world. Despite our focus on Africa and Europe we are aware of the thousands of similar incidents across the globe. Such are many recent cases that the description of certain countries or cities as the "kidnapping capital of the world" has fluctuated between the Americas and Asia. In 2007, that title belongs to Iraq with about 1,500 foreigners kidnapped. Three years earlier it had been Mexico before which it was Colombia which held the record.[49] What these countries had in common was that the kidnappers realized the financial reward attached to ransom payment and socio-economic and political leverage tied to kidnapping, piracy and ransom negotiations.

Endnotes

1 Rukmini Callimachi, "Paying Ransoms, Europe Bankrolls Qaeda Terror," *New York Times*, 29 July 2014. http://www.nytimes.com/2014/07/30/world/africa/ransoming-citizens-europe-becomes-al-qaedas-patron.html?_r=0. Accessed on 7 April 2015.

2 Géza Dávid and Pál Fodor (eds.), *Ransom Slavery along the Ottoman Borders: Early Fifteenth–Early Eighteenth Centuries* (Leiden: Brill, 2007); and Richard Wright, *Kidnap for Ransom: Resolving the Unthinkable* (Boca Raton, FL: Taylor & Francis, 2009), 23.

3 Christopher Harress, "Secret Flow of Somali Piracy Ransoms: 179 Hijacked Ships Generated Some $400M in Payments since 2005. So Where Has It All Gone?" *International Business Times*, 4 November 2013. http://www.ibtimes.com/secret-flow-somali-piracy-ransoms-179-hijacked-ships-generated-some-400m-payments-2005-so-where-has. Accessed 29 April 2015.

4 See "Afghanistan: Abducted Aid Workers Found Dead," *Toronto Star*, 12 April 2015, A8 and in late 2013, captors of American journalist, James Foley demanded over $100 million from his family. He was killed around August 2014 after ransom negotiations broke down. See Callimachi, "Before Killing James Foley, ISIS Demanded Ransom from U.S.," *New York Times*, 20 August 2014. http://www.nytimes.com/2014/08/21/world/middleeast/isis-pressed-for-ransom-before-killing-james-foley.html. Accessed 12 April 2015. Furthermore, recent media reports reveal that Boko Haram sell some of the Chibok girls to Central Africa for as low as $12 while ISIS released a price list for Yazidi women: Woman, 40-50 years: 50,000 dinars; Woman, 30-40 years: 75,000 dinars; Woman, 20-30 years: 100,000 dinars; Girl, 10-20 years: 150,000 dinars; Children 1-9 years: 200,000 dinars. Each buyer is limited to three "slaves" except for foreigners like Turks, Syrians and Gulf Arabs. See Abdelhak Mamoun, "Exclusive: ISIS document sets prices of Christian and Yazidi slaves," *Iraqi News*, 3 November 2014. Accessed on 7 April 2015. http://www.iraqinews.com/features/exclusive-isis-document-sets-prices-christian-yazidi-slaves/; "Yazidi 'slave' women captured by ISIS fanatics in Iraq," *Daily Mail Online*, 14 August 2014. Accessed on 8 April 2015. http://www.dailymail.co.uk/news/article-2719698/President-Obama-authorises-airstrikes-Iraq-defend-civilians-Islamic-militants-swarming-country.html; David Blair, "Nigeria's Boko Haram isn't just kidnapping girls: it's enslaving them," *The Telegraph*, 13 January 2015. Accessed on 6 April 2015; http://www.telegraph.co.uk/women/wom-

ens-life/11342879/Nigerias-Boko-Haram-isnt-just-kidnapping-girls-its-enslaving-them.html.

5 Claude Meillassoux, *The Anthropology of Slavery: The Womb of Iron and Gold,* trans. Alide Dasnois (Chicago: University of Chicago Press, 1991), 33, 101-109.

6 Thaddeus *Sunseri,* "Slave *Ransoming* in German East Africa, 1885-1922," *International Journal of African Historical Studies,* 26 (1993), 481-511.

7 Dávid and Fodor, *Ransom Slavery*; Nabil Matar, *Turks, Moors and Englishmen in the Age of Discovery* (New York: Columbia University Press, 1999); Paul Baepler (ed.), *White Slaves, African Master: An Anthology of American Barbary Captivity Narratives* (Chicago: University of Chicago Press, 1999); Daniel J. Vitkus, *Piracy, Slavery, and Redemption: Barbary Captivity Narratives from Early Modern England* (New York: Columbia University Press, 2001); Robert C. Davis, *Christian Slaves, Muslim Masters: White Slavery in the Mediterranean, the Barbary Coast and Italy, 1500-1800* (New York: Palgrave Macmillan, 2003); Wolfgang Kaiser (ed.), *Le commerce des captifs: les intermédiaires dans l'échange de le rachat des prisonniers en Méditerranée, XVe-XVIIIe siècle* (Rome: École française de Rome, 2008); and Lawrence A. Peskin, *Captives and Countrymen: Barbary Slaves and the American Public 1785-1816* (Baltimore: The John Hopkins University Press, 2009).

8 Sylviane Diouf, "The Last Resort: Redeeming Family and Friends," in Diouf (ed.), *Fighting the Slave Trade: West African Strategies* (Athens: Ohio University Press, 2003), 83.

9 Fodor, "Introduction," in Dávid and Fodor, *Ransom Slavery*, xiv.

10 Michel Fontenay, "Esclaves et/ou captifs: préciser les concepts," in Wolfgang Kaiser (ed.), *Le commerce des captifs: les intermédiaires dans l'échange de le rachat des prisonniers en Méditerranée, XVe-XVIIIe siècle* (Rome: 2008), 15-24.

11 Thomas J. Bowen, *Adventures and Missionary Labours in Several Countries in the Interior of Africa from 1849 to 1856* (London: Frank Cass, 1968 [1858]), 319-20.

12 A. Hone and D. Hone (eds.), *Seventeen Years in the Yoruba Country: Memorials of Anna Hinderer Gathered from Her Journals and Letters* (London: Religious Tract Society, 1872), 216.

13 Thomas J. Hutchinson, *Impressions of Western Africa* (London: Longman, 1858), 277.

14 George Bargery, *A Hausa-English Dictionary and English-Hausa Vocabulary* (London: Oxford University Press, 1934); Charles Robinson, *Dictionary of the Hausa Language*, vol. 1, 3rd ed. (Cambridge: Cambridge University Press, 1913) and Frederick *Lugard,* "*Memorandum No. 22:* The Condition of Slaves and the Native Law Regarding Slavery in Northern Nigeria," *African Economic History,* 40 (2012), 177-178.

15 Prof. Assan Sarr of Ohio University, Athens, provides the Mandinka terms. See Email communication, 12 April 2015.

16 Jennifer Lofkrantz, "Protecting Freeborn Muslims: The Sokoto Caliphate's Attempts to Prevent Illegal Enslavement and its Acceptance of the Strategy of Ransoming," *Slavery and Abolition*, 32 (2011), 109-110.

17 Igor Kopytoff and Suzanne Miers, "African 'Slavery' as an Institution of Marginality," in Miers and Kopytoff (eds.), *Slavery in Africa: Historical and Anthropological Perspectives* (Madison: University of Wisconsing Press, 1977), 3-81.

18 Mungo Park, *Travels in the Interior Districts of Africa...in...1795, 1796 and 1797* (London: John Murray, 1807), 441-42.

19 The resurgence of slavery in parts of the world (Syria, Iraq and Northeastern Nigeria under ISIS/ISIL and Boko Haram) might further complicate contemporary ransoming operations.

20 Rodanthi Tzanelli, "Capitalizing on Value: Towards a Sociological Understanding of Kidnapping," *Sociology*, 40:5 (2006), 929-947.

21 Meillassoux, *Anthropology of Slavery*, 103.

22 James A. O. C. Brown, *Crossing the Strait Morocco, Gibraltar and Great Britain in the 18th and 19th Centuries* (Leiden: Brill, 2012), 39-40, 98.

23 *An Historical Narrative of the Shipwreck and Captivity of Mr. De Brisson* (Perth: K. Morison, 1789), 79-80.

24 *Moriscos* (also "Moorish") were former Muslims who were forced to convert to Christianity rather than face death or expulsion from Spain. They served as ransom brokers because they understood the cultural dynamics of North African Muslim societies.

25 See James Brodman, *Ransoming Captives in Crusader Spain: The Order of Merced on the Christian-Islamic Frontier* (Philadelphia: University of Pennsylvania Press, 1986); Ellen Friedman, *Spanish Captives in North Africa in the Early Modern Age* (Madison: University of Wisconsin Press, 1983); Dávid and Fodor, *Ransom Slavery*; and Davis, *Christian Slaves, Muslim Masters.*

26 James G. Jackson, *An Account of the Empire of Morocco and the Districts of Suse and Tafilelt,* 3rd ed. (London: Frank Cass, 1968 [1814]), 274; and The National Archives, Kew (TNA), FO 174/20, M. Abithol to Peter Gwyn, 21 September 1811. Cf. Norman Stillman, *The Jews of Arab Lands: A History and Sourcebook* (Philadephia: The Jewish Publication Society, 1998), 370.

27 Robin Law (ed.), *The English in West Africa: The Local Correspondence of the Royal African Company of England, 1681–1699*, Parts 1-3 (Oxford: Oxford University Press, 1997-2006).

28 Ojo, "Amazing Struggle: Dasalu, Global Yoruba Networks, and the Fight against Slavery," *Atlantic Studies*, 12:1 (2015), 5-25.

29 Also see Anonymous, "Great Britain and the Barbary States in the Eighteenth Century," *Historical Research*, 29:79 (1956), 87-107; and Nabil Matar, *British Captives from the Mediterranean to the Atlantic, 1563-1760* (Leiden: Brill, 2014).

30 Friedman, *Spanish Captives*, 142; Weiss, "Barbary Captivity and the French Idea of Freedom," *French Historical Studies*, 28:2 (2005), 231-64; E. Nathalie Rothman, "Becoming Venetian: Conversion and Transformation in the Seventeenth-Century Mediterranean," *Mediterranean Historical Review,* 21 (2006), 39-75; Frederic Leiner, *The End of Barbary Terror: America's 1815 War Against the Pirates of North Africa* (Oxford: Oxford University Press, 2007); and Peskin, *Captives and Countrymen.*

31 Jeremy Keenen, *The Dying Sahara: US Imperialism and Terror in Africa* (London: Pluto Press. 2013); Jacob Zenn, "Boko Haram: Recruitment, Financing, and Arms Trafficking in the Lake Chad Region," *Combating Terrorism Center Sentinel*, 7:10 (2014), 5-9 and Jacob Zenn, "Boko Haram and the Kidnapping of the Chibok Schoolgirls," *Combating Terrorism Center Sentinel,* 7:6 (2014), 1-8.

32 Phillip D. Curtin, "Jihad in West Africa: Early Phases and Inter-Relations in Mauritania and Senegal," *Journal of African History*, 12 (1971), 12-13.

33 Curtin, "Jihad in West Africa."

34 James L. A. Webb, Jr., *Desert Frontier: Ecological and Economic Change along the Western Sahel, 1600-1850* (Madison: University of Wisconsin Press, 1995).

35 Mohammed Haji Ingriis, "The History of Somali Piracy: From Classical Piracy to Contemporary Piracy, c. 1801-2011," *The Northern Mariner,* 23 (2013), 239-66.

36 Allice Bettis Hashim, *The Fallen State: Dissonance, Dictatorship and Death in Somalia* (Lanham: University Press of America, 1997), xiii-xix; Douglas Guilfoyle, "Piracy off Somalia and Counter-Piracy Efforts," in Douglas Guilfoyle (ed.), *Modern Piracy: Legal Challenges and Responses* (Northampton, MA: Edward Elgar, 2013), 35-60; and Martin N. Murphy, "Petro-piracy: Predation and Counter-predation in Nigerian Waters," in Guilfoyle, *Modern Piracy*, 61-90.

37 See Eric Hobsbawm, *Social Bandits and Primitive Rebels* (Glencoe, Ill.: Free Press, 1960); and Franklin Graham IV, "Abductions, Kidnappings and Killings in the Sahel and Sahara," *Review of African Political Economy*, 38:130 (2011), 587-604.

38 John Anderson, "Piracy and World History: An Economic Perspective on Maritime Predation," *Journal of World History*, 6 (1995), 175-199; Markus V. Hoehne, "Counter-terrorism in Somalia: How External Interference Helped to Produce Militant Islamism," http://hornofafrica.ssrc.org/somalia/; Sarah Percy and Anja Shortland, "The Business of Piracy in Somalia," *Journal of Strategic Studies*, 36 (2013), 541-78; and Christopher L. Daniels, *Somali Piracy and Terrorism in the Horn of Africa* (Lanham, MD.: Scarecrow Press, 2012).

39 Michael Watts, "Petro-Insurgency or Criminal Syndicate? Conflict & Violence in the Niger Delta," *Review of African Political Economy*, 34:114 (2007), 637-60; Oarhe Osumah and Iro Aghedo, "Who Wants to be a Millionaire? Nigerian Youths and the Commodification of Kidnapping," *Review of African Political*

Economy, 38:128 (2011), 277-87; Ogbonna Onovo, "Combating the Crimes of Armed Robbery and Kidnapping in the South-East and South-South Zones of Nigeria: Strategies, Challenges and Prospects," *Igbinedion Journal of Diplomacy and Strategy,* 1:1 (2009), 12-21; Daniel A. Tonwe, Godwin Uyi Ojo, and Iro Aghedo, "Spoils Politics and Environmental Struggle in the Niger Delta Region of Nigeria," *Inkanyiso: Journal of Humanities and Social Sciences,* 4:1 (2012), 37-48 and Conway Waddington, "Kidnappings in West Africa: West Africa-issue in Focus," *Africa Conflict Monthly Monitor* (2013), 54-57.

40 See Attila Ambrus, Eric Chaney and Igor Salitskiy, "Pirates of the Mediterranean: An Empirical Investigation of Bargaining with Asymmetric Information" (DRAFT), 6 November 2014. http://scholar.harvard.edu/files/chaney/files/pirates.pdf and Claudio Detotto, Bryan C. McCannon and Marco Vanniniz, "Understanding Ransom Kidnapping and Its Duration," 11 July 2012. Available at SSRN: http://ssrn.com/abstract=2109941

41 Wadström, *Essay*, Vol. 2, 17.

42 See Michael Hastings, America's Last Prisoner of War," *Rolling Stone*, 7 June 2012, http://www.rollingstone.com/politics/news/americas-last-prisoner-of-war-20120607; "Taliban-held U.S. soldier released in exchange for Afghan detainees," *The Washington Post*, 31 May 2014. Retrieved 31 May 2014; John Hicks, "Guantanamo Prisoner Transfer for Bowe Bergdahl Violated Laws, Review Finds," *Washington Post*, 21 August 2014. Retrieved 22 August 2014; Zachary A. Goldfarb and Juliet Eilperin, "Obama: 'No Apologies' for Bergdahl Release Deal," *The Washington Post*, June 5, 2014. http://www.washingtonpost.com/politics/obama-no-apologies-for-bergdahl-release-deal/2014/06/05/a4c15fca-ec2a-11e3-9f5c-9075d5508f0a_story.html

43 Ivan Watson, "Lebanese Celebrate Return of Five Prisoners," *National Public Radio*, 16 July 2008. http://www.npr.org/templates/story/story.php?storyId=92586233. Accessed 20 April 2014; Barak Ravid, Avi Issacharoff and Jack Khoury, "Israel, Hamas Reach Gilad Shalit Prisoner Exchange Deal, Officials Say," *Haaretz*, 11 October 2011. http://www.haaretz.com/news/diplomacy-defense/israel-hamas-reach-gilad-shalit-prisoner-exchange-deal-officials-say-1.389404. Retrieved 20 April 2015 and Merle Robillard, "Gilad Shalit and Hundreds of Palestinians Are Released in Prisoner Swap," *National Post*, 18 October 2011. http://www.nationalpost.com/m/wp/news/blog.html?b=news.nationalpost.com/2011/10/18/gilad-shalit-and-hundreds-of-palestinians-are-released-in-prisoner-swap," Retrieved 19 April 2015.

44 Karen Yourish, "The Fates of 23 ISIS Hostages in Syria," *New York Times*, 10 Feb. 2015. http://www.nytimes.com/interactive/2014/10/24/world/middleeast/the-fate-of-23-hostages-in syria.html

45 Julian Borger, Kim Willsher and Stephen Burgen, "Terrorist Ransoms: Should Governments Pay Up or Stick to their Principles?" *The Guardian* (UK), 22 August 2014. http://www.theguardian.com/media/2014/aug/22/terrorist-ransom-government-pay-james-foley

46 Dapo Falade, "Wali, ex-NBA President, Regains Freedom," *Nigerian Tribune*,

25 October 2014. http://www.tribune.com.ng/news/top-stories/item/19549-wali-ex-nba-president-regains-freedom; and "Sister of Nigerian Petroleum Minister Alison-Madueke Kidnapped in Port Harcourt," *Sahara Reporters*, 24 Oct. 2014. http://saharareporters.com/2014/10/24/sister-nigerian-petroleum-minister-alison-madueke-kidnapped-port-harcourt

47 Jeremy Diamond, Sophia Saifi and Saima Mohsin, "Inside the Fight to Free Warren Weinstein," 24 April 2015. http://www.cnn.com/2015/04/24/politics/warren-weinstein-congress-hostage-release/index.html

48 Ifeanyi Okolie, "How kidnappers of Okonjo-Iweala's Mum Killed 72-yr-old Woman," *Nigerian Vanguard,* 21 Apil 2013. http://www.vanguardngr.com/2013/04/how-kidnappers-of-okonjo-iwealas-mum-killed-72-yr-old-woman/#sthash.9HcDBjU9.dpuf

49 "Colombia: Kidnap Capital of the World," *BBC News*, 27 June 2001.

SECTION I

The Mediterranean and the Maghrib

CHAPTER I

"Para Que Me Saque Cabesea Por Cabesa...":

Exchanging Muslim And Christian Slaves Across The Western Mediterranean[1]

Daniel Hershenzon

In the winter of 1613, the Algerian corsair Babaçain left the port of Algiers captaining a *saetia*, one of the ships with Latin sails used by North African corsairs, and headed north to the Spanish coast in the hope of capturing Christians to sell back at home. At the time, Babaçain was seventy years old and probably already had plans to retire. This could have been his last embarkation. Sadly, two leagues, around five miles, away from Cartagena, the Algerian ships ran into a Spanish royal squadron. After a brief battle, the Algerians had to acknowledge defeat. Babaçain was taken captive by the captain of the *Patrona Real*, the galley leading the squadron. He and his crewmembers were interrogated, enslaved, and put to work as oarsmen in the royal fleet. Two years earlier, in 1611, Sergeant Domingo Álvarez, a Spaniard serving Phillip III, was posted with his company, a body of close to 150 soldiers, in Oran, the largest Spanish fort-city in North Africa. Unfortunately, *en route*, his ship ran into Algerian corsairs. After a brief battle, the Spaniards had to acknowledge defeat, and Álvarez and his comrades were taken captive and enslaved as rowers on the galleys of the Algerians' corsairs, possibly of the kind that Babaçain had captained.[2]

For early modern ears, such heartbreaking stories sounded fairly common not to say trivial. After all, a few millions of Muslims and Christians were taken captive and enslaved in the early modern Mediterranean: 300,000 to 400,000 Moroccans and North African Ottoman Subjects passed through Portugal and Spain between 1450 and 1750; about 500,000 Muslims were enslaved in Italy between the beginning of the sixteenth century and the end of the eighteenth; in Malta alone, between 35,000 and 40,000 Muslims (around half of which were North Africans) were sold as slaves in the seventeenth and eighteenth centuries; and more than a million Christians were enslaved in the Maghrib between 1530 and 1780.[3] It is not always possible to distinguish between Muslims from the Maghrib, Mashriq and Anatolia but the fact that these calculations exclude the Spanish Balearic and Canary Islands, Sardinia and France means that the numbers of Maghribis enslaved in southern Europe must have been even higher. In any case, the sight of laboring slaves or recently ransomed captives begging in the town square was common for Mediterranean city dwellers.

Why juxtapose the captivity tales of Babaçain and Álvarez? Indeed, they are strikingly similar: on the one hand, a corsair, i.e., a "state" authorized pirate, taken captive and employed as a slave by his Christian enemies; on the other, a soldier, captured and enslaved by Muslim enemies. But does mere similarity justify subjecting these human trajectories to the same historiographical framework? And is resemblance the only relation between these trajectories? Most scholars of piracy and captivity answer the first question in the negative.[4] The underlying scholarly assumptions are that despite their parallels, these are two distinct historical phenomena: enslavement of Muslims in the northern shores of the Mediterranean, and captivity of Christians in North Africa. Empirically, the claim is based on the fact that Algiers, Tunis, and Morocco did not develop ransom institutions similar to the French and Iberian Orders of Redemption (the Trinitarians and the Mercedarians). In the absence of such institutions, Muslim captives, as opposed to Christians, had little hope of returning home and thus should be considered slaves. On a theoretical level, the treatment of captivity of Muslims and of Christians as two separate phenomena privileges a national rather than a trans-national perspective. Scholars' decision to focus on more "real" objects such as nations or states results in writing the histories of Spanish, French, Portuguese or Algerian captivity instead of a connected history of Mediterranean slavery.[5] Such perspective overshadows the interdependence and links between the two captivities and disconnects related processes, which were constantly in mutual formation.

It is time to answer the second question – is resemblance the only thing linking the captivity of Babaçain and Álvarez? The answer is no. If we keep on following what happened to them, we discover that their stories do intersect just before the moment of their ransom when they were exchanged, one for the other. Such exchanges, facilitated by the short distance separating Sicily from Tunis, Algiers from Majorca, or Gibraltar from Tangiers and Tétouan, weaved social and political links between the two captivities. They also demonstrate that the absence of ransom institutions did not prevent North Africans from ransoming their dear ones. Maghribi rulers often discussed the ransom of their subjects as part of the negotiations of peace treaties with European powers.[6] Beyond that, at irregular intervals, Algerian pashas or Moroccan sultans initiated negotiations with their Spanish counterparts over the exchange of large numbers of captives. This happened, for example, in 1612 when Muḥammad al-Shaykh al-Ma'mūn, ruler of Fez and one of three sons of Saadian Sultan Aḥmad al-Manṣūr, negotiated with the Portuguese governor of Tangiers the return of several of his subjects for Christian captives.[7] A similar deal was cut in 1629, when Morato Āghā, an Algerian emissary, was sent to the Spanish fort town of Oran in order to, among other things, barter five Turks for Christians.[8] And again in 1634, when a local Moroccan leader whose name the sources do not reveal negotiated with the governor of Larache (El Araich) the swapping of two Muslims for seventy Christians.[9] The exchange rate was not always in favor of the Christians. When in 1689, Alaouite Sultan Mawlāy Ismā'īl ibn al-Sharīf conquered Larache, he demanded one thousand Muslims in return for the hundred Spaniards he took captive.[10] Doubtlessly, such interactions occurred more often than we now know, and somewhere in the General Archive of Simancas documents recording them still lie buried, awaiting discovery.[11]

As little as we know about these diplomatic interactions, we know a lot less about how simple folks, men but more often women, negotiated the exchange of their spouses, sons, or siblings. The efforts of common Maghribis and Iberians towards liberating their kin, thus, stand at the heart of this chapter. On the basis of the reconstruction and analysis of such negotiations and exchanges, I argue that North African Muslims of all classes actively pursued the release of their family despite the absence of institutionalized Maghribi ransom mechanisms. Moreover and in light of the absence of institutional ransom mechanisms, the fact that barter, or the exchange of one slave for another, was the most common ransom modality North Africans pursued demonstrates how connected and interdependent the captivity of Muslims and that of Christians was.

That captivity of Muslims and Christians formed interdependent elements of a single Mediterranean system, however, does not mean they were identical. Far from that, the system was asymmetrical.[12] Christians were ransomed in greater numbers. The reason was that several institutions in

Christendom took care of the ransom of Christians: the Trinitarian and the Mercedarian Orders, church institutions charged with the liberation of Christians from the Maghrib, ransomed Portuguese, Spanish and French captives, while Italian urban fraternities ransomed Italian captives.[13] The absence of similar institutions on the Muslim side meant that the system offered Christians and Muslims uneven chances of retrieving their liberty.

Asymmetry also characterized the production and archiving of records that documented trafficking and ransom of Muslims. Whereas the Orders of Redemption, from the 1570s on, systematically recorded their missions, thus establishing serial documentary corpora that contained names of ransomed captives, ransom prices and detailed descriptions of ransom negotiations, it seem as if similar documentation for the seventeenth century North Africa was either produced in smaller quantities, not archived, did not survive or still awaits discovery and study.[14] That means that for now, at least, ransom of Muslims must rely on records written by Christians and Maghribi Muslims and Jews archived in Spanish archives. There are no inventories cataloging such transactions or bundles containing them alone neatly stacked on the archive's shelves. Relevant information appears irregularly in petitions of all sorts sent to the Council of War or now and then in notarial records. These can be complemented by searching data in the margins of autobiographies, inquisitorial investigations, intelligence reports and letters. Thus, while I do not make claims about the volume of such exchange practices, I argue that there are enough of them to justify their examination as a unified object of study. An analysis of the mechanics and use of these practices offers a new way of understanding captivity and how it linked North African powers and the Spanish Empire.[15]

Petitioning the Ruler

It is time to go back to Babaçain and Álvarez and their fate. In the years following his capture, Babaçain never lost hope, and kept writing letters and sending messages through a network of merchants, soldiers, and ransomed captives, both Christian and Muslim, that crisscrossed the Mediterranean. Such information had to be precise and include the address in which the slave was employed, his masters' name or the galley on which he rowed as an oarsman. In 1655 or a year earlier, for example, an unidentified Muslim slave wrote to his relatives in Algiers explaining that he was enslaved "in Sanlucar [de Barrameda in western Andalusia]...in the street of the Bretons, [and] his owner [was] called Nicolás Rubin."[16] In the case of Babaçain, the information he needed to provide was the name of the royal galley in which he pulled the oar. Providing his wife with this detail, however, was only the first step towards retrieving his liberty. From that point on, she was the one who had to take the lead in arranging his release. The chance of royal slaves, such as Babaçain, buying their liberty was even smaller than those held in urban households. Rather than negotiating independently, such slaves usually had to find a proxy who would do it on their behalves. The surest way of finding a Christian agent who would free her husband was to force someone to do it.

Yet how might an old Algerian woman force a Spaniard to act on her behalf and safely return her husband? Purchasing a Christian captive, preferably a soldier, was her best shot. Indeed, that is exactly what Babaçain's wife did. She bought Domingo Alvarez from his owner, neither to have him as a servant in her household, nor to profit from his ransom, but to use him to get her husband back. Her selection was not arbitrary; she must have first asked around, ascertaining that he would fulfill her needs. Alvarez belonged to the massive class of poor captives who rarely had the means to ransom themselves. Given this, his price would not have been too high and, if he wanted to return home, he would have to obey her demands. But there was another reason for which she preferred him over other captives: he was a soldier with many years of service behind him. As such, he was in a better position than "civil" captives to ask favors from the king. And that is exactly what he was expected to do: write to the king and ask to be exchanged in return for her husband. Poor Alvarez was happy to cooperate. In the petition he sent the Council of War (*Consejo de Guerra*) in April 1616, he wrote that "after serving his majesty for many years in the royal navy . . . he was captured by the Turks of Algiers,"[17] thus stressing his history of service. He added, likely at the urging of Babaçain's wife, that "he has no possessions with which to ransom himself, and the said moor, his mistress, was determined that no sum could convince her to give him his freedom other than her own husband's liberty."[18]

The crown was reluctant to accept this kind of deal, and the archive of the Council of War preserves many orders the king issued to the royal fleet throughout the seventeenth century, prohibiting the concession of galley slaves to individuals.[19] Rarely, did the king approve more than a handful of petitions. In 1630 it approved twenty-five such petitions and a similar, if not larger, number of petitions must have been approved in the preceding couple of years. These were exceptional years, however, that followed a successful Moroccan attack on the Spanish fort town of La Mamora (Mehedía), in which a large number of soldiers were taken captive.[20] The crown resisted such exchanges for three reasons. First, the royal fleet had a constant shortage of slaves; second, Spanish bureaucrats feared that Muslim ship captains would revert to their earlier practice of preying on Spanish ships and coasts and capturing Spaniards; third, although the crown usually prohibited handing over enslaved Muslim corsairs to Christians petitioners hoping to save their dear ones, it was occasionally involved in and even initiated such exchanges when the captives were influential powerful nobles, officers or a large group of soldiers. The somewhat confusing classification system of Muslim slaves developed by the bureaucrats of the Spanish fleet reflects these reasons. The fleet officers distinguished between "corsairs" or "captains of Arab ships" (*arraezes*), on the one hand, and "Moors of ransom" (*moros de rescate*) or "Moors of value" (*moros de consideración*), on the other. While the crown did not grant petitioners slaves classified as "corsairs" fearing they would return to attack Spanish ships, it also refused to provide petitioners with slaves classified "moors of ransom." Such slaves were of high value due to their status or wealth and thus were kept for future exchange of those the crown honored. Captives' kin, then, had a chance of obtaining the slave they wanted from the crown only if he was not a corsair nor or exceptional value. Petitioners, familiar with this system, employed the fleet's classifications when applying to the crown. For example, María de Puçeula, who hoped to exchange her husband captured in Tétouan, petitioned the crown in 1587 for the brother-in-law of her husband's master. In her petition, she wrote that the requested slave is "not an *arraez* or (a Moor) of importance."[21] Similarly, in 1616, Juan López Malvada stated in his petition that Hamete, the slave he asked for "was not an *arraez* or (a Moor) of ransom."[22]

The petitions Spaniards submitted to the crown placed in motion investigations regarding the status of the requested slave. The story of Elvira García, a widow from the city of the Puerto de Santa María near Cádiz, who negotiated with an unidentified Moroccan widow the exchange of their sons, illustrates the bureaucratic trajectories of these petitions. García's only son, Diego, enlisted as a cabin boy on a ship captured by the galleys of the Sultan of Morocco in 1593 when the eighteen-year-old youth was enslaved with the rest of the sailors. Despite her poverty, García did all she could to ransom Diego, but without success. Two years later, the Moroccan widow, whose son Amete was enslaved in 1583 on the Spanish royal galley *La Granada*, contacted García. The Moroccan wrote to her, saying, "she will ask the king (of Morocco) to give her as alms the other Christian (García's son) so [that in exchange for him] they will give her back her son."[23] García immediately addressed the king through his Council of War, recounting the sufferings of her child and the offer made to her by Amete's mother. She asked that, "in light of that the king will give her as a favor the... Moor in order to complete the exchange with her son."[24]

As in the case of Alvarez and Babaçain, the Council of War deferred to the king for instructions and was ordered to contact the *contador* of the royal galleys, the person in charge of the books listing the slaves working in the galleys, and to ascertain Amete's status. In this way, the Council would determine the Muslim slave's role on the ship on which he was held, the circumstances of his capture, and his current age. If the fleet officers decided that the slave in question was not "a Moor of ransom" and thus exchangeable, they would send their decision to the Council, which would in turn pass it on to the king. In response to García's petition, the fleet officers reported to the Council of War – "Hamete [sic] of Morocco, son of Ali, twenty two years of age, long eye lashes and thick brows, a birthmark on his throat and a burn scar on his right arm, a few cuts on his forehead and of small-size body, who was taken captive in the Almeria de Ceuta... on October 7, 1583... and as it seems in the books of our offices and we are informed he is not of value, or a corsair or of ransom."[25] In this case, then, the fleet officers gave the green light for proceeding to the next step towards exchanging the two slaves.

Problems arose when the petitioners and the *contador* or other fleet officers disagreed about a slave's status. Such disagreements resulted from incorrect or debated enlistment of Muslim slaves at the time of their capture, or when they were delivered to the fleet officers. Sometimes, captains who caught Muslims falsely claimed they were corsairs, in order to get a greater bonus. Juana de los Santos argued in her petition that the captain who caught Hamete Muxi lied when he listed him as an *arraez* – "and the captain who captured him, in order to increase his benefits, despite the fact he [the Muslim] was someone else, handed him to them [galleys' officers] as an *arraez.*"[26] When petitioners' requests were refused due to the status the crown attributed to the slave in question, they tried to trace Christian captives who had been previously held on the Muslim ship where the slave they wanted was captured. They took the testimonies of these ex-captives, hoping to convince the fleet officers of the petition's merit. Juana de los Santos acted differently: she provided the testimony of Luis de Guerra, a Portuguese Trinitarian who was held hostage in Tétouan for many years, who swore that Hamete Muxi, the Muslim slave de los Santos requested from the crown, was "of no importance (*baxo*)." Juana de los Santos soon discovered that even such a testimony was not enough—the *adelantodo* simply refused to hand Hamete Muxi over to her. In another petition to the crown, she complained that the *adelantado* was "always looking for excuses and not feeling the sufferings of the Christian captives."[27] The *adelantado* stood in the way of others as well. Ysabel Hernández, Antón Rodriguez's wife, claimed "that even though she went to the *adelantado* with the two said writs (*cedula*), he refused to give her the said Turk whom she demanded."[28] In other words, getting royal writs ordering the fleet officers to hand over slaves to petitioners was not always sufficient evidence, and different officers along the chain of command could prevent the execution of such exchanges.

Barring objections from the fleet officers, the petitioners could advance to the next step. These deals involved a twofold exchange. When and if the crown finally agreed to concede its galley slaves, it demanded alternative ones in return. While the slaves that petitioners sought were usually old, weak, and sick—or at least that was how petitioners portrayed them in their requests—the ones that the crown demanded in their place had to be young, healthy, and strong. In other words, in order to obtain a slave to exchange for kin held captive in the Maghrib, petitioners had to provide the crown with an alternative slave. The insistence of the crown on exchanging and never giving its slaves as gifts points at another asymmetry between captivity of Muslims and Christians and sheds light on a recent debate about whether Mediterranean bondage should count as captivity or slavery. The large majority of Christians imprisoned in the Maghrib, Robert Davis has argued, lived and died as slaves and should be studied as such.[29] Michel Fontenay has advanced the debate by insisting on the distinction between "slaves" defined by their use-value and "captives" by their exchange-value; the majority of captives were purchased by business-oriented traders who bought them as a shrewd investment, whereas slaves were bought by slave owners who solely sought to benefit from the fruits of their slaves' labor. Fontenay has explained that in the Mediterranean, as opposed to the Atlantic, captives were slaves waiting for their ransom whereas slaves were captives who gave up on the hope of being ransomed.[30] For this reason it was possible to distinguish a captive from a slave only in regard to those slaves who were ransomed and returned home. In other words, the distinction could be made only after the fact of ransom.[31] The case of Muslim slaves owned by the Spanish crown, however, demonstrates that even when such slaves faced a potential ransom – i.e. were about to become captives, they maintained their use-value. The king was willing to give up on them only for a young, healthy and strong alternative Muslim slave, treating slaves in terms of muscle mass.

The king's demand meant that before the petitioners got the slave they needed, they had to obtain another with whom they would pay the crown. This point is important, as it further complicates the distinction between captives and slaves, buyers who bought captives in order to sell them and those who bought them in order to exploit their labor. The dynamic examined here shows that at least some North Africans bought Christian slaves in order to exchange them for their dear ones enslaved in Spain; at least some Christians bought Muslim slaves in order to exchange them for another Muslim slave, by which they may obtain the release of their relatives. In their portrayal of the categories of "slave" and "captive" as exclusive and defined by use-value in the case of the former and exchange-value in the vase of the latter, the participants in the debate over Mediterranean bondage ignored the fact that these were dimensions of a single process. Enslaved captives constantly moved between the statuses of "slave" and "captive" and captives could and did have use-value while slaves could and did have exchange-value. Labor and market profit alone do not exhaust the motives of buyers of captives in the early modern Mediterranean. Perhaps more important, these multi-layered exchanges clearly manifest some of the links between enslavement of Christians and Muslims. That Spaniards who formed parties in such ransom coalitions had to provide the crown with alternative slaves further complicates this interdependence, and points out the self-perpetuating nature of these violent practices and exchanges.

The nature of the documentation is such that we know a lot less about the parallel communications between Muslim captives or their kin and Maghribi rulers, Algerian pashas or Moroccan Sultans.[32] It is clear that in different stages there was a religious and political obligation to provide captives and their families with aid. In eighteenth century Algiers, for example, a new category of endowment for Muslims held captive in Christian land appeared in the waqf income registers. Apart from that, a certain percentage of the booty captured by the corsairs was collected by the government for the same end.[33] How did captives' kin ask and receive that support, however? What if they needed a slave owned by the authorities or the Sultan? The few Spanish documents that echo such interactions suggest that rulers collaborated with their subjects by helping them upon request. This was the case for Hamete's mother, the Moroccan widow who negotiated a deal with Elvira García and who according to García intended to ask the Sultan for the captive Diego, Gacía's son. Other sources suggest that like their Spanish counterparts, Maghribi rulers often had ransom agendas opposed to their subjects' needs. One such source presents the critique Ridwān al-Janawī – the son of a Genoese convert, a healer who performed miracles, ransomed captives and was venerated as a holy man – launched in Fez against the ruler after the battle of Ksar El Kebir. The victorious Sultan, Ahmed al-Manṣūr, preferred selling the thousands of Portuguese captives he took rather than giving them to his subjects who had relatives held captive in Portugal. Riḍwān al-Janawī, condemned al-Manṣūr.[34] These are no more than scant hints pointing out allegedly similar tensions between rulers and ruled across the sea. More evidence and research are required in order to further tease out such a comparison.

Ransom Dealers

Getting the necessary information, most importantly where a captive was held and what his identity was, and obtaining the slave required for the exchange was the first step in a long process. Humble family members hardly ever had the means and knowledge needed to advance the transaction to the next stage transferring a slave across the sea and exchanging him or her for another. It was at this point that Maghribis and Iberians contacted and contracted intermediaries: Jews, Christians, Muslims, Moriscos, or renegades (Christians who converted to Islam). Everyone who was able to occasionally participated in the trade, a fact echoed, as we will see, in the fragmented nature of the information extant about the intermediaries. For many of these intermediaries, the positions of trader, pirate, ransomer, or captive meant different stages in complex professional trajectories often linked with commerce. This was the case of the Spaniard Gaspar de los Reyes, who after a few years of captivity in Algiers, ransomed himself, and struck an agreement with two local Algerian families and two Christian captives. To the Algerians he promised to buy their relatives held captive in the town of the Puerto de Santa María; to the Christians, to collect money for their ransom from their kin, also in the Puerto de Santa María. De los Reyes left Algiers to Spain, received the Muslim slaves, and got the money for the Christian captives. Then, he continued to Málaga where he received sixteen more "Turks" from Christians who bought them in order to exchange them with their beloved ones imprisoned in Algiers.[35] De los Reyes provides a typical example of a captive-turned-redeemer, literally capitalizing on the social contacts he established through his work as a slave in a tavern in Algiers, where he also came to master Arabic. That in Málaga a large number of people contracted him to transfer Muslim slaves to Algiers shows the pervasiveness of the practice. In one trip he was able to release eighteen Muslims! The large number of Muslim captives picked up in Málaga suggests that the port city served as a center for such transactions and that captives' kin knew where intermediaries like de los Reyes were to be found. And yet, the only reason for which we know of the case is that de los Reyes converted to Islam and ended up sentenced at the inquisitorial tribunal of the Canary Islands where he and other witnesses told his story. In this last regard, the case demonstrates the difficulty of studying such transactions, which in the absence of systematic recording and archiving requires the collection of data scattered at the margins of seemingly unrelated documentation.

Intermediaries of this kind often collaborated, forming partnerships that crossed confessional lines. Judas Malachi was a Jewish merchant from Tétouan and one of the suppliers of the Peñón de Vélez, a Spanish fort in Morocco. He operated as a Spanish royal ransom agent in the Maghrib between 1589 and 1595.[36] The contract Malaqui struck with the crown obliged him to send hostages to Málaga. Malaqui provided two Muslim business associates as hostages; one of them, the merchant Hamete Madan from Fez, stayed until at least 1595.[37] Like this merchant from Fez, Moriscos in Tunis, who were extremely active in the local ransom market throughout the seventeenth century, worked tightly with Jews from Livorno.[38] Some Muslims and former Muslims specialized in the ransom and rescue of Muslims from Christian lands. In 1571, a Muslim slave in Naples, who had converted to Christianity years earlier and was baptized as Aniello Tarantino, was accused by the Inquisition of blasphemy. During his trial, the inquisitors discovered that he had taken advantage of the liberty that conversion to Christianity provided him, and for a high price arranged for North African slaves to escape back to the Maghrib.[39]

For Christian merchants from Spain, ransoming Christians from the Maghrib was mainly a way of legitimating commerce with North Africa. As part of this commerce, they also ransomed or participated in the exchange of Muslims enslaved in Spain. Among the ransom intermediaries, Majorcan corsairs and merchants, who specialized in trade with North Africa, were renowned. For them, as for other Iberian subjects of the Spanish crown, the discourse of ransom, or more precisely that of the redemption of captives, was evoked in order to legitimize trade in other commodities with Tunis, Algiers, and Morocco. Spanish official discourses echoed religious rhetoric that prohibited direct trade with the infidel. However, in practice, trade with North Africa became a normal occurrence in seventeenth century Spain and the volume of direct and indirect trade between Spain and the Maghrib grew throughout the period.[40] This commerce functioned under a system of "permanent exception" – the special licenses that the crown issued over and over again for merchants trading with the Maghrib turned in fact into a form of tax.[41] In order to obtain a license, traders had to prove that part of the transaction was geared towards the ransom of Christians. The system had its limits, however, as is demonstrated by the case of the Majorcan skipper Già. In 1668, on behalf of a mercantile company from his island, Già exported tar to Algiers. Unlike other commodities, tar was deemed a material of war, and its sale to Muslims was absolutely prohibited. Già was arrested by the Inquisitorial tribunal of Majorca in 1669.[42] In his defense, he claimed that he used his profits to ransom captives. Sadly, since the majority of the captives that left Algiers with him claimed they paid for their liberty with their own money, the argument did not serve him very well.[43]

We see then, the difficulty of generalizing about the intermediaries' motives. Anyone who was on the spot might and often did engage in the ransoming process. Some did so out of compassion to their coreligionists. Others rescued their friends, kin, or fellow countrymen. Profit was central for many ransomers, but it would be wrong to reduce participation in the trade to simple economic motives. Maghribi Muslims and Jews, residents of the Spanish garrisons and of Moroccan and Algerians settlements, employed the ransom of captives to facilitate the commercial contacts with Spain; Già did so to whitewash his illegal arms export; and other Christian merchants ransomed co-religionists to lubricate commerce with North Africa.

Spaces of Exchange

Bustling port cities such as Málaga, Cádiz, or the Puerto de Santa María were known as trade centers in which one could commission a merchant to transfer Muslims south to the Maghrib and to return with liberated Christians, but the actual exchange often took place in the Christian enclaves dotted throughout the North African littoral.[44] In the western part of North Africa it was mostly the Portuguese (Ceuta, Tangiers etc.) and Spanish (Bougie [Béjaïa], Oran etc.) *presidios*, in the central part French and Genoese (Bastion de France, Tabarka) trading posts. They varied in their degree of autonomy and sovereignty, in the forms of social and ethnic life they generated, and hence in the kind of transactions they enabled. The idea behind the fifteenth century Portuguese and sixteenth Spanish *presidios*, the result of the continuation of the movement of the *Reconquista* to North Africa, was to establish a network of forts that supported each other while providing control over major maritime trading routes. Ironically, they ended up reproducing elements of *convivencia* Spain.[45] The Spanish fort town of Oran, for example, held a large Jewish community, whose members provided Christians with translation and interpretation services, money loans, food provisions, strategic information and trafficking of slaves. It also included a small number of Muslims, partly but not exclusively slaves.[46] Often, the Jewish leaders of the local community were asked to employ their connections in Algiers in order to ransom Christians held captives there.[47] In some cases, Algerian envoys were sent to the city to negotiate the exchange of captives.[48]

Ceuta, a Portuguese settlement from 1415 and part of the Spanish Empire from 1580, provides another example of such a trading zone. Only twenty-two miles away from Tétouan and nineteen from Algeciras in Spain, this fort town was ideal for exchanging Spanish subjects for Maghribis. Three cases from the mid-seventeenth century illustrate Ceuta's role as a center for the ransoming of captives. In the first, the mother of "English Mostafa," an Algerian Morisco captured by Christians in the early 1640s, bought Emanuel d'Aranda and two other captives in order to exchange them for her son and four other "Turks." She hired a "Turk" to take them with a ship to Tétouan but a short distance away from the city the ship sunk and the survivors had to proceed on land to Tétouan. There, they lodged in the house of a Jewish merchant and sent letters to Ceuta announcing their arrival in Tétouan. They soon discovered that the person they were waiting for had already left Ceuta for Gibraltar. However, before leaving he arranged credit for them in Tétouan through a local Morisco merchant.[49] This way, they did not have to wait in prison. Two Muslim merchants in Ceuta provided credit for the Turks with whom d'Aranda and his friends were to be exchanged, and the Turks also waited in freedom for the swap to take place. After further back and forth, and with the help of local merchants, the captives were exchanged and returned home.[50] In the same year, another Algerian family that hoped to ransom their kin enslaved in Spain bought Diego Hernández, a Christian captive, for that purpose. They hired one Zigamete [Sid Ahmed?], an Algerian residing in Tétouan, and ordered him to take Diego Hernández to Ceuta to meet Domingo Alvales, a Christian intermediary representing Hernández's wife, Juana Ramirez. Alvales had to hand over to Zigamete the relative of the Algerians whom he received from Juana Ramirez, and in return receive Diego Hernández.[51] A decade later, Diego López de Acosta, held captive in Algiers, was trying to engineer his exchange in return for a Muslim enslaved in Sanlúcar de Barrameda. He sent instructions to Tomas Velásquez de Oliver, asking him to buy the Muslim slave: "send him to Ceuta with heavy guard, and make him write [to me and order me when] to leave [Algiers] to Tétouan in order that the exchange will be executed there *as is the custom* (emphasis added)."[52] Beyond stressing the importance of Ceuta and Tétouan as spaces of exchange, De Acosta's words demonstrate how ransom procedures followed rules and created expectations among the parties involved. These cases also shed light on the complexity of such exchanges and on the collaboration required between Christians, Muslims, Moriscos and Jews. In some instances, it was the habitants of tiny settlements neighboring the *presidio* who walked there themselves to negotiate ransom independently. Amar ben Aabica (as Spanish sources spell his name) crossed the distance from his village to near Melilla several times in 1595 in the hope of ransoming his son, who was taken captive and now pulled an oar on one of the Spanish royal galleys. Ben Aabica purchased for that purpose two soldiers from Melilla who were taken captive by the Muslim neighbors of the fort. The governor of the *presidio* tried to ransom the soldiers for money but the father refused. Eventually, the governor wrote to the Council of War and asked for Amar ben Aabica's son explaining that otherwise the father would not release the captive soldiers.[53]

Tabarka, an island near Tunis, conquered by Charles V in 1535 and leased out in 1542 to the Genoese Lomellini who dealt in the coral fished there, was a similar haven.[54] The Spaniards knew exactly what the island was good for. In a report submitted to the Council of State in 1582, the Spanish ambassador in Genoa explained that "the only benefit of that place is the ransom of Christians, [since] the corsairs of Bizerte, Annaba, and all the coast of Barbary go there, and [we also receive] a few reports from the Levant."[55] The island's location, only 80 miles away from Tunis, 216 miles from Mazara del Vallo (located at the southwestern tip of Sicily), and 317 miles away from Algiers, was instrumental in its functioning as a trade zone but it also entailed shared sovereignty over its territory: Spanish and Genoese sovereignty embedded in the deed of leasing, and Ottoman sovereignty formed by the tribute Genoa paid Algiers and Tunis formalized in capitulations that the Sultan issued.[56] Jerónimo Gracián, held captive in Tunis in 1592 and 1594, portrayed the island as a safe exchange space that guaranteed the captives that they would not be sold back to slavery immediately upon paying the "go-between," while assuring the latter that he would be compensated upon releasing the captives he ransomed. In 1609, Fatima, an Algerian thirteen-years-old girl held captive in Livorno, was ransomed and sent back home. On the way, her ship stopped in Calvi in Corsica, where Fatima was forced to convert and baptized as Madalena. In response, the Algerian arrested three Trinitarian friars on a ransom mission and the hundred and thirty captives they had ransomed. In the negotiations that ensued, the Algerians insisted that Fatima be sent to Tabarka and questioned there by an Algerian envoy about the authenticity of her conversion– "if she was a Christian he would leave her, and if a Moor he would take her with him."[57] A few years later, the Algerians and Spaniards negotiated the ransom of the detained Trinitarians and their captives in return for the Bey of Alexandria and his wife, at the time held captive in the Spanish viceroyalty of Sicily. The parties struck an agreement that was never executed. According to the agreement the viceroy of Sicily had to transfer Mahamete Bey and his wife to the custody of the Genoese governor of Tabarka. In the meantime, the intermediary that cooked the deal had to arrange for a letter from the Sultan ordering the Pasha to release the Trinitarians and the captives they had ransomed. Once the Trinitarians and the captives were free, the governor of Tabraka was to free the

Bey and his wife and provide them with safe passes.[58] Despite the failure of these cases, they point out how Muslims and Christians perceived Tabarka as a middle ground that facilitated exchange and safe interaction.

Manipulating the System

In the preceding pages I have reconstructed some of the unwritten rules of the ransom economy and the procedures required to negotiate, strike, and execute a transaction. These protocols were institutionalized to the degree that the parties involved had certain expectations, in some cases explicitly articulated in the documentation that recorded the exchange. When these expectations were not fulfilled, captives took action and tried to amend the situation by evoking these unwritten protocols and the potential destructive effects of their violations. Such instances not only shed light on the rules and the expectations themselves but also on the way various actors – the King, royal bureaucracies and bureaucrats but more interestingly captives themselves – could manipulate the ransom economy or object to such manipulations.

One set of expectations which captives, kin, and sellers had pertained to the exchange rate in which captives changed hands. The title of the paper, "para que me saque cabesa por cabesa [sic]", taken form the above mentioned letter of Diego López de Acosta suggests that the rate was a slave for slave but the records show that on the ground things were messier. From the distance of four or five centuries and on the basis of the scattered archival fragments we now possess it is hard to know the exact rate and the reasons it changed, and yet, it is fair to assume that all interested parties had a good sense of what it was.[59] Moreover, the ransom economy was such that when captives felt that their sovereigns authorized deals in rates too low or too high in a way that influenced the ransom market for the worse, they complained.[60] In 1589, for example, Spaniards held captive in Algiers sent a complaint to the crown regarding the king's approval of several ransom deals, which included the exchange of Christians enslaved in the Maghrib in return for Muslims enslaved in Spain. The captives did not challenge the idea of an exchange of Muslims for Christians, but they expressed fury over the rates of exchange on which the deals were based. In the complaint they sent to the Council of War, they argued that the crown freed rich Muslims in return for poor Christians, in other words, that the king paid too much and got too little:

> In Barbary, they have been making a profit by giving a poor Christian for a wealthy Moor from your Majesty's slaves [,] and even if it is true that one

> engages in good works when a captive leaves [captivity] in return for a Moor, one causes damage to the rest of the captives because following that the [Moors] raise the ransom [prices] saying that if such a poor Christian won them a Moor that was worth that much... and as a result ransoms cost a lot.[61]

The crown, the captives argued, inflated ransom rates and sabotaged their chances of returning home. The king's actions signaled to Muslim slave owners that they could and should ask for more in return for their Christian slaves. In response to the complaint, the king ordered a halt to such exchanges for the reasons listed in the captives' complaint.

I do not want to overestimate the success of their letter, for the crown's policy remained indecisive on this subject throughout the seventeenth century. While orders against such exchanges were regularly issued, captives' kin continued to petition the crown for his slaves, and royal officers continued to provide them with slaves to ransom back their relatives. Despite this continued back and forth, the complaint brought at least a temporary halt of ransom deals, demonstrating its potential and power to provoke action. The complaint reflects how the king's actions had an immediate effect on the ransom market in Algiers and thereby on slaves' lives. The beauty of this record, however, is that in contrast to other sources that were part of the procedure of the exchange itself, this one forms a commentary on the system and an attempt to affect it. It shows how beyond the common knowledge required to petition a sovereign for one of his slaves or find information about slaves across the sea, common knowledge shared by Algerian and Spanish widows and mothers, captives occasionally attempted to define the rates on which exchange was based and they could do that from their captivity away from home. In other words, captives and their kin not only employed the system but also participated in its shaping.

Another set of captives' expectations regarded the fair execution of ransom agreements. The following case is not about the barter of captives per-se but rather about a manumitted Muslim slave. Despite the slightly different context, it is worth examining in detail as it sheds more light on the ways in which ransom linked Spain, Morocco and Algiers and on how captives could manipulate the situation by making references to these links. It concerned Yusuf of Tlemecen, the slave of a Sevilian noble, who was manumitted but arrested soon afterward, enslaved again and forced to pull an oar on one of the royal galleys. His enslavement stands out as he was detained without having committed a crime, and in spite of carrying manumission records that vouched for his freedom and proved that he was on his way back to the Maghrib. Instead of falling into desperation, Yusuf drafted a complaint and sent it to the Council of War on March 9, 1644. He explained that he was arrested immediately after his manumission on his way home and added that:

> In Barbary, they never detain Christians who paid their ransom; and by detaining in Spain the Moors who had paid their ransom, [the Spaniards] create a situation in which in Barbary they would do the same with the Christians, a thing that would result in notable damage to many Christians because there are much more Christians than Moors who are ransomed.[62]

This document is revealing. First, in contrast to Trinitarian and Mercedarian propagandistic images that portrayed Maghribi cities as lawless spaces in which capricious Muslims regularly violated agreements they themselves negotiated,[63] Yusuf's petition suggests that the execution of ransom agreements was fairer in the Maghrib than in Spain. His description, off course, might have been biased in the other direction. However, the fact that he was eventually released might suggest that the magistrates with whom he interacted believed him or at least acknowledged that there was some truth in his words. Second, the complaint shows how slaves were not entirely helpless, had access to paper and ink even while rowing on a slave galley and mastered and used, upon need, Spanish legal and administrative codes. Third, the petition did not merely express Yusuf's private anger and hope that the individual counselor, or more likely secretary, reading his petition would be kind enough to let him go. It echoed institutional norms and expectations that Yusuf knew his interlocutors shared with him. Yet, facing the violation of these norms, he added an implicit threat, reminding the Spanish magistrates how such incidents end – "that would result in notable damage to many Christians."[64] In so doing, he went beyond describing the system in which he was trapped, trying to affect it. Finally and perhaps more importantly, the success of the petition (Yusuf was released soon after) points out another way in which captivities of Muslims and of Christians were tightly connected: violation of ransom or manumission agreements struck with Muslims could result in reactive violation of agreements that Christians negotiated in the Maghrib. The threat Yusuf was giving was based on the asymmetry between Muslims and Christians' prospects of liberation. In making it, Yusuf showed how asymmetry could play in favor of Muslim slaves.

Conclusion

In his *Mediterranean and the Mediterranean World in the Age of Philip II*, Braudel described piracy, and *ipso facto* captivity and ransom, as having "its own familiar customs, agreements and negotiation. While robbers and robbed were not actually accomplices before the event, like the popular figures of the *Commedia dell' Arte*, they were well used to methods of bargaining and reaching terms, hence the many networks of intermediaries."[65] The case that opened the chapter, like other cases examined, illustrates the complicity between captives and captors as well as that between kin of captives on both sides of the sea. The Council of War, in its response to the crown regarding the exchange of Babaçain for Álvarez claimed that the former was a ferocious corsair whose release would risk the life and freedom of Spaniards. Nonetheless, and in light of Álvarez' many years of service and of Babaçain's old age, the king consented to the petition Babaçain's wife submitted via Álvarez, manifesting his generosity towards his subjects. The successful ransom of both veterans shows how the absence of institutions such as the orders of redemption, the Trinitarians and the Mercedarians, did not prevent Ottoman Maghribis or Moroccans from ransoming their relatives. Together with Iberians, Maghribis developed procedures and unwritten protocols that facilitated the return home of their relatives enslaved in the Habsburg Empire. Independent ransom intermediaries, whose dynamism demonstrates that the ransom economy was never limited to ecclesiastic institution actors, transferred captives across the Mediterranean and handed them over to other go-betweens in trading zones that provided safe spaces for these barters. By focusing on these negotiations and exchanges rather than on captives' religious confession, Maghribis' involvement in the ransom economy becomes visible. When examined from this perspective, not only does it become clear that North African Muslims made huge efforts to liberate their beloveds but also that the captivity and ransom of Moroccans and Algerians and that of Christians from Iberia but also France and Italy were tightly entangled.

The fact that barter was the most common form of exchange of liberation of Muslims operates as a reminder that the Mediterranean ransom economy was not based exclusively on the selling of captives, but also on swapping, gift exchange, and a combination of these modalities. Profits from ransom and slave labor, then, lose their exclusivity as the only reasons for the capture and enslavement in the Mediterranean. Captivity and ransom in the Mediterranean was never only a business and some bought slaves only in order to retrieve the liberty of their dear ones. Ironically, however, the execution of such barter agreements created a demand for more slaves. While the parties to such deals sought resolution to the violent effects of piratical practices, in so doing they perpetuated the same practices, since buying one slave in order to exchange him or her for a second required them to purchase a third to pay for the first. Such swapping geared towards separation, Christian slaves back to Christendom, Muslims back to Muslim territory, created endless links in the process. The chapter has pointed out three such instances: First, Algerians that interacted with Spaniards often involved royal authorities in such negotiations; second, the intervention of royal authority could immediately affect the ransom market across the sea by inflating exchange rates; third, violation of ransom deals of Muslims enslaved in Spain, often resulted in retaliation against Christians enslaved in the Maghrib. That these captivities formed elements of a single system did not entail their symmetry. First, because Christian captives enjoyed ransom services provided by the Trinitarians and the Mercedarians, services not available to Muslim captives. Second, Spanish royal politics regarding Muslim slaves and Spanish soldiers enslaved in the Maghrib furthered the prospects of ransom for Christians while diminishing them for Muslims. That happened because one hand the crown was reluctant to allow the ransom of certain classes of Muslim slaves. Third, asymmetry also dominated the production and archiving of information as well as its study in the present. The richness of Spanish archives allows the reconstruction of how Muslims and Christians negotiated and executed ransom agreements, but doubtlessly, further research in Ottoman Algerian and Moroccan archives would help recalibrate this history.

Captivity, as it emerges of the analysis, created a brutal rupture in the lives of individuals, but simultaneously, it helped make the Mediterranean into an economic, social and political space. Captivity forced Algerian and Moroccan mothers and wives to negotiate with Christian women in Europe the exchange of their sons and husbands; it allowed for the maintenance of kinship ties at home; it facilitated the entry of Maghribi Jews and Muslims into Spain, from which they were formally excluded since their expulsion; and thanks to paper and information flows, it permitted Spanish and Maghribi religious and political institutions to gain knowledge of what was happening in enemy territory. In that sense, the value of focusing on such exchanges goes beyond the study of captivity and ransom as such, also shedding light on how the sea, a socio-political space linking Iberia and North Africa, emerged out of the flow of such transactions.

Endnotes

1 I thank Naor Ben Yehoyada, Jessica Marglin, Martin Hershenzon, Gillian Weiss and the anonymous reader of *African Economic History* for their comments on earlier versions of the chapter. Research for this chapter was facilitated by generous funding from the Social Science Research Council, the Program for Cultural Cooperation between Spain's Ministry of Culture and American Universities, and the University of Michigan.

2 Archivo General de Simancas (here after AGS), Legajo 811, 5.16.1616 and Legajo 814, 4.9.1616.

3 Alessandro Stella, *Histoires d'Esclaves dans la Péninsule Ibérique* (Paris: Éditions EHESS, 2000), 78-79; Raffaella Sarti, "Bolognesi schiavi dei 'turchi' e schiavi 'turchi' a Bologna tra cinque e settecento: alterità etnico-religiosa e riduzione in schiavitù," *Quaderni Storici*, 107 (2001), 450; Michel Fontenay, "Il mercato maltese degli schiavi al tempo dei Cavalieri di San Giobanni," *Quaderni Storici*, 107 (2001), 397; Robert Davis, "Counting European Slaves on the Barbary Coast," *Past and Present*, 172 (2001), 87-124. Salvatore Bono conjectured that between the sixteenth and nineteenth century 2,000,000 slaves from the Muslim Mediterranean entered Europe and around a 1,000,000 Christians were enslaved in the Muslim world. Salvatore Bono, "Slave Histories and Memoirs in the Mediterranean World: A Study of the Sources (Sixteenth-Eighteenth Centuries)," in Maria Fusaro, Colin Heywood and Mohamed-Salah Omro (eds.), *Trade and Cultural Exchange in the Early Modern Mediterranean, Braudel's Maritime Legacy* (New York: I. B. Tauris, 2010), 105.

4 For two notable exceptions see these attempts to compare Christian and Muslim captivity and slavery: Michel Fontenay, "L'esclave galérien dans la Méditerranée des Temps Modernes," in Henri Bresc (ed.), *Figures de l'esclave au Moyen-Age et dans le monde moderne: actes de la table ronde* (Paris: Éditions L'Harmattan, 1996), 115-42 ; and Claude Larquié, "Captifs chrétiens et esclaves maghrébins au XVIIIe siècle: Une tentative de comparaison," in Gonçal López Nadal and María Luisa Sánchez León (eds.), *Captius i esclaus a l'antiguitat i al món modern. XIXe colloque du GIREA, Palma de Mallorca 1991* (Naples: Jovene Editore, 1996), 347-364.

5 The literature on early modern captivity is vast and a few examples will suffice. On Spanish captives; see Ellen G. Friedman, *Spanish Captives in North Africa in the Early Modern Age* (Madison: University of Wisconsin Press, 1983); Maximiliano Barrio Gozalo, *Esclavos y cautivos: Conflicto entre la cristiandad y el islam en el siglo XVIII* (Valladolid: Junta de Castilla y León, Consejería de Cultura y Turísmo, 2006); José Antonio Martínez Torres, *Prisioneros de los infieles: vida y rescate de los cautivos cristianos en el Mediterráneo musulmán (siglos XVI-XVII)* (Barcelona: Ediciones Bellaterra, 2004). On English, see Nabil I. Matar, *Britain and Barbary, 1589-1689* (Gainesville: University Press of Florida, 2005); and Matar, "English Accounts of Captivity in North Africa and the Middle East: 1577-1625," *Renaissance Quarterly*, 54 (2001), 553-572; Linda Colley, *Captives, Britain, Empire and the World, 1600-1850* (New York: Pantheon Books, 2002). On Algerians, see *Moulay Belhamissi, Les captifs algériens et l'Europe chrétienne* (*1518-1830*) (Alger: L'Entreprise Nationale du Livre, 1988). More broadly, on North African captives, see Matar, "Piracy and Captivity in the Early Modern Mediterranean: The Perspective from Barbary," in Claire Jowett (ed.), *Pirates? The Politics of Plunder, 1550-1650* (Basingstoke: Palgrave Macmillan, 2007), 56-73. On French, Gillian Lee Weiss,

Captives and Corsairs, France and Slavery in the Early Modern Mediterranean (Stanford: Stanford University Press, 2011).

6 Weiss, *Captives and Corsairs*; and Belhamissi, *Les captifs algériens.*

7 AGS, *Estado*, Legajo 246, 5.12.1612.

8 AGS, *Estado*, Legajo, 992, 10.30.1629.

9 AGS, *Estado*, Legajo 3446, 3.21.1633.

10 For documents and more about this case, see J. Vernet, "La embajada de al-Ghassni (1690-1691)," *Al-Andalus*, 18 (1953), 109-131; Tomás García Figueras, Carlos Rodríguez Joulia Saint-Cy, *Larache: datos para su historia en el siglo XVII* (Madrid: Instituto de Estudios Africanos. CSIC, 1972), 319-327; Arribas Palau, Mariano, "De nuevo sobre la embajada de al-Gassani (1690-1691)," *Al-Qantara*, 6 (1985), 199-289; Ubaldo de Casanova y Todolí, "Algunas anotaciones sobre el comportamiento de los esclavos moros en Mallorca durante el siglo XVII y un ejemplo de intercambio con cautivos cristianos," *Bolletí de la Societat Arqueològica Lul·liana: Revista d'estudis històrics*, 41 (1985), 323-332.

11 For documents and study of the ransom of Moroccans and Algerians in the second half of the eighteenth century orchestrated by the Sultan Muḥammad b.'Abdallāh al-Khaṭīb, see Ramón Lourido Díaz, "La obra redentora del sultán marroquí Sīdī Muḥammad b. 'Abd Allāh entre los cautivos musulmanes en Europa (siglo XVIII)," *Cuadernos de Historia del Islam*, 11 (1984), 138-183; and Mariano Arribas Palau, "Argelinos cautivos en España, rescatados por el sultán de Marruecos," *Boletín de la Asociación Española de Orientalistas*, 26 (1990), 23-54.

12 Wolfgang Kaiser, "La excepción permanente. Actores, visibilidad y asimetrías en los intercambios comerciales entre los países europeos y el Magreb (siglos XVI-XVII)," in José Antonio Martínez Torres (ed.), *Circulación de personas e intercambios en el Mediterráneo y en el Atlántico (siglos XVI, XVII, XVIII)* (Madrid: CSIC, 2008), 171-189; Daniel Hershenzon, "Plaintes et menaces réciproques: captivité et violence religieuses dans la Méditerranée du XVIIe siècle," in Jocelyne Dakhlia and Wolfgang Kaiser (eds)., *Les Musulmans dans l'histoire de l'Europe. Tome 2. Passages et contacts en Méditerranée* (Paris: Albin Michel, 2013), 441-460.

13 On Trinitarians and Mercedarians, see Friedman, *Spanish Captives*; Barrio Gozalo, *Esclavos y cautivos*; and Martínez Torres, *Prisioneros de los infieles.* On Italian confraternities, see Robert Davis, *Christian Slaves, Muslim Masters: White Slavery in the Mediterranean, the Barbary Coast, and Italy, 1500-1800* (New York: Palgrave Macmillan, 2003), 139-193.

14 On the state of seventeenth- and eighteenth-century Algerian archives and sources relevant for this history, see Fatiha Loualich, "In the Regency of Algiers: The Human Side of the Algerine Corso," in Maria Fusaro, Colin Heywood and Mohamed-Salah Omro (eds.), *Trade and Cultural Exchange in the Early Modern Mediterranean, Braudel's Maritime Legacy* (New York: I. B. Tauris: 2010), 69-96, esp. 93-96. On the problem of Moroccan documents from the early mod-

ern period, see the comments in Mercedes García Arenal, *Ahmad al-Mansur, The Beginning of Modern Morocco* (Oxford: One World, 2009), 144; and Daniel J. Schroeter, *The Sultan's Jew, Morocco and the Sephardi World* (Stanford: Stanford University Press, 2002), xiii.

15 During most of the period examined here, the Spanish Empire included Portugal, Sicily, Naples, Milan and several fort towns in Mediterranean and Atlantic North Africa.

16 "[E]n SanLúcar... en la calle de los Bretones, y se llama su amo Nicolás Rubin...." Archivo Histórico Nacional (hereafter AHN), *Inquisición*, Leg. 933/2, 11.13.1655. While the letter of the Muslim slave did not survive, the letters that the Christian captive with whom the Muslim slave was supposed to be exchanged has survived. In his letters, the Christian captive referred to the information the Muslim provided his Algerian relatives with. The title of this article, "para que me saque cabesa por cabesa [sic]," is taken from the letter of the Christian captive.

17 "...después haver servido a vuestra majestad muchos años en la harmada rreal... y el año de 611 fue captivo de los turcos de Argel," AGS, *Guerra Antigua*, Legajo. 811, 16.5.1611.

18 "...no tiene con que se poder rrescatar y la dicha mora, su ama, está determinada de no le dar por quanto tesoro hubiere en el mundo menos de por el rrescate de su marido" AGS, *Guerra Antigua*, Legajo. 811, 16.5.1611.

19 For example, AGS, *Guerra Antigua*, Legajo. 784, 31.3.1613. On the role of slaves in the royal galleys and the crown's position on their employment, see Manuel Lomas Cortés, "Les galériens du Roi Catholique: esclaves, forçats et rameurs salariés dans les escadres de Philippe III (1598-1621)," *Cahiers des Annales de Normandie*, 36 (2011), 111-124, esp. 9-13. In comparison with French policies, however, the Spanish crown was much more tolerant towards the idea of exchanging slaves, see Weiss' chapter, "Ransoming 'Turks' from France's Royal Galleys," in this volume.

20 AGS, *Guerra Antigua*, Libro 159, 1630.

21 AGS, *Guerra Antigua*, Legajo. 213, Fol. 546. "y no es arraez ny de consideración."

22 AGS, *Guerra Antigua*, Legajo. 810, 24.9.1616, "que no es arraez ni de rescate."

23 AGS, *Guerra Antigua*, Legajo. 442, 23.4.1594, "pedirá al rrey le dé de limosna el otro cristiano porque le dan su hijo."

24 AGS, *Guerra Antigua*, Legajo. 442, 23.4.1594 "que atento a esto le aga merced del otro moro para hazer el truque y rescate de su hijo."

25 AGS, *Guerra Antigua*, Legajo. 442, 23.4.1594, "Hamete de Marruecos, hijo de Ali, de hedad de 22 años pestañas y cejas grandes con un lunar grande en la garganta y una señal de fuego en el brazo derecho y unas sajaduras en la frente pequeño del cuerpo fue cautibo en la Almería de Ceuta... en siete de otubre de mil y quinientos y ochenta y tres años.... Y por lo que parece por este assiento y somos informados no parece que sea de consideración ni arráez ni de rrescate."

26 AGS, *Guerra Antigua*, Legajo. 274, fol. 116, 9.20.1589 "Y el capitán que le captivo por llevar mayor ynteres sea el ya otro los dio por arraez,"

27 AGS, *Guerra Antigua*, Legajo. 274, fol. 116, 9.20.1589 "buscando siempre excusas y doliéndose poco de los captivos cristianos,"

28 AGS, *Guerra Antigua*, Leg. 272, fol. 56 "...[Y] que aunque a acudido y rrequerido con las dichas dos cedulas al adelantado no le a querido dar el dicho turco,"

29 Atlantic slavery, he has added, was "above all a matter of business;" slavery in the Maghrib of "passion... almost of *jihad*." Davis, *Christian Slaves, Muslim Masters*, xxv. With a small variation, Davis has reproduced a long-criticized dichotomy in studies of slavery according to which slavery in America was economic, while in Africa it was social. On the dichotomy between the alleged economic nature of slavery in the Atlantic and the social nature of slavery in Africa, see Frederick Cooper, "The Problem of Slavery in African Studies," *Journal of African History*, 20 (1979), 103-125.

30 Michel Fontenay, "Esclaves et/ou captifs : préciser les concepts," in Wolfgang Kaiser (ed.), *Le commerce des captifs : les intermédiaires dans l'échange et le rachat des prisonniers en Méditerranée, XVe-XVIIIe siècle* (Rome: École Française de Rome, 2008), 15-24. Whereas in the Mediterranean, the terms "slave," "captive," "ransom," and "redemption" are used interchangeably, in West Africa they are sharply distinguished and related to distinct enslavement practices and procedures of manumission, ransom, and redemption, see Ojo's chapter in this volume.

31 Bono, "Slave Histories and Memoirs in the Mediterranean World," 100. On the distinction in Roman, Christian and Judeo traditions, see Andrés Díaz Borrás, *El miedo al Mediterráneo: La caridad popular valenciana y la redención de cautivos bajo poder musulmán 1323-1539* (Barcelona: CSIC. Instituto Milá Fontanals, 2001), 5-18. On the terms used in Arabic, see Nabil Matar, *Britain and Barbary, 1589-1689*, 114-115. On the terms in Ottoman Turkish, see Géza Dávid and Pál Fodor, "Introduction," in Géza Dávid and Pál Fodor (eds.), *Ransom Slavery along the Ottoman Borders (Early Fifteenth-Early Eighteenth Centuries)* (Leiden: Brill, 2007), xiv. The latter offer an alternative solution of this debate with "Ransom Slavery," Ibid. European understandings of the bondage of Christians in the Mediterranean were reshaped at the turn of the nineteenth century by the phenomenon of slavery of Blacks. Whereas in the early modern period the captivity of Christians in the Maghrib was perceived in religious or commercial terms, in the nineteenth century, it came to be understood in racial terms. It was no more the captivity of Christians but rather the slavery of whites. For a discussion of this shift, see: Weiss, *Captives and Corsairs* and Ann Thompson, *Barbary and Enlightenment: European Attitudes Towards the Maghreb in the Eighteenth Century* (Leiden: Brill, 1987),

32 Matar, "Piracy and Captivity in the Early Modern Mediterranean." On intellectual and religious approaches to ransom in West Africa during the period, see Lofkrantz's chapter in this volume.

33 Miriam Hoexter, *Endowments, Rulers and Community, Waqf al Haramayn in Ottoman Algiers* (Leiden: Brill 1998), 27 and 158.

34 P.S. Van Koningsveld, "Muslim Slaves and Captives in Western Europe during the Late Middle Ages," *Islam and Christian-Muslim Relations*, 6 (1995), 10.

35 AHN, *Inqisición*, Leg. 1824-2.

36 AGS, *Guerra Antigua*, Legajo. 271, fol. 304, 1589.

37 AGS, *Guerra Antigua*, Legajo. 448, fol. 206, 23.10.1595.

38 Míkel de Epalza, "Moriscos y Andalusíes en Túnez durante el siglo XVII," *Al-Andalus*, 34:2 (1969), 247-327, esp. 262-269.

39 Peter A. Mazur, "Combating 'Mohammedan Indecency': The Baptism of Muslim Slaves in Spanish Naples, 1563-1667," *Journal of Early Modern History*, 13 (2009), 25-48, esp. 32-33.

40 Martín Corrales Eloy, *Comercio de Cataluña con el Mediterráneo musulmán (siglos XVI-XVIII): El Comercio con los 'enemigos de la fe'* (Barcelona: Bellaterra, 2001); and *Roberto Blanes Andrés, Valencia y El Magreb: Las Relaciones Comerciales Maritimas (1600-1703) (Barcelona: Bellaterra, 2010).*

41 On the "permanent exception," see: Kaiser, "La excepción permanente," 171-189. For a brilliant analysis of the negotiations between the Majorcan administration and the Spanish crown regarding the right to trade with Muslims, see Natividad Planas, "La frontière franchissable: normes et pratiques dans les échanges entre le royaume de Majorque et les terres d'Islam au XVIIe siècle," *Revue d'histoire moderne et contemporaine,* 48:2 (2001), 123-147.

42 The Inquisition based its right to interfere on matters of commerce with Muslims on a papal bull prohibiting it. But Già's attorney claimed the bishop annulled the bull and hence it was in the Episcopal rather than inquisitorial jurisdiction. We do not know what was the bishop's response, but the claim of the attorney points to how interactions with Maghribi fell under a multiplicity of competing jurisdictions, a situation which the parties involved could employ to their favor, see Natividad Planas, "Conflicts de competence aux frontiers. Le contrôle de la circulation des homes et des marchandises dans le royaume de Majorque au XVIIe siècle," *Cromohs*, 8 (2003), 1-14.

43 AHN, *Inquisición*, Legajo 1714, carpeta 7.

44 Wolfgang Kaiser, "Zones de transit. Lieux, temps, modalités du rachat de captifs en Méditerranée," in Jocelyne Dakhlia and Wolfgang Kaiser (eds.), *Les Musulmans dans l'histoire de l'Europe. Tome 2. Passages et contacts en Méditerranée* (Paris: Albin Michel, 2013), 251-272.

45 Jean-Frédéric Schaub, *Les juifs du roi d'Espagne* (Paris: Hachette Littératures, 1999).

46 Beatriz Alonso Acero, *Orán-Mazalquivir, 1589-1639: una sociedad española en la frontera de Berbería* (Madrid: CSIC, 2000).

47 Schaub, *Les juifs du roi d'Espagne*, 94-5.

48 AGS, *Estado*, Legajo, 992, 10.30.1629.

49 On the role of credit in ransom operations in the context of Tunis, see Sadok Boubaker, "Réseaux et techniques de rachat des captifs de la course à Tunis au XVIIIe siècle," in Kaiser, *Le commerce des captifs*, 25-46.

50 Emanuel de Aranda, *Les captifs d'Alger: Relation de la captivité du sieur Emanuel d'Aranda* Ed. Latifa Z'rari Latifa (Paris: J. P. Rocher, 1997), 65-74.

51 Diego Díaz Hierro, *Historia de la Merced de Huelva: hoy catedral de su diócesis* (Huelva, 1975), 36.

52 "[M]andarle a Seuta con buena custodia, y hacerle escribir que baje yo a Tetuán para que allí se aga como es costumbre el trueque," AHN, *Inquisición*, Legajo 933/2, 11.13.1655.

53 AGS, *Guerra Antigua*, Legajo 432, fol 181, 10.22.1595.

54 For example, the lease from 1615, see: AGS, *Estado*, Negociaciones de Sicilia, Legajo 1169, fols. 18-20.

55 "[C]omodidad solo ay en aquel lugar de rescatar cristianos acudiendo allí los corsarios de Viserta, Bona, y toda la costa de Berbería, y algunos avisos de Levante," AGS, *Estado*, Legajo 1416, fol. 138/1-2.

56 Philippe Gourdin, *Tabarka: histoire et archéologie d'un préside espagnol et d'un comptoir génois en terre africaine (XVe-XVIIIe siècle)* (Rome: École Française de Rome, 2008), 245-269.

57 "Si fuere christiana la dexa y si mora la lleve consigo," AGS, *Estado*, Legajo 1882, fol. 245, 8.1.1617.

58 AGS, *Estado*, Legajo 259, 20.11.1614.

59 For economists' attempt to calculate and analyze ransom prices over the long term, see Attila Ambrus and Eric Chaney, "Pirates of the Mediterranean: An Empirical Investigation of Bargaining with Transaction Costs, 9.14.2010," http://www.economics.harvard.edu/faculty/chaney/files/barbary.pdf, accessed on July 10, 2011. See also: Jean Mathiex, "Trafic et Prix de l'Homme en Méditerranée aux XVIIe et XVIIIe siècles," *Annales,* 9 (1954), 157-64.

60 On the Mediterranean ransom economy, see Wolfgang Kaiser, "L'économie de la rançon en Méditerranée occidentale (XVIe-XVIIe siècle)," in Simonetta Cavaciocchi (ed.), *Ricchezza dal mare, secc. XIII-XVIII*, vol. 2 (Florence: Le Monnier, 2006), 689-701; and the chapters in Wolfgang Kaiser (ed.), *Le commerce des captifs: les intermédiaires dans l'échange et le rachat des prisonniers en Méditerranée, XVe-XVIIIe siècle* (Rome: École Française de Rome, 2008).

61 AGS, *Guerra Antigua*, Legajo 268, Fol. 200, 1.3.1589. "[Y] aunque es verdad que se haze buena obra al cautibo que sale por el moro, hazese mala a todos los cautivos porque con esto les suben los rescates diziendo que tal christiano pobre le dio un moro que valían tanto y quieren al respecto que cada uno vaya subiendo y con esto cuestan muchos los rescates..."

62 AGS, *Guerra Antigua*, Legajo 1541, 3.9.1644. "Pues en la Ververía a ningún christiano se le detiene después de haver pagado su rescate, y deteniendo en España a los moros después de haverse serrescatado será dar ocación a que en la Ververía hagan otro tanto con los christianos de que resultara notable perjuicio a muchos cristianos pues ellos son muchos los que por su rescate salen del cautiverio y muy pocos los moros."

63 For example, see the collection of early modern pamphlets related to Algiers: Ignacio Bauer Landauer, *Papeles de mi archive: Relaciones de África (Argel)*,

Vol. 4 (Madrid: Editorial Ibero-Africano-Americana, 1922/23).

64 On the dynamic of challenge and riposte within the context of captivity across the Mediterranean, see Hershenzon, "Plaintes et menaces réciproques: captivité et violence religieuses dans la Méditerranée du XVIIe siècle."

65 Fernand Braudel, *The Mediterranean and the Mediterranean World in the Age of Philip II*, Vol. 2 (New York: Harper & Row, 1972), 867.

CHAPTER II

Ransoming "Turks" from France's Royal Galleys

Gillian Weiss

Introduction

During the reign of Louis XIV, at least two thousand "Turks" (*Turcs*) labored for the Sun King.[1] Ottoman and Moroccan subjects, presumed to be Muslims, they helped power France's expanding fleet of galleys during the late seventeenth century. These oar-driven vessels possessed naval as well as penal utility, but their function was overwhelming symbolic. While gilded prows, fleur-de-lis flags, and intricate carvings displayed the monarch's majesty, chained rowers exhibited his authority. In fact, a small number of *mariniers de rame* (salaried oarsmen, previously known as *bonnevoglies* from the Italian) performed in this royal spectacle of subjugation for pay. All the others – about eighty percent convicts (*forçats*) and twenty percent slaves (*esclaves*) – acted for free. The criminals, vagabonds and heretics in the first category had been condemned by *parlements* throughout France, and then transported, mostly on foot, to the king's naval base in Marseille or one of several smaller maritime outposts. The *esclaves turcs* usually arrived by sea, having been seized or purchased in Mediterranean ports and near Habsburg battlefields by an extensive network of traffickers accountable to the ministry of the marine.

Thanks to the anti-monarchical memoirs of Huguenot exiles and other Protestant polemic, France's royal galleys have been notorious since the eighteenth century.[2] In the modern period, one American and at least two

French scholars have published major works, providing detailed overview of the institution and quantitative analysis of the galley corps.[3] Another corpus has focused on *forçats pour la foi* (convicts for the faith).[4] With one notable exception,[5] however, no study has focused on the slaves, whose presence exposes as myth the kingdom's supposed free soil.[6] More recently, historical studies of Mediterranean slavery on the one hand and Muslims in France on the other[7] have moved "Turks" out of the shadows. It is becoming increasingly clear that the legal maxim, "there are no slaves in France," little affected Ottomans and Moroccans in the *chiourme* (rowing force), even when at the end of seasons at sea, they descended on dry land. It is also coming to light that *esclaves turcs*, as well as their visual representations played a larger role in the propaganda of Louis XIV than previously understood.[8] In particular, by advertising the subjugation of alleged infidels, *Turc*-powered galleys answered critics of France's commercial ties with the Ottoman Empire that Europeans termed "Capitulations."[9] Instead, vessels and oarsmen projected an image of naval and religious domination and imperial ambition. Meanwhile, publicly celebrated *Turc* baptisms broadcast the king's Catholic supremacy – over Muslims as well as Protestants.

Ottoman and Moroccan slaves were integral elements in a Bourbon promotion strategy, and starting in the 1660s, Louis XIV expended tremendous financial and diplomatic resources on procurement. During his father's and his grandfather's reigns, whenever they could, aristocratic captains and even the queen had staffed their private galleys with *Turcs*.[10] Now, half a century later, intendants in Provence and proxies in Malta systematically signed supply contracts with merchants in France and abroad to achieve an ideal balance aboard the royal fleet.[11] They also bartered set numbers for naval commands and consular offices. Knight of Malta Jean de Saint-Hérem, for instance, pledged 150 "esclaves" at 250 *livres* apiece to head up a galley; Louis Maillet of Cassis promised 50 per year at 340 *livres* each to acquire an appointment to Candia.[12] Meanwhile, established consuls in Italian cities and ship captains who called at slaving ports came under intense pressure to obtain tall, healthy men aged twenty to forty. As marine minister Jean-Baptiste Colbert, marquis de Seignelay told consul François Cotolendi in Livorno, "There is no occasion for you better to demonstrate your zeal and more easily to enter his majesty's good graces than by sending a large number of slaves to Marseille."[13] Galley officials entertained experiments with Atlantic sourcing from the Guinea Coast and Canada but returned quickly to the Mediterranean.[14] And what the crown could not attain openly, it sought through subterfuge. Most common was buying or capturing, then keeping, men generally deemed un-enslavable by treaty or religion, even over the objections of the Maltese Inquisitor.[15] More daring was sending out clandestine scouts like the one code-named "Baptiste Fedeli" who bid for six hundred Hungarian prisoners-of-war at Vienna.[16] For three decades, 150-200 Tripolitans, Tunisians, Saletians, Anatolians, Bosnians, and even Russians, Poles and Greeks – but most of all Algerians – involuntarily joined the rowing force each year.[17]

Given the effort and expense of acquiring and training these *esclaves turcs*, and the grueling yet skilled work they executed on the galleys, the crown was highly resistant to freeing them, whether in exchange for money, political favors, or even some of the thousands of French Christians held across North Africa.[18] Indeed, royal representatives regularly shunned payments, risked foreign war and sacrificed fellow subjects rather than emancipate *Turcs* still capable of pulling an oar. Though for the sake of Mediterranean commerce and in pursuit of European domination, France signed bilateral treaties with each of the three western Ottoman provinces and Morocco that appeared to mandate reciprocal liberation, it seldom immediately or fully complied. Though individuals on both sides made regular, independent efforts to initiate trades, Louis XIV seldom consented. Though appearing to participate in a symmetrical, cross-confessional system of "ransom slavery"[19] French officials stationed in Versailles, Marseille and the échelles (trading ports) of North Africa were in fact upholding a set of asymmetrical foreign relations.[20]

This gap between principle and practice certainly confirms a growing power differential across the western Mediterranean. France's superior naval strength – violently demonstrated in the 1680s and 1690s – gave its government some cover for diplomatic violations. Yet its reluctance to release slaves also implies a rejection of a very premise of ransoming: that every human being possesses an individual, monetary exchange value. Though each *Turc* selling on the market had a proper price, during the late seventeenth century a *Turc* serving on the French royal galleys had become priceless.

Strong as a Turk

In his *Dictionnaire universel*, compiled between 1672 and 1684 and published in 1690, Antoine Furetière defines a *Turc* first as a person from Turkey and then as a subject of the Ottoman sultan. Examples of proverbial usage provide the only hints of servility. To be "fort comme un turc" (strong as a Turk) was to be "extremely robust," as all Muslims, but especially North Africans and even more especially Algerians were reputed to be.[21] For a *chiourme* to perform at its fullest potential required the brute force of slaves, as well as their strategic placement in technically difficult positions at end of the oar, naval administrators commonly believed.[22] Thus in context *Turc* served as shorthand for *esclave turc*, making "Turk" and "slave" virtual synonyms. In the world of the galleys, a *Turc* was a slave, though the status was not hereditary. A *Turc* was a public slave, recognizable by his red hat, long shirt, short pants and hooded cape. He might be hired out to private masters who gained prestige by having one as a personal valet or extracted labor by using one in local industry; or he might be allowed to work on his own account, maintaining a small shop along the quay.

More than a "living tool,"[23] a *Turc* was an administrative category, with distinct judicial and diplomatic standing. A *Turc* was a number recorded in bureaucratic registers, along with name, origin and distinguishing physical characteristics; a *Turc* was a partner, chained to a *forçat* to deter flight. In late seventeenth-century France, a *Turc* was invariably male but, in fact, not invariably Muslim. Both purchasing agents and galley officials had incentive to confuse religious origins – as they did geographical ones – allowing them to enslave not only diplomatic allies but also Orthodox and Jewish subjects of the Ottoman Empire who straddled the Crescent-Cross divide. Meanwhile, a *Turc fait chrétien* (Turk made Christian) was a convert who received special privileges. Whether he had formerly or still currently adhered to Islam, a *Turc* was a symbol. As a propaganda implement propelling a vehicle of propaganda, a *Turc* showcased the king's ability to dominate the bodies and occasionally the souls of infidels. As a financial instrument, a *Turc* operated like an abstract unit of account. As a counterpart for a French subject detained in North Africa, a *Turc* offered some security against abuse, while representing – a mostly fictive – potential for trade.

Ransom Slavery

These relational attributes gave *Turcs* on the royal galleys tremendous idealized power. Yet these relational attributes also largely denied them individualized status, a necessary condition for ransoming. Jennifer Lofkrantz defines ransoming as "the practice of paying for the release of a captive at the time of capture or soon afterwards."[24] In doing so, she insists on the time-bound particularity of one type of liberation, while implying a categorical differentiation between two forms of bondage. When the government of the Sokoto Caliphate promoted policies to buy back freeborn Muslims quickly, it was to ensure that temporary captives did not become permanent slaves. When the French government acted either to release Christians or to obtain ostensible Muslims, by contrast, linguistic and literal fluidity prevailed. Despite local, royal, religious and familial efforts to intervene, many French *captifs* spent lifetimes in servitude. Despite promises to free them, the subjection of *Turcs* often endured as long as their bodies held out. In principle, person-for-cash exchanges might occur at any moment, but in practice speeds of deliverance varied by timing and circumstance.

In Islamic West Africa, the ultimate fate of human booty distinguished ransoming from redemption, with beneficiaries of the first restored to "previous status" at home and the second kept in "subservient status" within an alien society.[25] In Catholic France, where multiple synonymous terms described the process of exit as well entry and experience, baptized rowers came the closest to achieving "redemption" in the sense Lofkrantz posits. During the second half of the seventeenth century, royal policy banned *Turcs faits chrétiens* (Turks made Christian) from repatriating and withheld free residency from those still fit to serve. Yet starting in the 1680s, coinciding with the Revocation of the Edict of Nantes that criminalized Protestantism, the crown offered limited privileges to Muslim slaves who joined the Church. While invalid neophytes received daily charity, valid ones received wages. *Mariniers de rame* remained bound to the galleys but enjoyed greater freedom of movement, the possibility of marrying and having children and the promise of full liberty upon retirement.[26] The goal of such an arrangement was to maximize the physical and symbolic contributions of converted "Turks" and to minimize spiritual backsliding. One of its results was to relegate them to a peculiar subservient but unsettled status – as religiously integrated foreign forced laborers.

Measuring Value

Muslim or Christian, Orthodox or Jewish, effective *Turcs* were all precious to Louis XIV. At slave markets and on military fronts outside the kingdom, however, they had variable costs. Depending on age, physical features, geographical origins, sale location and time period, their price might diverge by a factor of two or three. Yet once incorporated into the *chiourme*, a muscular eighteen-year-old Tunisian bought in Genoa and a slightly maimed Cypriot seized near Cairo were ascribed identical worth. Through this process Ottoman and Moroccan bodies fit to row lost their individuality, becoming fungible replacement labor, whether translated into currency to pay a fine or debt, or offered in kind for discharge from the galleys.[27] As idealized objects, they acted like money. Sometimes they even underwent "laundering" in Livorno, a city with one of the most important slave markets on the Mediterranean coast. There, French agents took advantage of diplomatic terms that prohibited the *capture* but permitted the *purchase* of particular subjects, so that, as sometimes happened, Algerians illegally taken at sea transmogrified into slaves legally acquired on land.[28] *Esclaves turcs* also fulfilled two widely accepted monetary functions: measuring value and, at least on paper, operating as a medium of exchange. As such, they joined a long tradition of slaves functioning as both non-metallic specie and mechanisms for bookkeeping.[29]

During the second half of the seventeenth century, the penalty for a negligent *argousin* (prison guard) or a careless employer who allowed a rower to escape vacillated between one, two or three times "the price of a Turk," a denomination that hovered for several decades around 300-400 *livres*, roughly the same cost as for a sub-Saharan or French *esclave*.[30] In the same period, ship owners received and refused a proposal "to reimburse in Turks" a portion of a royal loan for arming their vessels.[31] In the years up to 1684, the galley treasury also logged hundreds of deposits from disabled convicts; their release had to be endorsed by the marine ministry then implemented via royal orders for "detaching [them] from the chain."[32] Conversion rates into able *Turcs* differed according to sentence rendered and time served, with violent offenders and Huguenots banned from exercising this buy-out option. Followers of the R.P.R (*Religion Prétendue Réformée* or so-called Reformed Religion) were to remain incarcerated until they recanted. For petty criminals, by contrast, authorities who expressed few scruples about keeping valid ones decades past their terms eagerly took cash to liberate those from whom they could derive no further physical labor – and no longer wished to clothe and feed. Another alternative was to assign valetudinarians less strenuous tasks inside the arsenal, or else ship them off to France's American colonies.[33] Once struck from the *chiourme* and issued freedom certificates from the crown, ex-convicts received orders to leave the area immediately and permanently. Repeated expulsion edicts suggest that many did not.

Still, the disposal of incapacitated rowers endured. The difference was that from 1684 onwards, a diminished supply of slaves had created such a large discrepancy between paper valuation and market value that a new ordinance proscribed the receipt of funds, mandating the delivery of flesh. A freedom ticket for a *Catholic* invalid oarsman became, in principle, "an able-bodied Turk fit to serve in his place."[34] A valid Catholic *forçat* with a completed sentence had a shot at manumission only if he could lay his hands on multiples. The question is how. Given that French merchants had been explicitly forbidden from slave trading on their own accounts[35] and French consuls explicitly instructed to buy up the best candidates on the market, it would seem that purchasing agents for a convict stood at a strong disadvantage. Despite the odds, however, galley records indicate that some managed.

One method they used was to pay premiums that Louis XIV would not. There is little to support the contention that "there were always Turks for sale on the quays of Marseille,"[36] though it does seem likely that slave traders accepted furtive payments from convicts at higher than the going rate. Sometimes these private dealings worked to royal advantage. The marine minister was pleased, for example, when freedom-seeking *forçats* offered up prohibitively expensive "Turks from Livorno." That way, he explained, their procurement "cost the king nothing."[37] As such examples make clear, the interchangeability of money and slaves shifted over time. What remained constant was the idealized nature of usable "Turks." Within the closed economy of the galleys, a (healthy) *Turc* was a *Turc* was a *Turc* was a *Turc*: a substitutable object to be retained for propaganda purposes rather than a distinct subject to be freed for diplomatic ones.

Acting Diplomatically

In the diplomatic realm, sustained by gift and ransom economies open to foreign participants and governed by principles of reciprocity, it was harder for French authorities either to overlook particularities among servile "Turks" or to ignore repercussions for enslaved Frenchmen. Even though they continued to view Islam as an abstract commonality and physical prowess as a correlated attribute, they had no choice but also to acknowledge – even if they chose to ignore – the diverse ways Moroccan and Ottoman subjects self-affiliated and the diverse ways Moroccan and Ottoman leaders measured value.

When France's marine minister ordered extra food distributed to Tripolitan rowers on the galleys, therefore, he was offering recompense for special privileges accorded French captives in Tripoli.[38] When officials from coast to capital addressed complaints from the *dey* of Algiers about inaccessible Muslim burial grounds in Marseille, however, they were accepting that *esclaves turcs* held anywhere in Christendom behaved as standard securities for the good treatment of Christian slaves held across the lands of Islam.[39] In 1699, Moroccan ambassador 'Abdallah ibn 'Aisha explained the situation bluntly. He had received a letter about a galley captain who punished his [Muslim] slave by having him viciously whipped and then vinegar and salt rubbed into the man's wounds. "Inform the vizier [marine minister] Pontchartrain," wrote ibn Aisha, "that as soon as I return to my country I will administer two hundred blows to every [Christian] slave in my house, and as soon as I arrive at court, I will order the same done there."[40] In such cases, French officials had to recognize that *Turcs* kept *in* France had diplomatic worth unconnected to physical condition – but rather tied to political allegiance or religious standing or both. At the same time, representatives of the French crown knew very well that to make well-received presents for a Muslim ruler, *Turcs* sent *from* France had to possess appropriate social position as well. That is why, say, the repatriation of a vizier's kinsman garnered flowery thanks from Istanbul but the return of a handful of Moroccan subjects earned expressions of displeasure. As sultan Mulay Isma'il noted scornfully, "Do not think that among them is one of our servants, soldiers or relations. These are people 'without importance.'"[41]

From the 1660s through the 1690s, France signed numerous peace accords with the three Ottoman provinces of North Africa and the kingdom of Morocco. Negotiated by special envoys, resident merchants, dedicated friars, naval deputies; captives, converts and other sorts of marginal intermediaries, these settlements inscribed norms for safe travel and trade, granted refuge to vessels and peoples, and set terms for diplomatic privileges and changes of religion. They also required, if not always effected, large-scale slave liberations – whether by exchange, cash payment or some combination. Over three decades, publicly acknowledged terms trended in France's favor, though secret clauses sometimes made additional, controversial allowances. The official, French version of the 1665 accord between France and Tunis, for instance, provided for the liberation of "all the French slaves" and "only the janissary [elite military] slaves found to be from Tunis." The confidential one required a head-for-head trade of *every* soldier with Tunisian roots held in France for a portion of the French subjects held in Tunis, with Tunis sending an inspector to verify full compliance and France paying a fixed sum for each enslaved subject who remained. In this case, the necessary sums were raised through a royal grant, local collections and money amassed by the *Frères de la Merci* (Mercedarians), one of two orders devoted to freeing Catholic faithful from Muslim territories.[42] Twenty years and two French bombardments later, a treaty between France and Algiers still provided for slave exchange. In 1684, French firepower had already forced the release of several hundred captives for free; the agreement pertained to those Frenchmen left behind and an equal number of Algerians serving in Marseille.[43]

In such a context, from the viewpoint of liberating states, specific identities became paramount. Each polity sought its own subjects, though once satisfied a Muslim or Catholic ruler might claim non-native coreligionists to demonstrate charity or power.[44] Neither volunteered converts lest these trophies for the faith decide to recant or else face execution at home. Meanwhile, respective willingness to receive Christians converted to Islam (known as renegades) or *Turcs faits chrétiens* varied over time. As for the particular case of Huguenots, the crown's policy towards buying them back changed after the 1685 Revocation of the Edict of Nantes. Before then negotiators had orders to save Protestants as potential returnees to the Catholic Church. Afterwards they were instructed to abandon Reformed Christians in captivity.[45] Skill, rank and roots also counted to *deys*, *beys*, *pashas*, sultans and the king. Facing a labor shortage in his navy, Louis XIV prioritized sailors; given imperial politics, Ottoman appointees in North Africa regularly favored janissaries; the Moroccan sultan Mulay Isma'il subjects from loyal territories. Finally, rulers on both sides yielded to pressure from high-placed family members to seek the release of relatives.

This time, Louis XIV first sent emissaries to rescue a group of French mariners and only then showed off his emancipatory abilities to European rivals by directing an admiral, as well as the *Frères de la Sainte Trinité* (Trinitarians), the second Catholic order dedicated to slave "redemption," to deliver multinational groups of Christians that included English and Dutch Protestants. In return, Hajj Hussein's ambassadors accompanied back to Algiers boatloads of both able-bodied and crippled rowers. To the *dey*'s chagrin, however, few of them were "our janissaries." Instead, he protested in 1684, "The other slaves...are foreigners who do not belong to us at all."[46] Frustration over France's non-release of promised Algerian rowers was the grounds for another outbreak of maritime hostilities, leading to another round of negotiation after the violence had ended and a new treaty with articles that regulated the ransom of slaves. For up to thirteen hundred Frenchmen in captivity, the Algerians insisted on getting market value; for a hundred acknowledged Algerians on the royal galleys, the French agreed to accept one set price for "Turks" (which here implied Ottoman soldiers) and another lower one for "Moors" (which here indicated members of indigenous populations).[47]

Yet seven years later, despite additional envoys, many letters and some manumission, the agreement had not been fully executed. Algerian diplomat Suleyman Buluk Bashi complained to the French marine minister Louis Phélypeaux de Pontchartrain in 1696: "The slaves we get back are Arabs from Egypt, Moors from Salé, Tripolitans and others from whom [French officials] get money, and they are liberated while our brothers and our children remain in irons." What is worse, French representatives lie to the *diwan* about [the slaves'] fate, he continued, saying they are dead when, in fact, "They have written letters to their families in Algiers and told them their news and about their health." French officials like Pontchartrain who made the decision to dispatch non-Algerian invalids in place of usable Algerian rowers, arguing that the *dey* had no valid claim to slaves bought at Malta or elsewhere seized under foreign flag,[48] knew very well that outside the galleys, a *Turc* was not a *Turc* was not a *Turc*. Sometimes, however, they made the calculated decision to pretend that he was.

A Fiction of Equivalency

Franco-North African agreements of the last third of the seventeenth century, whatever their precise terms, articulated a fiction of equivalency: that subjects of Christian and Muslim powers had the same worth. Yet they also masked an imbalance in naval power, in diplomatic staff, in numbers and in motives for wanting slaves in the first place. Proponents of the jihad theory of Mediterranean slavery aside,[49] Western scholars have largely accepted the idea that North Africans were in it for the money. As a former French captive noted, "The Turks, but especially the corsairs of Algiers, Tunis and Tripoli and other coasts of Barbary, make war more for interest than for glory."[50] Clearly, the Ottoman Empire and Morocco derived some economic profit from ransom, though how much has not been conclusively measured. To a degree their inhabitants also acquired status, technology and various sorts of terrestrial labor. What they did not get or seek were rowers. By this period, a more complete transition to the sail had dried up demand.[51] The mismatch between the French quest for Muslims whose bodies incarnated royal authority and the North African quest for Christians whose bodies represented ransom potential was a lopsided recipe for dissimulation.

French subjects carried to North Africa held greater future than current value, which public and private investors tried to gauge by scrutinizing appearance, language, knowledge and skills. Before they did, France's resident consul verified origins and circumstances of capture. This royal representative's success in getting some arrivals declared invalid prizes depended upon in-person access backed by credible threat of force. At diplomatic audiences, some non-French captives tried to pass for Catholic natives. At the *badistan* (slave market), everyone attempted to conceal high birth and any capacities that would rate a high ransom. "To hear these poor unfortunates talk," remarked a Trinitarian friar, "they are all cripples, all beggars, all invalids in the lands of these corsairs."[52] According to one former consul, playing down social status worked: "The French are usually those sold the most cheaply because besides always appearing poorer than they really are, masters always worry that the king will withdraw them by some treaty, obliging [their release] for purchase price."[53]

Treaties from the 1680s and 1690s generally brought even less favorable provisions for North Africa, since France had shifted tactics in the Mediterranean. No longer confined to the corsair chases and brief salvos that had characterized earlier periods, royal fleets equipped with the latest technology mounted a series of prolonged attacks against Algiers and Tripoli, inspiring Tunis to sign a pre-emptive agreement. In the aftermath, French representatives buoyed by longstanding diplomatic infrastructures, were well positioned to push through accords and force slave liberations. Given verbal and paper assurances of reciprocity, emissaries from the Ottoman provinces and also Morocco, expected to repatriate at least some compatriots. Arriving in France with lists of names in Arabic and Latin transliteration and variously comprised entourages, they made every effort to visit the galleys and identify countrymen. Yet a relative lack of personnel on the ground and gunboats on the water meant vulnerability to French equivocation. The most North African diplomats could do was to threaten retaliation against Frenchmen, whether overseas or on the sea.

Knowing they would come under pressure to manumit subjects of certain powers, agents of the French crown did for brief periods refrain from buying them in the first place.[54] However, the temptation for subterfuge ran deep and extended far. It was more than a matter of proxies fudging, clerks misregistering and intendants dissembling, which they did. After learning that a deputy from Algiers and another from Tunis was en route to Marseille in the 1680s, the marine minister sent orders "to prevent as much as possible that he has communication with the Turks on the galleys," taking particular care to intercept any letters they tried to pass him.[55] Insisting that all the Moroccan ambassador's countrymen were on campaign rather than, in fact, hidden on the galley hospital's upper floors, royal officers "stroked him on one side and stole his shirt on the other," in the words of one slave.[56] It was more than a matter of Ottomans pretending to be, say, natives of Moroccan Salé; or of valid oarsmen pretending to be invalids, which happened too.[57]

By the late seventeenth century, France's very participation in Mediterranean faith-based "ransom slavery" was based on an untruth: that Louis XIV would accept the valuation of a usable *Turc* at "the price of a Turk." Inside the world of the galleys, "Turks" circulated like money, changeable into credits and debits. Yet approached from the outside, *esclaves turcs* seemed permanently fixed to their benches. Thus even if envoys to North Africa did negotiate in good faith, domestic officials resisted compliance: to feign ignorance of a slave's sovereign allegiance or social status was to deny the reciprocal, individualized logic of ransom in favor of the one-sided, idealized logic of the galleys. The first accounted for personal attributes. The second, assuming Islam, allowed viability as the only variable.

Thus *Turcs* serving on France's galleys had few paths to liberty, besides escape. So long as they kept all limbs intact – and draconian punishments including the death penalty discouraged self-maiming[58] – they faced decades if not lifetimes in servitude. As instructions to the galley intendant put it, "Freedom should never be proposed [to healthy Turks], and when they are absolutely crippled and useless, it is up to you to extract the ordinary price of a Turk or more if possible, and on your recommendation, the king will grant them liberty."[59] Some valid slave rowers did attempt to flee, and despite distinctive appearances and linguistic limitations, enough succeeded to warrant multiple ordinances that threatened fines for aiding runaways or offered rewards for catching them. Only the exceptionally well-connected *esclave turc*, however, could influence the criteria by which his liberation case would be judged. Only credible threats of reprisal could force authorities intent on maintaining the power of the royal *chiourme* into fulfilling promises for group trades.

Within a system that assessed worth by physical-cum-symbolic utility and associated strength with perceived faith, experienced, healthy "Turks" possessed greater value to the king than the great majority of French Christians. Individually, it took enormous social and financial capital to balance the scales. Given that only the rare Franciscan friar or Knight of Malta won release for a serviceable *Turc,* Benjoumar Amet Gigery, for instance, offered a replacement slave plus "a man of condition from Provence" held by the *dey*.[60] Never imagining their relative would escape from Tunis in 1672, the family of Jean Bonnet of Cassis in Provence, he later recounted, "had bought a slave for my exchange with great difficulty because he was the sedan carrier for Madame Arnoul," the galley intendant's wife.[61]

But the wife of a Marseille man carried off to Salé a few years later had no such success when she offered 400 *livres* for her husband's master's son, a galley slave held in France. A royal appointee who may have been willing to compromise the comfort of a spouse was not willing to compromise the strength of the *chiourme*. Learning that Aly Bonamen was 39-years-old and occupied an elite position as "vogue-avant," Jean-Louis Habert, seigneur de Montmort declined to let him go. Such "Turks being rare," he wrote in 1686, so "it would not be appropriate to accord any more, at least not for 400 *livres*."[62] Indeed, after French corsairs landed a Moroccan prize in 1695 and a local merchant received permission to buy a would-be slave to exchange for a French one in Meknes, it was on the explicit condition that the man not be suited to serve as *vogue-avant.*[63] The preponderance of evidence suggests that most effective rowers whom French families managed to trade for relatives in North Africa must have been purchased in foreign slave markets, not liberated from the royal galleys.

Crippled Commodity Money

In the later seventeenth century, it was slaves too old or too infirm to pull an oar who moved most freely along Mediterranean and even Atlantic circuits. Unfit to serve as rowers but too precious simply to let go, invalid *Turcs* were turned into presents for a chartered company based off the Algerian coast, sent to the Caribbean, put up for sale in Italy or traded for French captives.[64] To derive some economic utility from otherwise idle workers who remained behind, some were employed in the production of naval fixtures and the construction of naval vessels.[65] Unlike their able counterparts, disabled *esclaves turcs* never operated as units of account, but were assigned mostly catalytic value in the ransom economy – unless they turned out to be renegades. For the most part, if the crown did not execute Christians "turned Turk," it kept them in perpetuity.[66] For crippled *Turcs* who stayed true to their first religion by contrast, officials eager to compensate for lost use value through exchange nonetheless expressed some qualms about the tactical dangers of allowing repatriation: the risk that returning slaves might reveal the true number of compatriots in bondage. Such intelligence disseminated in Algiers or Tunis "could lead the *diwan* to reclaim them and the king to refuse," fretted a letter from Versailles, giving North African corsairs cause to attack French merchant vessels.[67]

In the end, the conversion rate between invalid *Turcs* and valid replacements, money to obtain them, Christian captives, or all of the above, rested on ministerial judgment bent on maximizing profit and galley strength.[68] Still limited to self-barter in 1677, an incapacitated "Turk" had to supply either one serviceable substitute or one French Christian, and that year three did so.[69] But a register from the next year lays out an additional route to freedom. It lists the names and origins of sixty-six "invalid Turks who will be liberated after each one puts a healthy Turk in his place, or three hundred *livres*, or a French slave in his place."[70] By the 1690s, with supplies of rowers scarcer, the king loosened the rules from one direction – releasing three invalids for a single valid *esclave turc* – but tightened them from another. Whereas the crown had earlier accepted head-for-head swaps, it now insisted on a French slave *plus* "the price of a Turk" for one cripple.[71] During the same period, after a breakdown of Franco-Moroccan negotiations, in part over the sultan's own reticence to accept ransom, numerous Frenchmen held in Meknes complied, paying out the extra four-hundred-*livre* sum to the galley treasury.[72]

By this new arrangement, even if the two parties to a cross-Mediterranean ransom deal split the monetary cost of the extra slave, the terms were fundamentally imbalanced. Here, an actual French subject, whatever his physical condition, possessed exchange value equal to a powerful, idealized

Turc. By contrast, a real Ottoman or Moroccan subject in poor physical condition – however treasured by his sovereign or his family – had use value to Louis XIV only as instigator of the transaction. For the Sun King who saw his glory reflected in the sweat of toiling North African slaves, an invalid became useful as a conduit once he became useless as rower. Finally freed from servitude, he then had a choice either to go home or "to renounce Mahometanism and establish [himself] in Marseille."[73] For "the Most Christian King" who wanted his fervor reflected in the souls of former infidels, a liberated invalid gained symbolic value when he joined the Catholic Church. Those who stayed in the city could claim ongoing rations and, by tradition, a yearly set of clothing, "taken from *forçats* who die at the hospital."[74] While disabled converts fit to serve received a small sum each day, disabled converts compelled to retire could anticipate a minimal annuity for life.

Conclusion

What might we conclude from this evaluation of the value of *esclaves turcs* on France's royal galleys during the reign of Louis XIV? How to explain conflicting Franco-North African expectations of reciprocal manumission expressed in bilateral agreements? Sanjay Subrahmanyam has argued against incommensurability as a useful frame for "understanding inter-imperial dynamics."[75] Wolfgang Kaiser has argued for asymmetry as a means for understanding ransoming practices. Here, I have suggested that we cannot accurately assess how Ottoman and Moroccan rowers, healthy or handicapped, were swapped for cash or in kind without considering where they fit and how much and how far they circulated in the market, galley, gift and ransom economies of the seventeenth-century Mediterranean.

For several decades during his reign, Louis XIV rejected what would seem a foundational idea for ransoming: that it is always possible to put a price on freedom. Certainly, royal officials of the 1660s-1690s had no difficulty putting a price on people, aggressively buying prime specimens for the *chiourme* and conveying them to France, where in the guise of accounting units, commodities, counterparts, currencies, partners, men, numbers, securities, subjects and slaves, they flowed among categories, alternating between individual and ideal. Because the monarchy judged value by the standard of replacement rather than monetary exchange, an *esclave turc* could be worth more than a denomination of a "Turk."

Endnotes

1 Pierre Boyer, "La Chiourme turque des galères de France de 1685 à 1687," *Revue de l'Occident musulman et de la Méditerranée,* 6 (1969), 55-56.

2 See Jean Marteilhe, *Mémoire d'un protestant condamné aux galères de France pour cause de religion (1700-1713)* (Amsterdam, 1757), first published in French and Dutch; and Jean François Bion, *Relation des tourments qu'on fait souffrir aux Protestants qui sont sur les galères de France...* (London: Henry Ribotteau, 1708), also released in Amsterdam and translated into English.

3 Paul Masson, *Les Galères de France, 1481-1781: Marseille, port de guerre* (Paris: Hachette, 1938); Paul Bamford, *Fighting Ships and Prisons: The Mediterranean Galleys of France in the Age of Louis XIV* (Minneapolis: University of Minnesota Press, 1973); André Zysberg, *Les Galériens: vies et destins de 60,000 forçats sur les galères de France, 1680-1748* (Paris: Editions du Seuil, 1987).

4 Notably, Gaston Tournier, *Les Galères de France et les galériens protestants des XVIIe et XVIIIe siècles*, 3 vols. (Cévennes: Musée du Désert, 1943).

5 Boyer, "La Chiourme," 53–74.

6 Sue Peabody, *"There Are No Slaves in France": The Political Culture of Race and Slavery in the Ancien Régime* (New York: Oxford University Press, 1996).

7 See Jocelyne Dakhlia, Bernard Vincent and Wolfgang Kaiser, eds. *Les Musulmans dans l'histoire de l'Europe*, 2 vols. (Paris: Albin Michel, 2011-2013), particularly Dakhlia's essay, "Musulmans en France et en Grande-Bretagne à l'époque moderne: exemplaires et invisibles" in vol. 1: *Une integration invisible*, 231-407.

8 Gillian Weiss, "Infidels at the Oar: A Mediterranean Exception to France's Free Soil Principle," *Slavery & Abolition* 32 (2011): 397–412, and with Meredith Martin, "'Turks' on Display during the Reign of Louis XIV," *L'Esprit Créateur,* 53, 4 (2013), 98–112.

9 Gilles Veinstein, "Les Capitulations franco-ottomanes de 1536: sont-elles encore controversables" in *Living in the Ottoman Ecumenical Community: Essays in Honour of Suraiya Faroqhi*, eds. Vera Costantini and Markus Koller (Leiden, Netherlands: Brill, 2008), 71–88.

10 On the galleys under Kings Henry IV and Louis XIII, see Alan James, *The Navy and Government in Early Modern France, 1572-1661* (Suffolk, UK: Royal Historical Society, 2004), chap. 5. On earlier employment of "Turks" see Marie de Medici's request to her uncle, the Grand Duke of Tuscany, for 50-60 "Turcs forçats" for her personal galley under construction (Medici Archives, Filza 4728, 2 August 1605, cited in Berthold Zeller, *Henri IV et Marie de Médicis: d'après des documents nouveaux tirés des archives de Florence et de Paris* (Paris: Didier et Cie., 1877), 268-269); and the Cardinal of Richelieu's 1636 announcement that a prize from Salé had yielded 230-240 "Turcs et Maures" to be distributed across the fleet (Eugène Sue, ed., *Correspondance de Henri d'Escoubleau de Sourdis*, archevêque de Bordeaux, chef des conseils du roi en

l'armée navale... 3 vols. (Paris: Crapelet, 1839), 77.

11 Galley officials strived for a 4:1 ratio of *forçats* to *esclaves* (Boyer, "La Chiourme," 55). References to slave supply contracts abound in the Archives nationales [hereafter AN], Marine B^6. For the precise terms of one held at the Archives départementales des Bouches-du-Rhône [hereafter ADBR], 9B3, f. 270v, reproduced by Joseph Fournier, "Un Marché de turcs pour les galères royales (1685)," *Bulletin philologique et historique,* 1/2 (1901), 571-574. See also Masson, *Les Galères de France,* 279-283. Louis XIV seized the property of one merchant who had been advanced 36,000 *livres* but did not fulfill the terms of his *Turc* supply contract and went bankrupt (*Arrêt* for sale of house and other possessions of Béranger, 6 April 1688, AN, Marine $A^3$12, n.p.).

12 AN, Marine $B^6$4, f. 58v; $B^6$11, f. 47r-49r.

13 See numerous examples of such orders to merchants and correspondence with consuls in AN, Marine B^6 and B^7, including marine minister Jean-Baptiste Colbert, marquis de Seignelay to Livorno consul François Cotolendi, Versailles, 6 August 1686, $B^7$59, f. 98v. Also, Salvatore Bono, "Forniture dall'Italia di schiavi musulmani per le galere francesi (1685-1693)," *Annali delle facoltà di scienze politiche dell'Università di Cagliari* (1983), 83–97.

14 Documents about the incorporation into the *chiourme* of purchased sub-Saharans Africans and kidnapped Iroquois starting in the 1670s can be found in AN, Marine $B^6$9-14 and 19-20, respectively. See also Bamford, *Fighting Ships*, 154-165 and Brett Rushforth, *Bonds of Alliance: Indigenous and Atlantic Slaveries in New France* (Chapel Hill, NC: University of North Carolina Press, 2012), 145-152.

15 On the Maltese Inquisitor's interference and the French king's bid for papal dispensation in 1679-1680, see AN, Marine $B^6$12, ff. 188v-216v.

16 For the clandestine journey of Swiss Guard Chevalier de Salis, who in 1688 managed to transport just 164 slaves to Marseille on English vessels see AN, Marine $B^6$19 and 20.

17 As André Zysberg has shown ("Un Audit rétrospectif: analyse du budget des galères de France entre 1669 et 1716" in *Histoire des familles, de la démographie et des comportements*, ed. Jean-Pierre Poussou and Isabelle Robin-Romero (Paris: Presses de l'Université de Paris-Sorbonne, 2007), 1068), the acquisition of *Turcs* in the late seventeenth century consumed two to three percent of the annual galley budget. For representative geographic origins of 76 "Turks" aboard the *Capitaine* in 1672, for example, see Zysberg, "Un Esclavage d'Etat: le recrutement des rameurs sur les galères de Louis XIV," in *Contraintes et libertés dans les sociétés méditerranées aux époque modernes et contemporanéennes,* *XVIe-XXe siècles*, ed. Zysberg and Sadok Boubaker (Tunis: Faculté des sciences humaines et sociales de Tunis; CRHQ, CNRS-Université de Caen, 2007), 80.

18 For counts of French slaves held across North Africa in the sixteenth-nineteenth centuries, see Weiss, *Captives and Corsairs: France and Slavery in the Early Modern Mediterranean* (Stanford, CA: Stanford University Press, 2011), app. 1.

19 Dávid Géza and Pál Fodor (eds.), *Ransom Slavery along the Ottoman Borders: Early Fifteenth-Early Eighteenth Centuries* (Leiden, Netherlands: Brill, 2007).

20 On asymmetry as a condition of Christian-Muslim relations in the early modern period, see Kaiser, "Asymétries méditerranéens: présence et circulation de marchands entre Alger, Tunis et Marseille" in *Les Musulmans*, 1: 417–442.

21 Antoine Furetière, *Dictionnaire universel, contenant généralement tous les mots françois tant vieux que modernes, & les termes de toutes les sciences et des arts*, 3 vols. (The Hague, Netherlands: Arnout & Reinier Leers, 1690), Vol. 3, 759. See also François Lebrun, "Turcs, barbaresques, musulmans, vus par les français du XVIIe siècles, d'après le 'Dictionnaire' de Furetière," *Cahiers de Tunisie* 44, 3–4 (1991): 69–74.

22 René Burlet, Zysberg, and Jean Carrière, "Mais comment pouvait-on ramer sur les galères du Roi-Soleil," *Histoire et Mesure,* 1:3/4 (1986), 147–208.

23 Aristotle, *Politics*, Book 1, chaps 4-7.

24 Jennifer Lofkrantz, "Protecting Freeborn Muslims: The Sokoto Caliphate's Attempts to Prevent Illegal Enslavement and Its Acceptance of the Strategy of Ransoming," *Slavery & Abolition* 32, 1 (2011), 109.

25 Ibid., 110.

26 The *sol* per day accorded converted *Turcs* starts appearing on galley expenditures in 1686 (AN, Marine $B^6$86, f. 572r). The first offer that they became *mariniers de rame* dates from 1684 (AN, Marine $B^6$16, ff. 156r-158v).

27 For examples of the costs and values of *Turcs* from 1669-1700, see AN, Marine $B^6$1-33.

28 Marine minister Jean-Baptiste Colbert to galley intendant Nicolas Arnoul, Saint Germain-en-Laye, 1 April 1670, AN, Marine $B^6$2, f. 39. In another instance, the king gave permission for merchants (with foreign commissions) in Malta to swap Algerians and Tunisians captured in violation of standing treaties for other "Turks" the French reportedly had license to buy. Louis XIV to marine intendant Jean-Louis Girardin de Vauvré, Versailles, 11 January 1685, AN Marine, $B^2$54, f. 9.

29 In theory, see Paul Einzig, *Primitive Money in Its Ethnological, Historical and Economic Aspects* (London: Eyre & Spottiswoode, 1948). In practice, see Linda A. Newson, "The Slave-Trading Accounts of Manoel Batista Peres, 1613–1619: Double-Entry Bookkeeping in Cloth Money," *Accounting History,* 18:3 (2013), 343-365.

30 A 1681 royal ordinance, renewed in 1695, for instance, set the penalty for a runaway at 3 replacement *Turcs* or 1000 *livres* (AN, Marine $A^3$12, n.p.; $B^6$13, f. 260); one from 1689 fined a guard who beat his charge with a stick rather than a lash 400 *livres* "pour acheter un turc" (AN, Marine $A^3$12, n.p.; $B^6$21, 87r). On price comparisons, see Ernest Dottain, "Un Chapitre de l'histoire de la marine sous Louis XIV: la justice et les galères," *Revue contemporaine,* 29 (1862), 493 ; and Peabody, *"There Are No Slaves,"* 13.

31 Louis XIV to Vauvré, Versailles, 11 January 1685, AN, Marine $B^2$54, f. 9.

32 In 1677 Colbert called the bluff of a valid *forçat* named Fronnet, promising his

freedom if he really came up with *thirty Turcs* to replace him (AN, Marine B[6]8, f. 175). More typical was a "rôle des invalides" (1683, AN, Marine B[6]15 ff. 121r-125v) divided into categories: those who have done their time and supply a *Turc*; invalids who have not done their time but offer a *Turc*; crippled salt smugglers who have done their time.

33 The marine ministry notably implemented the exile option in 1687-1689 when it sent groups of invalid *forçats* to Canada and invalid *forçats* and *Turcs* to the Caribbean (AN, Marine B[7]59, ff. 185r; B[6]21, ff. 4-5).

34 Royal ordinance, Versailles, 20 March 1684, AN, Marine A[3]12, n.p. and B[6]16, ff. 52v-53r.

35 Royal ordinance, Versailles, 15 February 1678, AN, Marine A[3]12, n.p.

36 Tournier, *Les Galères de France et les galériens protestants*, Vol. 1, 195.

37 Cited in Ernest Lavisse, "Sur les galères du roi," *Revue de Paris,* 4 :22 (1897), 257.

38 Pontchartrain to intendant of Provence, Pierre-Cardin Lebret, Paris, 27 May 1693, Archives de la Chambre de Commerce de Marseille [hereafter ACCM], G50.

39 Pontchartrain to Jean-François Croiset, Versailles, 1 October 1698, AN, Marine B[6]31, ff. 527r-530r; and French consul Philippe-Jacques Durand to the Marseille Chamber of Commerce, Algiers, 18 October 1698, discussed in Régis Bertrand, "Les Cimetières des 'esclaves turcs' des arsenaux de Marseille et de Toulon au XVIIIe siècle," *Revue des mondes musulmans et de la Méditerranée,* 99-100 (2002), 205-217.

40 Moroccan ambassador 'Abdallah ibn 'Aisha to French merchant Jean Jourdan, Brest, 24 May 1699, AN, Marine B[7]223, f. 12.

41 Mulay Isma'il to Louis XIV, 22 July 1684, reprinted in Henry de Castries, Pierre de Cenival and Philippe de Cossé Brissac, eds., *Les Sources inédites de l'histoire du Maroc de 1530 à 1845*, 30 vols. (Paris: Ernest Leroux, 1905–1960), 2nd ser., 3: 444.

42 The text of both the official treaty, signed on 25 November 1665, and the secret accord signed the following day are reproduced in Eugène Plantet, ed., *Correspondance des beys de Tunis et des consuls de France avec la cour, 1577-1830* [hereafter *CBT*], 3 vols. (Paris: Félix Alcan, 1893-1899), 1: 182-192; financial details can be found in 1: 199, 204-205 n. 3, 219-220 n. 3.

43 On France's bombardments of North Africa and negotiations with representatives of Ottoman North Africa and Morocco, see Weiss, *Captives and Corsairs*, chap. 4. For the 25 April 1684 Franco-Algerian treaty, see Edgard Rouard de Card, *Traités de la France avec les pays de l'Afrique du Nord: Algérie, Tunisie, Tripolitaine, Maroc* (Paris: A. Pédone, 1906), 45-52.

44 On a large-scale Moroccan rescue mission of the late eighteenth century, see Thomas Freller, "'The Shining of the Moon': The Mediterranean Tour of Muhammad Ibn Uthman, Envoy of Morocco, in 1782," *Journal of Mediterranean Studies,* 12:2 (2002), 307–326.

45 Instructions for envoy Guillaume Marcel, 16 November 1689 (Copy from Versailles, AN, Affaires étrangères [hereafter AE] B[I]116 ff. 163-165) and Marcel to Seignelay, 14 February 1690 (AN, AE B[I]116, ff. 236-242).

46 AN, Marine, Registres de dépêches, 1684, f. 109; Archives coloniales de la Marine (Compagnies du Bastion de France, 1639-1731), cited in Plantet, *Correspondance des deys d'Alger avec la cour de France, 1579-1833* [hereafter *CBA*], 2 vols. (Paris: Félix Alcan, 1889), 1: 111 n. 2, 96-98.

47 The treaty, dated 24 September 1689, is reproduced in Rouard de Card, *Traités de la France*, 52-60. For further details about the lead-up and aftermath, see Weiss, *Captives and Corsairs*, chap. 4.

48 Algerian envoy Suleyman Buluk *Bashi* to Pontchartrain, 18 June 1696 and report from Pontchartrain, [1696], AN, Marine B7 220, f. 63v, 66v.

49 Robert C. Davis, *Christian Slaves, Muslim Masters: White Slavery in the Mediterranean, the Barbary Coast, and Italy, 1500-1800* (New York: Palgrave Macmillan, 2003).

50 First published (La Flèche: Gervais Laboe, 1665), excerpted by Louis Piesse (ed.), "L'Odyssée ou diversité d'aventures, encontres en Europe, Asie et Afrique par le sieur du Chastelet des Boys," *Revue africaine,* 10 (1866), 98.

51 Michel Fontenay, "Le Maghreb barbaresque et l'esclavage méditerranéen aux XVIe et XVIIe siècles," *Cahiers de Tunisie,* 44:3/4 (1991), 17.

52 Pierre Dan, *Histoire de Barbarie et de ses corsaires...* (Paris: Pierre Rocolet, 1637), 372.

53 Laurent d'Arvieux, *Mémoires du chevalier d'Arvieux...*, ed. Jean-Baptiste Labat, 6 vols. (Paris: Charles-Jean-Baptiste Delespine, 1735), 5: 267-268.

54 For example, Commission for Jacques Hayet, Commissaire ordinaire de la Marine, Saint Germain-en-Laye, 17 December 1680, AN, Marine B[6]12, f. 270.

55 Colbert to galley intendant Jean-Baptiste de Brodart, Versailles, 26 July 1681, AN, Marine B[6]13, ff. 163r-164r; Seignelay to galley general Louis Victor de Rochechouart, duc de Mortemart, 27 August 1684, cited in Plantet, *CDA*, 1: 111 n 2. On other tricks for avoiding contact between *esclaves turcs* and envoys, see AN, Marine B[6]16, ff. 101v-102v; B[6]29, ff. 345v-347v.

56 Muhammad bin 'Ha'ider' to Ali 'Mercher,' Marseille, 9 May 1682, reproduced in Castries, *Sources inédites* (1922), 2nd ser., Vol. 1, 691-693. On this thwarted contact, also see AN, Marine B[6]14, ff. 5r-8r, 82v-83v, ff. 91v-96v.

57 Pontchartrain to galley intendant Jean-*Louis Habert*, seigneur de Montmort, Versailles, 30 April 1692, AN, Marine B[6]24, ff. 136r-138r; same to same, Versailles, 9 February 1691, Marine, B[6]23, 49r-50v.

58 On royal ordinances against self-mutilation promulgated in 1683 and 1692, see AN, Marine B[6]16, f. 37r and B[6]25, f. 346v-347r, B[6]55, f. 43r.

59 Seignelay to Montmort, Versailles, 12 December 1691, AN, Marine B[6]23, ff. 356r-v.

60 For examples of approved exchanges see, AN, Marine B[6]6, f. 46r; B[6]10, 90v; and rejected ones: B[6]15, ff. 139v-140r; B[6]18, ff. 242r-244v. On Benjoumar Amet Gigery, whose fate after 1678 remains unknown, see B[6]8, f. 39v and B[6]10,

f. 116r. The Provençal gentleman in question may have been Claude Auxcousteaux de Fercourt (author of Relation *de l'esclavage des sieurs De Fercourt et Regnard, pris sur mer par les corsaires d'Alger (1678-79)*, ed. M. Jean-Baptiste Targe (Toulouse: E. Privat, 1905) or his friend, the playwright, Jean-François Regnard who fictionalized his experience in the posthumously published *La Provençale* (1709). Both men did agree to large ransoms, whose payment is confirmed in Plantet, *CDA*, 1: 81.

61 Antoine Galland, *Histoire de l'esclavage d'un marchand de la ville de Cassis, à Tunis*, ed. Catherine Guénot and Nadia Vasquez (Paris: Editions de la bibliothèque, 1992), 134.

62 Annotated list of "Forçats qui demandent leur liberté," [n.d], AN, Marine D^{5}1, n.p.

63 Pontchartrain to Sieur du Puy, Versailles, 7 December 1695, AN, Marine B^{6}27, f. 474r.

64 Colbert to Arnoul, Versailles, 29 January and Compiègne, 28 December 1672, AN, Marine B^{6}4, ff. 12v-14v, 232; lists of invalid *esclaves turcs* to be sold in Livorno and Genoa, Versailles, 19 September and 15 November 1686, AN, Marine B^{6}18, f. 189r, f. 240r.

65 Seignelay to galley intendant Michel Bégon, Fontainebleau, 31 October 1685, AN, B^{6}17, f. 469r. During the plague of 1720, galley officials were willing to risk the lives of invalid, not valid, *Turcs* in caring for the sick and burying the dead. Conseil de Marine to échevins de Marseille, Paris, 25 August 1720, Archives municipales de Marseille, GG 321.

66 Seignelay to Brodart, Versailles, 2 November 1683, AN, Marine B^{6}15, f. 116r.

67 Louis XIV to intendant Arnoul, Versailles, 31 August 1674, AN, Marine B^{6}6, f. 119v. Seignelay made a similar point in letters to French ambassador to Istanbul Pierre Girandin, Versailles, 16 June and 8 December 1686, AN, Marine B^{7}59, ff. 83r, 132v.

68 Thus Hamet de Tunis, as he was known, and Pierre Gaillard won their respective freedoms in 1678 only after turning over an additional *Turc* each. AN, Marine B^{6}10, ff. 90v.

69 Colbert to Brodart, Fontainebleau, 9 September; and roll of invalid forçats accorded liberty, Saint Germain-en-Laye, 1 December 1677, AN, Marine B^{6}9, f. 175, ff. 242v-243r.

70 Register of October 1678, AN, Marine B^{6}10, ff. 154v-158v.

71 Seignelay to Montmort, Versailles, 14 February 1690, AN, Marine B^{6}22, f. 46.

72 On the drawn-out negotiations between France and Morocco, see Charles Penz, *Les Captifs français du Maroc au XVIIe siècle, 1577-1699* (Rabat, Morocco: Imprimerie officielle, 1944), 189-196 and Weiss, *Captives and Corsairs,* chaps. 3 and 4. For multiple examples of slave exchange deals of the 1690s sweetened with 400 *livre* payments, see AN, Marine B^{6}26-29.

73 Pontchartrain to Montmort, Versailles, 20 January 1694, AN, Marine B^{6}26, f. 18.

74 Jérôme Phélypeaux, comte de Pontchartrain to Père Maisontier in Bordeaux, Versailles, 25 March 1699, AN, Marine $B^6$32, ff. 135v-136r; marine minister Jean-Frédéric Phélypeaux, comte de Pontchartrain to galley intendant Nicolas-François Arnoul, chevalier, seigneur de Vaucresson, 10 January 1725, $B^6$55, ff. 5r-6r.

75 Sanjay Subrahmanyam, "Par-delà l'incommensurabilité: pour une histoire connectée des empires aux temps modernes," *Revue d'histoire moderne et contemporaine,* 54:4 (2007), 34-53.

Map 3.1: Morocco in the Eighteenth Century

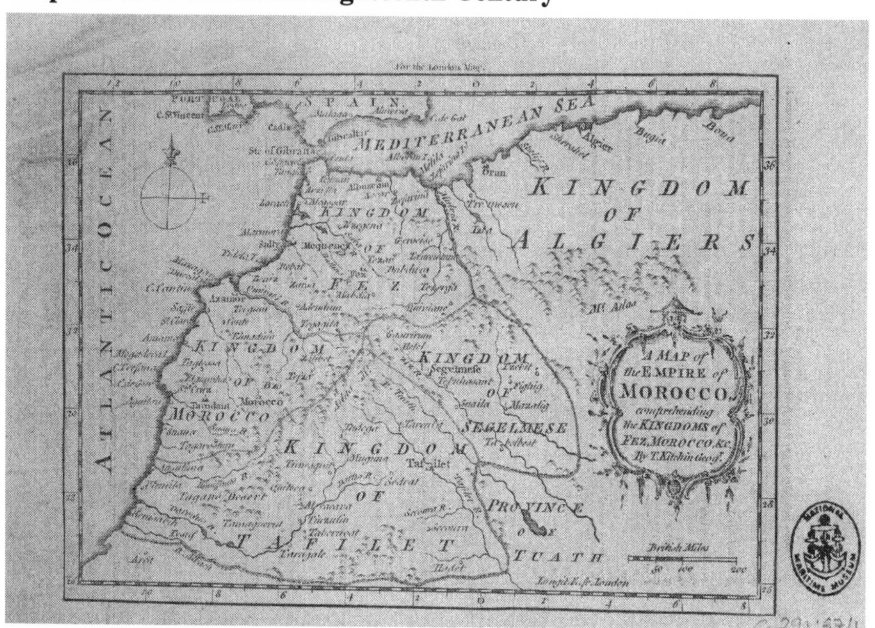

Source: "A Map of the Empire of Morocco Comprehending the Kingdom of Fez, Morocco etc. by T. Kitchin, Geogr.," c. 1790. National Maritime Museum, Greenwich, London

CHAPTER III

Ransoming Practices and "Barbary Coast" Slavery:

Negotiations relating to Liverpool Slave Traders in the Late Eighteenth Century[1]

Suzanne Schwarz

The shipwreck and ransom of the officers and crew of two Liverpool slave ships (the *Anna* and the *Solicitor General*) on the "Barbary Coast"[2] of Morocco in the last two decades of the eighteenth century took place in a context of growing metropolitan debate on the moral and legal justifications for the enslavement of Africans in the transatlantic slave trade.[3] Two years before the schooner *Anna* foundered on the shore at Wad Nun (Wād Nūn) south of Agadir in May 1789, the Liverpool abolitionist and former slave trade mariner Edward Rushton published a poem in which he pointed to the hypocrisy of those who cherished their own liberty but were prepared to deny it to others. Using the voice of a fictional slave in the West Indies, he criticized men who "Think ... that liberty is bliss," but who were motivated by "base av'rice, to make others slaves." These men had wrenched Africans from their "native shore Which (dreadful thought!)" they "must behold no more."[4] Bound to the Gold Coast on his maiden voyage as captain of this newly-constructed vessel designed to carry 83 enslaved Africans,[5] James Irving appeared to be aware of the broad parameters of abolitionist debate in Britain and attempted in his subsequent correspondence with the Vice-Consul at Essaouira (al-Sawīra) to use this borrowed language of liberty to secure his own release.[6] He urged John Hutchison to "Let that spirit of humanity which at present Manifests itself throughout the realm actuate you to rescue us speedily from the most intollerable [*sic*] Slavery."[7]

In the same year that Irving was shipwrecked, Gustavus Vassa's *Interesting Narrative* urged "nominal Christians" to consider how they could reconcile the brutality and suffering imposed on Africans with the biblical injunction to "Do unto all men as you would men should do unto you."[8] For Irving, his Christian faith was used in captivity in Morocco not to reconsider the legitimacy of his earlier role in transporting some three thousand Africans to the Americas but rather as a form of resistance and a clear signifier of his cultural superiority over his Muslim captors whom he repeatedly represented as "infidels," "barbarians" and "savages."[9] In describing his captivity to his intended readers, he set his experiences in a wider biblical context by commenting on how he had "languished and pined in sorrow" for "40 days." The Bible was also presented as a source of solace, which enabled the mariners to withstand their inhumane treatment at the hands of the "tyrants." Shortly after the men's capture on the beach at Wad Nun in May 1789, Irving noted in his journal how "One of us had saved a Bible, from which we selected some Psalms and Chapters, suited to our forlorn situation; and received considerable comfort and benifit [*sic*] from reading them."[10]

Irving considered that his detention represented a reversal of the natural social order, and he was incensed by the notion that "Negroes" could exert control over his crewmen. In a journal entry for 17 June 1789, he reported how some of his crew were required to work in a garden near to Guelmim "under the direction of a Mahomitan negro, who beat them frequently."[11] With no cognisance of Islamic traditions of slavery and contemporary debate in West Africa on the rights of freeborn Muslims,[12] Irving interpreted his captivity narrowly within the framework of metropolitan assumptions on the rights of Britons to freedom.[13] Cultural assumptions about European entitlement to liberty and African eligibility for enslavement which Liverpool traders would have regarded as normative were at odds with the prevailing climate of opinion in this "ransoming frontier between the worlds of Christianity and Islam."[14] As Jennifer Lofkrantz has noted, in "Muslim regions of West Africa the slavery debate was centred on religious identity; in other words, on social and cultural categories, rather than on 'race' and Enlightenment ideals as in European and European-derived societies."[15] Irving was aware that his Christianity attracted the ire and disdain of his captors, but seemed not to comprehend fully that his non-Muslim identity made him vulnerable to enslavement and potentially forced conversion.[16] The pattern was more complex still in eighteenth-century Morocco. Chouki El Hamel points to examples of Muslims being enslaved by other Muslims; the "most outstanding Moroccan example being the enslavement of the Muslim Haratin – the so-called free blacks or ex-slaves - during Mawlay Isma'il's reign."[17]

The cases of the *Anna* and the *Solicitor General* bring into sharp relief the confrontation between entrenched pro-slavery attitudes and emerging abolitionist ideas which were shaping debate on the transatlantic slave trade in late eighteenth-century Britain.[18] The rich corpus of surviving documentation relating to the negotiations for the eleven-man crew of the *Anna* also offers a clear insight into the strategies deployed by different interest groups engaged in the process of ransoming, as well as the assumptions which underpinned the responses of captors, captives, relatives and those acting as ransom brokers and mediators. These Liverpool slave traders were among an estimated 20,000 Britons taken captive by Barbary corsairs or captured following shipwreck in the seventeenth and eighteenth centuries, although as Linda Colley points out Irving's account is one of a relatively small number of surviving narratives written by Britons held in North Africa.[19]

This chapter draws on consular correspondence, as well as several journals written by Captain Irving to describe his experiences in captivity for his father, brother-in-law and uncle.[20] Irving's use of language suggests that, not surprisingly for a mariner en-route to West Africa, he was aware of the popular genre of Barbary captivity narratives and the "corsair hysteria" surrounding them.[21] In recounting the circumstances following the shipwreck on 27 May 1789, Irving describes how he "saw the print of a human foot in the Sand" after they waded ashore from the wreck, a phrase which is strikingly similar to one used in Daniel Defoe's *Robinson Crusoe*. Irving may well have used this as a shorthand device for reminding his readers of the eponymous character's experience of captivity by the Barbary corsairs and his subsequent escape.[22] As Davis points out, "popular broadsheets and simple word of mouth circulated throughout Europe, telling and retelling of Christians taken by the hundreds and by the thousands, on the high seas or during coastal sorties, and hauled off in chains to a life-in-death of hard labor in Morocco, Algiers, Tunis or Tripoli."[23] The multiple versions which Irving created of his narrative indicate that he was eager to disseminate knowledge of his experiences widely among friends and family, although there is no evidence to indicate that he intended to publish his narrative for a national audience.[24] His younger cousin and namesake, surgeon on the *Anna*, also compiled a supplementary narrative entitled "A very short account of what happened to me after the seperation [*sic*] on the 16th of June 1789."[25]

Ransom negotiations for the release of mariners from the *Anna* and the *Solicitor General* were successful in the long run, yet the process was faltering, delicate and protracted. Negotiations were delayed not only by the complex political interplay between the imperial court and the dissident southern territories of Morocco, but also by the use of ransom negotiations by the Sultan to exert diplomatic pressure on the British government to concede to various demands. In the case of the *Anna,* the halting progress of negotiations spanning a period of fourteen months raised the prospect in Captain Irving's mind of inflated ransom demands and a breakdown in communications which would render him vulnerable to permanent enslavement. In West Africa, Lofkrantz and Olatunji Ojo note how protracted negotiations could lead to the failure of the ransoming process and enslavement for captives.[26] In his first petition to the Vice-Consul on 24 June 1789, Irving referred to his fear of being "lost forever to ourselves, our Wives and familys, our Country and all we hold dear," and the use of the term "lost" in this context may well have denoted his fear not only of geographical separation but also of being absorbed into an alien Islamic culture and society.[27]

Negotiations were still more protracted in the case of the *Solicitor General* wrecked "10 leagues to the Northward of Cape Bayodore [Boujdour]...."[28] It was reported in *Lloyd's List* on 22 December 1795 that the ship en-route from Liverpool to Africa was "totally lost" on the Barbary Coast on 11 August 1795. A breakdown in communications between the Sultan, consular officials and the southern territories meant that the Consul General was not able to confirm to the British government that the men had been "finally redeemed" until almost two years after their shipwreck in July 1797.[29] The Sultan, Mawlay Sulayman, also had other concerns as the political situation in Morocco was disrupted by rebellion and a period of "dynastic crisis."[30] Seven months after the shipwreck, Matra was unable to offer any positive news on the redemption of the crew. The delay in commencing ransom negotiations meant that the men had been sold a number of times to "Arab speculators," with the result that their prices had increased markedly. Two months later on 28 May 1796, Matra again expressed regret that he had no further information on the seamen. Reports in British newspapers in July 1796 indicated that the men had been ransomed from "slavery," but they were still detained at Agadir.[31] Even though Matra reported on 10 September 1796 that the Sultan had sent troops to redeem the men, they were not transferred north to Essaouira until May or June 1797.[32]

Whilst maritime misadventure on a stretch of coastline noted for its treacherous currents was the initial cause of the crewmembers' captivity, they were subsequently drawn into a highly organized and complex ransoming economy which generated profits and political leverage for a number of different interest groups in Morocco. The crewmembers would have been unaware that shipwreck "was often perceived by Moroccan officials as deliberative trespassing." As Mohamed H. Mohamed explains in his chapter in this volume, "European mariners who ventured into, or were shipwrecked at, the south of Essaouira were routinely charged with trespassing and treated accordingly." According to Christopher Robson, a Liverpool slave trade surgeon appealing on Irving's behalf in September 1790, it was "chance" which had given Irving "an Opportunity to write to the English Consul at Mogodore."[33] In reality though, routes for trading mariners from the littoral to inland areas were well established as were networks of communication for initiating ransom negotiations with consular officials at Essaouira and Tangier.[34] The trading of shipwrecked mariners was coordinated through the commercial networks of the powerful Bayruk family centred on the town of Guelmim.[35] This was a carefully regulated enterprise and not the product of chance; as Lofkrantz points out, "the Bayruk operated as regional wholesalers, purchasing shipwrecked sailors from coastal fishermen and Saharan nomads" and then arranging for ransom negotiations with European consuls and the Sultan. Their networks included Jewish traders who played a central role in the bargaining processes for hostages and their purchase, housing and movement in Morocco.[36]

The frequency of shipwreck, averaging two vessels a year according to James Grey Jackson, provided several sources of profit for fishermen and nomadic peoples who apprehended European and American mariners on shore.[37] In a violent struggle on 28 May 1789 with men described as "copper coulered [*sic*] naked savages," the crewmembers of the *Anna* were stripped of their personal possessions and some of their clothing. In addition to a "loaded Blunderbuss" which Irving had brought ashore for protection, the men carried with them "1000 Dollars ... all of which fell into the hands of the Arabs."[38] Subsequent searches for money were carried out on the following day, and Irving recorded his indignation that his "most secret places and hair underwent the search" by women and some "strange Arabs, who passed that way, on their journey to the wreck." The stricken vessel was regarded as a prize, and immediately after the crew's capture on the beach "the men mounted themselves on Camels, and went in quest of the Vessel." The cargo of the *Anna*, assorted for the purposes of trade in enslaved Africans on the Gold Coast, was comprised of "India, Manchester and Hardware Goods with about 20 tons Salt." The salt was washed out as the vessel sank, but some of the remaining cargo was retrieved for sale as Irving recorded that on 1 June "the men were by this time returned from the wreck, with several pieces of Cloth etc. of the Cargo." One of Irving's "own shirts that had been carried from the wreck" was later "sold at Mogodore to the vice Consul."[39] The value of the wreck's contents was the focus of questioning by several travellers Irving encountered during his journey to Guelmim on 12 June 1789. His captors clearly felt they had established a proprietary interest in the vessel, and were pleased that Irving indicated to the travellers they encountered that there were no watches or money in the vessel. The ship's log book seemed to have some value to their captors, as they resisted with "threats and blows" requests by Irving and his crew to retrieve the document; it is conceivable that the ship's log may have been used in subsequent negotiations to verify the identity and relative value of the men in their possession.[40]

The clustering of wrecks in the area around Wad Nun suggests that mechanisms for trading Christian captives inland to Guelmim were well developed. Within two days of their capture, intelligence of the men's captivity was transmitted southwards. The second mate and apprentice were "marched about 20 miles, to the Southward ... where a man wrote something on a piece of paper with a stick, which he sent away with a messenger."[41] During their twelve day detention on shore at Wad Nun, Irving knew that his crew had been separated and allocated to different owners but he had no insight into the strategic decisions which influenced the choice of men and the monetary value placed upon them. Status informed the selection of the men, as the three most senior officers were initially kept together. The importance of appearance and status on the fate of captured mariners was noted by Jackson in his *Account of the Empire of Morocco.* He described how quarrels frequently broke out "among the Arabs, about the possession of the sailors, disputing for the captain or mate because he is better dressed, or discovers himself to them in some other way, and because they expect a larger ransom for him."[42]

On 8 June 1789 the captain, his chief mate and surgeon were "march'd in 9 Days more thro[ugh] barren parch'd Desarts and Mountaneous Wilds" to the town of Guelmim located some thirty miles to the south-east of the position of their shipwreck.[43] Matthew Francis Dawson, the second mate, was probably not considered particularly valuable and had been "marched to the Southward" with the apprentice Samuel Beeley on 28 May 1789. Yet, as the nephew of John Dawson, one of Liverpool's leading slaving merchants, he had the potential to command the highest ransom payment among the crew.[44] Silvin Buckle, James Drachen and Jack Peters, described as "Portuguese Blacks," were also kept together and this may indicate that their captors were aware of the differential status and value of crewmembers.

The mariners were transferred on foot for sale at Guelmim, a market centre and a focal point for caravan routes in the trans-Saharan trade.[45] On the day before their arrival at the town, Irving and his officers were made more presentable for sale as they were given a "pair of scissars" and the captain was instructed to cut his beard which "was by this time very long, and troublesome." In a comment, which directly reflected Irving's earlier role as a surgeon in inspecting enslaved Africans gathered together for sale on the coast, he described how, "That action as it too much resembled the practice followed by the Slave traders, gave us much trouble."[46] Eight of the crew of the *Anna* were purchased by Mawlay 'Abd al-Rahman, the exiled son of Sayyidi Muhammad Ibn Abdallah (Sidi Muhammad), Sultan of Morocco and, according to an account written by the ship's surgeon, they "were conducted to a place belonging to Muly Abdrauchman, about 5 miles from Gulimeme, where we were employed digging the ground ... with things like pick axes, from sun rise till sun set."[47]

Irving, separated from his chief mate and surgeon, was sold for a second time at Guelmim to Shaykh Brahim. This is consistent with Jackson's account, as he noted how after travelling to market the men "at length become objects of commercial speculation."[48] Successive ownership by different masters was a common pattern in the experience of ransomed mariners, including Captain Thomas Smith of the *Solicitor General* and the French captives Follie and Saugnier.[49] Although it is not possible to establish the identity of Irving's owner with any degree of certainty, it is clear that the person who purchased him would have required a degree of status and the approval of "Takna notables *(ayan)*." Mohamed Mohamed notes how, "it would be hard to imagine the existence of a 'commoner' in Wady Nun who could 'buy' or 'sell' shipwrecked Europeans."[50] Irving also reported in his journal how he was lodged with a Jew at Talaint where "12 families of Jews" were under his "master's protection."[51]

After almost a month in Morocco, the formal commencement of ransoming negotiations can be traced to the instructions Irving received at Talaint on 24 June 1789 to write to the British Vice-Consul "informing him of my misfortunate situation." The letter written "with a reed, on course wrapping paper" informed Hutchison that Shaykh Brahim demanded 500 dollars per head for each of the men in his possession, although this figure was the subject of ongoing dispute during Irving's captivity.[52] Aware of the pivotal role that the consul played in starting and sustaining the ransoming process, Irving's appeal was formal and respectful, yet plaintive and inviting empathy for his men's suffering. He conveyed as much information as possible about his good character, background and current location, but also communicated forcibly his expectation that it was the consul's duty to secure their release as "good and Loyal" Englishmen. A meeting earlier in the day with some French mariners who had been wrecked five months earlier had impressed upon Irving the potential frailty of the ransoming process and the likely consequences of its failure.[53] Criticizing the shortcomings of the French consul and the negation of his duty, Irving urged Hutchison to "Suffer us not any longer like some poor Frenchmen About 10 or 12 Miles from hence to be the Slaves of Negroes, which reflects an unpardonate [*sic*] Negligence on the man who should see them liberated."[54]

Irving's attempts to exert some control over the ransoming process included conveying to Hutchison a clear sense that he was sufficiently well-connected in England to ensure that any ransom money would be reimbursed. He named the merchant John Dawson as his main supporter, and emphasized how "Our Merchants are very Affluent." Family members who could act as surety were also named, and his uncle's employment by the East India Company was used to demonstrate his reputable credentials and financial status. Irving indicated initially that his own resources would enable him to cover the ransom costs of his younger cousin the surgeon, but later extended this to include the nephew of John Dawson. In making strategic choices, he also encouraged Hutchison to prioritize the white crewmen over the three Portuguese blacks. The identity he presented to Hutchison was deliberately selective; he made no reference to his employment as a slave trader and presented himself as a loyal Englishmen rather than as a Scotsman. This was a tactic used by Irving to persuade diplomatic officials to act swiftly to secure his release, and it was unlikely to have had any impact on the ransom price demanded as Irving was entitled to seek British assistance in any case.[55] The selective construction of national identity was also characteristic of American mariners held captive in North Africa; they typically claimed to be English in negotiations for their release, as this was perceived by their captors as a more reliable basis for securing ransom payments through the British consular officials stationed in Morocco.[56]

Irving's expectation that it was responsibility of government to secure the crew's release was central to his appeal to Hutchison. This was a reasonable assumption, as Ressel notes that by the eighteenth century it was "commonly accepted throughout Western Europe that states had the responsibility to buy back their subjects from captivity among the Muslims." This entitlement was accepted by Hutchison who urged Irving to write to the Consul-General stating that it is "proper for every British Subject in this Country to apply for Protection to the person, who has His Majesty's Commission for that purpose."[57] These rights, although accepted in theory, could be difficult to secure in practice.[58] Irving showed an awareness of other private and charitable means used in seventeenth- and eighteenth-century England to secure the release of captives through fundraising by subscription. One option he proposed to Hutchison was that if sufficient funds could be raised for his ransom and that of his cousin, he could return home to England and "redeem" the others "by subscription if Government does not." Irving was clearly perplexed by the failure of the ship's Mediterranean Pass (number 7469) to provide protection from captivity. Regarding this as a valuable document, he concealed it for almost a month in the "head-band" of his "drawers" which he noted always escaped the searches for money.[59] The system of issuing passes reflected efforts by Britain and other European nations to reach agreements through treaties "to protect their shipping, providing their vessels with duly certified passes," and Lofkrantz notes how arrangements for the "treatment of shipwrecked individuals and prisoners were prominent in treaties with England (1760) and Spain (1767)."[60] However, the possession of a pass did not guarantee protection from capture. In his correspondence with Hutchison, Irving noted how "We are not on Hostile Terms with the Moors, and I have a pass granted by the Lords Commissioners of the Admiralty therefore why are we detained my good Sir."[61]

Shaykh Brahim also exerted control over the ransoming process by threatening Irving and his crew with slavery if the sum demanded was not paid, and Irving reported to Hutchison on 25 June 1789 how "the people here tell me if you do not pay for me or get me Released, in Ten days I go out to the fields to work at the Corn."[62] Pressure on Irving was also exerted through his crew, as on 2 August Irving reported that "My Master will not allow me to Close[?] the letter till I inform you that the Muley Abdrackman means to send them into the Gum Country if not redeemed soon."[63] This threat to send his crew to the Senegal valley considerably increased Irving's anxiety, and was a deliberate strategy used by his captors to create a sense of urgency in the minds of captives and consular officials. The ransom price of the men was probably higher than their market value as slaves, but this pressure was also intended to maximize the profit that could be secured from ransoming the men.[64]

Shaykh Brahim and Mawlay 'Abd al-Rahman, acting independently of the Moroccan government (Makhzan), sought to establish direct negotiations with the consular officials but this was circumvented by the intervention of Sidi Muhammad who prohibited private ransoming initiatives. This was one of the means by which Sidi Muhammad sought to impose and demonstrate his authority over the dissident southern territories in the area surrounding Wad Nun.[65] By July 1789, Hutchison apprized Irving of his powerlessness to act without Sidi Muhammad's permission. In response to Irving's increasingly desperate appeals, Hutchison explained how "no money I could offer, and would chearfully advance, can effect the purpose without the intervention of the Emperor, who will be very soon informed concerning you."[66] Sidi

Muhammad insisted that all ransom negotiations for European and American hostages should be channelled directly through him. Moreover, the ransom of Christian captives as leverage to secure the release of freeborn Muslims held by European powers was a central feature of his reign and was a policy which informed the negotiation of peace treaties with various Christian states.[67] The consular correspondence makes no reference to any specific requests by Sidi Muhammad for the release of freeborn Muslims in exchange for the crew of the *Anna*, but discussions centred instead on the acquisition of a frigate and armaments.[68] Sidi Muhammad wrote to George III in August 1789 drawing attention to how the crewmembers of a "Merchantman that was shipwrecked to the southward of our Territories" were in his possession, and that their release depended on the supply of "several pieces of small cannon, mortars etc."[69]

The intervention of Sidi Muhammad, however, generated lengthy delays linked to disputes over the level of ransom payments and tended to inflate the costs of securing a captive's release.[70] Irving reported that Shaykh Brahim refused to sell the men to the Sultan as he pays only a "trifling sum for Christians," and Hutchison had to reassure him that he would make good the difference "betwixt the Emperor's Allowance and your real ransom."[71] Hutchison was careful not to supply Irving with clothes that would give him "any superior Appearance," as he explained that "would only tend to augment the difficulties of your redemption." In his correspondence, Matra pointed out to William Wyndham Grenville, Vice-President of the Board of Trade and Commissioner of the Board of Control, that they needed to be careful in the bargaining process not to give the impression that the men were of more "consequence" than they actually were as this could lead to a higher ransom price.[72] Negotiations for the crew of the *Anna* also became embroiled in a dispute between the British and Moroccan government regarding tariffs and terms of trade. Sidi Muhammad considered that the formalities and courtesies of diplomatic exchange had not been observed properly by the British authorities. He pointed out that when he had redeemed men in the past, he did not even receive a letter thanking him for his assistance.[73] Sidi Muhammad insisted that he would not act in the case of the *Anna* until he had received a letter from the Court naming all of the men held in captivity.[74] Consular officials had to maintain pressure on British government officials to respond to the requests of the Moroccan court, and Matra urged Evan Nepean at the Home Office in December 1789 to send a request for the men so that they could be "restored" to their relatives.[75]

Maintaining Sidi Muhammad's good offices and interest in the crew of the *Anna* shaped the strategies deployed by consular officials. Matra reported to government that he had "many irons in the fire," but the most successful involved persuading William Lemprière, a doctor with the garrison in Gibraltar, to travel to Taroudant to provide medical treatment for Mawlay 'Abd al-Salam, the favorite son of the Sultan who was almost blind.[76] Matra was convinced that this device was pivotal in securing the release of the men, as without it they would have probably remained with the "Arabs" until they "perished." He explained how ten Frenchmen who had been shipwrecked some eighteen months earlier were now "so dispersed" that it would be impossible to recover them.[77] Matra thereby acknowledged that the men's position could have transformed from hostage to slave if the ransoming negotiations had been unsuccessful. Sidi Muhammad's personal interest in the crew of the *Anna* is reflected in the audience with Irving once the men had been transferred to Marrakesh. Whilst no doubt one-sided and reflecting his prejudice towards his Muslim captors, Irving's journal account reflected his chagrin at how the Sultan:

> sent for a Chart of the Atlantic Ocean and pointed out the courses I ought to have steered, in order to have avoided shipwreck. This is a Lesson he gives to every one, who has the misfortune to come before him in this light, however he does it in a very ignorant lame manner....[78]

For relatives and friends in England, their role in the ransoming process focused on using any influence or connections at their disposal to keep the cases fresh in the minds of political figures at a local and national level. With little progress in negotiations for the release of the crew of the *Solicitor General* eight months after its shipwreck, Daniel Backhouse, a prominent Liverpool merchant, wrote to John Tarleton M.P. in April 1796 asking him to intervene in the case of Captain Thomas Smith and his crew.[79] Backhouse was writing on behalf of the captain's wife, whose situation was "pitiable." Personal and business contacts informed the content of the letter, as Backhouse pointed out that Smith had been trained by Tarleton's father and that he had "sail'd Mate & Master in our employ several Voyages to Old Calabar."[80] Smith's status as a freeman of Liverpool was also used to bolster his case. Backhouse informed Tarleton that he had reassured Mrs. Smith:

> that she may depend that you will exert your utmost endeavours to procure her unfortunate Husband's release & that you probably would step forward in the Service of his unfortunate Crew, who I hope you will agree with me, ought not to be lost to their Country & familys for want of friends to procure their release if possible.[81]

The appeal that George Dalston Tunstall, brother-in-law of Captain Irving, sent to Matra in November 1789 drew attention to the suffering experienced by his "unhappy only sister who labours under the greatest anxiety of mind for her Dear husbands liberty." The letter also placed emphasis on the family's tradition of service in the Royal Navy and the loss of his father in active service at Madras in 1771 to encourage the Consul General to respond favorably to his appeal.[82] A petition written by William Sherwood, a leading captain in the Liverpool slave trade, emphasized Irving's good character as a "Carefull, Sober and Industrious" man, but did not include any reference to personal connections.[83] Other than lobbying influential contacts and raising money, family and friends in Britain were relatively powerless in the ransoming process. Their distance from the site of captivity precluded any direct intervention by individual family members to redeem hostages in the event of the failure of ransom negotiations, and they were dependent on state action and military intervention.[84]

The status and national origin of mariners had a direct bearing on the response of consular officials to the process of ransoming.[85] Although two of the three "Portuguese Blacks" who sailed as crew on the *Anna* were released from captivity, it was clear that the British consul treated their release as a far lower priority than the other crewmen. In his correspondence with Grenville, Matra stated that he would "have them thrown into the bargain, or left over for after consideration," which reflects their perceived inferiority.[86] On 19 December 1789, Matra informed Grenville that he was attempting to get the men to make an application to the Portuguese agent, as this would be a means of reducing the expenses of the British consulate. Reflecting a wider debate about whether consuls were obliged to redeem foreign seamen serving on vessels carrying their national flag,[87] Matra emphasized that he thought it was the responsibility of a Portuguese agent to treat for the release of Silvin Buckle, James Drachen and Jack Peters.[88] In 1807, this issue was debated by the Ironmongers' Company of London, which deployed charitable funds for the ransoming of captives in North Africa. They questioned whether their funds should be used to redeem only British-born captives or people of all nationalities serving on British vessels, other than those nations at war with Britain. After consulting with James Grey Jackson, they reached the conclusion that "any person employed fairly in the British service, and falling into slavery may properly be redeemed by the Company without reference to the Birth place of the captive."[89]

Irving's deliberate construction of his identity as a heroic figure resisting the tyranny of his Muslim captors was central to the way in which he recounted his experiences of captivity in several journals written on his return to England.[90] He emphasized how he was subject to, but resisted, an "intolerable" form of slavery using the strength derived from his Bible and his

Christian faith. Yet, despite this use of language he was aware throughout his captivity that his value lay principally in his ransom price and that it was the failure of negotiations which would mark his transition from hostage to slave. This awareness is reflected in his first appeal to Hutchison on 24 June 1789, in which he asked him to satisfy "me with respect to future Expectations, and whether we are or are not to be slaves." Irving was clearly unsure about their status, as he asked again on the following day for the consul to "Send me a Note relative to the Nature of our state."[91] When Matra wrote to Grenville from Tangier on 21 July 1789 to inform him about the loss of the *Anna*, he did not employ the term slavery to describe the men's condition but outlined the political devices he could use to secure their release. In a letter to Irving dated 27 September 1789, Matra explained that he had authorized the "sums demanded for your Ransom" and that their "redemption" would be secured through every means possible. Similarly, the Vice-Consul used the term "captivity" rather than "slavery" to characterize the captain's situation.[92]

Yet, Irving repeatedly used the terms slave and slavery in his correspondence. It was not until he was transferred to Marrakesh in January 1790 that he acknowledged directly that he was a hostage rather than a slave. He urged his wife Mary to "bear up under your sufferings with the fortitude of a good Christian, and to encourage you let me assure you that I am no longer a Slave but enjoy my liberty in every respect (that of leaving the country excepted)." He restated this in a letter from Essaouira two months later, saying that he had "little reason to call myself a Slave, but rather a prisoner at large."[93] For Irving, the point of transition from slave to hostage was when he was transferred from the ownership of his captors in the southern Saharan provinces to the control of the Sultan and the Vice-Consul. He defined himself as a slave throughout the period from June 1789 to January 1790 based principally on his fear that he was out of reach of redemption and thereby vulnerable to enslavement. A meeting with some Frenchmen who had been shipwrecked earlier in 1789 emphasized the possibility that he might be left to languish in slavery. He recorded in his journal how the realization that the French consul was unable to redeem the men "almost petrified me:"

> Could have died rather than devote my life to be spent in so abject a state, bereft of all Christian Society, a slave to a savage race, who dispised [*sic*] and hated me, on account of my beleif [*sic*].[94]

Irving's use of the term "slave" was also a device that he used deliberately to make his appeals for liberty more powerful, such as when he wrote to Matra craving "with the Humility of a poor slave your Assistance and protection." In this doleful petition, he pointed out that he was suffering in slavery "with people who are Scarsely a degree better than Savages, Strangers to [...] better affection of the Heart...." In attempting to convey the depth of his suffering, he claimed that "a Sensible heart may in some degree feel that no pen or the Tongue of a Cicerco can express, first a dreadfull shipwreck then siezed [*sic*] by a party of naked savages with drawn knives expecting every moment to be deprived of a painfull existence."[95] Describing himself as a "slave" to his friends and family also added to the dramatic impact of his tale and was a means of placing himself in the longer tradition of Barbary captivity narratives. Although Irving and the other crewmembers were required to undertake a variety of menial tasks, it was in the interests of their captors to ensure they remained in reasonably good condition and that their labor was not as arduous as that imposed on other captives in North Africa.[96] Clarence-Smith and Eltis suggest that the treatment of captives "probably improved slightly in the eighteenth century. As ransoming became more significant, the asset value of captives increased, providing an incentive for better treatment."[97] Irving was not required to undertake fieldwork, unlike other members of his crew, which points to the higher value placed on him by his captors. There is no doubt that Irving was sold on a number of occasions and required to undertake coerced labor in a domestic context, but his frequent reference to his slavery obscures the clear intention of his captors to facilitate his return to his previous status through the ransoming process.[98]

Despite the complaints by Irving and his cousin about their suffering at the hands of the "unfeeling moors," the cases of the *Anna* and *Solicitor General* provide examples of successful ransom negotiations. Of the nineteen mariners on the *Solicitor General,* eighteen were ransomed.[99] Ten of the eleven crewmembers of the *Anna* returned home, although James Drachen, one of the "Portuguese blacks," died in captivity.[100] Not all negotiations were as successful, and James Grey Jackson attempted to identify the key obstacles which prevented the positive completion of the ransoming process in other cases.[101] Based on knowledge built up from "observations made during a residence of sixteen years in different parts of the Empire of Marocco," he pointed out that forty English seamen shipwrecked between 1790 and 1806 were "dispersed in various parts of the Desert, after a lapse of time, in consequence of the Consul making no offers sufficiently advantageous to induce the Arabs to bring them to Mogador [Essaouira]." Jackson stressed the importance of acting swiftly, and that the transfer of captives north to Essaouira "should always be done as soon as possible after the wreck."[102] Other seamen were held for far longer periods than the mariners on the *Anna* and the *Solicitor General.* Jackson estimated that some eighty seamen on

English vessels were "redeemed after a tedious existence among the Arabs of from one to five years, or more, originating from various causes, such as a want of application being made through the proper channel, want of remitting money for their purchase, or want of a competent agent settled on the coast." In Jackson's opinion, the process of ransoming would have been speeded up by the employment of a specialist negotiator or agent who had access to a fund of money specifically for ransom payments. He argued that:

> by allowing a sum rather above the price of a black slave, the Arabs would immediately bring them to Mogodor, knowing they could depend on an adequate price; by this means they might be procured for half what they now cost; and it would be an infinitely better plan than that of soliciting the Emperor to procure them through the Bashaw of Suse; for, besides the delay, and consequent protracted sufferings of the captives, the favour is undoubtedly considered by the Emperor as incalculably more than the cost and charges of their purchase.[103]

Implicit in Jackson's comments is a criticism of the amateurish and uncoordinated efforts of consular officials to secure the release of seamen. If such improvements had been put in place, Jackson questioned, "how many an unfortunate Englishman would have been delivered from bondage?"[104]

The crewmembers of the *Anna* and the *Solicitor General*, particularly the captains and officers, were well practised in categorizing individuals according to their financial value. Thomas Smith, captain of the *Solicitor General*, had experience of trading at Old Calabar, an area characterized by face to face trade with African suppliers.[105] When the *Solicitor General* was wrecked in August 1795, Smith was en-route to Bonny in the Bight of Biafra "for Negroes."[106] In their roles as surgeon and surgeon's mate on slaving voyages to the Bight of Biafra between 1787 and 1788, Irving and his younger cousin would have gone on shore with the captain and participated in direct negotiations with African merchants for the supply of enslaved Africans.[107] By inspecting the medical condition of the Africans gathered for sale, they played a direct role in assessing the economic value of individuals destined for export in the transatlantic slave trade as well as the profits that would accrue to the officers through payments based on the survival rates of the slaves in the Middle Passage. This capacity appears not to have been diminished by their period in captivity and their own treatment as commodities. After casting off his "Arabic Rags," on his return to England in November 1791, Irving returned to sea in command of the *Ellen* just two months later.[108] When James Irving junior, the younger cousin and namesake of the captain, accepted the position of surgeon on the *Ellen*, he calculated the profits he expected to receive from the purchase and sale of 253 enslaved Africans.[109] As the ship sailed from port, he informed his "Honoured Parents" in Langholm in Scotland that "My wages is £4 S*terling* per month besides if it please God we make a good voyage, I get head Money, and if we only bury 6 slaves my Couzin will receive £100 and I £50 Bounty." Showing his awareness of the terms of the Dolben Act of 1788, which rewarded captains and surgeons for keeping slave mortality at 3% or lower, the surgeon explained how the death of "not more than nine slaves" would result in the payment of bonuses of £25 for him and £50 for his older cousin. In stark contrast to his financial calculations, the death of 47 of the 253 African men, women and children (18.6%) embarked on the *Ellen* in 1791 points to the devastating human impact of the trade.[110]

In pleading for his own release from captivity in Morocco, Captain Irving referred to the "sordid avarice" of his captors and how he had been "consigned over to a Slavery more detestable than Death."[111] Yet, he drew no parallels with the financial rewards he had accrued during his slave-trading career, which had generated sufficient capital to purchase property in his home town in Scotland following his first slaving venture on the *Vulture* in 1784.[112] His correspondence with his wife Mary is punctuated frequently with his concern that their wealth and future plans had been severely undermined by his period in captivity. The first letter sent home following his capture in Morocco lamented how the shipwreck had shattered their "hopes and prospects," and that he would need with "Gods Assistance" to undertake another slaving voyage "to retrieve what I've lost."[113]

As a result of his period in captivity, Irving travelled to a number of urban and rural settlements and developed some awareness of the economy, society and culture of Morocco. His journals include reference to the wealth and splendour of the royal court at Taroudant, the appearance and productivity of the Moroccan landscape, as well as the religious devotion shown by Muslims with whom he came into contact. In some respects, Irving emerged from his period in Morocco with some factual understanding of local peoples and societies, and he exhibited a clear awareness of social gradations in Morocco. Yet, his cultural conceit was such that he dismissed any evidence which challenged his worldview of European superiority. When he visited the court of Mawlay 'Abd-al-Salam at Taroudant, for example, he recorded his surprize at the appearance of the Prince and struggled to reconcile the evidence of wealth and cultural advance with his preconceived ideas of European civilization and African savagery:

> In the afternoon I was taken before the Prince where I was much surprised to find the defferance and respect that was shown him. I expected to find him only one degree removed from a Savage, as all the other moors or Arabs are...

> His dress was rich and graceful. His menial servants stood at the door, and the chief scribe with other Grandees sat at some distance from him on a Carpet. He was served with a cup of coffee poured from a Golden Pot, and the rest of the service was of plate. The chamber was large and spacious. The wall was hung round with a kind of Tapestry, and the floor tiled with various coulered [*sic*] Tiles, arranged in differant [*sic*] figures, and covered with a rich Turkey carpet.[114]

In order to counter such evidence of civilization, Irving provided frequent examples of the backwardness of the people. After recounting details of the court at Taroudant, for example, he followed this swiftly with an entry in which he ridiculed the "ignorance" of the "uncivilized moors" who asked him to diagnose and cure their illnesses by examining their pulses. His disparaging comments on the women he encountered in Morocco also added to his general depiction of an uncivilized society. The women at Wad Nun were described as a "disgrace to humanity, possessing nothing human, but shape," and he highlighted their lack of feminine qualities by referring to how they spat on him, "severely tormented" him, stripped him of his clothing and conducted intimate searches for money.[115]

Other than recording the occasional phrase to support his narration of events, Irving made no attempt to learn any Arabic. His comments on the Muslim faith were also sparse and typically supported the dramatic purposes of his narrative. Although he remarked on the presence of a school held in one of the tents on the beach, his main purpose was to point out how the teacher was an "inhospitable pedant" who would not allow them to shelter there. On those occasions where he commented on the Muslim faith, it was typically used to illustrate their captors' lack of humanity and compassion.[116] In an entry for 8 June 1789, for example, Irving described how their captors spat in their faces when they begged for water and then "obliged us to drink out of our hats as the dish would have been poluted [*sic*], had any of us touched it with our lips."[117] A few days earlier, Captain Irving described how they were forced at knifepoint to "sing, and say part of their prayers which we did not then understand."[118] Rather than challenging his cultural prejudices, Irving's period in Morocco reinforced his sense of identity as a Briton caught up in the long-running conflict between the Christian and Islamic worlds.[119] As such, his journals exhibit similar characteristics to those written by other British captives in the early modern period. As Vitkus points out, these captivity narratives viewed Moroccan culture and society through "an anti-Islamic lens...."[120] This is reflected in his choice of language for the final entries in his journal in which he recorded the crew's departure on several English vessels from the harbour at Essaouira on 24 September 1789.

Although his men were "bare and pennyless," he anticipated that returning to England would lead to "better days." He drew on his Christian faith through his "cordial prayer, that we might never again visit those Barbarious regions in a similar predicament."[121]

Endnotes

1 I would like to thank Robin Law, Jennifer Lofkrantz, Olatunji Ojo and David Pope for their helpful comments on a draft of this chapter. I am also grateful to Paul Lovejoy and Mohamed Mohamed for their valuable advice on a number of issues.

2 The term "Barbary Coast," used by European commentators in the early modern period to refer to a large coastal area of North Africa, reflected limited contemporary understanding of the diversity of local societies and cultures. Until the nineteenth century, the term was also closely associated with corsair attacks on shipping. In a letter written to the Consul General at Tangier, George Dalston Tunstall referred to "that barbarous coast which from all accounts is so deserving of its title." Lancashire Record Office [hereafter LRO], DDX 1126/1/22, George Dalston Tunstall to J.M. Matra, Consul General at Tangier, 9 November 1789. Transcript in Suzanne Schwarz, ed., *Slave Captain. The Career of James Irving in the Liverpool Slave Trade,* 2nd ed. (Liverpool: Liverpool University Press, 2008), 106-107. For a discussion of the characteristics of the "Barbary Captivity Narrative," see Mohamed H. Mohamed, "'The Disgrace of Christendom:' Shipwreck and Ransoming in Southern Morocco (1780s-1820s)," in this volume.

3 James Walvin, "The Public Campaign in England against Slavery, 1787-1834," in David Eltis and James Walvin (eds.), *The Abolition of the Atlantic Slave Trade. Origins and Effects in Europe, Africa, and the Americas* (Madison: The University of Wisconsin Press, 1981), 63-68; Christopher Leslie Brown, *Moral Capital. Foundations of British Abolitionism* (Chapel Hill: University of North Carolina Press, 2006), 1-9, 17-19, 23-24.

4 Edward Rushton, *West-Indian Eclogues* (London: W. Lowndes and J. Philips, 1787), 3. *The English Review* noted that, "These eclogues are four in number, viz. Morning, Evening, Noon, and Midnight. The persons introduced are unfortunate negroes, who, having been carried away forcibly from their native shores, are dragging on their miserable lives in all the horrors of slavery. They are represented as either bewailing their wretched state, or planning the destruction of their tyrants." *English Review, or, An Abstract of English and Foreign Literature, 1783-1795*, 10 (October 1787), 315.

5 The *Anna* was a schooner of fifty tons burthen owned by John Dawson, which set sail from Liverpool on 2 May 1789. Under the terms of the Dolben Act, the vessel was entitled to carry 83 enslaved Africans. David Eltis et al., *Voyages: The Trans-Atlantic Slave Trade Database,* www.slavevoyages.org, voyage identification number 80295; F.E. Sanderson, "The Liverpool Delegates and Sir

William Dolben's Bill," *Transactions of the Historic Society of Lancashire and Cheshire,* 124 (1972), 75.

6 For a discussion of Captain Irving's career, see Schwarz, *Slave Captain.* Information on the second slave ship commanded by James Irving (the *Ellen*) is available in Eltis, *Trans-Atlantic Slave Trade Database,* voyage identification number 81242.

7 The National Archives, Kew [hereafter TNA], FO 52/9, Morocco Series, Various 1772-1792. Captain Irving at "Telling" to John Hutchison, Vice-Consul at Mogador [Essaouira] in Morocco, 24 June 1789, ff. 115-16. Transcript in Schwarz, *Slave Captain*, 92-94.

8 Olaudah Equiano, *The Interesting Narrative and Other Writings* (New York: Penguin Books, Vincent Carretta, ed., 2003), 61. *The Interesting Narrative* was first published in March 1789, two months after the motion to abolish the slave trade. Paul E. Lovejoy, "Autobiography and Memory: Gustavus Vassa, alias Olaudah Equiano, the African," *Slavery and Abolition,* 27:3 (2006), 317.

9 Irving made frequent use of these terms in journals written on his return to England, but he was careful not to employ this language in correspondence written during his captivity in Morocco. In his first petition for help to John Hutchison, Vice-Consul at Essaouira, he describes how they were being held by "Arabs and Moors in a condition miserable beyond Conception." Irving at "Telling" to Hutchinson, 24 June 1789, in Schwarz, *Slave Captain,* 92. In a letter to his mother-in-law, Mrs. Mary Tunstall, he described his captors as "Natives." LRO, DDX 1126/1/13, James Irving to Mrs. Tunstall, 1 August 1789. Transcript in Schwarz, *Slave Captain*, 97-98.

10 Beinecke Rare Book and Manuscript Library, Yale University, Osborn Shelves c. 399, "A Narrative of the Shipwreck of the *Ann*, Capt[ai]n Irving." Transcript in Schwarz, *Slave Captain*, 127-48 (131, 143).

11 TNA, FO 52/9, Morocco Series, Various 1772-1792, James Irving at "Telling" in Morocco to Mr. Hutchison, Vice-Consul at Mogador, 2 August 1789, fol. 117. Transcript in Schwarz, *Slave Captain*, 99-100; "Narrative of the Shipwreck of the *Ann*," in Schwarz, *Slave Captain,* 139. El Hamel identifies the presence of black slaves and free blacks in Morocco, and their important contribution to Moroccan society. Irving's reference to "Negroes" in close proximity to Guelmim is not surprizing, as the town was closely linked to the trans-Saharan trade; the "usual route was Timbuktu, Arawan, Taghaza and Tafilalt." Chouki El Hamel, *Black Morocco. A History of Slavery, Race, and Islam* (Cambridge: Cambridge University Press, 2013), 4-5, 7-9, 109, 154, 233. The late seventeenth-century captivity narrative written by Francis Brooks includes reference to "*Black-a-moors*" set over European captives "as Task-masters," cited in Adam R. Beach, "African Slaves, English Slave Narratives, and Early Modern Morocco," *Eighteenth-Century Studies,* 46:3 (2013), 336.

12 Definitions of legal and illegal enslavement had been the subject of debate by "Muslim scholars in the western and central Sudan regions of West Africa ... from at least the fifteenth century." Jennifer Lofkrantz, "Protecting Freeborn

Muslims: The Sokoto Caliphate's Attempts to Prevent Illegal Enslavement and its Acceptance of the Strategy of Ransoming," *Slavery and Abolition,* 32:1 (2011), 111; Jennifer Lofkrantz and Olatunji Ojo, "Slavery, Freedom, and Failed Ransom Negotiations in West Africa, 1730-1900," *Journal of African History,* 53 (2012), 26-28; Paul E. Lovejoy, *Transformations in Slavery. A History of Slavery in Africa,* 3rd ed. (Cambridge, Cambridge University Press, 2012), 86-87. In the 1820s, the Sokoto Caliphate withdrew from "participation in the Atlantic slave trade" on "its own initiative." Paul E. Lovejoy, "Diplomacy in the Heart of Africa. British-Sokoto Negotiations over the Abolition of the Atlantic Slave Trade," draft paper, supplied in email correspondence; Jamie Bruce Lockhart and Paul E. Lovejoy (eds.), *Hugh Clapperton into the Interior of Africa. Records of the Second Expedition, 1825-1827* (Leiden: Brill, 2005), 56-61.

13 David Eltis, *The Rise of African Slavery in the Americas* (Cambridge: Cambridge University Press, 2000), 1-18.

14 Call for papers, "Perspectives on Historical and Contemporary Ransoming Practices," 25-26 April 2014.

15 Lofkrantz, "Protecting Freeborn Muslims," 111.

16 Jennifer Lofkrantz, "Scholars, Captives and Slaves: Ransoming Prisoners in Muslim West Africa," Draft chapter supplied in email correspondence, 5, Lofkrantz, "Muslim Intellectual Reactions to Illegal Enslavement and the Strategy of Ransoming," Paper presented at conference on "Perspectives on Historical and Contemporary Ransoming Practices," York University, 25-26 April 2014. In his narrative, Robert Adams referred to the harsh treatment of Christians and attempts to convert captives to Islam. *The Narrative of Robert Adams, a Sailor, who was wrecked on the Western Coast of Africa, in the Year 1810* (London: Printed for John Murray by William Bulmer and Co., 1816), 73, 146. For a discussion of the reliability and significance of Adams's account, see Charles Hansford Adams (ed.), *The Narrative of Robert Adams, A Barbary Captive* (Cambridge: Cambridge University Press, 2005), ix-lv. James Grey Jackson considered that the young males among a ship's crew were particularly vulnerable. He described how, "the young lads, of which there are generally two or three in every ship's crew, are generally seduced by the Arabs to become Mohammedans; in this case, the Sheick or chief of the duar adopts him, and initiates him in the Koran, by sending him to the (Mdursa) seminary, where he learns to read the sacred volume, and is instructed in the pronunciation of the Arabic language." James Grey Jackson, *An Account of the Empire of Morocco,* 3rd ed. (London: Frank Cass 1968 [1814]), 277.

17 El Hamel, *Black Morocco*, 9.

18 Seymour Drescher, "The Slaving Capital of the World: Liverpool and National Opinion in the Age of Abolition," *Slavery and Abolition,* 9:2 (1988), 128-29.

19 It is estimated that fifteen "substantial narratives" survive for this period. Linda Colley, *Captives: Britain, Empire and the World, 1600-1850* (London: Jonathan Cape, 2002), 88-89. Vitkus indicates that 23 captivity narratives were written by British captives between 1577 and 1704. Daniel J. Vitkus and Nabil Matar

(eds.), *Piracy, Slavery and Redemption. Barbary Captivity Narratives from Early Modern England* (New York: Columbia University Press, 2001), 3. A consensus has yet to be reached on the total number of people who were held in captivity in North Africa. Robert C. Davis estimates that in the period between 1530 and 1780, there were "almost certainly a million and quite possibly as many as a million and a quarter white, European Christians enslaved by the Muslims of the Barbary Coast." Robert C. Davis, "Counting European Slaves on the Barbary Coast," *Past and Present,* 172 (2001), 118.

20 The "Narrative of the Shipwreck of the *Ann"* held at the Beinecke Rare Book and Manuscript Library was purchased from a dealer in London in 1954. Another eighteenth-century version of Irving's journal has recently come to light in the North Yorkshire County Council Record Office [hereafter NYCC]. This account is "written on 29 pages" and the "paper is watermarked 1794." The first page of the journal includes reference to "Mr. Irving's journal wrote in Barbary." The journal is held in the collection of Tot Lord of Settle, NYCC, ZXF 34/5. I am grateful to Keith Sweetmore for this information contained in email correspondence, 10 March 2011. A twentieth-century copy of Irving's journal is held at the Lancashire Record Office, and a nineteenth-century copy is held at The Beacon, Whitehaven.

21 Davis, "Counting European Slaves," 89.

22 "Narrative of the Shipwreck of the *Ann,*" in Schwarz, *Slave Captain,* 129. In *Robinson Crusoe,* reference is made to how Crusoe was "exceedingly surprised with the print of a man's naked foot on the shore, which was very plain to be seen in the sand." Daniel Defoe, *Robinson Crusoe* (Ware: Wordsworth Editions, 1995 [London, 1719]), 117-18.

23 Davis, "Counting European Slaves," 89.

24 In the early modern period, captives who were ransomed successfully and returned home told their stories numerous times. Vitkus and Matar, *Piracy, Slavery and Redemption*, 2-3.

25 "Narrative of the Shipwreck of the *Ann,*" in Schwarz, *Slave Captain,* 149-51.

26 Lofkrantz and Ojo, "Slavery, Freedom, and Failed Ransom Negotiations in West Africa," 26.

27 Irving at "Telling" to Hutchison, 24 June 1789, in Schwarz, *Slave Captain,* 92.

28 TNA, FO 95/1/3, Barbary States, 1766-1801, Letter from John Foxcroft to Messrs. Forbes & Co., Liverpool, fol. 203; TNA, FO 52/11, Morocco Series, Consul James M. Matra, 1795-1810, James Matra to the Duke of Portland, 31 October 1795, fol. 48; James M. Matra to the Duke of Portland, 18 November 1795, fol. 51.

29 TNA, FO 52/11, Morocco Series, Consul James M. Matra, 24 July 1797, fol. 118.

30 Mohamed El Mansour, *Morocco in the Reign of Mawlay Sulayman* (Wisbech: Middle East and North African Studies Press, 1990), 88-98.

31 *St. James's Chronicle or the British Evening Post,* July 19, 1796-July 21, 1796, Issue 6019, 17th-18th Century Burney Collection Newspapers, Gale reference

number Z2001330268 (accessed 30 January 2015); *Lloyd's Evening Post (London, England)*, July 20, 1796 – July 22, 1796, Issue 6070, 17th-18th Century Burney Collection Newspapers, Gale reference number Z2000538431 (accessed 30 January 2015).

32 TNA, FO 52/11, Morocco Series, Consul James M. Matra, 24 March, 28 May and 10 September 1796, ff. 59, 64, 112.

33 LRO, DDX 1126/1/29, Letter from Christopher Robson to William Graham, 22 September 1790. Transcript in Schwarz, *Slave Captain*, 115-16.

34 Essaouira was founded by Sidi Muhammad in 1764 as a focus for European trade. Other European consuls were based in the port, including those of France, Denmark and Portugal. El Hamel, *Black Morocco*, 222, 225.

35 Mohamed Hassan Mohamed, *Between Caravan and Sultan: The Bayruk of Southern Morocco. A Study in History and Identity* (Leiden: Brill, 2012), 1-3, 278-335.

36 Lofkrantz, "Scholars, Captives and Slaves," 12-13. For a discussion of Jews in Morocco, see El Mansour, *Morocco in the Reign of Mawlay Sulayman*, 14-16, 42, 44-46.

37 Jackson described how, "soon after a ship strikes, some wandering Arabs strolling from their respective duars in the Desert, perceive the masts from the sand hills; and without coming to the shore, repair to their hordes perhaps 30 or 40 miles off, to apprise them of the wreck; when they immediately assemble, arming themselves with daggers, guns, and cudgels." Jackson, *Account of the Empire of Morocco*, 270.

38 Irving at "Telling" to Hutchison, 24 June 1789, in Schwarz, *Slave Captain*, 92-94.

39 "Narrative of the Shipwreck of the *Ann*," in Schwarz, *Slave Captain*, 131, 147.

40 Ibid., 133.

41 Ibid.

42 Jackson, *Account of the Empire of Morocco*, 270.

43 This explanation was set out in a letter written by Captain Irving to J.M. Matra. LRO, DDX 1126/1/16, Draft of a letter from James Irving to J.M. Matra, undated.

44 Between 1772 and 1795, John Dawson "probably invested in 129 voyages." Information supplied by David Pope in email correspondence, 28 January 2015. This includes an additional thirteen voyages to those indicated in David Pope, "The Wealth and Social Aspirations of Liverpool's Slave Merchants of the Second Half of the Eighteenth Century," in David Richardson, Suzanne Schwarz and Anthony Tibbles (eds.), *Liverpool and Transatlantic Slavery* (Liverpool: Liverpool University Press, 2007), 197.

45 El Hamel, *Black Morocco*, 233; El Mansour, *Morocco in the Reign of Mawlay Sulayman*, 57-58.

46 "Narrative of the Shipwreck of the *Ann*," in Schwarz, *Slave Captain*, 138. The shaving of their beards and heads was regarded as the "highest indignity" by two Africans enslaved on the Gambia in the early 1730s. Lofkrantz and Ojo,

"Slavery, Freedom, and Failed Ransom Negotiations in West Africa," 29.

47 "A very short account of what happened to me after the seperation [*sic*] on the 16th of June 1789," in Schwarz, *Slave Captain,* 149. Mohamed Mohamed notes how Mawlay 'Abd al-Rahman was "arguably, the maternal cousin of Ubaydallah Ibn Salim, Bayruk's father." He had taken "refuge in al-Sus but was there only from 1779 to 1789." Information supplied in email correspondence, 12 January 2015.

48 Jackson, *Account of the Empire of Morocco*, 272.

49 Lofkrantz, "Scholars, Captives and Slaves," 18-19; *Voyages to the Coast of Africa, by Mess. Saugnier and Brisson; Containing an Account of their Shipwreck on Board Different Vessels, and Subsequent Slavery* (London: G.G.J. and J. Robinson, 1792), 10, 17. In a letter from Daniel Backhouse to John Tarleton, it was noted how Captain Thomas Smith "has been sold three times & is now Slave to a Jew." TNA, CO 267/10, Daniel Backhouse to John Tarleton, 19 April 1796.

50 I am grateful for this information supplied in email correspondence by Mohamed Mohamed, 14 August 2014; Mohamed, *Between Caravan and Sultan,* 1-2, 278-335.

51 "Narrative of the Shipwreck of the *Ann,*" in Schwarz, *Slave Captain,* 141.

52 Ibid.

53 A number of French mariners who were shipwrecked on the coast of North Africa were slave traders. Gillian Weiss, *Captives and Corsairs. France and Slavery in the Early Modern Mediterranean* (Stanford: Stanford University Press, 2011), 131, 134, 139; William G. Clarence-Smith and David Eltis, "White Servitude," in David Eltis and Stanley L. Engerman, eds., *The Cambridge World History of Slavery, Volume 3, AD 1420-AD 1804* (Cambridge: Cambridge University Press, 2011), 152.

54 Irving at "Telling" to Hutchison, 24 June 1789, in Schwarz, *Slave Captain,* 92.

55 Ibid., 92-94.

56 Christine Sears, "'Arab Speculators:' Arab-African Masters and Slave Ransoming in the Late Eighteenth and Early Nineteenth Centuries," Paper presented at conference on "Perspectives on Historical and Contemporary Ransoming Practices," 25-26 April 2014.

57 LRO, DDX 1126/1/15, John Hutchison, Vice-Consul, to James Irving at "Telling" in Morocco, [28] August 1789. Transcript in Schwarz, *Slave Captain,* 101-102.

58 Marcus Ressel, "Conflicts Between Early Modern European States about Rescuing their Own Subjects from Barbary Captivity," *Scandinavian Journal of History,* 36:1 (2011), 2-3.

59 "Narrative of the Shipwreck of the *Ann,*" in Schwarz, *Slave Captain,* 133; Irving at "Telling" to Hutchison, 24 June 1789, in Schwarz, *Slave Captain,* 93.

60 Clarence-Smith and Eltis, "White Servitude," 152; Lofkrantz, "Scholars, Captives and Slaves," 10.

61 Irving at "Telling" to Hutchison, 24 June and 25 June 1789, in Schwarz, *Slave*

Captain, 93-94.

62 TNA, FO 52/9, Morocco Series, Various 1772-1792, Captain Irving in Morocco to either John Hutchison, Vice-Consul at Mogador, or James M. Matra, Consul General at Tangier, 25 June 1789, fol. 116, in Schwarz, *Slave Captain*, 94.

63 James Irving at "Telling" in Morocco to Mr. Hutchison, Vice-Consul at Mogador, 2 August 1789, in Schwarz, *Slave Captain*, 100; TNA, FO 52/8, Morocco Series, Consul James M. Matra, 1789-1790, James Matra to William Wyndham Grenville, 12 September 1789, fol. 130.

64 In West Africa, the "ransom prices were usually at least twice the price the captive would fetch on the slave market and often more." Lofkrantz and Ojo, "Slavery, Freedom, and Failed Ransom Negotiations in West Africa," 33.

65 Lofkrantz, "Scholars, Captives and Slaves," 10-11, 13-14.

66 LRO, DDX 1126/1/11, John Hutchison, Vice-Consul, to James Irving at "Telling," Morocco, 10 July 1789. Transcript in Schwarz, *Slave Captain*, 95.

67 Lofkrantz, "Scholars, Captives and Slaves," 2, 5, 9-10.

68 There is reference to a request from the Sultan for Matra to supply information demonstrating how he had reimbursed the "losses of the three Moors wrecked on our coast," but the circumstances are unclear. TNA, FO 52/8, Morocco Series, Consul James M. Matra, 1789-1790, James Matra to William Wyndham Grenville, 11 March 1790, fol. 194.

69 TNA, FO 52/8, Morocco Series, Consul James M. Matra to Evan Nepean, 22 October 1789, ff. 152-54, 160-62.

70 Hershenzon notes that royal intervention in ransoming negotiations could inflate prices. Daniel Hershenzon, "Ransoming Muslims: North African Captives and their Ransom in the Early Modern Period," Paper presented at conference on "Perspectives on Historical and Contemporary Ransoming Practices," York University, 25-26 April 2014.

71 LRO, DDX 1126/1/17, John Hutchison, Vice-Consul, to James Irving at "Telling" in Morocco, 13 August 1789. Transcript in Schwarz, *Slave Captain*, 100-101.

72 P. J. Jupp, "Grenville, William Wyndham, Baron Grenville (1759-1834)," *Oxford Dictionary of National Biography,* http://www.oxforddnb.com/view/article/11501?docPos=1 (accessed 30 January 2015); LRO, DDX 1126/1/12, John Hutchison, Vice-Consul, to James Irving at "Telling," Morocco, 21[?] July 1789. Transcript in Schwarz, *Slave Captain*, 96-97; TNA, FO 52/8, Morocco Series, Consul James M. Matra, 1789-1790, James Matra to William Wyndham Grenville, 7 August 1789, fol. 108.

73 TNA, FO 52/8, Morocco Series, Consul James M. Matra, 1789-1790, James Matra to William Wyndham Grenville, 22 October 1789, ff. 150-52; James Matra to Evan Nepean, 22 October 1789, ff. 152-54, 160.

74 TNA, FO 52/8, Morocco Series, Consul James M. Matra, 1789-1790, enclosed with a letter from James Matra to William Wyndham Grenville, 19 December 1789, fol. 180; Matra to Evan Nepean, 27 December 1789, fol. 184; Matra to William Wyndham Grenville, 14 February 1790, fol. 190.

75 Elizabeth Sparrow, "Nepean, Sir Evan, first baronet (1752-1822)," *Oxford Dictionary of National Biography,* http://www.oxforddnb.com/view/article/19894?docPos=1 (accessed 30 January 2015); TNA, FO 52/8, Morocco Series, Consul James M. Matra, 1789-1790, James Matra to Evan Nepean, 20 December 1789, ff. 181-82.

76 TNA, FO 52/9, Morocco Series, Various 1772-1792. Extracts of Letters from Consul Matra dated Tangiers [*sic*] the 9th Aug[us]t and 5th Sept[embe]r 1789, ff. 113-14. The surgeon subsequently wrote an account of his experiences in Morocco. William Lemprière, *A Tour from Gibraltar to Tangier, Sallee, Mogodore, Santa Cruz, Tarudant, and Thence over Mount Atlas to Morocco*, 3rd ed. (London, 1804).

77 TNA, FO 52/8, Morocco Series, Consul James M. Matra, James Matra to William Wyndham Grenville, 26 January 1790, fol. 188.

78 The Beacon, Whitehaven. "Journal of Voyage and Shipwreck," 98-99.

79 Daniel Backhouse organized an estimated one hundred slaving ventures between 1773 and 1799, and also participated in the direct trade to the West Indies. Pope, "The Wealth and Social Aspirations of Liverpool's Slave Merchants," 185, 194. For a discussion of the career of John Tarleton MP, see "Tarleton, John (1755-1841), of Finch House, nr. Liverpool, Lancs," Published in *The History of Parliament: the House of Commons 1790-1820,* ed. R. Thorne, 1986, available on the website: *The History of Parliament. British Political, Social & Local History,* http://www.historyofparliamentonline.org/volume/1790-1820/member/tarleton-john-1755-1841 (accessed 29 January 2015).

80 This firm included Thomas Tarleton, John Tarleton and Daniel Backhouse. The partnership was dissolved in 1794, although the business was carried on by John Tarleton and John Backhouse until 16 July 1802. I am grateful to David Pope for this information contained in email correspondence, 28 January 2015.

81 TNA, CO 267/10, Daniel Backhouse to John Tarleton, 19 April 1796, ff. 132-34.

82 LRO, DDX 1126/1/22, George Dalston Tunstall to J.M. Matra, Consul General at Tangier, 9 November 1789. Transcript in Schwarz, *Slave Captain*, 106-107.

83 Liverpool Record Office, 387 MD 54, William Sherwood to an unnamed individual, 2 May 1790. Transcript in Schwarz, *Slave Captain*, 113.

84 Lofkrantz and Ojo, "Slavery, Freedom, and Failed Ransom Negotiations in West Africa," 26-27, 29, 33, 35-37.

85 The impact of social inequalities on ransoming policy can be traced in West Africa. Lofkrantz and Ojo, "Slavery, Freedom, and Failed Ransom Negotiations in West Africa," 26.

86 TNA, FO 52/8, Morocco Series, Consul James M. Matra, 1789-1790, James Matra to William Wyndham Grenville, 7 August 1789, fol. 108.

87 Given the diverse international origins of mariners on ships in the eighteenth century, this lack of clarity about responsibility was "an important legalistic gap." Ressel, "Conflicts Between Early Modern European States," 3.

88 TNA, FO 52/8, Morocco Series, Consul James M. Matra, 1789-1790, James

Matra to William Wyndham Grenville, 19 December 1789, fol. 177.

89 TNA, FO 174/14, Letters from the Ironmongers' Company of London Regarding the Redemption of British Slaves and Shipwrecked Mariners in Morrocco, 7 July 1807.

90 This was typical of a number of captivity narratives written by British subjects in the early modern period. Vitkus and Matar, *Piracy, Slavery and Redemption*, 4, 37, 359.

91 Irving at "Telling" to Hutchinson, 24 June 1789, in Schwarz, *Slave Captain*, 92-93; Irving in Morocco to either Hutchison or Matra, 25 June 1789, in Schwarz, *Slave Captain*, 94.

92 LRO, DDX 1126/1/19, James M. Matra to Captain James Irving, 27 September 1789. Transcript in Schwarz, *Slave Captain*, 104; Matra to Grenville, 21 July 1789, in Schwarz, *Slave Captain*, 95-96.

93 LRO, DDX 1126/1/25, James Irving to Mary Irving, 31 January 1790, LRO, DDX 1126/1/26, James Irving to Mary Irving, 26 March 1790, in Schwarz, *Slave Captain*, 109-13.

94 "Narrative of the Shipwreck of the *Ann,*" in *Schwarz, Slave Captain,* 140.

95 LRO, DDX 1126/1/16, Draft of a letter from James Irving to J.M. Matra, undated.

96 Ellen G. Friedman, "Christian Captives at 'Hard Labour' in Algiers, 16th-18th Centuries," *International Journal of African Historical Studies,* 13:4 (1980), 618-28.

97 Clarence-Smith and Eltis, "White Servitude," 155.

98 Ransoming is defined as "the release of a captive prior to enslavement in exchange for payment." This process involves "the ransomed captive returning to their previous status in their own society." Lofkrantz and Ojo, "Slavery, Freedom, and Failed Ransom Negotiations in West Africa," 25-26, 29; Jennifer Lofkrantz, "Intellectual Discourse in the Sokoto Caliphate: The Triumvirate's Opinions on the Issue of Ransoming, ca. 1810," *International Journal of African Historical Studies,* 45:3 (2012), 386; Lofkrantz, "Protecting Freeborn Muslims," 109-110.

99 TNA, FO 52/11, Morocco Series, Consul James M. Matra, 1795-1810, James Matra to the Duke of Portland, ff. 48, 51, 112, 118.

100 "Narrative of the Shipwreck of the *Ann,*" in Schwarz, *Slave Captain*, 143, 148.

101 In West Africa, the failure of ransom negotiations could be caused by "time constraints, disputes over price or with brokers, captor disinterest, or the prohibition of ransoming by the state." Lofkrantz and Ojo, "Slavery, Freedom, and Failed Ransom Negotiations in West Africa," 26.

102 Jackson, *Account of the Empire of Morocco*, v, 279-80.

103 Ibid., 280.

104 Ibid., 274, 279-81.

105 TNA, CO 267/10, Daniel Backhouse to John Tarleton, 19 April 1795, ff. 132-34.

106 TNA, FO 95/1/3, John Foxcroft to Messrs. Forbes & Co., 16 October 1795.

The *Solicitor General* was a brig of 186 tons owned by William Forbes, Thomas Rigmaiden, William Gregson junior, Joseph Ward and William Begg. The ship sailed from Liverpool on 17 July 1795 bound to the Bight of Biafra to purchase 310 enslaved Africans. Eltis et al., *Trans-Atlantic Slave Trade Database*, voyage identification number 83572.

107 Paul E. Lovejoy and David Richardson, "African Agency and the Liverpool Slave Trade," in Richardson, Schwarz and Tibbles, *Liverpool and Transatlantic Slavery,* 43-65.

108 LRO, DDX 1126/1/32, James Irving in London to Mary Irving, 12 November 1790. Transcript in Schwarz, *Slave Captain*, 118-19.

109 The *Ellen*, a ship of 152 tons burthen owned by John Dawson, sailed from Liverpool on 3 January 1791. After purchasing enslaved Africans at Cape Coast Castle and Anomabu, Captain Irving sailed from West Africa bound for Trinidad on 16 September 1791. Of the 253 enslaved Africans carried on board the *Ellen,* just over one half of those transported were adult males (50.2%). Eltis et al., *Trans-Atlantic Slave Trade Database,* voyage identification number 81242. In contrast to the *Anna*, it is unlikely that the *Ellen* was purpose-built for the slave trade. The Certificate of British Registry dated 14 December 1790 indicates that the *Ellen* was a "prize captured from the Americans," which had been "legally condemned in the High Court of Admiralty" in July 1782. This "square sterned ship" had three masts, and two decks with a height of four feet between the decks. The ship was "pierced for sixteen guns" and also had a figurehead. In contrast, the *Anna* was a British built "square sterned schooner" with one deck, two masts and no figurehead. Merseyside Maritime Museum Archives, Certificate of British Registry, C/EX/L/4, vol. 8, no. 133, 14 December 1790; Certificate of British Registry, C/EX/L/4, vol. 7, no. 20, 16 April 1789.

110 Letter in private ownership, James Irving junior to his parents in Scotland, 2 January 1791. Transcript in Schwarz, *Slave Captain*, 119-20; Stephen D. Behrendt, "The British Slave Trade, 1785-1807: Volume, Profitability, and Mortality," Ph.D thesis, University of Wisconsin-Madison, 1993, 161-63; Sanderson, "The Liverpool Delegates," 75-76.

111 LRO, DDX 1126/1/16, Draft of a letter from James Irving to J.M. Matra, undated.

112 Schwarz, *Slave Captain*, 35, 78.

113 LRO, DDX 1126/1/14, James Irving at "Telling" in Morocco to Mary Irving in Liverpool, 1 August 1789. Transcript in Schwarz, *Slave Captain*, 98-99.

114 "Narrative of the Shipwreck of the *Ann*," in Schwarz, *Slave Captain*, 144.

115 Ibid., 131, 133-34.

116 This approach is also characteristic of the narrative of Robert Adams. Charles Hansford Adams, *Narrative of Robert Adams*, xv.

117 In an entry for September 1789, Captain Irving's younger cousin urged his readers to "Judge of my situation now, amongst unfeeling moors who would spit in my face, and call me an infidel or unbeliever when I spoke." "A very

short account of what happened to me after the seperation on the 16th of June 1789," in Schwarz, *Slave Captain*, 151.

118 "Narrative of the Shipwreck of the *Ann*," in Schwarz, *Slave Captain*, 134-35.

119 Muslim captives were held in Spain and other European countries, and were sometimes exchanged for Christian captives. Friedman, "Christian Captives," 616-18, 631-32.

120 Vitkus and Matar, *Piracy, Slavery and Redemption,* 4, 16, 37; Colley, *Captives*, 116-17; Lofkrantz, "Scholars, Captives and Slaves," 2; Russell Hopley, "The Ransoming of Prisoners in Medieval North Africa and Andalusia: An Analysis of the Legal Framework," *Medieval Encounters,* 15 (2009), 337-38; Friedman, "Christian Captives," 617-18; Charles Hansford Adams, *Narrative of Robert Adams*, xv, xlviii-xlix.

121 "Narrative of the Shipwreck of the *Ann,*" in Schwarz, *Slave Captain*, 148.

CHAPTER IV

"The Disgrace of Christendom":

Shipwreck and "Ransoming" in Southern Morocco (1780s-1820s)[1]

Mohamed H. Mohamed

In "Protecting Freeborn Muslims," Jennifer Lofkrantz defined ransoming as "the practice of paying for the release of a captive at the time of capture or soon afterwards." She went on to differentiate ransoming from redemption. While "a redeemed slave remains in a subservient status" in the host society, a ransomed captive is likely to regain his original free state.[2] This definition and the concomitant distinction of ransoming from redemption, are also the twin grids of the recent conference on "Perspectives on Historical Ransoming Practices" hosted by the Harriet Tubman Institute at York University (April 25-26, 2014). In this instance too, ransoming was defined as "the demand for payments (in cash or kind) to secure the release of hostages." And in comparison to "redeemed slaves who often remain in a subservient position of the former master's society, the victims of ransoming usually return home." But the steering committee also elected the "ransoming frontier between the worlds of Christianity and Islam" as the overarching contextual frame for conceptualizing ransoming.[3] At face value, there seems to be split between the definitive, and rather materialist, definition of ransoming and its somewhat permissive contextual and conceptual frameworks. The definition may give the reader the impression that ransoming is about 'pure' economics and, as such, lends itself to quantitative analysis—i.e. who ransomed whom, from whom, when, and for what, and for how much. Conversely the invocation of the "ransoming frontier" spawned by pre-modern duels between "Christianity and Islam" suggests the ideological imperative as a complimentary, if not rival, frame of reference. In as much as economic analysis usually dwells on the calculable, ideology veers towards the realm of the intangible. A possible exit strategy is to leave the resolution of the split between the definition of ransoming and its relevant contextual framework to the sources. In any case, student of history could venture only as far as the available evidence would allow. Otherwise s/he risks reading into, rather than out of, his/her sources.

In this chapter I seek to put the above economic conception of ransoming to the test. To this end, I deployed a set of European and American narratives of shipwreck and captivity in Northwest Africa from the early modern period. For context, I will first map out the geopolitical setting for shipwreck and then identify the textual heritage that could gainfully be used to sort out the realistic and rhetorical about discourses on captivity and ransoming. This section is followed by an overview of the main features of this type of travelogue. It is geared to highlight whether and how these captivity narratives live up to the twin benchmarks of "paying for the release of a captive" and the "demand for payments (in cash or kind) to secure the release of hostages." I will conclude with some tentative thoughts pertaining to the credibility of captivity narratives that also mandate their cross-referencing with the type of sources which may accentuate their evidential value.

Geopolitical and Textual Imperatives

The explorer's text ... follows a path prescribed by tradition.
V.Y. Mudimbe[4]

European encounters with the people of what is, today, the Atlantic seaboard of Morocco and Mauritania were the byproduct of the opening of the Atlantic Ocean to navigation back in the late fifteenth and early sixteenth centuries. In fact, we can hardly explain the emergence of Morocco as a separate dynastic realm at the beginning of the sixteenth century without reference to the Moroccan-Portuguese duel along the Atlantic coast of *al-Sus* that spawned the first *Shurafa* dynasty: the *Sa'dians* (1510s-1650s). Recognition of the growing significance of the Atlantic mercantilist system inspired the successors of the Sa'dians, the *Alawites* (1650s-2000s), to open *Casablanca* in 1760 and *Essaouira* (al-Sawīra) (Mogador) in 1765 to cater to trade with western Europe. The Alawites designated Essaouira as the southernmost official Moroccan port of trade.[5] To enhance its commercial status, the Alawite court discouraged the European ships Essaouira had begun to attract from docking anywhere to the south of this port--namely, in the Atlantic shore of al-Sus and "its" (Western) Saharan backyards. European mariners who ventured into, or were shipwrecked at, the south of Essaouira were routinely charged with trespassing and treated accordingly. As further determent, the Alawite court cajoled the dignitaries of *Susian* and Saharan groups such as the *Takna, Awlad Dulaym* and *Awlad Busuba*ʿ to monitor this coastal strip and to arrest the crew of foreign vessel that trespass to the south of Essaouira. Indeed, the Alawite sultan *Mawlay Sulayman* (1792-1822), dismissed one of his most versatile deputies to al-Sus, *Muhammad Yahya Aghnaj* (r.1806-1821), mainly for his inability to find a "remedy" to the Atlantic's propensity to spew "Nazarene" (Christian) ships on Morocco's Saharan backyards. In an ironic twist, what European pamphleteers lamented as shipwreck and captivity was often perceived by Moroccan officials as deliberative trespassing. The term used to refer to such violators of Alawite fiscal/foreign policy is indicative of this apprehension: they were consistently labeled *asra* (war captives).[6] The long history that spawned *Nazarene* and *Moor* as "providential" protagonists, and hence, demarcated the Mediterranean as "a ransoming frontier," seems to have also produced ample room for mistaken intentions. Not surprisingly, European and Moroccan discourses on shipwreck and captivity tend to hark back to the *Moorish* conquest of the Iberian Peninsula and the *Nazarene* Reconquista it had, posthumously, inspired. Discourses on early modern shipwreck, then, can best be understood in the context of the textual tradition inspired by the prolonged pre-modern encounters across the Mediterranean Sea. This is also the encounter that spawned the so-called *Barbary Captivity Narrative*.[7]

The combination of pre-modern links across the Mediterranean and the increasing encounters via the Atlantic ought to have rendered Morocco, as *Barbary*, and Moroccans, as *Moors*, sufficiently familiar to Europe's intellectual vanguard. As late as 1809, however, the British literati and long-time resident of Morocco, James Gray Jackson, could still concur with the complaints of the British Consul-General, James Matra, that "there are more books written on Barbary than on any other country, and yet there is no country with which we are so little acquainted." Jackson blamed the prevalence of European "misconception and misrepresentation" of the *Moors* on linguistic incompetence and "servile" copying from pre-modern authors such as Leo Africanus (w.1526).[8] He could have just as well invoked narratives of shipwreck to adumbrate the notion of recycling. In the same way that it paved the way for encounters with "wandering" or "wild" Saharan Arabs, the opening of the Atlantic also sanctioned their concomitant representation as mere copies of the textual *Moor* conceived in the womb of perennial conflict across the Mediterranean. This, in fact, is one of the most striking features of early modern European accounts of captivity in Northwest Africa.

The shipwreck and captivity narratives of the two French men, Pierre-Raymond de Brisson (1785) and Charles Cochelet (1819), and their American counterparts, Robert Adams (1812) and James Riley (1815), are replete with anecdotes that hark back to the textual *Moor* already incarcerated in the *Barbary Captivity Narrative*.[9] In fact, even Jackson's rather empathetic rendition of early modern encounters between British "seamen" and "wild Arabs" hardly violates the discursive parameters of this literary genre—it exudes a priori knowledge:

> Sometimes, the poor seamen perceiving what savages they have to contend with (though they are far from being savage and inhospitable as their appearance indicates) determine in making resistance, and by means of cannon and small arms, maintain a temporary defense.[10]

Neither the Francophone nor the Anglophone (British and Americans) survivors of shipwreck were overly interested in secular identities. Instead, they tend to conceive their captors as *Moors, Moselimin* or *Monselimene* (Muslims) and, then, locate the site of encounter in the outskirts of a dysfunctional Alawite dynastic realm—what de Brisson called "the deserts of Africa" and Jackson, Adams and Riley depicted as "the western coast of Africa."[11] In that sense, the porous identification of their captors as "wandering Arabs" or "wild Arabs" is the only distinguishing variable in such pliable definitions. At the discursive level, captivity narratives are riveted on a torturous trek across the "deserts of Africa" and encounter with neo-*Moors* of a somewhat different (darker) hue— alas, the "blacke" *Moors* of the *Barbary Captivity Narrative*. Entrapment in "holy cause" facilitated the elevation of Saharan Arabs to allegories of what David Hume called "men wholly different."[12] The narrator usually posits landing in the "barbarous coast of Africa" as the inevitable prelude to his encounter with, or rather abduction by, "wild Arabs." In these accounts, Islam is the common denominator between the "wild Arabs" (the Sahara), the "superstitious Berbbers" (al-Sus) and the "fanatic Moors" (the Mediterranean basin) and, in that capacity, the sinew of their immutable identity. The sanctification of identities often enables the narrators to skew differences in the usable names of their protagonists. One can glean this consensus on the centrality of sanctified difference to the conception of Saharan or Susian identities from the accounts of de Brisson, Cochelet and Riley.

Notwithstanding occasional allusions to the portable or spatial identities of their captors/hosts, narrators of shipwreck routinely trade such contingent signifiers for the familiar profile of the textual *Moor*. In the process, the encounter with "wild Arabs" becomes part of a sequel leading to passage through Wady Nun (Wād Nūn), arrival at Essaouira, and ultimately, repatriation to Europe.[13] The journey from the site of shipwreck to Europe takes the guise of a linear transfer from the den of infidelity and barbarism to the bastion of Christendom and civility. Conversely, being a wild Arab or fanatic *Moor* is a signifier of domicile in cursed terrains and, hence, lack of redeeming qualities. Discursively, the indictment of the *Moor* "wild Arab" with baneful dispositions such as enslavement or the pursuit of ransom had the added advantage of fortifying the shipwrecked *Nazarene's* sense of scriptural superiority. The location of the site of ordeal beyond the reach of Alawite sultans often eases the imagination of ransoming in terms of the transfer of rights in the bodies of "poor Christians" from "wild Arabs" to itinerant "Jew or Moor" traders. Jackson provided a brisk summary of this relay:

> The Arabs… carry the Christian captives about the desert, to different markets to sell them …. They [Christians] at length become objects of commercial speculation, and the itinerant Jew traders, who wonder about Wedinoon [Wady Nun] find means to barter for them *tobacco, salt, a cloth garment, or any other thing...* and then return with the purchase. If the Jew have a correspondent at Mogador [Essaouira], he writes to him … and requests him to inform the agent, or consul of the nation of which the captain is subject, in the meantime flattering the poor men that they will shortly be liberated and sent to Mogador ... along and tedious servitude, however, generally follows, for want of a regular fund at Mogador for the redemption of these people (emphasis added).[14]

It is perhaps worth noting that without reference to sanctification, it will be difficult to decode Jackson's deft invocation of *Semitic* conspiracy to underscore the dual (physical and spiritual) plight of "Christian captives." Yet, the fact remains that the construction of the "wild Arabs" as sacrilegious protagonists became possible mainly because of the recycling of the imagery of the "fanatic" *Moor*. Fittingly, contingent differences between the early modern "wild Arabs" of the Sahara and the "Wedinoon Jew or Moor traders," and the pre-modern *Moors* of the "cities" pale beside the mere fact that they were not Christians. The presentation of the "wild Arabs" as dark and ferocious was sanctioned by the pre-modern introduction of the "swarthy" *Moor* as an indefatigable and sensual corsair. In early modern captivity narratives, Saharans tend to be insidiously ferocious precisely because of their religious affinity to the pre-modern *Moors* Europeans had come to both dread and revile.[15]

Given the primacy they assign to religiosity, the testimonies of survivors of shipwreck are circumscribed by current reservations regarding the traveler's infatuation with, and simultaneous intolerance of, difference. They can best be utilized with two precautions in mind. Firstly, linguistic differences proscribed the narrators' ability to transcend visual observation. In this context, reported speech is a rhetorical device that elevates what was, in essence, a recyclable textual trope to a contingent utterance. At the time of first encounter, for example, de Brisson knew only "a few Arabic words" he picked up during his "preceding voyages to Senegal."[16] In contrast, Riley invoked differential aptitude to infer "affinity between the Arabian and Spanish" to tout his ability to "learn" Arabic while it continued to elude his comrades:

> I had, previously, learned the French and Spanish languages, both by grammar and practice, and had also been accustomed to hear spoken the Russian and different dialects of the German, as well as the Portuguese, Italian, and several other languages; so that my ear had become familiar with their sounds and pronunciation. Perceiving an affinity between the Arabian and Spanish, I soon began to learn the names of common things, in Arabic and to compare them in my mind with those I had met with in Turkish and other Oriental history.... My four companions, however, could scarcely comprehend a single world of Arabic, even after they were redeemed.[17]

Coincidentally, both de Brisson and Riley's accounts teem with reported speech. Linguistic incompetence also seems to have enhanced sensual faculties. Survivors of shipwreck often compensate their linguistic limitations by descriptions of fearful landscapes and, the terrific attire (or lack of it) and physique of their barbarian occupants. On this occasion too, the "wandering Arabs" became knowable courtesy of their approximation of the stylized profiles of the barbarian already incarcerated in pre-modern travelogue.

In fact, these *neo-Barbary* captivity narratives teem with evidence of knowledge before encounter. For instance, de Brisson was haunted by the prospect of "meeting with some hordes of the tribe of the Labdesseba [*Awlad Busuba*ʿ], a ferocious people." These apprehensions were duly fulfilled: "I was," he melancholically noted, "much affected to learn that we had fallen into the hands of the most ferocious people who inhabit the deserts of Africa."[18] Conversely, Jackson blamed the inclination of the British sailor to rush to his "cannons" on a pre-existing "persuasion that he must either perish in fighting a horde of wild Arabs or submit to become their captive." In contrast, Riley had already "been taught to consider" the *Moors* "the worst of barbarians." Yet it was precisely because of his ability to deliver the terrific "half-Indian and half-Negro" *Moor* to his Euro-American audience that Riley also became one of the celebrities of his time:

> We saw a human figure approach our stuff.... It was a Man! ... He appeared to be ... of a complexion between the American Indian and Negro.... His hair was long and bushy ... His face resembled that of an Ourang-outang more than a human being; his eyes were red and fiery, his mouth ... stretched nearly from ear to ear, well lined with sound teeth.... I could not but imagine that those well set teeth were sharpened for the purpose of devouring human flesh![19]

Secondly, one should not take the element of sameness oozing from the profiles of different peoples, from different geo-political settings and at different times, as a confirmation of the perseverance of particular cultural mores or economic norms. Rather, given the facilities of translation and mass-publication that were the hallmark of modernity, it became possible for European travelers to anticipate the fearful spaces and barbarian hordes incarcerated in their texts. For instance, the French version of de Brisson's account was published in 1789. The English translation was released early next year: March 1790. Two years later (1792), the English version of de Brisson's narrative was supplemented by the almost identical account of his (French) compatriot, Francois Saugnier.[20] Likewise, Cochelet's narrative was promptly translated into English. In that sense, the high degree of consensus exhibited by the neo-*Barbary Captivity Narratives* does not necessarily mean that their authors were reporting observable realities. If anything, we are not witnessing the birth of novel ideas about Northwest Africa or its inhabitants. After all, the fanatic, sensual and predatory *Moor* has long become a permanent fixture in pre-modern European discourses on both the space and its occupants.

These reservations could enable the researcher to make narratives of shipwreck and ransoming thinkable. For instance, from captivity narratives one gets the impression that animosity between early modern worshipers of the *same but different* deity on "the western coast of Africa" was pre-ordained by what happened in the basin of the Mediterranean at an earlier time (the pre-modern period). Such reservation may help in the deconstruction of discourses on captivity and ransoming. The question then is not simply whether there is a case to be made for "ransoming" or not. Rather, the discursive posture permeating such captivity narratives begs the pertinent questions of who initiated the "demand for payment" and who stood to benefit the most from it? In the meantime, one could conceptualize early modern discourses on ransoming as malleable formula that, to borrow from Mudimbe, "follows a path prescribed by tradition." De Brisson and Jackson's accounts provided imitable simulations of this formula.

Of "Wild Arabs" and "Poor Christians"

Perfidy and treachery are also two vices inherent in every Arab.
De Brisson[21]

It is, perhaps, because of their entrapment in pre-modern textual conventions that narratives of shipwreck teem with discordant statements when it comes to the question of captivity in foreign lands. One should, of course, expect the *Barbary Captivity Narrative* to cast its shadow over the issue of ransoming too. And it did. Accounts of captivity and ransoming are replete with metaphors of religiosity, and at this plane it is an exercise in futility to try to peel the material content from its rhetorical form. Discursively, both the "deserts of Africa" and its "savage" occupants seem to be designed to inflict maximum pain. For the British translator of de Brisson's narrative, for instance, "the dangers and difficulties the author [de Brisson] encountered were indeed extraordinary, but they are such as might be expected in a country like Africa, and among a people equally brutal and ferocious as the Arabs."[22] Consequently, the "wild Arabs" were, by design, incapable of recognizing calculable self-interest. Wanton cruelty and perpetual starvation come across as the pathologies underpinning their pursuit of "Christian captives." They routinely shrug promises of hefty ransoms if only they were to drive their French captives to St. Louis, Senegal, and their British or American counterparts to Essaouira. Almost simultaneously, however, these same impulsive protagonists "would have" promptly shipped their "Christian captives" all the way to Essaouira if there was the faintest hope that they would get better deals than the trifles the roving "Jew or Moor traders" were in the habit of offering. De Brisson and Jackson set the tone for this discordant polemics, and later narrators of shipwreck and captivity such as Riley kept it alive.

De Brisson's rather prolonged captivity was partly the byproduct of his own conceit and miscalculation. And a priori knowledge was the bedrock of this posture. He, for instance, deployed a combination of the "few Arabic words" he knew and "gestures" to earmark the "master" he thought would most likely respond to an offer of a hefty reward and conduct him to Senegal. In the midst of the "dreadful massacre" of the crew on the site of the shipwreck, he "perceived an unarmed Arab" and, by his attire, he mistook him for "one of those who had accompanied prince Allicory on a visit which he had formerly paid me [de Brisson] at … St. Louis." That was also how and why de Brisson squandered his chance to be promptly repatriated to Essaouira:

> By the help of the few Arabic words ... and my gestures, I made him comprehend that I solicited his assistance to conduct us to the place of our destination [Senegal]. Having added that I had about me wherewith to compensate for his trouble, he seemed to understand this part of my communication much better than the former; for, he directly thrust his fingers through mine, to inform me that we were friends from that moment... I then gave him two beautiful watches ... two pair of silver sleeve buttons; a ring ... a silver goblet; and two hundred and twenty livres... The precaution I had taken, to save these effects in hope of procuring the good will of those into whose hands I might fall proved to me an inexhaustible source of sorrow and uneasiness.[23]

The last statement suggests that de Brisson was, *mentally*, prepared to "fall" into the hands of "the most ferocious people who inhabit the deserts of Africa." One is also left wondering about the utility of what de Birsson himself had valuated as "trinkets" to Arabs like the "Labdesseba" and "Ouadelims" who "live upon nothing but the milk of their camels." In either case, whether the dowry of de Brisson's contorted "communication" with an unarmed Arab could be conceived as ransom or an attempt to procure services is more important than its utilitarian value. Arguably, this display of affluence stirred a rumor amongst the spectators of his performance that de Brisson was "a Christian who must be exceedingly rich." After "surveying" de Brisson, for instance, "a troop of women and children" shrieked "he is a king!" Being "exceedingly rich" or a "king" seems to have been the impression de Brisson wanted to impart to his "wild" audience. He, probably, believed it was also tantamount to expedite his speedy delivery to St. Louis or, at least, to "Prince Allicoury."[24]

De Brisson actually "begged" his hand-picked "master," Sidy Mahammat, not to accept a rival "proposal" made by his "brother-in-law who was also one of the chiefs of the horde," Sidy Sellem. According to de Brisson, "chief" Sidy Sellem wanted to add him to his collection. De Brisson considered this "proposal" objectionable because it "seemed to announce a ridiculous captivity."[25] To further dissuade his "master," Sidy Mahammat, from acceding "chief" Sellem's offer, de Brisson assured him that "he would receive more for my [de Brisson] ransom than his brother-in-law would give him." The irony here is that it was de Brisson who first advertised ransoming as an adequate frame of reference for the relation between the *Nazarene* captive and his *Moorish* captor. According to de Brisson, this "chief of the horde," Sidy Sellem, told him that he would regret "not accepting his offer."[26] And he did! For it was "chief" Sidy Sellem who would eventually, deliver de Brisson to Essaouira and then Marrakesh. In the meantime, de Brisson's chosen "master" kept on evading the tiresome trip to either Senegal or Essaouira. And this was despite de Brisson's repetitive endeavors to tempt him with the prospect of a hefty ransom. In response to a question by a despondent de Brisson "what he was waiting for, in order to conduct me to Senegal" for instance, Sidy Mahammat, invoked the lack of "vigorous camels." On another occasion, the "master" fell back on a trio of "excessive heat," lack of "provisions" and, "above all, water." For good measure, he also pleaded that it would be impossible to "approach Senegal" because the "river has inundated all neighboring plains." Besides, there was the looming threat "from the Arabs of the tribe of Trargea (Trarza)." These evasive tactics confirmed de Brisson new-found suspicion that Sidy Mahammat was nothing but a "fanatical priest" who would stop at nothing "in order to convince me to embrace his religion."[27]

Over time, de Brisson developed conflicting apprehensions about the agenda of his 'sly' master. Despite the lack of any concerted attempt at conversion, de Brisson concluded that the "fanatical priest," simply wanted him to give up and become *Moor.* Simultaneously he could not shake off the impression that his patron/captor "sincerely wished to get rid of" him but simply did not want to embark on an arduous journey, and not to Senegal in particular. This latter conviction became stronger after what might have seemed a surprising response to his incessant complaints. According to de Brisson, his "master" eventually asked "whether at Mogador, which they call Soira, a large ransom would be given for each of us. I told him that he would have no occasion to be dissatisfied." He then informed de Brisson that "a Jew merchant will pass this way, tomorrow," and de Brisson could ask him "for some paper" to write to "those from whom you [de Brisson] expect assistance." The "Jew merchant" did arrive on time. Contrary to Jackson's prediction, he did not "purchase" or even offer to "purchase" de Brisson. Instead he took from him a letter addressed "to the French consul, at Soira, or … whomsoever represented him." In the letter, de Brisson laid out "the surest and best means of sending to us, and the only method he [the consul] could employ to procure our deliverance." To his chagrin, the French consulate did not enact "the only method" he prescribed—the dispatch of an emissary armed with a "ransom."[28] As a result, de Drisson had to languish in "the deserts of Africa" much longer. As if that was not enough, de Brisson also lost one of his comrades to a "furious reptile": a venomous snake. Naturally, de Brisson added this calamity to the long list of objections against his "fanatical priest": if he had only delivered them to Senegal.

By this time, de Brisson had plenty of allies from amongst the "tribe of Labdesseba." According to de Brisson, they took turns to admonish their kinsman for hanging on to "the Christian slaves" and, then, posed the pertinent question of "what pleasure or what profit you [Sidy Mahammat] procured?" The question was particularly pressing because it came on the heels of another emphatic assurance by a visiting "sheriff of Trargea [Trarza]" that "everything at Senegal belongs" to de Brisson! Interestingly, this "sheriff of Trargea" did not try to "purchase" de Brisson. Nor was de Brisson's own "master" overly excited by this seemingly fortuitous assurance. For instance, he did not take advantage of this opening to *mortgage* the prospect of "a large ransom" to the august visitor from the "neighboring plains" of Senegal. Instead, it was the "brother in law" of his "master," and, according to de Brisson, his most consistent detractor, "chief" Sidy Sellem, who, this time, carried the day. Seeing that de Brisson had indeed regretted "not accepting his [earlier] offer" Sidy Sellem prepared another surprise for him. De Brisson "did not know that this bargain was concluded," but he still inferred that "chief" Sidy Sellem had offered "his brother" Sidy Mahammat, "five camels in exchange." And "one day" he, called on de Brisson and instructed him "to prepare to set out with him next mourning for Mogador."[29]

According to de Brisson's own calculation, it took them "fifty-six" days to reach Essaouira. The trip confirmed his former host's apologetic farewell that "you [de Brisson] will soon perceive how great reason I had to be afraid of it [the trip]." It was "long, painful and dangerous."[30] On the same day they reached Essaouira, de Brisson and his shipmate were "presented to the governor of the place." The "governor" ordered them to promptly proceed to Marrakech in order to meet the "emperor" and "hear the orders for their liberty from his mouth." In contrast, the "emperor" could not wait to chastise de Brisson that it was their "fault" that they were shipwrecked "upon his coast." They should have stayed away from "the shore." He, then, asked de Brisson "with whom didst thou come?" De Brisson mentioned "chief" Sidy Sellem and the "emperor" interjected by saying "I know him."[31] Then, the "emperor" interviewed "chief" Sidy Sellem. Once the conversation turned to the "purchase" price for de Brisson and his mate, however, "chief" Sidy Sellem "artfully replied that, he had no other view in exposing himself to the danger of travelling these immense countries than to go and prostrate himself at the feet of his sovereign." Ironically, de Brisson endorsed this lofty discourse. He too had, finally, come to the conclusion that had "chief" Sellem not been "desirous of rendering homage to the emperor … I should never have been restored to my country."[32] At the pedantic level, such subversive revelation suggests that ransoming per se did not loom prominently in the "wandering" Arabs' perception of *Nazarene* trespassing in their own backyards. Yet, one does not have to believe that *pilgrimage* to the "sovereign" was "chief" Sellem's primary quest to ponder the scope of the relation between the Alawite court and the "wild Arabs." It goes without saying that de Brisson did not know, and could not have known, what is it exactly that the "emperor" had offered "chief" Sellem if only to offset the "five camels" he, supposedly, lost to the "fanatical priest" that was de Brisson's "master." This is not to mention the "large camel" "chief" Sellem had procured to transport de Brisson besides the provisions and labor for "fifty-six days."[33]

In fact, de Brisson did not disclose what is it exactly that the French consul at Essaouira had *donated* to "chief" Sellem either. Notwithstanding his frequent invocations of "purchase" and "large ransom," all he had to offer was an opaque statement that Sellem left to his barren homeland "very well satisfied with the generosity of the consul." Yet, this was the same miserly consul, Mure, de Brisson stridently rebuked for "paying his court to the emperor of Morocco and his officers" instead of the more efficacious ransoming recipe that "would have" expedited de Brisson's prompt repatriation:

> This agent might have procured us our liberty by dispatching to Gouadnum [Wady Nun/ Gulimeme] any Arab or a Jew merchant, who for *a hundred piastres … would have* travelled all the desert, and who consequently *would have* been contented with much less, had he made researches only in the neighborhood of Morocco. Had he issued an order for bringing all Christian slaves to Mogador, the Arabs *would have* conducted them there from all parts, *in order to receive the ransom*, which they *would have* gladly employed in purchasing wheat and barley.… But the consul … prolonged our misfortune, *for the Arabs, our masters, were very cautious not to undertake a long, painful, and dangerous journey, without some hope of being rewarded.* Mr. Mure was contented … with writing back to the minister, that he was using every exertion to find us out.… I am proud of having represented him to his employers in a proper light.[34] (Emphasis added)

Sanctimonious fixation on "the ransom" goes a long way to highlight the discursive tenor of the early modern *neo-Barbary captivity narrative*. One could hardly decode the comforting, albeit elusive, "would have" spine of this polemic without reflecting on de Brisson's stance on the function of the state, or the merits of "free enterprise." For almost simultaneously de Brisson had nothing but laudatory commendations for "Messrs. Duprat and Cabannes, merchants at Mogadore." According to de Brisson, the "extensive trade… they carry on in the interior parts of the country gives them great influence." Surprisingly, he did not dwell on the predictable question of why did not the "great influence" of the "merchants at Mogador" expedite his own rescue from "the deserts of Africa"?[35] From this vantage point, it is impossible to reconcile de Brisson's prescription of what either "the Arabs" or an "Arab or a Jew merchant" *would have* done in response to modest offers of "ransom," and his own failure to educate his "fanatical priest" on the merits of shipping him to Senegal. This mismatch between discursive posture and mundane experience is, however, one of the main fixtures of captivity narratives. In Anglophone literature, it was Jackson who first laid out the parameters of this polemic.

One significant difference between Jackson and de Brisson's take on captivity and ransoming is that Jackson was not shipwrecked and, as such, is not recounting a personal experience. But by virtue of his prolonged sojourn in Morocco (1790-1806), proficiency in "African Arabic" and encounter with multiple shipwrecked-British sailors, he is, probably, a more credible witness. In so far as the issue of ransoming is concerned, however, de Brisson and Jackson's discourses were strikingly similar. According to Jackson, for instance, about thirty ships were shipwrecked at Morocco's Saharan backyards in the period from 1790 to 1806. Of these thirty ships, seventeen were flying the British flag, five were French and five were American. Jackson computed the number of crew on board the British ships as about two hundred sailors. Of these two hundred mariners, "forty young men and boys" were, ostensibly, either killed during the initial scuffle with "wild Arabs" or were "induced to embrace the Mohammedan religion" and, as such, presumed socially dead. Another "forty" were mostly "old men" who were, probably, "killed" by the same "wild Arabs." And yet another "forty" were "dispersed in the desert" due to the inability of the British consul to make "offers sufficiently advantageous to induce the Arabs to bring them to Mogador." Conversely, only eighty were "redeemed after a tedious existence among the Arabs." Once more, it was exceptionally long before these "poor Christians" were repatriated mainly because of the "want of remitting money for their purchases."[36] In that sense, Jackson tended to endorse de Brisson's advocacy of ransoming as the most efficient mode of extricating shipwrecked sailors from their "Arab" captors. Unlike de Brisson, Jackson provided his "wild Arabs" with an alibi of sorts. The improvident "wild Arabs" desperately want to get rid of their overfed "Christian captives" because it did not take them long to discover that they were "unserviceable":

> The Arabs going nearly in state of nature, wearing nothing but a cloth or rag to cover their nakedness, immediately strip their unhappy victims, and march them up the country bare-footed, like themselves.... The Europeans suffer the pains of fatigue and hunger in a most dreadful degree, for the Arab will go 50 miles a day, without tasting food, and at night will content himself with a little barley meal mixed with cold water: miserable fare for an English seaman, who ... eats meat every day....They carry the Christian captives about

> the desert, to the different markets to sell them, for they very soon discover that their habits of life render them altogether unserviceable.[37]

According to Jackson, it was at this juncture that the "wild Arabs" also dump their "Christian slaves" on the first "Wedinoon Jew or Moor trader" willing to give up trifles like "tobacco, salt, a cloth garment, or any other thing." There was nothing the British vice-consuls at Essaouira could have done besides writing to "the consul-general at Tangier."

In comparison to de Brisson, Jackson concocted an alibi for the British vice-consuls at Essaouira, who were, first and foremost, fellow traders. According to Jackson, British traders at Essaouira could not afford "a sum rather above the price of a black slave" because they had "various other uses for their money." In any case, a loan at "the European interest of five percent" was simply not tempting enough. In Essaouira, money was often lent at "six percent per month."[38] Like de Brisson Jackson went on to advocate the *free-market* stratagem he believed was more conducive to the repatriation of "unfortunate" British sailors:

> If the interest of the munificent bequest of Mr. Thomas Betton … had been appropriated, agreeable to his will, to the alleviation of the dreadful sufferings; to shortening the duration of captivity; small sum would be sufficient at Mogador … if deposited in the hands of the Vice-Consul, or any merchant of respectability, where it might remain ready to be employed in the purchase of these unfortunate people, and by allowing a sum rather above the price of a black slave, *the Arabs would immediately bring them to Mogodor, … by this means they might be procured for half what they now cost;* and it would be an *infinitely better plan than that of soliciting the Emperor to procure them through the Bashaw of Suse; for, besides the delay, and consequent protracted sufferings of the captives, the favour is undoubtedly considered by the Emperor as incalculably more than the cost and charges of their purchase....* It is generally a month or two before the news of a shipwreck reaches Mogador, at which time, if a fund were there deposited, in the hands of a competent agent, *a hundred and fifty* [Spanish] *dollars would be sufficient to purchase each man.*[39] (Emphasis added)

In as much as it rests on the "would have" discursive posture, this recipe is identical to the one de Brisson has already invoked. Like de Brisson, Jackson did not disclose the "purchase" price for an actual, rather than hypothetical, captive. The deft assurance oozing from "half of what they [sailors] now cost" tends to impart the same discursive effect as de Brisson's invocation of "a hundred piasters" or "much less" as a bench-mark for what "would have" motivated "any Arab or a Jew merchant … to travel all the desert." After all, Jackson did not proffer any specific case where a "wild Arab" had "immediately" delivered "unfortunate people" to Essaouira in response to the publication of an "adequate price" or "a hundred and fifty dollars" for that matter. The closest he came to such disclosure was his recounting of a case he had personally handled. One British trader, James Renshaw of Essaouira, "advanced the money" for an anonymous captive who, "had his ransom not been paid to the Arab," he *would have* been "sold or compelled to embrace the Mohammedan religion." The British vice-consul at Essaouira, Joseph Dupuis, simply did not have "the purchase money" at hand. Jackson, however, had a very hard time recouping Renshaw's loan. Yet, the total sum repaid, "including the cost of clothing" and, one may add, "the European interest" rate of 5% for "two years ... did not amount altogether to forty pounds"! One is left wondering how much trader Renshaw had actually paid out to the nameless "Arab" who delivered this captive to the British consulate in Essaouira? Interestingly, adumbration of Renshaw's sacrificial deed contrasts sharply with the complete silence on the expenditure and labor of the "Arab" protagonist. According to Jackson, such delays tend to discourage British merchants "however philanthropically disposed" they were, of sinking their capital in the business of ransoming.[40]

Jackson's proposition fell on sympathetic ears in London. The *Iron Mongers' Company* of London not only assumed full responsibility for trader Renshaw's debt but also forwarded one thousand pounds to the British consulate in Essaouira. The company also proposed the establishment of direct contact with the Arab "Sheiks" in Wady Nun and the Sahara to convey the *good news* that "would have" expedited the prompt delivery of shipwrecked British mariners. This proposition was, however, promptly vetoed by both the British consul-generals in Tangier (Douglas and Green) and their deputies in Essaouira (Gwyn and Dupuis). In the opinion of the Consul-General "the Emperor [of Morocco] not only makes a point of delivering to the British consul any subjects of that nation who may be shipwrecked upon the coast of his empire, but also of extending his influence to redeem individuals who may experience a similar misfortune to the southward of his Dominions."[41] As a practice, then, ransoming was mired in the hitherto mystified links between the Alawite court (center) and the "wild Arabs" (margin). Besides, there was the web of trade-offs with various European states.[42]

Whether Jackson was aware of it or not, British consuls in Morocco were actually adhering to, and one may add, 'milking' article 35 of the Anglo-Moroccan treaty of 1791, which was, in essence, an updated version of article 6 of the treaty of 1760. According to this article, the Alawites were expected to "restore" any British subjects "forced on shore, or wrecked on any part of the Emperor's dominion." Indeed, the sultan was obligated to use his "utmost power and influence" to "restore" British subjects "wrecked at Oed Nun [Wady Nun], or on the coast to the southward among the Arabs." Moreover, the British consul-general was entitled "to use his best endeavors to procure the men" who might be shipwrecked amongst the "Arabs" to the "southward" of Wady Nun. But on such occasion too, he could count on the "assistance" of the "Emperor's subjects."[43] It goes without saying that "the Arabs" enshrined in this treaty were the same "wild" or "wondering" Arabs of the *neo-Barbary captivity narrative*. Ironically, Jackson himself cited an instance where "the Emperor has … ordered his Bashaw of Haha to purchase the British slaves that had been wrecked there (Wady Nun)."[44] One could assume that there were similar tradeoffs between Morocco and other European countries. If there were, indeed, considerable funds specifically earmarked for ransoming, they might have been used to cover the hospitality expenses and "European interest" charged by the "philanthropically disposed" trader-consuls advocating it. Without falling back on the 'irrationality' of *the native* cliche, it would also be impossible to explain the inclination of "wild Arabs" to forgo hefty cash rewards and, instead, settle for the trifles offered by nameless "Jew or Moor" traders. One reasonable exit strategy is to suspect some form of collusion between politicians and traders. Like their European counterparts, the dignitaries of the "wild Arabs" and the roving "Jew or Moor" traders were enthralled to the Alawite state and/or its deputies in al-Sus. In short, the "wild" Arab freelancer is a creature of metropolitan delusions and textual lore.

Taken together with what we know about the Alawites' endeavor to secure the caravan trade routes and to shore up the commercial status of their new port at Essaouira, these subaltern arrangements tend to explain the, seemingly, inexplicable riddles and silences in narratives of shipwreck. At the pedantic level, for instance, it helps the student of history to dispose of the inevitable question of why "poor Christians" who were, ostensibly, stranded beyond the jurisdiction of the Alawite sultans consistently show up at Essaouira and were regularly paraded before its seemingly non-involved "governor" and, occasionally, before the "emperor" in Marrakech. Alternatively, one can understand why de Brisson did not go to Senegal, and was, eventually, turned over to the "brother-in-law" of his "master" whom the "emperor" just happened to "know." And why he was silent on whether either the "emperor" or the French consul in Essaouira, Mure, had actually paid off "the ransom" to his Saharan escort. In contrast, Jackson came close to understanding the intricacies of this *politicized* mode of repatriation. He, for instance, first disparaged the act of "soliciting the emperor to procure them [captives] through the Bashaw of Suse." In his mind, this was particularly objectionable since, "besides the delay and consequent protracted sufferings of the captives," the value of the favor the sultans bestowed on British officials was "incalculably more than the cost and charges of their purchase." Almost simultaneously, Jackson advocated the merits of "an alliance with the present Emperor," Mawlay Sulyman, who consistently "gives them [captives] up to the British Consul without exacting such kind of remunerations."[45] Jackson, of course, was not privy to the treaties of 1760 and 1791. Otherwise, he would not have proffered what was already an established practice. At about the same time his account was published, the British consuls were commending the sultan and his "Bashaw of Suse" for defraying the full "purchase" price of the surviving crew of the British ship, the *Montezuma*. Yet, in the name of gifts to the sultan the consul-traders still dipped into the trust fund the Iron Mongers' Company had left in their care. The Alawite court promptly retaliated by allowing Britain to export an extra two thousand oxen to Gibraltar at the same discounted customs rate.[46] By virtue of his profession as trader, Jackson probably knew that favors to the sultan or "Bashaw of Suse" also had the nasty habit of begetting favors to Britain and its merchant-consuls.

I have already noted that de Brisson and Jackson's accounts tend to anticipate Cochelet, Adams and Riley's presentations of their mode of encounter with "wild Arabs" and prolonged captivity in the "western coast of Africa." On this occasion too, captivity is conceived in terms of prolonged "suffering," and eventual ransoming and delivery of "Christian slaves" to Essaouira. There are hefty doses of thrilling, albeit stylized, description of perpetual starvation and torturous treks across the scorching "desert of Africa." From this vantage point, one could gainfully take de Brisson and Jackson's accounts as the immediate textual role models for the narratives of Cochelet, Adams and Riley. Like de Brisson, for instance, Cochelet too had been to Senegal and, as such, also thought he had a working knowledge of "African" Arabic. In fact, he too was shipwrecked while on his way to (St. Louis) Senegal and had the inkling that he had fallen into the hands of the same "most ferocious" Arab wanderlusts.[47] Cochelet and four French comrades were 'traded' off to anonymous *Monselimene* affiliates of *Shaykh* Bayruk (r.1825-1858) of Wady Nun who, then, forwarded them to Essaouira. Cochelet and his comrades too were presented to the "governor" of Essaouira and, subsequently, paraded in front of the "emperor." Cochelet's presentation of *Shaykh* Bayruk is also indicative of knowledge before encounter. In any case, both *Shaykh* Bayruk and his father, *Shaykh* Ubaydallah Ibn Salim, were well-known to successive French and British consul-traders stationed in Essaouira-- their names had become perennial fixtures in consular reports.[48]

In so far as the issue of ransoming is concerned, Cochelet's account is also bereft of specific evidence that could be used to ascertain its monetary value. Without naming his participant observer, Maurice Barbier put the "ransom" the French consul-traders had, ostensibly, paid out in exchange for Cochelet's "party of five" at 12500 francs per sailor.[49] Yet, according to Cochelet himself, stalling in the negotiations preceding their shipment to Essaouira led a frustrated *Shaykh* Bayruk to call them a "useless burden." Like de Brisson, he too wanted to be repatriated to Senegal but his offers of a hefty reward failed to impress his Saharan captors and he had to settle for Essaouira. At Gulimeme, Cochelet, thought *Shaykh* Bayruk was trying to groom him as a trading partner and, to that end, assaulted him with a daring "harangue":

> Do you think your captains of vessels, instead of repairing to the ports of the sultan, at Soueirah {Essaouira] for instance, would consent to steer their course towards that part of the coast where you were shipwrecked? ... By it, the merchandise brought from your country, and those, which the desert produces, would no longer ... be subjected to duties, which double the value of them.[50]

If *Shaykh* Bayruk was mesmerized by the prospect of an alternative port to Essaouira, it is not difficult to imagine why Alawite officials were reluctant to treat shipwreck as an accident rather than evidence of a concerted *Nazarene* endeavor to evade "duties" at Essaouira. After all, the French consul, Jacques Denis Delaporte, not only dreamed of, but actually explored the prospects of, such alternative port with *Shaykh* Bayruk.[51] The statement also mystifies the idea that *Shaykh* Bayruk was merely holding out for the "ransom." It does not mesh with his reported attempt to goad his (French) 'captives' to venture to where their current ordeal had unfolded. The narratives of Cochelet's American counterparts, Adams and Riley also team with similar signs of textual entrapment. One could say that Adams and Riley merely *Americanized* European modes of reporting on "the deserts of Africa" and their "wild Arabs."

Like Cochelet, Adams and Riley seem to have benefited from the robust literary tradition underpinning de Brisson and Jackson's accounts. In fact, there are no substantive differences in their conception of the mode of captivity and eventual ransoming of "Christian slaves." Adams and Riley's accounts also range from the belief that ransom *had* to be the primary query of their improvident "Arab" captors to the deft refusal to disclose its exact value or, alternatively, to conceive it in terms of trifles like blankets. The same textual tradition seems to have enabled Adams and his redeemer, the British trader and vice-consul at Essaouira, Joseph Dupuis, to turn the carcasses of European ships into saviors in an otherwise cursed terrain.[52] For example, Adams' "Musslimin" *Moors* were "quite black" and "extremely indigent" that one would not expect them to turn down any prospect of ransom. On this occasion too, the "wild Arabs" routinely refuse to undertake the trip to where the ransom could be collected. After a prolonged period of "suffering" in the Sahara, Adams was left with no option but to flee from captors who, in any case, refused to pursue him! In the course of this "fake" flight, he reportedly, stumbled on "Musslimin" affiliates of "Governor ... Amedallah Salem" [Ubaydallah Ibn Salim] who subsequently delivered him to the commercial hub of Wady Nun: Gulimeme. According to Adams, he encountered a number of the British sailors the sons of "the Governor ... Boadick [Bayruk] and Brahim" had reduced to "property." Adams himself was, ostensibly, "offered ... for sale to the Governor, ... Amedallah Salem, who consented to take him upon trial but after ... about a week ... was returned to his old master, as the parties could not agree about the price."[53] Ironically, Adams did not disclose "the price" his anonymous "masters" considered too low and "Governor ... Amedallah Salem" considered too high. Nor does his narrative disclose how much *Shaykh* Ubaydallah had charged Dupuis for Adams and whether it was a "ransom" or a refund for expenditure and services.

From the narrative, Ubaydallah seems to have fallen for Adams' claim that he was British and, consequently, forwarded him to Essaouira where he was paraded in front of its "governor" and then turned over to Dupuis. Dupuis dressed up Adams as British and, possibly, in order to persuade the *Iron Mongers' Company* to accept his bills, he pressed Adams to map-out his narrative and, indeed, encouraged him to embellish the original account of his ordeal. If there was a ransom, its monetary value is one more riddle that could be resolved only by recourse to the *Iron Monger's* registers. In the revised chain of events he submitted to "the African Committee" in London, however, Adams seems to have gone too far! According to Adams, for instance, his own refusal to go to work enraged his "masters" in Gulimeme who would have "entirely killed him had it not been for the interference of Boadick [Bayruk], the Shieck's son."[54] Conversely, Boadick's brother, "Brahim," turned refusal to "work" into the capital crime that also justified his execution of the British sailor Dolbie. Adams used Dolbie's death in Gulimeme to regale his British interviewers with irksome, albeit familiar, anecdotes about *Moorish* cruelty:

> His master (named Brahim, a son of the Shieck), ordered him to get up and go to work, and upon Dolbie declaring that he was unable, Brahim beat him with a stick ... But as he still did not obey, Brahim threatened that he would kill

> him, and upon Dolbie replying that he had better do so.... Brahim stabbed him in the side with a dagger and he died in a few minutes.

In a moment of fitful rage, then, the *Moor* "Brahim" had squandered his father's chance at a hefty ransom. Yet, it was probably because of such glaring structural contradictions that Adams' story also began to fall apart. Upon further inquiry, "the African Committee" also discovered that Adams was not British but rather an American with a dubious record. Dupuis was reprimanded for this oversight. In response to an inquiry into the second anecdote, Dupuis informed "the African Committee" that the story negates what Adams himself, as well as other British sailors, had told him about the actual cause of Dolbie's death: "a fever or a cold" contracted "during heavy rain."[55] Notwithstanding the embellishment Adams has added at the behest of Dupuis, his narrative still did not make it to the 'best-seller' list. This was hardly the case for the next shipwrecked American who, ostensibly, also passed through Wady Nun but without encountering either *Shaykh* Ubaydallah or his sons, "Brahim" and Bayruk: James Riley.

Riley's account is strikingly similar to that of de Brisson in the sense that they both exude knowledge before encounter. By his own admission, Riley tried, albeit unsuccessfully, to elude falling into the hands of a people he had already been educated to consider "the worst of Barbarians." He was hardly clear on the temporal identity of the "worst barbarians" he first encountered. Yet, he was sure that his captors were "*ElMusselmine*" and went on to chart a mesmerizing *road-map* of his treks in the Sahara that included encounter with the "Labdessebah" [Awlad Busubaʿ] and passage "across Wadelims" [Awlad Dulaym].[56] Like de Brisson, his captors were so indigent that they fought over the sailors and their effects. From his description of the indigence of his captors, it is difficult to imagine how they could have possibly turned down any prospect of "ransom." Ironically, that was exactly the unexpected outcome of his first feeler. The signs of affluence exuding from his appearance led his captors to anticipate what Riley, probably, wanted them to believe: that he was, indeed, the "*rais*" (captain) and, as such, worth his weight in ransom. In mimicry of de Brisson, it was Riley who first suggested ransoming as starting point for verbal communication between the shipwrecked "Englesis" and "wondering Arabs." The proposal itself came on the heels of an attempt by Riley's captors to verify his identity and is laced with the looming shadow of the Alawite dynastic realm:

> They wanted to know what country we belonged to; I told we were ... Englesis [English] ... they next desired to know if I knew anything about Marocksh [Marrakech]; this sounded something like Morocco: I answered yes; next of

> the sooltaan [sultan].... They wanted me to tell his name, soo Mook, but I could not understand them until they mentioned Moolay Solimaan; this I remembered to be the name of the present emperor of Morocco, as pronounced in Spanish.... I tried to intimate to them, that if they would carry me there, I should be able to pay them for my ransom.... They shook their heads-- it was a great distance, and nothing for the camels to eat or drink on the way.[57]

Riley's presentation does not support Jackson's proposition that the "wild Arabs" tend to ferry their "Christian captives" to different markets, much less transform them into "objects of commercial speculation." Instead we are led to believe that Riley's first master, "Hamet," traded him off to one of his relations, "Bickri." Hamet, subsequently came back and "after talking" to Bickri, he "took off the blanket from his back and gave it to Bickri," and retrieved Riley. Riley was, ostensibly, sold for the second time to "a tall old man, nearly as black as a negro, one of the most ill-looking and disgusting [he] had yet seen." Shortly after, he was once again returned to his first master, Hamet. Riley did not disclose the terms of the last two "transactions".[58]

If Riley's reported circulation amongst his hosts qualifies as ransoming, it still falls short of the "commercial speculation" Jackson had conjured up. It also goes a long way to dispel the idea that the "wild Arabs" were in the habit of pursuing "Christian captives" for "pure" economic reasons. From the narrative, one could not help but conclude that *investment* in "poor Christians" was not worth the "wild" Arabs' effort either. Riley and his mates were neither shopped around in local markets, nor advertised to "itinerant Jew traders." According to Riley, he found his way to Essaouira courtesy of a chance encounter with a roving "Arab" trader from Wady Nun also called Sidy Hamet. In comparison to de Brisson, Riley did not get the news of the impending arrival of trader Hamet from his male master, Hamet. Rather, it was "the old woman" who tipped him off. Ironically, Riley classified trader Hamet as a member of "a tribe surnamed by the Moors, sons of lions, on account of their unconquerable spirit."[59] Yet, "sons of lions" is a cryptic translation of the name of the same "most ferocious" Arabians both de Brisson and Riley had identified as *Labdessebahs* [Awlad Busubaʿ]. In this instance too, it was Riley, rather than his "master," Hamet or trader Hamet, who initiated the bargain on ransoming.

By dolling "a large offer of money," Riley hoped to persuade trader Hamet to both "buy" and "carry" them "up from the desert." In a manner reminiscent of Jackson's representation of the dispositions of British traders at Essaouira, trader Hamet also seemed to prefer "other uses" for his meager funds. He was hardly as eager for the "ransom" as Riley might have expected. Riley had to entice, implore, cajole, pray and patiently wait for a positive response. He was ecstatic when he, finally, *saw* trader Hamet surrender "two blankets or course haicks, one blue cotton covering and a bundle of ostrich feathers" to his "master" Hamet.[60] This cumbersome revelation does not encourage any attempt to posit such bedding essentials as an adequate ransom for valued captives. Nor does it help one to deduce a coherent economic explanation for the tendency of either the "wild" Saharans or the roving Arab and Jew traders from Wady Nun to consistently export "Christian captives" to Essaouira. For in addition to the "two blankets or course haicks" and "one blue cloth," trader Hamit-- like de Brisson's chaperon before him-- had to procure provisions and transport camels for the exacting trip to Essaouira. Riley, perhaps inadvertently, provided his two Hamets (master and trader) with an alibi of sorts. While they did not qualify for his gratitude, the "barbarous" (captor) and "thieving" (trader) Arabs still figured as part of "the ways of providence" that plotted the end of his ordeal. In the end, it was the "merciful God," rather than the lure of ransom, that "disposed the hearts of the barbarous Arabs in our favour." Likewise, it was the same "merciful God," rather than the "large offer of money" that prevailed upon a "thieving Arab" such as trader Hamet to shelve his quest for "ostrich feathers (which was his whole business there)" and instead, toil for more than fifty days to ferry Riley to the safety of Essaouira.[61] Fittingly, in his letter to the British trader and acting-vice-consul, William Wilshire, Riley asked only for "an interpreter and a guard." He did not disclose the "large offer of money" he made to trader Hamet. Nor did Riley conjure a possible role for the "Sooltaan" (sultan) his inquisitive captors "wanted" him to "tell his name."[62] Yet, he too was promptly paraded before the "governor" of Essaouira. Like de Brisson, Cochelet and Adams, Riley did not dwell on who exactly paid off his "thieving" escort, trader Hamet, or how much was the total "purchase" price.

Conclusion

The forgoing discussion mandates two tentative conclusions pertaining to the conceptual and evidential merits of early modern European narratives of shipwreck and captivity in Northwest Africa. At face value, none of these conclusions tends to live up to the precision implied by the twin definitions of ransoming cited in the preamble to this chapter: that is, "paying for the release of a captive at the time of capture or soon afterwards" and/or "the demand for payments (in cash or kind) to secure the release of hostages." But they do justify the proposition of the duel between the "worlds of Christianity and Islam" as the proper contextual backdrop for the study of discourses on captivity during the early modern period. Firstly, in all five narratives, presentations of the mode of encounter between "wild Arabs" and "poor Christians" are laden with metaphors that hark back to the pre-modern *Barbary Captivity Narrative*. One could, indeed, argue that what we are dealing with are demonstrations of how pre-modern textual norms continued to orient authorial discourses on European captivity in Northwest Africa during the early modern period. The element of sameness oozing from these accounts could then be taken as evidence of entrapment in textual traditions rather than a signifier of contingent and verifiable "ransoming practices." At the discursive level, differences in the conditions of social existence invariably fail to induce the early modern "wild Arabs" to do things differently from the pre-modern "fanatical" *Moors* trapped in the Mediterranean "ransoming frontier." It is perhaps, because of their entrapment in pre-modern textual traditions that early modern captivity narratives also tend to join the ranks of what Mudimbe has called the "visible and recent reasons" that validate the literary heritage that spawned them.[63] Ultimately, it is textuality that enabled these authors to overcome linguistic barriers and, thereby, decorate their testimonies with the kind of reported speech that also enliven their narratives. This, of course, was also the main marker of their success.

Secondly, entrapment in textual traditions may also explain the deft refusal of captivity narratives to yield the mundane information that render discourses on ransoming amenable to statistical tabulation. For example, all five accounts are replete with signifiers of quantifiable economic gain like "ransom," "reward," "purchase money," "price," "offer of money," "sell" and "buy." Yet, the narrators either refuse to specify the exact monetary value of the ostensible transaction or conceive it in porous terms like "generosity" or exotic trinkets such as "beautiful watches," or mundane consumables like "tobacco," "salt" and "blankets or course *haicks*." In fact, even in such instances of disclosure, what the reader usually gets are, at best, speculations of what the itinerant "Jew or Moor" trader from Wady Nun, rather than the absentee European redeemer, had surrendered to "wild Arabs." Indeed, neither the "Christian captives" nor European agents (traders/consuls) in Morocco were directly involved in the negotiations/bargaining between "wild Arabs" and roving traders leading to repatriation to Essaouira. It goes without saying that they were not in a position to pay up either "at the time of capture or soon afterwards," if ever. This silence is further compounded by the inexplicable, but unanimous, refusal to assign any value to the foreseen expenditure or manual labor of either the itinerant Wady Nun trader or the "wild Arabs." They come across as mere barbarian scavengers. Assuming that the "wild Arab" was, if we believe Jackson, pathologically designed to "go fifty miles a day" on a diet of "barely meal mixed with cold water," he was still in the *bad* habit of assigning value to his labor and time. Yet, at the end of a torturous trek across "the deserts of Africa" for almost two months, the "poor Christians" regain their liberty, while their "thieving" escorts seem to be content with the experience. To bypass this deft silence on how the "wild Arabs" and roving "Jew or Moor" traders might have recouped their losses, one needs to examine the scope and term of their relations with the Alawite court and its deputies. In fact, one does not have to venture beyond the precautionary measures the Alawites had taken to secure Essaouira and its life-line, the caravan trade routes, to speculate why both dignitaries of "wild Arabs" and roving "Jew and Moor" traders opted to dump their cargo of "poor Christians" either at Wady Nun or Essaouira rather than (French) Senegal. In most cases, the trip to the latter was both shorter and less risky. It would be naive to attribute the rather high success rate of such strategies on the Alawites' ability to manipulate the "philanthropic" or "fanatic" dispositions of their adjutants. Almost simultaneously, the European merchant-consuls at Essaouira assiduously tally their expenses (lodging, food, cloth …) with the "European interest" in mind and file the total as ransom. And yet, in captivity narratives, they usually come across as paragons of "Christian" empathy and/or national pride. A circumvention of such anachronistic mismatch entails the tracing of ransoming from the European end and following the money trail back to Morocco, and more specifically, to the doorsteps of the consul/traders stationed at Essaouira.[64] This way, one may get a better grip on who paid what, how much, to whom and where or when. After all, ransoming was one of the tried *industries of fear* of its time. It too tended to feed off the advocacy of eminent danger and the dire need for mutual trust and cooperative behavior. In this capacity, it was deployed to generate significant resources and, simultaneously, to justify their abuse. Fittingly, some of its main beneficiaries were also amongst its most vociferate 'non-governmental' advocates.[65] A cross-referencing of the records of the Alawite court and European consulates with the registers of financiers such as the *Iron Mongers Company* may rectify the mismatch between the trifles reportedly ceded to "wild Arabs" and the exorbitant funds ostensibly earmarked for the ransoming of "poor Christian."

Endnotes

1 "[T]he tardiness and supineness of diplomacy," James Jackson wrote, "effaces all hope, and after producing dispondency, they [shipwrecked Europeans] are at length … induced to abjure Christianity and accordingly become Mooselmin [Muslims], after which their fate is sealed and they terminate their miserable existence … in the Desert, to the disgrace of Christendom." See James G. Jackson,

An Account of the Empire of Morocco and the Districts of Suse and Tafilelt 3rd ed. (London: Frank Cass, 1968 [1814]), 273.

2 Jennifer Lofkrantz, "Protecting Freeborn Muslims: The Sokoto Caliphate's Attempts to Prevent Illegal Enslavement and its Acceptance of the Strategy of Ransoming," *Slavery & Abolition*, 32:1 (2011), 109-10.

3 Paul Lovejoy, Jennifer Lofkrantz, Olatunji Ojo and Jeff Gunn, "Perspectives on Historical and Contemporary Ransoming Practices," Harriet Tubman Institute, York University, Canada (April 25-26, 2014). There was a lively exchange among conferees on the difference between ransoming and redemption.

4 V. Y. Mudimbe, *The Invention of Africa: Gnosis, Philosophy and the Order of Knowledge* (Bloomington: Indiana University Press), 13.

5 The Alawite drive to turn Essaouira into a sole outlet for southern Morocco led to the simultaneous closure of Agadir and the transfer of its inhabitants to Essaouira. Essaouira's prosperity was, however, contingent on the Alawite ability to secure the caravan network of communication linking *al-Sus* (southern Morocco) to the Niger-Senegal basins. See Daniel J. Schroeter, *Merchants of Essaouira : Urban Society and Imperialism in Southern Morocco, 1844-1866* (Cambridge: Cambridge University Press, 1988), 85-108, 117-32; Mohamed H. Mohamed, *Between Caravan and Sultan: The Bayruk of Southern Morocco* (Leiden: Brill, 2012), 213-14, 256-277; Mohammed Ennaji and Paul Pascon, *Le makhzen et le Souss al-Aqsa, la correspondence politique de la maison d'Illigh, 1821-1894* (Paris-Casablanca: C.N.R.S et Toubkal, 1988), 12-17, 19-23.

6 See, Mohamed, *Between Caravan and Sultan,* 297-301. In narratives of shipwreck, the "emperor" routinely goes out of his way to meet and lecture European mariners on how they could/should have avoided shipwreck on "his coast." According to the British slave trader, James Irving for instance, the sultan "sent for a chart of the Atlantic Ocean and pointed out the courses I ought to have steered, in order to have avoided shipwreck. This is a lesson he gives to everyone, who has the misfortune to come before him in this light." For Irving's narrative, see Suzanne Schwarz, ed., *Slave Captain: the Career of James Irving in the Liverpool Slave Trade* (Liverpool: Liverpool University Press, 2008).

7 On the *Barbary Captivity Narrative*, see Paul Baepler (ed.), *White Slaves, African Master: An Anthology of American Barbary Captivity Narratives* (Chicago: University of Chicago Press, 1999); Nabil Matar, *Turks, Moors and Englishmen in the Age of Discovery* (New York: Columbia University Press, 1999); Daniel J. Vitkus, ed. *Piracy, Slavery and Redemption: Barbary Captivity Narratives from Early Modern England* (New York: Columbia University Press, 2001); Nabil Matar, *British Captives from the Mediterranean to the Atlantic, 1563-1760* (Leiden-Boston: Brill, 2014)

8 Jackson, *An Account*, v-vii; Jackson spent sixteen years in Morocco (1790-1806); Leo Africanus is the "Latin" name of the Moroccan author of the much translated text *Description de l'Afrique*: al-Hasan Ibn Muhammad al-Wazan (1488-1550). In 1520 al-Wazan, was taken captive by Italian corsairs who sent him as a gift, slave, to Pope Leo X. He was baptized as Giovanni Leone but

came to be known simply as Leo Africanus (Leo the African). For an early English translation of this text, see Leo Africanus, *The History and Description of Africa*, trans. John Pory (London: Hakluyt Society, 1896). For an Arabic edition, see Mohamed Hajji and Mohamed al-Akhdar (ed., trans.), *Wasf afriqiya li al-Hasan Ibn Muhammad al-Wazan al-ma'ruf bi Jan Leon al-Afriqi*, 3 vols. (Rabat: al-sharika al-maghribya li-dur al-nashr, 1980).

9 De Brisson, Pierre-Raymond, *An Account of the Shipwreck and Captivity of Mr. de Brisson with a Description of the Desert of Africa, from Senegal to Morocco and his own Observation, While Harassed from Place to Place by the Wondering Arabs* (London: Robert Barker, 1790); Charles Cochelet, *Narrative of the Shipwreck of the Sophia* (London: Richard Philip, 1822); Robert Adams, *The Narrative of Robert Adams, An American Sailor Who was wrecked on the Western Coast of Africa in the year 1810* (London: John Murray, 1816); James Riley, *An Authentic Narrative of the Loss of the American Brig Commerce* (London: Richard Philip, 1822). In the U.S.A, Riley's narrative was published under the tantalizing title of *Suffering in Africa: Captain Riley's Narrative*, Gordon Evans, ed. (New York: Clarkson N. Potters Publishers, 1965).

10 Jackson, *Account*, 270.

11 According to Riley, for instance, his (Muslim) captors also "wanted to know … if we had seen any of the natives whom they called Moselimin (Muslims)." See Riley, *Suffering*, 65.

12 "Should a traveler returning from a far country," Hume wrote, "bring us an account of men wholly different from any whom we were ever acquainted … we should immediately … detect the falsehood and proven him a liar." Ralph Cohen (ed.), *The Essential Works of David Hume,* (New York: Bantam Books, 1965), 105.

13 De Brisson, *Account*, 12-50; Cochelet, *Narrative*, 6-78; Adams, *Narrative*, 53-72; Riley, *Authentic Narrative,* 34-348. By virtue of their prolonged presence in Senegal and familiarity with some Saharans, French authors are more likely to credit their captors with "tribal" identities.

14 Jackson, *An Account*, 272.

15 For an example of the parallelism between conceptions of the pre-modern *Moor* and the early modern "wild" or "wandering" Arabs, see Mohamed, Mohamed, "Africanists and Africans of the Maghrib II: Casualties of secularity," *Journal of North African Studies*, 17:3 (2012), 409-431; Francis Brooks, *Barbarian Cruelty* (London: Salisbury and Newman, 1693).

16 De Brisson, *Account,* 14-40.

17 Riley, *Suffering*, viii; As late as 1835, the British Consul-General in Morocco, Drummond Hay, voted against a Foreign Office proposal that requires his deputies to be (like their French counterparts) sufficiently fluent in Arabic. Arabic was deemed very difficult because it was "wholly new to a native of Europe." The National Archives, (TNA) FO 174/167, Drummond Hay to Foreign Office (Tangiers, 11 July 1835).

18 De Brisson, *Account,* 12, 18.

19 Jackson, *An Account*, 270; Riley, *Authentic Narrative,* 278; Riley, *Suffering,* 18; "Riley," Evans wrote, "became one of the best known men in the United States ... His description of foreign places and barbarism caught the public's imagination." Riley, *Sufferings*, vi.

20 *Voyages to the Coast of Africa, by Mess. Saugnier and Brisson; Containing an Account of their Shipwreck on Board Different Vessels, and Subsequent Slavery* (London: J. Robinson, 1792).

21 Ibid., 93.

22 Ibid., v.

23 Ibid., 15.

24 Ibid., 12, 15, 18, 28.

25 Cumbersome as it is, the statement tends to underscore De Brisson's culpability in his own captivity! According to de Brisson, his "master's brother-in-law, who was also one of the chiefs of the horde, took particular care of all the slaves. He ordered camel's milk to be given us, and the flesh of the ostrich dried in the sun and cut into small pieces. I do not know how he happened to be prepossessed in my favour; but having approached me, he addressed me in the following manner: 'unfortunate stranger, my brother has been indebted to me for a long time; if you will attach yourself to me, I shall make the necessary arrangements with him'." De Brisson, *Account,* 31.

26 De Brisson, *Account*, 31. De Brisson later discovered that "Sidy Sellem" did not waste time to deliver those he collected at the site of shipwreck to Essaouira. By the time he arrived in Essaouira, they had long been repatriated to France. The precision implied by what seems to be full names like "Sidy Sellem" and "Sidy Mahammat" is deceptive. *Sidy* is (like Mr.) a term of endearment used to address prominent *sufi* (*zawaya*) figures. It is futile to speculate which "Sellem" or "Mahammat" from amongst all the "wandering Arabs" De Brisson was referring to!

27 De Brisson, *Account*, 35-39.

28 De Brisson, *Account*, 40-41. De Brisson split the blame for this failure between the French consulate at Essaouira and the "Jew merchant" of his hosts. In the footnote, he identified two types of "Jews." There are those "who live in the cities," and those "born in the desert," and hence, "live in the same manner as the Arabs." This distinction lurks beneath his conception of "the only" guaranteed mode of redemption: "If ever the French government, or any other, should hear of vessels lost upon these coasts, their agent, either at Tangiers or Mogadore, must make application to a Jew named Aaron, who resides at Gouadnum [Gulimeme/ Wady Nun], and who sends emissaries into different parts of Africa to reclaim wrecks." De Brisson, *Account*, 41.

29 De Brisson, *Account*, 49-58

30 Ibid., 61.

31 Ibid., 75-79. It is doubtful that de Brisson actually "talked" to either sultan Sidy Muhamad Ibn Abdulla (r.1757-90) or Mawlay Yazyd (r.1790-92). The "emperor" in question was most probably, the Alawite deputy (*khalifa*) to al-Sus. But

this invocation of the "emperor" is not unique: it is standard cliché in captivity narratives.

32 De Brisson, *Account*, 76-80. From this account, much seems to have been 'lost in translation.' Still one could deduce that "chief" Sidy Sellem was one of the Saharan dignitaries the Alawites had deputized to monitor the Atlantic coast and round up *Nazarene* trespassers. The reprimand "why did you not keep further from the shore" and Sellem's reported statement that "there were some more [captives] whom I could easily collect, if your majesty will give me an order for that purpose" tend to point in that direction; see De Brisson, *Account,* 79.

33 De Brisson and his comrades had also cost their "masters" an undisclosed number of sheep. According to De Brisson, they were driven by hunger to consume carrion and that "suggested to us the idea of strangling a few kids [lambs] in the night time persuaded that our masters would throw them away, as their law does not permit them to eat the flesh of any animal, unless it has died by the knife. This stratagem occasioned frequent deaths, and it was observed that those kids, which appeared best in the evening, were … those which were found dead in the mourning … We were at length caught in the act." De Brisson, *Account*, 46.

34 Ibid., 49

35 Ibid., 50.

36 Jackson, *Account*, 279.

37 Ibid., 272.

38 Ibid., 273-275.

39 Ibid., 274. In the British Foreign Office records, Thomas Betton was introduced as a "Turkey Merchant" who tested *Moorish* captivity and, in effect, "left in his will dated in 1724 a trust to the Iron Mongers' Company of London" to be "perpetually employed in the redemption of British captives from Moorish slavery." See TNA, FO 174/153: 3 November 1813; TNA, FO 174/155 (Consul Douglas' copy book, Tangier), 17 June 1818- 2 August 1823.

40 Jackson, *Account*, 275-281.

41 See Peter Gwyn to James Green (Mogador), 23 September 1811, "Iron Mongers' proposal to open a correspondence with the Sheiks to the Southward," TNA FO 174/20, James Green to Joseph Dupuis (Tangier), 3 November, 1811, TNA FO 174/153; Douglas (Tangier) to the Right Honorable, The Earl of Bathurst, 6 April 1815, TNA FO 174/154. The idea was initially (6/04/1811) rejected because it "would most certainly occasion the holders of such unfortunate men, to retain them in order to exact very large sums." TNA, FO 174/20

42 On the diplomatic parameters and "worth" of repatriation in the pre-modern Mediterranean front see the chapter by Gillian Weiss, "Ransoming 'Turks' from France's Royal Galleys ," 51-72.

43 For this article (35), see TNA FO 52/42-44 (26 December 1791).

44 Jackson, *Account*, 276. *Haha* is the province/region that also includes Essaouira.

45 Jackson, *Account*, 280-281 (footnote).

46 On the shipwreck of the *Motezuma*, see TNA, FO 174/14, Peter Gwyn to James

Green, 5 March, 1811, 27 June, 1811; TNA, FO 174/153, James Green to Joseph Dupius, 3 November 1813.

47 Cochelet, *Narrative,* 7, 52-53.

48 Ibid., 53-54, 61-63; On the Bayruk family, see Mohamed, *Between Caravan and Sultan;* For this mode of French reporting on the "chiefs of Wady Nun," see *Archive des affaires etrangères, correspondance commerciale Mogador, 1836-1844; tome I,* 182-185.

49 Maurrice Barbier (ed.), *Trois français au sahara occidental au XIXe siècle* (Paris: L'Harmattan, 1984), 95.

50 Cochelet, *Narrative*, 86-87.

51 On *Shaykh* Bayruk's quest for an alternative, local, port, see, Mohamed, *Between Caravan and Sultan*, 310-22.

52 Adams, *Narrative*, 8-9; notes, 85-88.

53 Ibid., 68. Ubaydallah Ibn Salim (d. approx. 1817-1818) of the Bayruk family was the key trader and most powerful leader of the Takna ensemble, a devotee of the Alawite court and the main contact of the British consulate in Essauira.

54 Adams, *Narrative*, 71-73.

55 Ibid., 73. For Dupuis' rejoinder see, note n. 144.

56 Riley, *Suffering,* 318-19.

57 Ibid., 66-67.

58 Ibid., 73.

59 Ibid., 73; It would be an exercise in futility to try to "certify" the identity of either of these two "Hamets"!

60 Riley, *Suffering*, 86, 88

61 Ibid., 247, 256-8.

62 Ibid., 171; Riley presented himself as English to both his captors and trader Hamet and that was, probably, why his letter was addressed to the British consulate in Essaouira. According to Riley, trader Hamet rebuked him: "the English are good for nothing—you see even our women and children can walk and run"! Riley, *Suffering*, 141.

63 Mudimbe, *Invention*, 15-16.

64 Drummond Hay struggled to exonerate "Christian" expatriates from the "bad faith" that pervaded "all classes of natives" in Morocco. But he still had to concede that "Christians of certain classes seem too frequently to take the immoral infection." Drummond Hay to FO, 11 July 1835, TNA, FO 174/167.

65 Matar synthesized some "cases of duplicity" from the pre-modern period: "In October 1636, Charles FitzGeffry pleaded with his … congregation to be charitable and help raise the ransom money for captives. There is some evidence that parishioners, clergy, and sometimes lords of manors, contributed, but such ad hoc collections were riddled with dishonesty. In 1618 Edward Eastman pocketed money earmarked for captives; only a few months before FitzGeffry preached, merchants who had been given £942 to spend on captives were discovered to have spent £424 only, and had kept the rest; in December 1670, collections were fraudulently made under the guise of ransoming captives … A

year later, a petition was presented to the king regarding the case of John Pile who had collected money for captives, but then absconded. Ten years later, in Algiers, John Nevell complained about Lionel Croft who claimed to have paid ransom for captives redeemed by others," Matar, *British Captives*, 47.

SECTION II

Ransoming in Western Africa

CHAPTER V

Idealism and Pragmatism:

The Related Muslim West African Discourses on Identity, Captivity, and Ransoming

Jennifer Lofkrantz

Introduction

As has been demonstrated in recent scholarship, the ransoming of captives has been a widespread practice throughout West Africa.[1] Underpinning ransoming practices, including who and how a person should be ransomed and the conduct of ransom negotiations, is intellectual thought and debate on ransoming. As I have stated elsewhere, ransoming is defined as the paying for the release of a captive, with cash or kind, at the time of capture or soon afterwards. Moreover, the ransoming of a captive is differentiated from the redemption of a slave in that a redeemed slave usually remains in their former master's society in a subservient position.[2] This chapter is primarily concerned with intellectual discourse on ransoming rather than ransoming practices. In sixteenth to nineteenth century Muslim West Africa, the issue of ransoming was intimately linked to the question of captivity and enslavement. Captivity could result in both the ransoming of the captive and the enslavement of the captive as well the execution, free release, and prisoner exchange of the captive. Therefore, the discourse on ransoming was strongly affiliated with the debate on who could and could not be legally enslaved and particularly with discussion on remedies for illegal captivity. Moreover, the discourse on ransoming highlights the tension, for intellectuals, between the ideal and the pragmatic in seeking the release of illegally taken captives.

Considering the role of slavery and the slave trade in West Africa it is not surprising that enslavement, and particularly the enslavement of freeborn Muslims, provoked a response by Muslim intellectuals. Scholars based their arguments within accepted interpretations of the Mālikī *madh'hab*, the school of Islamic law preponderant in West Africa and the Maghrib, and within the context of the scholarly debate on the issue. Not only were West African jurists reacting to the enslavement of freeborn Muslims but they were also reacting to a North African argument that defined individuals identified as "black" as being enslaveable which informed their discourse on enslaveability. West African jurists argued that freeborn Muslims, regardless of racial categorization, should never be enslaved and that Muslims who came into possession of captive or enslaved Muslims should release them. Yet, many jurists acknowledged that ransoming was a useful tool in obviating enslavement and encouraged the ransoming of Muslims. The discussion of the issues of race, religious identity, captivity, enslavement, and ransoming were therefore entwined. Ransoming was a tactic against captivity and enslavement. Jurists who viewed ransoming as a pragmatic response to the problem of enslavement perceived ransoming as a means of re-attaining the freedom of captives, in particular freeborn Muslims, whose enslavement they viewed as illegal. Ransoming as a remedy for illegal captivity and enslavement became especially important in the nineteenth century, an era where enslavement, including that of freeborn Muslims, was pervasive. Therefore, in order to discuss scholarly opinion on ransoming which was perceived by many Muslim scholars primarily as a means to protect freeborn Muslim from enslavement, one must first delve into intellectual thought concerning legal and illegal enslavement.

Scholars and the Issue of Legal and Illegal Enslavement and its Remedy

In studying the historical West African scholarly discourse on slavery and ransoming, the concept of a "discursive tradition" is applicable. Talal Asad views Islamic discourse as a continuous engagement and reflection on the past and on previous scholarship in order to develop meaningful solutions to the problems of a particular time and place. For Asad, Islam is "neither a distinctive social structure nor a heterogeneous collection of beliefs, artifacts, customs and morals" but a set of discourses "that seek to instruct practitioners regarding the correct form and purpose of a given practice."[3] Similarly, Scott Reese views the Islamic cannon as a "living body of knowledge continuously employed and interpreted."[4] The concept of a "discursive tradition" has been used by anthropologists such as Adeline Masquelier, Roman Loimeier and Abdulkader Tayob, among others, to address how Muslim scholars and laypeople across Africa have navigated between "tradition," religious reform, and the modern world.[5]

Informing the debate on legal and illegal enslavement in Islamic West Africa were local interpretations of the Mālikī madh'hab and the North African discourse on race and slavery.[6] As the West African debate on legal and illegal enslavement exemplifies, the discursive tradition in West Africa was informed by the combination of the interpretation of core texts and by local religious and socials contexts. Issues of debate included who was considered to be a Muslim, the onus for proving freeborn Muslim status, and the fate of illegally-captive individuals. In the southern Sahara and in West Africa we see that scholars both adamantly reiterated that the only reason for enslavement was unbelief in Islam and rebutted a North African argument that equated "blackness" with original unbelief and therefore enslavement.

In seventeenth to nineteenth century southern Sahara, Sahel and Sudan, racial difference was obvious but the meaning changed depending on place and time. Generally, in the Maghrib, the Sahara, and the Sahel conceptions of racial difference as well as religious identity were used as a means to categorize difference. Usually ethnicity and religious identity were used in combination south of the Sahara. James Webb argues that Saharans developed a race-based identity as desertification in the seventeenth century forced migration to the southern desert edge and into closer proximity with Sudanese. Webb views racial identity along the desert edge as developing in tandem with nomadic Saharans asserting control over agricultural Sudanese with "white" masters and "black" slaves.[7] However, as shown by Bruce Hall, conceptions of race in the southern Sahara and Sahel region of West Africa changed over time as local populations integrated North African and later European notions of race into their understandings of the significance of racial difference.[8] After the seventeenth century, notions of racial difference had become important to the social discourse of the region as some Berber and Tuareg populations became increasingly Arabized. Moreover, racial categories had more to do with genuine or ascribed genealogy than actual skin tone. Individuals who belonged to actual or ascribed Arab genealogies, no matter their skin tone, were deemed as "white" and those who did not were designated as "black." Yet, even as the terms used to mark racial difference and the social implications of that difference changed, a common feature was the negative and servile connotation of those identified as "black." However, just as "blackness" was being more and more associated with social inferiority, there was a counter-discourse, in the southern Sahara and Sudan, that argued that skin color and the ability to trace one's genealogy to the original Muslim community in Arabia, ought not to denote social status and one's standing as a Muslim. West African writers, or those who had experience in the region, were dealing with a much more ethnically diverse population where an Arab forefather, whether real or imagined, did not denote social status.

West African legal opinion and advice was grounded in the fundamental principle of Islamic jurisprudence that the natural condition, and hence the default status of an individual, is that of freedom. Therefore, theoretically, a person is supposed to be presumed to be free unless he or she is proven to be a slave. In theory, a person could only be enslaved if he or she were born to slave parents or if he or she was captured during a jihad. A jihad, a "just war," is a war of self-defence conducted under certain conditions against non-Muslims. The Mālikī madh'hab, also permitted a proselytizing war against non-Muslims if the target community refused to convert, or, if they were *ahl al-kitāb* (People of the Book), refused to either convert or to pay the *jizya* (poll-tax paid by non-Muslims).[9] Whether or not a particular war met the legal requirements for a "legal" or "just" war, a jihad, was also a subject of debate with proponents of any particular war obviously arguing that the conflict in question did meet the basic requirements. The Sunni Islamic schools of law agree, including the Mālikī madh'hab, that enslavement is only one option for dealing with prisoners of war, the others being execution, ransom, exchange against Muslim prisoners, taxation (applicable to the ahl al-kitāb) and free release.[10] In the Mālikī madh'hab and the other four major Sunni *madhāhib*, it was illegal to enslave someone as punishment for a crime or as payment for a debt, and it was forbidden for a free person to sell him or herself or his or her children into slavery.[11] People could only be enslaved if they were taken captive during a legal war or if they were born into slavery. West African scholars continually emphasized that the natural condition of a person was freedom and that enslavement could only be imposed on a select few under specific conditions.

Four writers who probably had the most influence on seventeenth to nineteenth century West African Muslim ideas on race, religious belief, and slavery are Abū Zayd 'Abdu Raḥmān b. Muḥammad b.Ibn Khaldūn (d. 1406), 'Abd al-Raḥmān al-Suyūtī (d. 1505), Muḥammad al-Maghīlī, (d. 1504) and Aḥmad Bābā (d. 1627). All four emphasized that religious identity trumped racial identity. Ibn Khaldūn, the fourteenth century historian from Tunis, whose *Kitāb al-'ibar*, (History of the Berbers) would provide later Arabized Berbers much of the historical material needed to connect local genealogies to important Arab Muslim figures in North Africa and the Arabian Peninsula, argued that adherence to Islam outweighed all other differences.[12] In the *Muqaddima* (1377), he fervently argued against the popular idea amongst thirteenth and fourteenth century Arabs that blackness was related to descent from Ham, the son of Noah who had been cursed, and therefore the subsequent inferiority of blacks and their inherent enslaveability.[13] Instead, Ibn Khaldūn accepted the theory of climes, that skin color and barbarism, were directly related to geographic location as the explanation of racial difference. In the version of the theory of climes generally accepted in Mediterranean communities at the time, the farther one moves northwards or southwards, the more barbaric the population. Therefore, both northern European paleness and sub-Saharan African blackness were associated with barbarism. Ibn Khaldūn however, rejected the direct correlation between skin color and climate and argued that the barbarism produced by climate could be ameliorated through the adoption of a revealed religion.[14] For Ibn Khaldūn, the real mark of civilization was not genealogy, climate, or skin color but religious identity.

Both the Cairo scholar al-Suyūtī and the Tlemscen scholar al-Maghīlī influenced the development of West African Islamic thought on enslavement and remedies for illegal enslavement even though they represented different sides of the orthodox spectrum. Al-Suyūtī was admired in West Africa for his command of the Islamic sciences but also for his acceptance of syncretism and local traditions in Islamic practice.[15] In contrast, even though al-Maghīlī is known for his influence in spreading Islam and the Mālikī school of law in Hausaland and for advising several political leaders throughout western Africa including the Askia al-hāj Muḥammad of Songhay, the Emir Muḥammad Rumfa of Kano and the political elite of Tuwāt, he is also known for battling against syncretic and non-orthodox practices throughout West Africa and especially in the Songhay Empire.[16] Yet, both of these men, one approaching the question from a liberal interpretation of Mālikī law and the other from a strict legalistic interpretation of law, argued that belief was the great equalizer and that the largest factor in ascertaining religious status in society was personal religious belief. Al-Suyūtī used hadith to counter negative stereotypes of blacks and while accepting that the genealogy of blacks could be traced to Ham, he dismissed the idea that their black skin was the result of a curse by Noah.[17]

For al-Maghīlī, race was also a non-issue. He divided people strictly on the grounds of personal belief and non-belief. He heavily promoted the rights and protections of Muslims while advocating discrimination against non-Muslims. By the time that he was advising the Emir Muḥammad Rumfa of Kano and had written *Taj al-Din yajib 'ala-mulūk*, al-Maghīlī was already known for his harsh interpretations of Khalīl's *Mukhtaṣar*, which laid out the Mālikī view of proper relations between Muslims and non-Muslims.[18] Al-Maghīlī was heavily influenced by the political events in the dār al-islām of the late fifteenth century, especially the loss of al-Andalūs and the expulsion of Muslims and Jews from now Catholic Iberia. Due to these events, he took a particularly rigid view of the rights and obligations of *dhimmī*, protected peoples, living in Muslim territories and viewed the protection of freeborn Muslims as paramount no matter their racial identity. Al-Maghīlī emphasized the responsibility of the state in freeing Muslim captives. He advised in *Taj al-Din yajib 'ala-mulūk*, that "if wealth abounds he [the prince] will preserve a surplus in the treasury for possible emergencies, for building mosques, *ransoming captives*, discharging debts, marrying women, aiding pilgrims and other necessities."[19] In terms of ransoming, al-Maghīlī's opinions, which had consistently fallen within accepted bounds of Mālikī interpretation, illustrate the point that many jurists were of the opinion that it was incumbent upon Muslim leaders to free their captive followers by paying ransom if necessary.

Similar to al-Maghīlī, Bābā's scholarship of the late sixteenth and early seventeenth centuries, which was based on his training in Mālikī law, was also heavily influenced by the events surrounding him and his personal experiences. Bābā, a Timbuktu jurist of Sanhāja origin and member of the powerful and scholarly Aqīt family, wrote his treatise after his own illegal captivity and enslavement in Morocco following Morocco's invasion of the Songhay Empire in 1591. He wrote this text in order to rebut North African ideas concerning skin color, religious belief and enslaveability. While it was accepted that Muslims were protected from enslavement, a question had arisen in sixteenth century North Africa about whether or not "black" Africans from south of the Sahara were legitimate freeborn Muslims based on how Islam spread in the region. In 1699, this discourse culminated in Morocco when Sultan Mawlāy Ismā'īl ordered the enslavement of the entire free black population in Morocco for his army on the basis that all "blacks" in Morocco were enslaveable because of their supposed servile ancestry.[20] Basically, those who argued that "black" Africans were enslaveable based their argument on the idea that since "black" populations had been forcibly converted to Islam, which was untrue, that their descendants were not true freeborn Muslims and were therefore enslaveable. To counter this argument, in *Mi'rāj al-Ṣu'ūd* (1615), Bābā relied on accepted histories of the spread of Islam in West Africa, and the undisputed Muslim status of West African states such as Ancient Ghana, Ancient Mali and Songhay, while also emphasizing that one's religious status was based on personal belief or non-belief.[21]

Bābā's *Mi'rāj al-Ṣu'ūd*, which was a series of responses to questions posed to him about slavery, became the most famous and most important work on slavery in West Africa and the Maghrib in the pre-nineteenth century period. This treatise not only revealed the thinking and interpretation of one of the most learned and respected scholars of Timbuktu but also exposed the internal debates about enslavement within the early seventeenth century intellectual and ruling elite in the region.[22] In *Mi'rāj al-Ṣu'ūd* Bābā addresses two key points: the question of "blackness" and enslaveability and the responsibility for proving a person's freeborn or non-freeborn Muslim status. It is important to note, that Bābā was not against slavery or enslavement per se, but was against the enslavement of freeborn Muslims. Bābā not only situated his judgements within the general corpus of Mālikī law but actively engaged the scholarship of those who came before him. This can be seen in his references to important scholars such as Maḥmūd b. 'Umar b. Muḥammad Aqīt and Makhlūfi b.'Alī b Ṣāliḥ al-Balbālī's (d. 1533-1534). Bābā's reference to Maḥmūd Aqīt and al-Balbālī indicates not only Bābā's scholarly context but also the long tradition of debate on issues surrounding illegal enslavement and their remedies. Indeed *Mi'rāj al-Ṣu'ūd* can be seen as a culmination of southern Saharan and West African intellectual thought on the non-equation of "blackness" and enslavement.

Even though the emphasis was placed on religious identity, there was an ethnic component to the West African discourse on enslaveability, as evident in *Mi'rāj al-Ṣu'ūd*. While Bābā insisted that personal belief and unbelief trumped all other considerations, he divided West Africa into two broad categories of Muslim and non-Muslim ethnic groups. In doing so, Bābā followed the southern Algerian scholar al-Balbālī's lead.[23] However, where they differed significantly is that where al-Balbālī argued that no one from a known Muslim state should be enslaved for fear of enslaving a freeborn Muslim, Bābā acknowledged that not all people coming from known Islamic states were Muslims nor would all people claiming to be Muslim actually be freeborn Muslims.[24] In order to err on the side of freedom and not to mistakenly enslave a freeborn Muslim, al-Balbālī advised against enslaving anyone from regions that were predominantly Muslim. Bābā advised to use extreme caution to make sure one did not enslave or purchase an enslaved freeborn Muslim but did not suggest the complete avoidance of purchasing people from predominantly Muslim states. This can be seen in Bābā's reply to a question on the lawful enslavement of individuals from certain states posed by a Moroccan, Yūsuf b. Ibrāhīm al-ʻĪsī, he stated that,

> what I think regarding your question is that you ought to know first that some of these groups (aṣnāf) are mixed together. Those whom we have ascertained to be Muslim are all of the people of Songhay and its kingdom [stretching for a distance of] some two months in length. Similarly all of Kano are Muslims since ancient times, likewise, Katsina and Zakzak [Zaria] and Gobir [?]. However, close to them are unbelieving people whom the Muslims may raid because of their extreme proximity, so we have heard, and they bring them to their place as unbelievers and slaves. As regards these people, if it is established among you that a slave woman or man is from these unbelievers and was merely raised in the city of Kano or Katsina or Zakzak or Kabi [Kebbi], and subsequently converted to Islam, then there is no harm in buying him, since he was taken captive while an unbeliever. Similarly, all the people of Bornu are Muslims, but close to them also are unbelievers whom the people of Bornu raid. The ruling is as before.[25]

According to Hall, one of the reasons why *Mi'rāj al-Ṣu'ūd* became so popular with later scholars was because of Bābā's precise categorization of different types of "blacks."[26] On the eve of the nineteenth century, the Fodiawa, 'Uthmān b. Fodiye, his brother, 'Abdullāhi b. Fodiye and 'Uthmān's son Muḥammad Bello, who were instrumental in leading the Sokoto jihad, accepted Bābā's premise that ethnicity could be used as a means for ascertaining an individual's Muslim status. However, the Fodiawa disagreed with some of Bābā's classifications. In a text written either by 'Abdullāhi or 'Uthmān b. Fodiye, but attributed to Uthmān, *Taḥqīq al-'iṣma li-jamī'*, undated, but most likely preceding the jihad, some of the ethnicities that Bābā listed as being Muslim were missing from the later list. Notably missing from the category of freeborn Muslims from the Fodiawa list are the Hausa and Gobirawa whom Bābā had included in his. Nevertheless, 'Uthmān b. Fodiye, echoing al-Balbālī's caution, and in agreement with Bābā's list, insisted that all Fulbe were to be protected from enslavement even though he recognized that not all Fulbe were Muslim.[27]

In *Mi'rāj al-Ṣu'ūd*, Bābā also addressed the question of who was responsible for proving a captive's freeborn or non-freeborn Muslim status. One of the disagreements among jurists, and Bābā discusses the opposing opinions, was whether the onus to prove an enslaved person's original status was the responsibility of the slave or the owner. According to Bābā, the general consensus was that it was the responsibility of the owner to prove that a captive was not a freeborn Muslim, however there was a minority opinion that disagreed. He reiterated that it was the responsibility of captors to prove their captive's non-freeborn Muslim status and not the responsibility of the captive to prove their freeborn status. He believed that Muslims who could be proven to be freeborn Muslims should not be enslaved under any circumstances and should be freed immediately upon their free origin being verified. He counselled al -'Īsī, to only purchase slaves whose status was clear and not to buy a slave whose origin or status was in doubt.[28] For Bābā, Muslim status was based on the personal belief or unbelief of an individual. If a free person was a Muslim then that person was not enslaveable regardless of ancestry or where he or she lived. Muslims holding captive freeborn Muslims or individuals who might be freeborn Muslims ought to immediately release them.

Remedies for Illegal Enslavement and the Practice of Ransoming

By the beginning of the seventeenth century, if not earlier, there was clear Muslim West African consensus that the only justification for enslavement was personal non-belief. Therefore, the enslavement of Muslims, including freeborn Muslims categorized as "black" was viewed as illegal. This was the culmination of an intellectual discourse that countered a North African discourse that tried to associate enslaveability with "blackness." Moreover, scholarly opinion was that it was the responsibility of the captor to ensure that a captive was not a freeborn Muslim and not the captive's responsibility to prove their freeborn Muslim status. Likewise, it was generally accepted that Muslim leaders had a responsibility for preventing enslavement that was illegal according to Mālikī law and for ensuring the rights of freeborn Muslims. Among scholars it was accepted that one of the duties of a Muslim leader was to ensure the freedom of fellow freeborn Muslims. Here, however, were two points of dispute. The first point of contention was how freeborn Muslims ought to be freed from illegal captivity. The second point of debate was what constituted personal belief and non-belief and therefore who was a freeborn Muslim worthy of protection. "Idealists" such as Bābā, argued that Muslims in possession of freeborn Muslims ought to freely release their captives without compensation. "Pragmatic" scholars such as al-Maghīlī agreed that the correct remedy for suspected wrongfully captive or enslaved individuals held by Muslims was free release. They accepted, however, that this was not necessarily a practical remedy as only the most pious Muslim captors would voluntarily freely release captives and slaves. Moving from the "idealistic" to the "pragmatic," in the eighteenth and nineteenth centuries, in an era of increasing enslavement, methods of Muslim scholar-activists for ensuring the freedom of freeborn Muslims, included moral suasion, rescue, political reform, as well as ransoming. Ransoming was one tactic on a continuum of strategies to prevent the enslavement of freeborn Muslims.

Throughout the eighteenth century, West African Muslim scholars attempted to use moral suasion to convince rulers to prevent what they perceived to be illegal enslavement of freeborn Muslims and to protect their rights. Scholars throughout the Islamic World, and not just in West Africa, viewed the normal relationship between scholar and government as being one of advisement. Scholars and jurists usually insisted that not only themselves but also rulers conduct themselves with piety and often viewed themselves as the protectors and spokespeople for the disadvantaged and non-elites.[29] For example, the noted Tuareg scholar, Jibrīl b. ʻUmar was an agitator for Muslim rights in both Hausaland and Aïr, trying to convince the political elites to ensure the safety and well-being of freeborn Muslims. He passed this quest to his nephews and students ʻUthmān and ʻAbdullāhi b. Fodiye. Jibrīl equated the selling of free men with adultery, wine drinking and manslaughter.[30] Muḥammad Tukur, a scholar contemporaneous to ʻUthmān, included the sellers of free men in his categories of unbelievers.[31] Indeed, prior to the launching of his jihad, ʻUthmān had repeatedly tried to convince Hausa political leaders to protect the rights of freeborn Muslims. Their failure, as seen by the Fodiawa, to uphold their duty as Muslim leaders to protect Muslims from captivity and enslavement was a major cause of the jihad. Muslim intellectuals also advocated and practiced the physical rescue of freeborn Muslims from enslavement. In this they were following in the footsteps of al-Maghīlī who had admonished the Emir of Kano that a good King reserved treasury funds for the rescue of freeborn Muslims. For example, Sulaymān Bāl, the Fulbe scholar who initiated the jihad in Fuuta Toro that led to the overthrow of the Denyanke ruling class in 1776, prior to the jihad, used physical force on the Senegal River to free a Muslim man who was being transported to the Atlantic coast to be sold after failing to convince the man's captors to freely release him or to allow his ransom.[32] Prior to the start of the conflict with Gobir, and in the early days of his jihad, ʻUthmān sent his students to intercept caravans and rescue trafficked Muslims, whereas Muḥammad Bello made clear in his writings that it was the responsibility of all Muslims to ensure the freedom of their fellow Muslims.[33]

Likewise, attempts at political reform and actual political reform, the West African jihads, inspired and led by intellectuals, was also a strategy to protect freeborn Muslims from enslavement. In instigating political reform, scholars stepped outside of their traditional role of advising rulers by becoming rulers themselves. Starting with Nāṣir al-Dīn's jihad of the 1670s in the

Senegal River valley, and continuing into the mid-nineteenth century with movements in Fuuta Jallon, Fuuta Toro, and the western and central Sudan, a series of jihads took place throughout Muslim West Africa to protect perceived freeborn Muslims rights.[34] The new governments that arose out of the successful jihads attempted to control and facilitate legal enslavement and trade while preventing illegal enslavement and trade. The Fuuta Jallon government, in the late eighteenth and early nineteenth centuries, for example, only permitted the slave trade to the coast to be conducted through the use of sanctioned caravan leaders.[35]

However, in an era where governments were tasked with permitting the enslavement of individuals deemed non-Muslim in order to facilitate economic growth, especially the plantation sector and international trade, and at the same time protect certain individuals from enslavement, scholar-rulers needed to balance the ideal with the pragmatic. The scholar-rulers of the Sokoto Caliphate exemplify the attempt at this balancing act. The Sokoto Caliphate was the largest state in nineteenth century sub-Saharan Africa but it did not have a strong central government. Instead, the emirate governments, who had their own priorities and unique issues of governance, cooperation, and control, held the bulk of economic and military power. The central government maintained unity through careful diplomacy and the maintenance of the respect for the intellectual foundations, based on the Mālikī madh'hab and the Qādiriyya *ṭarīqa* (Sufi order), of the state.[36] Despite the fact that a major impetus of the jihad was the protection of freeborn Muslims from enslavement, in order to maintain the unity of the state, Sokoto scholars and officials behaved pragmatically in dealing with the issue of illegal captivity and enslavement. Being pragmatic, but basing their opinions on earlier scholarship, Muslim scholars such as 'Uthmān b. Fodiye and later, 'Umar Taal who initiated his own jihad in the western Sudan in the 1850s, condoned the strategy of ransoming as a means of freeing captives instead of demanding their free release.[37]

The Sokoto government supported ransoming efforts by facilitating communication between captors and payers of ransom at government sanctioned markets, by providing mediators for the ransom negotiations and by directing that local funds should be established for the ransoms of those whose families could not afford the cost. On average, the price of ransom was twice the price the individual would have fetched on the slave market.[38] The government would have preferred that people taken captive whom they considered to be freeborn Muslims attain their freedom through free release, however, they condoned ransoming as a pragmatic strategy to free people whom the government deemed unenslaveable. The captive regained his or her freedom while the captor did not suffer a financial loss. Another benefit of condoning and facilitating ransoming is that it helped free captives who were at risk of being enslaved within the state. For example, while the Sokoto Caliphate forbade the export of slaves to the Atlantic Coast and checked northbound caravans, it did not have a mechanism for enforcing full compliance nor for checking the domestic slave trade.[39]

It is important to note, though, that both Sokoto and Umarian officials held a very narrow view of who was considered to be a freeborn Muslim. According to them, only individuals who followed "pure" Islamic law were freeborn Muslims. Both the Fodiawa and Taal based their definition of a freeborn Muslim on al-Maghīlī's definition of a non-Muslim. Al-Maghīlī defined as non-Muslim someone who was non-Muslim by origin such as a Christian or whose father was non-Muslim by origin, an "apostate," and anyone who "pretended" to be a Muslims but whose behavior indicated otherwise.[40] Al-Maghīlī's third category of non-Muslims allowed for people to define as non-Muslim, individuals who would define themselves as Muslim. The narrowness of Sokoto's definition of a freeborn Muslim is outlined in a series of letters exchanged by 'Uthmān, Bello and Muḥammad al-Amīn al-Kānimī of Borno between 1810 and 1812, on the eve of Sokoto's invasion of Borno. In these letters, the concepts of *takfīr* (declaring a self-professed Muslim an infidel) and *taqlīd* (the emulation of the ideal Muslim leader) were paramount to the Sokoto leaders. They considered as non-Muslim anyone who included syncretic forms in their practice of Islam and who attacked those who considered 'Uthmān b. Fodiye as the ideal Muslim leader.[41] 'Umar Taal adapted 'Uthmān's strategy of defining a leader and a state that considered itself to be Muslim as a non-Muslim in his justification for attacking Aḥmadu b. Aḥmadu, the third amīr al-mu'minīn of the Caliphate of Ḥamdullahi in 1862. Taal argued that a leader who supported a non-Muslim state against attack from a Muslim state such as Ḥamdullahi's earlier support of Segu against 'Umarian attack, had rejected Islam and was therefore a non-Muslim and a legitimate target of jihad.[42] The jihad leaders were only concerned with protecting individuals from enslavement whom they considered to be freeborn Muslims and who conformed to their interpretation of proper Muslim behavior.

The nineteenth century scholar-rulers of the newly established jihad states supported, facilitated and encouraged the ransoming of individuals they considered to be freeborn Muslims. Even so, like many who were in charge of state funds, they were not keen on paying the financial costs associated with ransoms.[43] They supported their decisions regarding who was responsible for ransom payments in the discursive tradition and found intellectual justification for their decisions. The two scholars who influenced nineteenth century West African intellectual thought on ransom payments were the Andalusian scholar Muḥammad b. Aḥmad b. Juzay (d.1340) and the Egyptian scholar Khalīl b. Isḥāq (d. 1374). Both scholars agreed that it was the responsibility of Muslims to pay the ransom of fellow Muslims but disagreed under which conditions the family and the state were responsible for the payment. Juzay argued that the payment of ransom was first the responsibility of the captive, second the state treasury, third the Muslim community and fourth non-Muslim residents.[44] In contrast Khalīl argued that the payment of ransoms was primarily the responsibility of the state and the Muslim community.[45] Khalīl's opinion was especially important since he was the author of the common abridged version of Mālikī law, *Mukhtaṣar al-shaykh Khalīl*, which was a foundational text of jurisprudence in the core curriculum of Muslim scholars in West Africa, including the Fodiawa, and which generated numerous commentaries which were also studied in the region. Al-Maghīlī, in advising that governments ought to maintain a fund for ransom payments and maintaining that it was the responsibility of rulers to free their followers was following Khalīl's reasoning. Nevertheless, despite the general adherence to both Khalīl's and al-Maghīlī's interpretations of Mālikī law, the Sokoto Caliphate scholars, finding Juzay's thought more in line with government budget concerns, followed Juzay's advice. They adopted the policy that rich captives and their families should pay for their own ransoms whereas the state should be responsible for the ransom payments of poor Muslims.[46]

However, while the scholar-rulers of the early Sokoto Caliphate agreed that they needed to prevent illegal enslavement while facilitating legal enslavement, and to ransom back their followers who had been taken captive, preferably with private funds, they differed on the advice they gave regarding the ransoming of captives held by their forces. Just as in the scholarly discussion on ransoming as a remedy for illegal captivity, in the discussion on ransoming as an option for dealing with war prisoners, we see the demonstration, especially by Muḥammad Bello and 'Uthmān's brother, 'Abdullāhi b. Fodiye, of Asad's view of Islamic intellectual thought as dynamic and adaptable to the issues of their time and place.[47] Bello and 'Abdullāhi drew upon the same Islamic intellectual cannon but, due to the differing circumstances that they were addressing, developed opposite advice on the ransoming of enemy captives.[48] Yet, a uniting factor between them seems to be prudency and pragmatism and the following of Khalīl's advice to only permit the ransom of enemy prisoners held by their forces from a position of strength. They ignored, though, Khalīl's opinion that governments should be the primary payer of the ransoms of their subjects.[49]

Even though Sokoto forces were able to conquer a large swath of territory in a relatively short period of time, the control they exerted over that territory varied. 'Abdullāhi wrote *Ḍiyā' al-ḥukkām* (ca. 1807), where he outlines his ransoming policies, upon request of the Kano jihad leaders who were in firm control of the territory and population of Kano emirate but were fighting amongst themselves and needed guidance in how to govern. Bello, on the other hand, wrote his opinion on ransoming in the form of an undated letter, most likely written between 1809 and 1817, to Ya'qūb b. Dādi, the founder of Bauchi Emirate (r.1808-1845).[50] Unlike, the situation in Kano, in Bauchi Emirate, there was no in-fighting between the governing elite but between 1808 and 1837, Ya'qūb was first conquering the region, then solidifying his control as he fought both internal rebellions and Muḥammad al-Kānimī's Borno forces.[51]

In *Ḍiyā' al-ḥukkām*, his legal treatise that he wrote for Kano's rulers and also in *Tazyīn al-waraqāt* (1813), his narrative of the jihad's military campaigns, Abdullāhi argued in favor of permitting the ransoming of war prisoners held by Sokoto forces. He viewed ransoming as a legitimate means for dealing with prisoners of war. In accordance with the Mālikī madh'hab, in *Ḍiyā' al-ḥukkām*, he listed five options for dispensing with non-Muslim adult male prisoners in accordance with the public interest. The prisoners could be executed, freed, ransomed, forced to pay the jizya, or enslaved. He left the fate of the prisoners to the discretion of the local imam. Abdullāhi's main concern was how the options dealing with war prisoners affected the division of the *ghanīma* (war booty). Depending on whether a captive was enslaved, executed, ransomed or freed affected the division of booty differently. Abdullāhi was concerned with explaining the legal options for dealing with war prisoners and the proper distribution of "profit" or "booty" if the ransoming option was exercised. Like 'Abdullāhi, Taal also took a rather pragmatic view to ransoming and did not object to the ransoming of non-Muslims as long as the profits were properly distributed.[52]

Bello outlined his opinion on ransoming in a letter that seems to be in response to Ya'qūb's request for advice on what to do with war prisoners captured by his forces. In this letter Bello retold the story of the victory over Tabūk and the debate over the fate of the prisoners taken by Muslim forces than ensued. The story of the victory over Tabūk is an important story in the oral tradition of the central Sudan.[53] According to Bello, the Prophet Muḥammad told the Companions that there were three possible fates for the captives that were acceptable to the interests of Islam. They could either ransom, enslave or execute the prisoners. According to Bello, the Prophet Muḥammad initially favored ransoming the prisoners but 'Umar argued that the prisoners should be executed. ‘Umar reasoned that the prisoners deserved neither ransoming nor enslavement and that they should be killed so that they would no longer be a threat. In Bello’s retelling of the story, after the Companions debated the issue, God descended a Qu’rānic verse that said to execute the prisoners. In advising Ya‘qūb on what to do with the prisoners in his custody, Bello counselled that the decision must be based upon the will of God, and the interests of Islam and of justice.[54] From this it can be inferred that Bello had advised Ya‘qūb to execute his prisoners instead of ransoming them. In Bello’s opinion it was clearly not prudent for Ya‘qūb to ransom back prisoners of war. The question in the early years of the jihad was not about the legitimacy of ransoming captives held by one’s forces, but whether or not it was pragmatic.

Conclusion

Muslim West African ransoming practices were based on interpretation of law and intellectual perceptions of the purposes and uses for ransoming. The discourse on ransoming, as a remedy for illegal enslavement, was linked to the intellectual discourse on slavery. West African scholars of the sixteenth to nineteenth centuries grappling with the issue of illegal enslavement were dealing with a complex situation. They were operating in an environment where there was increasing demand for slave labor over previous centuries in North Africa and the Americas, and especially in the nineteenth century, in West African markets. They were also dealing with a North African discourse and a changing southern Saharan discourse on the relationship between racial identity, unbelief, and enslaveability. In dealing with these issues, West African scholars drew upon and engaged with the Islamic intellectual cannon, the “discursive tradition” to develop advice, rooted in the Mālikī madh’hab, suitable for the socio-economic situations they were addressing. In this sense, they were balancing idealism with pragmatism. West African scholars and those familiar with the West African socio-political-religious environment, consistently reiterated that only unbelief was a legitimate reason for enslavement and that racial categorization was irrelevant. In the West African jihad era of the eighteenth and early nineteenth centuries, enslaveability was firmly based on perceived personal belief and not racial identity. Moreover in this time period, Muslim scholars, even if they held a narrow view of who they considered to be a freeborn Muslim, also advocated, through both their writings and their actions, a series of remedies for illegal captivity and subsequent enslavement of freeborn Muslims. These included moral suasion of both captors and government to prevent illegal enslavement, political reform, physical rescue of freeborn Muslims, and paying for the freedom of freeborn Muslims. Basing their intellectual thought on the intellectual cannon developed from at least the fifteenth century in order to address the socio-economic issues confronting their societies, the late eighteenth and early nineteenth century scholars argued that ideally individuals suspected to be freeborn Muslims ought to be granted free-release yet they recognized ransoming as a practical means for ensuring the freedom of freeborn Muslims. The only debate was on who should pay the ransoming costs and on the prudency of permitting the ransoming of enemy captives. On these questions, pragmatism also won out as the nineteenth century governments of the central Sudan passed the costs of ransoming from government coffers to private families and supported the ransoming of prisoners held by their own forces only when the prisoners did not pose a future threat.

Endnotes

1 Jennifer Lofkrantz, "Protecting Freeborn Muslims: The Sokoto Caliphate's Attempts to Prevent Illegal Enslavement and its Acceptance of the Strategy of Ransoming," *Slavery and Abolition,* 31:1 (2011), 109-27; Jennifer Lofkrantz and Olatunji Ojo, "Slavery, Freedom, and Failed Ransom Negotiations in West Africa, 1730-1900," *Journal of African History,* 53 (2012), 25-44; Olatunji Ojo, "[I]n Search of their Relations, To Set at Liberty as Many as They Had the Means: Ransoming Captives in Nineteenth Century Yorubaland," *Nordic Journal of African Studies*, 19:1 (2010), 58-76; Sylviane Diouf, "The Last Resort: Redeeming Family and Friends," in Sylviane Diouf (ed.), *Fighting the Slave Trade, West African Strategies* (Athens: Ohio University Press, 2003), 82-92.

2 Lofkrantz, "Protecting Freeborn Muslims," 109-110.

3 Talal Asad, *The Idea of an Anthropology of Islam* (Washington DC: Center for Contemporary Arab Studies Georgetown University, 1986), 14.

4 Scott S. Reese, "Islam in Africa/Africans and Islam," *Journal of African History,* 55:1 (2014), 19.

5 Adeline Masquelier, *Women and Islamic Revival in a West African Town* (Bloomington: Indiana University Press, 2009); Roman Loimeier, *Between Social Skills and Marketable Skills: The Politics of Islamic Education in 20th Century Zanzibar* (Leiden: Brill, 2009); Abdulkader Tayob, *Islam in South Africa: Mosques, Imams and Sermons* (Gainesville: University of Florida Press, 1999).

6 For a more detailed discussion on race and slavery in the Arab world and in the Maghrib see John Hunwick, "Islamic Law and Polemics over Race and Slavery in North and West Africa (16th -19th century)," in Shaun Marmon (ed.), *Slavery in the Islamic Middle East* (Princeton: Markus Weiner Publishers, 1999), 29-52; John Hunwick, "Arab Views of Black Africans and Slavery," presented at conference, "Collective Degradation: Slavery and the Construction of Race," Yale University, November 2003; Bernard Lewis, *Race and Slavery in the Middle*

East (Oxford: Oxford University Press, 1992); Chouki el Hamel, *Black Morocco: A History of Slavery, Race, and Islam* (Cambridge: Cambridge University Press, 2013).

7 James L.A Webb Jr., *Desert Frontier: Ecological and Economic Change along the Western Sahel 1600-1850* (Madison: The University of Wisconsin Press, 1995), 47-55.

8 Bruce S. Hall, "The Question of 'Race' in Pre-colonial Southern Sahara," *Journal of North African Studies*, 10:3/4 (2005), 339-367. Also see Bruce S. Hall, *A History of Race in Muslim West Africa 1600-1960* (Cambridge: Cambridge University Press, 2011).

9 Khalīl b. Ishāq, *Mukhtaṣar,* ed. and trans. Georges Henri Bousquet (Paris, 1962), 206-215.

10 Ishāq, *Mukhtaṣar,* 206-215. Further, the decision on what to do with one's share of captives rested fully with the owner. For example after one battle during the Moroccan invasion of Songhay, the qāḍī 'Ali ben Abdallah chose to free his captives whereas the qāḍī al-Mustafa brought his to Timbuktu and sold them. See Abd al-Rahmān al-S'adi, *Tārikh al-Sūdān*, trans. O. Houdas (Paris: Librairie d'Amerique et d'Orient Adrien-Masonneuve, 1964), 275-276.

11 Jonathan E, Brockopp, *Early Mālikī Law, Ibn 'Abd al-Ḥakkam and his Major Copendium of Jurisprudence* (Leiden: Bill, 2000), 144. Unlike the Sunni *madhāhib*, Shi'i fiqh continued to view slavery as a temporary condition and recommended that slaves be freed after a maximum of seven years in slavery. See for example the writings of the twelfth century Shi'i Iraqi scholar Ja'far ibn al-Hasan al-Muhaqqiq al-Hilli, *Droit Musulman: Recuil de lois concernant les Musulmans Schyites*, trans., Amédée Querry (Paris: Impremerie nationale, 1871) Vol. 2, 109.

12 For discussions on how Ibn Khaldūn's *Kitāb al-'ibar* was used by later Sahelian and Sudanese writers see Ralph Austen and Jan Jansen, "History, Oral Transmission, and Structure in Ibn Khaldun's Chronology of Mali Rulers," *History in Africa,* 23 (1996), 17-28; H.T Norris, *The Arab Conquest of the Western Sahara, Studies of the Historical Events, Religious Beliefs and Social Customs which Made the Remotest Sahara a Part of the Arab World* (London: Longman, 1986), 13-14; Raymond Taylor, "Of Disciples and Sultans: Power, Authority and Society in the Nineteenth-Century Mauritania Gebla" (Ph.D diss., University of Illinois at Urbana-Champaign, 1996), 23.

13 For more on the Hamitic hypothesis see Humphrey J Fisher, *Slavery in the History of Muslim Black Africa* (New York: New York University Press, 2001), 26-27; Hall, *A History of Race in Muslim West Africa*, 46-47.

14 Ibn Khaldūn, *The Muqaddimah: An Introduction to History*, trans., Franz Rosenthal (Princeton: Princeton University Press, 1967).

15 Bruce S. Hall and Charles C. Stewart, "The Historic 'Core Curriculum' and the Book Market in Islamic West Africa," in Graziano Krätli and Ghislaine Lydon (eds.), *The Trans-Saharan Book Trade, The Trans-Saharan Book Trade, Manuscript Culture, Arabic Literacy and Intellectual History in Muslim Africa*

(Leiden: Brill, 2011), 164. For more on al-Suyūtī's background and correspondence with West African scholars, see E. M Sartain, *Jalāl al-dīn al-Suyūtī: Biography and Background* (Cambridge: Cambridge University Press, 1975); and E. M Sartain, "Jalal ad-Din As-Suyuti's Relations with the People of Takrur," *Journal of Semetic Studies,* 16:2 (1971), 193-198.

16 Muḥammad al-Maghīlī, *Taj al-Din yajib 'ala-mulūk*, trans. T.H Baldwin, (Beyrouth-Liban: Imprimerie Catholique, 1932); John Hunwick (ed. and trans.), *Shari'a in Songhay The Replies of al-Maghīlī to the Questions of Askia al-hājj Muḥammad* (Oxford: Oxford University Press, 1985); John Hunwick, "Al-Maghīlī and the Jews of Tuwāt: The Demise of a Community," *Studia Islamica,* 61 (1985), 155-183.

17 Al-Suyūtī's defense of blacks is outlined in his treaty, *Raf' sha'n al-ḥubshān* (Raising the Status of the Ethiopians) and the abridged version, *Azhār al-'urūsh fī akhbār al-ḥubūsh* (The Flowers of the Throne Concerning Information about the Ethiopians). See 'Abd al-Raḥmān al-Suyūtī, *Raf' sha'n al-ḥubshān*, eds. Ṣafwān Dāwudī and Ḥassan 'Ubajī (Jedda: Dār al-qiblah li-'l-thaqāfa al-islāmiyya, 1991), and 'Abd al-Raḥmān al-Suyūtī, *Azhār al-'urūsh fī akhbār al-ḥubūsh*, ed.'Abd Allāh 'Īsā al-Ghazālī (Kuwait: Markaz al-makhṭūṭāt wa-'l-turāth wa-'l-wathā'iq, 1995).

18 Hunwick, "Al-Maghīlī and the Jews of Tuwāt," 155-183. His attitude towards dhimmī was not helped when his son was murdered in Tuwāt, allegedly by members of the Jewish community. See also Hunwick, *Shari'a in Songhay*, 31-39.

19 al-Maghīlī, *Taj al-Din yajib 'ala-mulūk*, 21. My emphasis.

20 Hunwick, "Islamic Law and Polemics over Race and Slavery in North and West Africa," 52-59; Chouki el Hamel, "The Register of the Slaves of Sultan Mawlay Isma'il of Morocco at the Turn of the Eighteenth Century," *Journal of African History,* 51:2 (2010), 89-98; Chouki el Hamel, "Race' Slavery and Islam in Maghribi Mediterranean Thought: The Question of the Haratin in Morocco," *Journal of North African Studies,* 7:3 (2002), 29-52; Hamel, *Black Morocco*, 155-185.

21 John Hunwick and Fatima Harrack eds and trans., *Mi'rāj al-Ṣu'ūd: Aḥmad Bābā's Replies on Slavery* (Rabat: Université Mohammed V Souissi Institute of African Studies, 2000).

22 For more on his personal history, see Paul Lovejoy, "The Context of Enslavement in West Africa: Aḥmad Bābā and the Ethics of Slavery," in Jane Landers and Barry Robinson (eds.), *Slaves, Subjects and Subversives: Blacks in Colonial Latin America*, (Albuquerque: University of New Mexico Press, 2006), 9-38; "Introduction" in John Hunwick and Fatima Harrack (eds. and trans.), *Mi'rāj al-Ṣu'ūd Aḥmad Bābā's Replies on Slavery* (Rabat: Université Mohammed V Souissi Institute of African Studies, 2000); el Hamel, *Black Morocco*, 82-83.

23 Al-Balbālī was from Tabelbala in present-day southern Algeria, studied in Walāta and Fez and taught in Kano, Katsina Timbuktu and Marrakesh. For more

information on him see John Hunwick ed., *Arabic Literature of Africa* vol. 2, *The Writings of Central Sudanic Africa* (Leiden: Brill, 1995), 25.

24 Hunwick and Harrack, *Mi'rāj al-Ṣu'ūd Aḥmad Bābā's Replies,* 28-29.

25 Ibid., 43-44.

26 Hall, *History of Race in Muslim West Africa 1600-1960*, 84.

27 'Uthmān or 'Abdullāhi b. Fodiye, *Taḥqīq al-'iṣma li-jamī'* Institute of African Studies, Ibadan C.A.D./20. Also see Muḥammad Bello, *Infāq al-Maysūr fī Tārikh bilād al-Takrūr*, ed. Bahiji Hadli (Rabat: Publications of the Institute of African Studies, 1996), 288-299. 'Uthmān b. Fodiye stated his injunction against the enslavement of Fulbe in his 1802 treatise, *Masā'il muhimma.* See Paul Lovejoy, "The Bello-Clapperton Exchange: The Sokoto Jihad and the Trans-Atlantic Slave Trade," in Christopher Wise (ed.), *The Desert Shore: Literatures of the Sahel*, (Boulder CO: Lynne Reiner Publishers, 2001), 201-229.

28 Hunwick and Harrack, *Mi'rāj al-Ṣu'ūd Aḥmad Bābā's Replies,* 53. See also 21.

29 For a discussion on the tension between Muslim rulers and scholars see Wael B. Hallaq, *The Origins and Evolution of Islamic Law* (Cambridge: Cambridge University Press, 2005), 178-194. See also Vincent J Cornell, "Ibn Battuta's Opportunism: The Networks and Loyalties of a Medieval Muslim Scholar," in Miriam Cooke and Bruce B Lawrence (eds.), *Muslim Networks from Hajj to Hip Hop* (Chapel Hill: The University of North Carolina Press, 2005), 31-51.

30 See ADH Bivar and M Hiskett, "The Arabic Literature of Nigeria to 1804: A Provisional Account," in *Bulletin of the School of Oriental and African Studies University of London*, 25 (1962), 143.

31 Muhammad Tukur, "Busuraa'u" in J. Haafkens, *Chants Musulmans en Peul* (Leiden: Brill, 1983), verse 8-15.

32 Muusa Kamara, *Florilège au jardin de l'histoire des noirs, Zuhūr al-Basātīn: l'aristocraties peule et la revolution des clercs musulmans, vallée du Sénégal*, ed., Jean Schmitz, trans., Saïd Bousbina (Paris: Centre National de Recherche Scientifique, 1998), 316-317.

33 Guy Nicolas, "Détours d'une conversion collective. Ouverture à l'Islam d'un bastion soudanais de résistance à une guerre sainte," *Archives de sciences sociales des religions,* 24, 48.1 (1979), 83-105; Muḥammad Bello, *Risāla ilā ahl al-ḥaramayn al-sharīfayn wa ilā ahl al-mashriq,* in 'Umar al-Naqar, *The Pilgrimage Tradition in West Africa* (Khartoum: Khartoum University Press, 1972), 142.

34 On the jihad movements in West Africa, see Martin Klein, "Social and Economic Factors in the Muslim Revolution in Senegambia," *Journal of African History,* 13:3 (1972), 419-441; Martin Klein, *Islam and Imperialism in Senegal* (Stanford: Stanford University Press, 1968); Michael Gomez, *Pragmatism in the Age of Jihad* (Cambridge: Cambridge University Press, 1992); Murray Last, "Reform in West Africa: The Jihad Movements of the Nineteenth Century," in Jacob Ajayi and Michael Crowder (eds.), *History of West Africa*, vol. 2, (London: Longman, 1974), 1-46; Mervyn Hiskett, *The Sword of Truth: The Life and Times of the Shehu Usuman dan Fodio* (New York: Oxford University

Press, 1973); John Hanson, *Migration, Jihad, and Muslim Authority in West Africa* (Bloomington: University of Indiana Press, 1996); Rudolph T. Ware III, *The Walking Qu'ran, Islamic Education, Embodied Knowledge and History in West Africa*, (Chapel Hill: University of North Carolina Press, 2014); and Paul E. Lovejoy, *Jihad in West Africa during the Age of Revolutions* (Athens: Ohio University Press, 2016).

35 See Bruce Mouser, "Walking Caravans," *Mande Studies,* 12 (2010), 19-104; Thierno Diallo, *Institutions politiques du Fouta Dyalon* (Dakar: IFAN, 1972); Winston McGowan, "The Development of European Relations with Futa Jallon and the Foundation of French Colonial Rule 1794-1897" (Ph.D. thesis, University of London, 1978); Jennifer Lofkrantz and Paul Lovejoy, "Maintaining Network Boundaries: Islamic Law and Commerce from Sahara to Guinea Shores," *Slavery & Abolition*, 36:2 (2015), 211-232.

36 For more on the constitutional set-up of the Sokoto Caliphate, see Murray Last, *The Sokoto Caliphate*, (London: Longmans, 1967); Hiskett, *The Sword of Truth*, 110-15; R.A. Adeleye, *Power and Diplomacy in Northern Nigeria 1804-1806* (London: Longman, 1971), 43–51; Philip Burnham and Murray Last, "From Pastoralist to Politician: The Problem of a Fulbe 'Aristocracy,'" *Cahiers d'Études Africaines,* 34, 133/135 (1994), 313-57; and Lovejoy, *Jihad in West Africa.*

37 'Uthmān b. Fodiye, *Bayān wujūb al-hijra 'alā 'i-'ibād*, ed. and trans., F.H. El-Masri (Khartoum: Khartoum University Press), 123; 'Umar Taal, *Bayān mā wa'qa'a*, eds, and trans., Mohamed Mahibou and Jean-Louis Triaud (Paris: Éditions du centre national de la recherches scientifiques, 1983).

38 Lofkrantz, "Protecting Freeborn Muslims," 109-127.

39 Lovejoy, "The Bello-Clapperton Exchange."

40 'Uthmān b. Fodiye, *Nūr-al-albāb*, trans. Ismail Hamet, *Revue Africaine*, 41 (1897), 300–303; 'Umar Taal, *Bayān mā waqa'a*, 98.

41 See Murray Last and M.A. Al-Hajj, "Attempts at Defining a Muslim in 19th Century Hausaland and Bornu," *Journal of the Historical Society of Nigeria,* 3:2 (1965), 231-49; Thomas Hodgkin, *Nigerian Perspectives: An Historical Anthology* (London: Oxford University Press, 1960), 198, n. 1; Louis Brenner, "Muhammad al-Amin al-Kanimi and Religion and Politics in Bornu," in John Ralph Willis (ed.), *Studies in West African Islamic History,* vol. 1, *Cultivators of Islam* (London: Frank Cass, 1979), 160-76; Louis Brenner, "The Jihad Debate between Sokoto and Borno: An Historical Analysis of Islamic Political Discourse in Nigeria," in J.F. Ade Ajayi and J.D.Y. Peel (eds.), *People and Empires in African History: Essays in Memory of Michael Crowder* (London: Longman, 1992), 21-45.

42 Taal, *Bayān mā waqa'a*, 107-138. See also the correspondence between Aḥmadu b. Aḥmadu and 'Umar Taal in Muhammad al-Hafīz al-Tidjāni, *Al-Hadj Omar Tall (1794-1864) Sultan de l'etat Tidjanite de l'Afrique Occidentale* trans., Fernand Dumont (Abidjan: Les Nouvelles Editions Africaines 1983).

43 Government avoidance of paying ransoms was common. See for example János J Varga, "Ransoming Ottoman Slaves from Munich (1688)," in Géza Dávid and Pál Fodor (eds.), *Ransom Slavery along the Ottoman Borders*, (Leiden: Brill, 2007), 169-183.

44 Muḥammad b. Aḥmad b. Juzay, *al-Qawānīn al-fiqhiyya* ed., Muḥammad Amīn al-Dannāwi (Beirut: Dar al-kutub a-Ilmiyya, 2006).

45 Ishāq, *Mukhtaṣar*, 1: 207-218.

46 'Uthmān b. Fodiye, *Irshād al-'ibād ilā ahamm masā'il al-jihād*, A/AR/43/2 Nigerian National Archives Kaduna (NAK), 44–45, Abdullāhi b. Fodiye, *Ḍiyā' al-ḥukkām*, in Shehu Yamusa, "The Political Ideas of the Jihad Leaders: Being Translation, Edition and Analysis of (1) Usal al-syayasa by Muhammad Bello, and (2) Diya' al-Hukkam by Abdullhah B. Fodio," (M.A. thesis, Bayero University Kano, 1975), 5. For an Arabic edition, see Abdullāhi b. Fodiye, *Ḍiyā' al-ḥukkām* (Zārīya: Maktab Nūlā, 1956)

47 Asad, *The Idea of an Anthropology of Islam*; Reese, "Islam in Africa/Africans and Islam," 19.

48 Jennifer Lofkrantz, "Intellectual Discourse in the Sokoto Caliphate: The Triumvirate's Opinions on the Issue of Ransoming ca. 1810," *International Journal of African Historical Studies*, 45:3 (2012), 385-401.

49 Ishāq, *Mukhtaṣar*, 1: 217-218.

50 According to USA Ismail and AY Aliyu, *al-qawl al-mawhūb fī ajwibat as'ilat al-amīr Ya'qūb*, was most likely written between 1809 and 1817 and therefore this letter was also most likely written during this time period due to the similar content. See USA Ismail and AY Aliyu, "Muhammad Bello and the Tradition of Manuals of Islamic Government and Advice to Rulers," *Nigerian Administration Research Project: Second Interim Report* (Zaria: 1975) 24-73. Reprinted in Uthman Sayyid Ahmad Ismail al-Bili, eds., *Some Aspects of Islam in Africa* (Reading UK: Ithaca Press, 2008) 65-80. However, it is possible that the letter was written any time before Bello's death in 1837.

51 For more on the political situations in both Kano and Bauchi see M.G. Smith, *Government in Kano* (Boulder: Westview Press, 1997); Joseph Smaldone, *Warfare in the Sokoto Caliphate: Historical and Sociological Perspectives* (Cambridge: Cambridge University Press, 1977), 36, 57, 75, H.A.S. Johnston, *The Fulani Empire of Sokoto* (London: Oxford University Press, 1967); Last, *The Sokoto Caliphate.*

52 John Ralph Willis, *In the Path of Allah: The Passion of Al-Hajj 'Umar* (London: Frank Cass, 1989), 170.

53 For a discussion of the importance of the story of the battle of Tabūk in the oral tradition of the central Sudan see Dalhatu Muhammad, "The Tabuka Epic (?) in Hausa: An Exercise in Narratology," in Ibrahim Yaro Yahaya, Abba Rufa'I and Al-Amin Abu-Manga (eds.), *Studies in Hausa Language, Literature and Culture: Proceeding of the Second Hausa International Conference* (Kano: Centre for the Study of Nigerian Languages, Bayero University, Kano, 1982), 397-415.

54 Muḥammad Bello to Yakubu Bauchi, undated, in Boubou Hama, "journal novembre 1964 à mars 1965," 397-400, Archives Nationales du Niger (ANN).

CHAPTER VI

European Captives and African Captors On The Gold Coast, 1869-1874

Olatunji Ojo

Introduction

In 1872, three years after Asante soldiers took four Europeans into captivity negotiations for their release had gone nowhere because the European contact agency, the British colonial administration in the Gold Coast colony, was reluctant to pay a huge ransom in exchange for the detainees' release. Therefore, Asante chiefs sent a messenger with a simple but tough message to the British Governor of the colony in Cape Coast, John Pope Hennessy: "[i]f the Governor has no money to pay the amount we ask let him give the Assin[,] Ackims [Akyem] and Decirras [Denkyira] in the place of the white men, and we will give them up to him. But not any less money."[1] For the chiefs it was not whether they could seize the captives but whether they should tie their release to a ransom payment or the return of coastal territories recently annexed by Britain. For the British, however, the bone of contention was the holding of Europeans for ransom at a time of European ascendancy in Africa. Britain later used the detention of the white captives as a justification for the conquest of Asante in 1874.[2]

Prior to the modern reports of European captives in the Nigerian oil-rich Niger Delta, the Nigeria/Cameroon Adamawa and Lake Chad region as well as Niger and Mali (see section 3 in this volume) the presence of Europeans held for ransom in West Africa has received little scholarship.[3] Thus European captives in Africa were historically associated with the Mediterranean and Maghrib regions.[4] Yet, evidence abound, dating back to the initial contacts between Europeans and West Africans, that Europeans were held variously as captives, hostages, prisoners, and as slaves and their release was sometimes tied to ransom payment. Without directly addressing the topic of ransom, Robin Law has criticized the erroneous notion that Europeans always had their way in West Africa pointing out how they relied on Africans for permission to settle, build forts, trade, and recruit labor among other activities. Recalcitrant Europeans faced sanctions for flouting African authorities.[5] Punishments ranged from expulsion to death, imprisonment, fine in lieu of deportation or death, or a combination of fine and deportation. At times, the fine was a form of ransom. Those who refused to pay sometimes died in captivity or were treated like slaves. In 1786, agents of the Dahomean king seized fifteen French and Portuguese traders and 80 of their Akan employees from their post in Porto Novo. M. Gourg, the head of the French post in Ouidah, paid £4,600 in ransom to secure their release. Four years later, Gourg himself was in trouble for violating certain local rules. He was "seized, bound, and exposed on the beach, till a canoe could be found to deport him. He died on "board the ship *Rouen*, en 'route towards Cape Francois."[6] Reports of European captives continued into the nineteenth century resulting in friction between West African chiefs and Europeans on the eve of European conquest of Africa.

In this three part essay on the neglected topic of European captivity in coastal West Africa, I explore why the freedom of European detainees in the Gold Coast was tied to ransom payment and what negotiations for their release reveal about the making of captives and ransoming negotiations in Africa. Due to the divergent conceptions of "ransoming" and "captives" among scholars and the often common conflation with related practices like "redemption," "manumission," "emancipation" of slaves part one clarifies how these are applied in this essay. Section two provides an overview of Afro-European relations on the Gold Coast before 1869 a period covering early European settlers in the late fifteenth to early sixteenth centuries and their commercial operations and how British ascendancy in the mid-nineteenth century altered the balance of power between Africans and Europeans. The third section discusses the seizure of white prisoners and the negotiation for their release within the context of contested Afro-European power relations. It argues that the seizure and demand for the ransoming of white captives indicates how some prisoners were seized not to be enslaved but for ransom payment.

Ransoming as Antidote to Enslavement

Studies on the ransoming of captives especially those concentrated on the Mediterranean world, the Maghrib and Central Europe have usually conflated the practice with the redemption of slaves and hostage negotiations. These are related but separate slaving tactics. The slave/captive divide is vital to understanding ransoming operations, the question of identity in slavery, and the concepts of legal/illegal enslavement and insider/outsider in Africa. One of the questions often raised is when does a person become a slave and when is a slave no longer a captive. Jennifer Lofkrantz separates slaves from captives based on post-release status and residency: captives returned to their old homes and to their original social status but former slaves remained within the slave society in a subservient position.[7] For captives, the period of detention (captivity) was relatively brief but longer for slaves. The passage of time subjected slaves to treatments that most captives never had to endure. Thus, by closely examining the anthologies of European detainees in North Africa, a distinction between captives and slaves would be that those held for a few months should be considered captives and those held for years were essentially slaves. Hence, one of the concerns for Africans was how to prevent the removal of captured relatives to distant locations and long detention due to the direct correlation between such removal and the possibility of enslavement.[8] In 1856, Samuel Crowther, a Yoruba liberated African and pastor cited the dangers of removal and enslavement as he cautioned European authorities to soften their anti-pawnship rhetoric. Human pawning, he said, was necessary "to ransom…captured relative from going into foreign slavery thus thousands have been kept back from being removed out of the country."[9]

Beyond where people lived, there is another distinction between captives and slaves. In West Africa, the process of turning captives into slaves involved some rituals. A new slave got a haircut, pair of clothing, and new names as part of the transition.[10] In 1730, Ayuba Suleiman Diallo of Bundu described his resentment when his captors shaved his and other captives' heads and beards, which in the Mandingo culture "make them appear like slaves taken in war."[11] The act of shaving a man's head and beard had similar ideological connotation as "castration." It reduced men to women, adults to children, aristocrats to commoners, and a freeborn to a slave. Furthermore, slaves also suffered humiliation when they were strip-searched in preparation for sale. Around 1700, William Bosman, a Dutch slaver in West Africa noted that ship surgeons thoroughly examined "naked men and women, without the least distinction of modesty."[12] While redemption, manumission and emancipation ended a period of enslavement ransoming obviated enslavement. Although each practice involved some form of payment ---financial or non-financial terms, both, prisoner exchange and any other compensation to captors or slave owners in exchange for the release of a captive or slave, ransom cost more because it returned captives to their original social status. A captive was worth more than his/her value as slave. Ransom payment gained a captive his freedom while the captor earned greater financial reward than selling the captive into slavery.[13] Due to these cultural nuances and to facilitate ransom payment captors held their victims near the place of captivity or moved to regionally designated meeting points like market towns and shrines where they could be easily found and ransomed. At times captives were transferred to mutually agreed third parties to broker ransom negotiations. In Yorubaland, Oko, an Egba town served this purpose for Oyo, Egba, Owu and Ijebu soldiers while Badagry, Ketu and Ilaro served Oyo, Egba, and Dahomean kingdoms. Comparable locations in North Africa included Algiers, Tunis, Tripoli and Marrakesh. The site of the market and negotiation rules had to be respected by all parties as described by Claude Meillasoux as the "same society" where hostile states shared common rules to facilitate prisoner release.[14]

For some states and individuals ransom was a legitimate source of revenue when the main purpose of taking a captive was to demand ransom rather than enslaving the victim. In such situations, ransom became a symbolic wealth transfer like tax or tribute payment by the weak to the powerful. Thus, during periods of declining slave prices, slavers targeted for seizure people with aristocratic and wealthy pedigrees from whom they could extract huge ransom. North African captors and slavers alike traded in their victims by transferring them to merchants in exchange for a fee. These merchants many of whom also sold slaves engaged in commercial speculation by buying European captives and selling them to higher bidders such that the cost of ransoming and redemption increased with each transfer or sale value. To ensure payment the merchants allowed captives they wanted ransomed to send letters to Europe as long as this would facilitate ransom or redemption payment.[15] In nineteenth century West Africa, ransom became highly profitable so that captors seized some people including Europeans whom they had no plans of enslaving or for whom they could not find a market to sell as slaves. Their seizure was to secure huge ransom payment. This trend foreshadowed contemporary piracy and kidnappings in Somalia and Nigeria where ransom is geared toward protecting captives from being murdered since they could not be enslaved.

Ransoming operations fluctuated due to the status and power of captives and their supporters. Powerful individuals were more effective in escaping bondage and when captured to be ransomed and avoid enslavement. They usually had the resources to pay ransom and/or secure support of their home states to regain freedom since strong states had better means of protecting their citizens from danger including bondage. Thus, while Europeans historically ransomed their citizens held by North Africans, as the balance of power began to tilt in Europe's favor from the seventeenth century they began to condemn such detentions and to deem ransom and redemption payment and enslavement of Europeans obnoxious and illegal.[16] As shown below these issues surfaced in the capture of Europeans by Asante and Britain's quest to free them *sans* ransom.

Afro-European Relations on the Gold Coast, 1471-1869

European merchants reached the Gold Coast in the late fifteenth century and over the next four centuries they played major roles in shaping the region's history from trading in gold and slaves to establishing agricultural estates and intervening in local and regional political and economic disputes. By 1874, the entire Gold Coast region and its hinterland had become a British possession. When the first Europeans, the Portuguese, arrived on the Gold Coast in 1471 they encountered a variety of Akan societies organized into multiple states. The region, named after its rich gold mines consisted of fifteen to twenty-five kingdoms of different sizes. In 1481, the Portuguese built the fort São Jorge da Mina, and later re-named El Mina after the Dutch seized it in 1637. The fort or castle was built on land purportedly leased from the *Denkyirahene* (king) of Denkyira. From here they traded in gold which they paid for in knives, beads, mirrors, rum, guns, ivory, and most importantly, textiles and slaves bought from the Bight of Benin and Sao Tomé to work the gold mines and plantations around the forts. News of the successful gold trade spread quickly, and later the British, Danes, Dutch, Swiss, and Germans also arrived.

The Gold Coast, as the name suggests, was known for the gold trade until the mid-seventeenth century when it also began to export slaves. Europeans recruited slaves from the interior for sale in the Americas and brought in slaves. Before long, the Gold Coast also became a hub for European trade with other parts of Africa. It re-exported to Europe and the Americas goods including slaves and textiles imported from the Bight of Benin and distributed to other African regions Europe-derived cowries, gold, textiles, metals, liquor and tobacco.[17] Drawing on the Atlantic slave trade voyage database embarkation figures remained generally low at about 2,000 slaves annually between 1660 and 1695. The number rose astronomically after 1695, perhaps due to the rise of Akwamu and Asante kingdoms, wars among coastal states and the consolidation of Akan trade networks, resulting in average annual export number of 2000 slaves between 1661 and 1695, 6000-12,000 slaves between 1696 and 1800 with periodic spikes in 1765-1775 and the late 1780s. By 1705, a Dutch trader wrote that gold had become so scarce that the Gold Coast should be renamed the "Slave Coast" after the neighboring Bight of Benin where slave was the most important item of trade since the seventeenth century.[18] On the eve of the British abolition the Gold Coast was still selling about 5000 slaves per year before export figures fell sharply to barely 200 slaves after the British abolition of the slave trade in 1807.[19]

If trade with Europeans was attractive and exciting it also produced tension when trade interfaced with politics. For the purpose of trade and defense, European traders built several forts or castles along the coastline to defend their various national and commercial interests against opposition from Africans and rival Europeans from land and the sea. The plurality of forts, about twenty-five in the eighteenth century, and less than ten miles from each other if we counted the smaller and less fortified posts scattered between major castles, was an indication of the political fragmentation and trade rivalry in the region. Indeed the guns mounted to defend the forts were pointed to the sea and not inland because potential threats from rival Europeans states and privateers were greater than the dangers posed by neighboring African communities.[20] On the African side, the plurality and smallness of coastal polities increased their vulnerability, hence the overlapping and shifting alliances with nearby European and African powers. Each state had trade and military pacts with Europeans allowing trade on its territory in exchange for military aid when necessary. Europeans and the more powerful inland kingdom of Asante exploited the fluid political situation on the Gold Coast to divide, rule and sometimes conquer the region.[21]

Though rich and powerful, the fact that Asante was landlocked meant its economic well-being depended on securing and maintaining access to the Atlantic Ocean. This was achieved in two ways: military conquest/annexation of coastal states and by peaceful negotiations for trade passage. Just as the Europeans had exploited fractured relations among the coastal states Asante also pursued both military and peaceful methods. In 1701, she conquered Denkyira kingdom, which rose to power in the seventeenth century. The conquest was significant because it gave Asante control of the gold-rich field of modern Grong-Ahafo, and direct contact with Dutch traders at Elmina. Other traditions claim Asante paid the Dutch about £9000 in debt owed by Denkyira chiefs thereby justifying the seizure of Elmina as a trade-off between Asante and the Dutch. The payment, the traditions indicate, symbolized Asante's ownership of Elmina. Whatever the claim, from the 1690s, if not earlier, Elmina was the commercial meeting point for Asante, Denkyira and Dutch traders and by 1699, a formal alliance existed between Asante and the Dutch West Indies Company. It is not unlikely the alliance contributed to Asante's conquest and annexation of Denkyira two years later.[22] Asante followed its success at Elmina with attacks on Asebu in 1726 and the Ga-state of Akyem in 1742. Access to the coast boosted Asante's power and brought it into closer but tense proximity to other powers, especially the kingdom of Fante and British traders around Cape Coast which Asante also sought to annex. Fante had British support as both became more scared of Asante after it launched successive attacks on coastal states between 1806 and 1816.[23]

Buoyed by its strong military and economy, Britain abolished the slave trade in 1807 after which it nudged other Europeans to follow suit. As the dominant foreign power on the Gold coast Britain expanded its territories by annexing other European forts and parts of Asante territory on the excuse that it was seeking to end local slave raids. Thus, after nearly four centuries of Afro-European relations, during which Africans mostly had the upper hand, the period after 1807 saw a shift in power relations in favor of Europeans, especially Britain.[24] For instance, in 1821 the British Company of Merchants at Cape Coast handed its forts on the Gold Coast (Cape Coast, Anomabu, Accra, Beyin, Dixcove, Kommenda, Winneba, Sekondi, Prampram and Tantamkweri), to the British Crown as represented by the Governor of Sierra Leone. Britain also added territories gained through military conquest and diplomatic negotiations from Fante, Denmark and Holland. At the same time Asante was unlike the coastal states. Though starting to feel the pinch of British imperial expansion, it still had the resources to fight back against foreign aggression. Thus, the 1842 report of the Select Committee of the British Parliament exaggerated in claiming that Britain had "very wholesome influence over a coast not much less than 150 miles in extent, and to a *considerable* inland; preventing within that range external slave-trade maintaining decent security, exercising a *useful* though *irregular* jurisdiction."[25] Truly, Britain reduced the Atlantic slave trade but its control, in 1842, did not extend "considerabl[y] inland." Asante and British armies clashed in 1824, 1826, 1863 and 1874 with Asante winning in 1824 and 1863 and Britain in 1826 and in 1874 when it earned a decisive victory turning Asante into a colony.

It is important to understand the economic basis of Anglo-Asante conflicts after 1807. Subsequent to the withdrawal of British slave traders and subsequent anti-slavery policies, Britain gradually reduced slave exports.

Although the collapse of the Atlantic slave trade had the ultimate paradoxical effect of encouraging domestic slave production and use, and a consistently high or stable slave price in some West African societies, one of its initial aftermath was a glut in the slave market with attendant low price, declining economy, and socio-economic chaos. For instance, in Yorubaland, the late development of alternatives to the slave trade led to an endured period of socio-economic disruptions. So slave raiding continued as a means of tribute payment and ransom extraction as warlords increasingly relied on revenue from ransom payment or the exchange of captives for a fee fixed usually more than the market value of the captive as a slave. In 1854, as warfare raged between various Yoruba factions, reports reaching the British consul in Lagos, Benjamin Campbell, showed that the captives were not sold into slavery because "slaves brought a very low price."[26] Hence soldiers kept the captives and "their friends [ransomed] them at a price considerably above the mere value of slave." The informant told Campbell the reason for seizing war prisoners was a "matter of money."[27] In Asante there were two elements to the British abolition of the slave trade. First, it led to a sharp drop in Asante's revenue from the slave trade. According to Paul Lovejoy and David Richardson "abolition had an initial severe impact on the commercial elites of the Gold Coast…in the form of a sudden decline in income… The severity of the decline in export earnings…had a strong, negative impact on the coastal economies and societies until the 1820s."[28] Second, though Asante had income from its extensive gold and kolanut fields and ivory trade and had potentials for engaging in palm oil production, the production of these products depended on a regular supply of slave labor. However, British abolitionism, which aimed at ending future slave raids made it potentially difficult for Asante to recruit new slaves for sale and productive ventures.[29] Therefore it should not be too surprising that Asante launched attacks on coastal societies repeatedly during the "initial crisis of adaptation."

However, economics alone do not explain Asante's challenges in the eighteenth and nineteenth centuries. There also existed political and strategic considerations. Asante's quest for access to the coast was intertwined with its territorial ambitions part of which was to subjugate and annex coastal territories and European settlements therein and deal with other enemies. Therefore, at the peak of its military power and expansionist ambitions in the early nineteenth century, what Asante did not need was an obstacle to its political momentum. Additionally, for Africans, the slave trade whether local, regional, or global was a tool for punishing real and imagined enemies. The slave trade was a form of exile for unwanted elements and for removing enemy soldiers so they would not return to battle. British anti-slavery stood in the way of achieving these goals. Violence intensified because Britain threatened Asante territorial integrity, hence its soldiers held some Europeans in captivity to strengthen their hands in negotiations with Britain—hardball politics *par excellence*. So, we must not assume that Asante did not resist British aggression and that European military superiority was not without its limitations. While on paper Britain possessed the military wherewithal to win a pitched battle, Asante soldiers adopted hit and run tactics launching offensive wars and retreating before Britain could mobilize decisive retaliation. In 1824, at Esamako, Asante soldiers killed the Governor of the Gold Coast, Charles MacCarthy who had led a British expeditionary force in contests related to Asante power to enforce its rules on satellite states and fugitive offenders.[30] While the various southern states on the Gold Coast, especially those in the Fante Confederation, did not want to give up their hold on trade brokerage between Europeans and hinterland societies they were also afraid of been subjugated by Asante. For the help rendered to Ameki, the king of Beyin, in a war against Fante in the early nineteenth century, Asante merchants earned the right to trade at the ports of Beyin near Fort Apollonia and Assin near Elmina at concessionary rates.[31] But the Asante also pointed to an older claim, subsequently referred to as the Elmina note, dating to about 1701 in which Dutch authorities pledged to pay the Asante king 960 Dutch guilders (20 gold ounces or £80 annually) for the right to trade at Elmina. With the payment Asante viewed Dutch as a junior partner and tenant on its property.[32] Asante assumed Britain would ignore the status quo. The nature of the payment and the full ramification of Asante-Dutch relations at Elmina formed part of the issues in the conflict with Britain

War between Asante and coastal states became more complicated as Holland, Denmark, Sweden, Portugal and Britain, whose merchants were invested in the region, supported coastal communities with weapons and logistics against Asante. By the 1860s the question was no longer whether Asante would invade the coast but when. In 1866, relations between Asante and coastal states and Europeans had so deteriorated that Denkyira, perhaps inspired by Europeans, blocked trade with Asante. Asante responded immediately with a punitive action. If Denkyira's trade embargo was enough provocation to warrant retaliation from Asante other events in the region made this even more urgent.

There was a radical shift in the Gold Coast political landscape and in Asante-European relations between 1867 and 1872. Whereas the Dutch forts on the Gold Coast were a colonial backwater in the nineteenth century, the British forts were slowly developed into a full colony, especially after Britain took over the Danish Gold Coast in 1850. The presence of Dutch forts in an area that became increasingly influenced by the Britain was deemed undesirable, and in the late 1850s British officials began pressing for either a buyout or trade of the Dutch forts, so as to produce more coherent areas of influences. In the Dutch political landscape of the time, a buyout was not a possibility, so a trade of forts was negotiated. In 1867, the "Convention between Great Britain and the Netherlands for an Interchange of Territory on the Gold Coast of Africa" was signed, in which Britain exchanged Beyin (Fort Apollonia), Dixcove (Fort Metal Cross), Sekondi (Fort Sekondi), and Komenda (Fort Komenda) for the Dutch posts of Mouri (Fort Nassau), Kormantin (Fort Amsterdam), Apam (Fort Lijdzaamheid), Accra (Fort Crevecoeur), Senya Beraku (Fort Goede Hoop), and Osu (Christiansborg). The transfer gave the forts on the western and eastern sides of the Sweet River and Cape Coast to Holland and Britain respectively.

The exchange was not as profitable as the Dutch had expected. Shortly after the transfer, Dutch officials secretly began negotiating a handover of all their forts, which they considered too costly to maintain, to Britain. In a February 1871 treaty, the whole Dutch colony in the Gold Coast was sold to Britain for 46,939.62 Dutch guilders in addition to some British holdings in Indonesia and the right to recruit labor from the Gold Coast.[33] The sore point of this last transfer was that it ceded to Britain Denkyira, Elmina and other coastal towns which Asante viewed as part of its territory. In a letter to the British Governor of Cape Coast, Herbert Ussher, the King (Asantehene) Kofi Karikari (British: Coffi Calicali) objected to the transfer

> the fort of that place [Elmina] ha[s] from time immemorial paid annual tribute to my ancestors to the present time by right of arms, annual tribute to my ancestors to the present time by right of arms, when we conquered Jutim Gackidi [Ntim Gyakari], King of Denkera. Jutim Gackidi having purchased goods to the amount of nine thousand pounds ... from the Dutch, and not paying for them before we conquered Jutim Gackidi, the Dutch demanded of my father, Os[e]i Tutu I., for the payment, who paid it full the nine thousand pounds ..., and the Dutch delivered the Elmina to him as his own, and from that time tribute has been paid us to this present time. I hope therefore your Excellency will not include Elmina in the change, for it is mine by right.[34]

Asante chiefs claimed payments from Holland constituted a tribute but the head of the Dutch post, Cornelis Johannes Marius Nagtglas, said it was "not a tribute, but more as a present to keep on friendly relations of trade... of slaves, gold dust, and ivory."[35] Irrespective of the nature of Asante-Dutch relations and whether the payment was a gift or tribute, land rent, tolls or tax there was no doubt that the Dutch had previously made some payments to the king of Asante. However, by denying or not being conversant of the full nature of the payment, Britain interpreted this as something that could be ignored. Thus, the Anglo-Dutch territorial pacts of 1867-1872 cost Asante its most profitable port town and gateway to the Atlantic world. Also by transferring Elmina to the Britain, an ally of Asante's foe, the Fante people, who controlled coastal trade, Asante would have to deal with Akan brokers whose cost of trade was 50% higher than what Asante used to pay at Elmina before the transfer. Thus, Britain was the enemy bent on undermining Asante's economy. Perhaps the conflict would not have escalated had Britain not ignored all of Asante's claims to Elmina and going as far as producing fake documents declaring that Asante "ceded" Elmina to the Dutch. The Asante council was split on how to respond to British expansion. A party wanted diplomacy but others refused.[36]

Politics, Economy, and Ransom Negotiations

Asante's opportunity to reassert control over the Gold Coast came in early 1868 and again in June 1869 when the kingdoms of Anlo and Akwamu around the lower Volta declared war on the Ewe of Krepi. In the ensuing war Asante soldiers sacked Krepi towns including Wegbe, Sokode, Anum and Ho and seized many captives including four European missionaries of the Basel Christian Mission: a Swiss, Frederick Augustus Ramseyer and his pregnant wife and infant son; a German, S. Johannes Kühne and Marie-Joseph Bonnat, a French trader based in Ho and one Smith, a merchant at Anum. They also seized Kuhne's African assistant, R[ichard?] Palmer and his wife, Kokoo, who worked for the Ramseyers. Ramseyer and Kühne had been in the Gold Coast since 1864 and 1866 but only six and two months respectively in Anum before their seizure.[37] At this stage Asante soldiers considered every European on British-held areas as British or their sympathizers and enemies of Asante.

The European captives did not think they would be in captivity for a long time. Initially they considered their seizure a mistake and assumed to be set free as soon as their identities became known to the captors, led by the State treasurer who was also a military commander, Adu Bofo, whom a British Officer, Francis Fuller, claimed "was a junior officer when he ventured on his Krepi campaign, but his successes had raised him to a position of great importance. He was now a large slave owner and had acquired a great wealth."[38] They were wrong because their seizure had both economic and political motivations and to ignore one was to escape the intricacies of ransoming negotiations. The Europeans' sin was that they had common cultural traits and by extension were the "kin" of the British with whom Asante was at war. It was no surprise that Asante chiefs interviewed some of the Africans captives at Anum to know if they (Europeans) sold or supplied weapons to Anlo people.[39] As an indication of the political factor, shortly after the Europeans were captured, Adu Bofo handed his nephew, Kwame Opoku, to the Krobo people, as guarantee the Europeans would be returned.[40]

The first five weeks of captivity saw the captives marching at a daily pace of about 30 miles as they journeyed from Krepi toward Kumasi. This was difficult for the European captives who had to walk in scorching heat from the blazing sun and burning houses and whose food consisted of local diets —yam, meat, beans, maize, cassava, and some milk for the children. Hence, it was not surprising that Ramseyer's baby had a fever and Kühne had a deep wound on his heel from heavy chains. The child died before the captives got to Kumasi in April 1870 after stopping in a village for several months. Their fate changed as soon as they entered Kumasi as what they expected to be a short detention dragged on for more than four years of captivity during which Ramseyer's wife gave birth to their second child in September 1870. However, if the Europeans considered their treatment poor they fared better than many freeborn citizens of Asante and much better than the hundreds of Krepi captives receiving little food.[41] During their four-year captivity in Kumasi, Kühne's claim that the allocation of only four and half dollars (£1 0s 3d) feeding allowance for him and two African captives every forty days was barely enough for food was reflective of his illness—he suffered from liver disease.[42] His fellow captive, Ramseyer, was of a different mindset. He claimed this particular food allowance was only for their early days in Kumasi and that the amount jumped to nine dollars for four captives every forty days. At other times he described regular visits and supply of food and other resources including gold dust and palm wine from local people, chiefs, the king and Queen Mother. Though the Ramseyers lost their child during the early days of captivity they had another one shortly afterwards. Also in 1871, they were allowed to rehire Kokoo, their old helper, who though captured together but subsequently separated and then reunited, to help with baby care duties.[43] They also had separate apartments and had permission to communicate with and receive gifts from the coast. They were allowed to receive the *Daily Telegraph*. Once they received "soap, metal plates, knives and forks, preserved meats, ham, cheese, tea, sugar, biscuits, and, above all, writing materials; gold dust, in value £22…and three umbrellas."[44] Eventually, they also had a private house built for them, two servants and freedom to preach and establish farms. Perhaps impressed with the house they also made furniture and built houses for the king. With this, it is clear these were special captives.

One reason for the long captivity was that they became hostages of Euro-Asante relations as their release was predicated on Britain recognizing Asante coastal interests. The captors also wanted a huge ransom. Even though this case is unique in that it involved Europeans detained in West Africa, how Asante chiefs, especially Adu Bofo, the *Gyaasewahene* (Treasurer) and officer in the Asante army viewed the situation reinforces the argument that in West Africa politics was also central to ransoming operations.[45] These chiefs delayed the release of the captives by stalling ransoming negotiations as a tactic to forcing concessions out of Britain including ending Fante attacks on Asante traders, releasing Asante captives detained by coastal societies and ending the trade embargo placed on Asante since 1863.[46] As we shall see below, the captives stayed long in captivity because their allies: the Basel Mission and both the Dutch and British governments refused to pay what they viewed as an exorbitant ransom fee and could not compel Bofo to release them.[47]

Like many ransoming cases, plans for negotiations to free the Europeans commenced after they were traced to Kumasi three months after their seizure. The captives were detained in a special house and had permission to contact their friends. On 21 October 1869, four months after their seizure, one of the captives, Kühne, met a man from Cape Coast, who had brought letters and some champagne for the king as negotiations to release the captives commenced. Six months later, in Kumasi, the captives again received a letter purportedly meant for them but which somehow was intercepted by the Asantehene which again confirmed knowledge of their captivity, information about the captor, and willingness to pay ransom. Written by David Asante of the Basel Mission, the letter highlights other aspects of ransoming operations such as the possibility of release taking place at the place of seizure and the value of frontier towns as spots for gathering information about relatives taken in battle. In his words

> We have taken all possible pains since your captivity to effect your deliverance. Twice have we sent messengers to the Ashantee camp offering money for your release, but in vain. I have been sent to Begoro, on the frontier of Akem, to try and come into communication with you, as up to the present… we have only heard of you by reports. I give the bearer a pencil, paper, and scissors that you may write; or…, send some of your hair, as an assurance that you are still alive.[48]

With lack of success on the part of the Basel Christian Mission, the British colonial administration for Gold Coast who now had responsibility for Krepi following cession by the Dutch took charge for securing release of the captives. One of the first decisions taken was that Britain took possession of

Asante captives on the Gold Coast including Bofo's nephew whom British officials retrieved from Krobo chiefs and moved to Cape Coast in late 1869. The plot, it seemed, was to swap these captives for the Europeans in Kumasi. Hence, in June 1870, the British governor of the Cape Coast, John Pope Hennessy released and sent back to Kumasi, a batch of Asante prisoners seized in a previous Anglo-Asante war around Akem with a promise to free more Asante captives upon the release of the Europeans.[49] At another time, he sent to the Asantehene a gold embroidered silk worth about £100 to facilitate release of the captives.[50] Another thirty Asante captives released by the British returned home in September 1870. Yet no serious negotiation took place for a long time due to two separate but related reasons. First, negotiations began late because Adu Bofo, whose troops had seized the captives, returned late from battle. Asante chiefs could also be hard negotiators wanting to extend negotiations and extract more concessions. Perhaps it was no surprise that Ramseyer "considered the capacity and intelligence of the Asante to be far superior to that of other Negroes."[51] It is interesting that while Asante authorities claimed they would not negotiate behind Adu Bofo's back evidence suggests they did and had agreed to demand about 100 ounces of gold in ransom for each European captive or £1440 for the four and that though the king might not want to attach "ransom" to the release of the captives "[b]ut money was an important thing in the eyes of the chiefs."[52]

On 4 September 1871, Adu Bofo entered Kumasi triumphantly two years after the missionaries were taken into captivity. Although his campaign was less successful than he planned since he lost more than 1000 men, he still returned with wealth in booty, slaves and skulls as war trophies. Perhaps, with some exaggeration, his troops arrived with over 2000 captives, mostly women and children. The king was impressed with Bofo's victory that he awarded him twenty *peregens* of gold, £162, three gold bracelets, two large umbrellas, 20 sheep and 20 loads of salt and liquor among others.[53]

Days after Bofo returned home, European officials on the Gold Coast sent to Kumasi one Henry Plange, a native clerk and Prince John Owusu-Ansa, an educated, Christian member of the Asante royal family, to negotiate peace between Elmina and Kumasi and for the release of the captives. Plange represented Dutch authorities while Ansa was the agent of the British administration. The choice of these two men as negotiators must be considered significant and tactical. As I have argued elsewhere, depending on the circumstances, a captor had more cards to play in ransoming negotiations. To the extent that failed negotiations meant the enslavement of captives and for Europeans in West Africa, death, pressure was usually on a captive's friends to agree to pay ransom for they usually put a higher premium on the life of the captive than the material value of ransom. The practice was to keep the captor interested in reaching an agreement by offering attractive payments. In Africa, where kinship was the engine of interpersonal relationship ransom brokers were usually men and women of influence with the captor.[54] The choice of local personnel was to remind Asante chiefs of past assistance o Asante subjects, including training Owusu-Ansa in Britain in the 1830s and the king's own grandmother released after her capture in the war of 1826.[55]

A related negotiation tactic was to put pressure on Asante by threatening its citizens held by the British. For instance, in December 1871, Opoku, Bofo's nephew, held by the British in Cape Coast sent a letter to Asante chiefs requesting that the Europeans be released so he could gain his freedom and return home.[56] Ransom negotiations opened a window into Asante official policy making process and how complex this could be depending on the issues at stake. In an essay on the Sokoto Caliphate, Lofkrantz highlights divisions among policy makers with each faction basing its decision on sound legal and historical precedent. As Sokoto leaders discussed whether ransoming should be granted to war prisoners the two most senior leaders of the Caliphate advised different actions. Mohammadu Bello instructed one of his senior lieutenants, the Emir of Bauchi to kill enemy prisoners while his uncle Abudullahi Fodio provided for the ransoming of prisoners irrespective of their loyalty. Lofkrantz attributes their views to differences between a pragmatic Bello who had to deal with rebellion in his territory and an idealist Fodio interested in raising money for the caliphate.[57] There are some similarities between Sokoto and Asante in their handling of ransoming decisions.

At a meeting of the Asante chiefs and the negotiators for Britain attended by the Asantehene, Adu Bofo, the Queen Mother, provincial kings from Bekwi, Duabin, Mampon and Fommena, and senior military officers among others held in the summer of 1872 the Asantehene told Plange that he and his chiefs would be satisfied with the payment of £1000 in ransom. However, the king was alone. Soon after he announced his decision there was murmuring and the meeting adjourned. Bofo rejected the king's offer instead demanding 1800 ounces of gold (£6480) as ransom. After more negotiations a faction within the council fixed ransom at 600 *peregens* or £1500. Four months later, another wing of the ruling class said the minimum amount payable in ransom was £2000.[58] The king was unhappy with this new demand saying it was too high but the chiefs ignored him saying emphatically "we will keep the white men…if the said amount was not…sent to redeem [sic] them."[59] The multiplicity of opinion within the Asante council symbolized the degree of opinions in the kingdom making it more difficult for the king to negotiate meaningfully with people outside the kingdom. By extension it was evidence of the king not being in full control of his subordinates and the policy process.

The tension at the meetings of Asante chiefs was palpable enough that Plange hurried back to Elmina to submit his report. He advised the Dutch government to pay the £1000 fee set by the king "for the expenses that the captives have occasioned at Coomasie." Since Britain had taken over Elmina, Plange's report was sent to Charles Salmon, the acting British administrator, who urged his boss, Governor John Pope Hennessy to pay the chiefs all they wanted (£2000) to speed up release of the captives.[60]

It is unclear why Asante chiefs failed to reach an agreement but it seems they discussed the merits of confronting British power. Lofkrantz and I have argued elsewhere that whether societies or individuals chose to release a captive or contest unsuccessful ransom negotiations depended partly on the opportunity cost of the alternative option/s or the reward from lack thereof.[61] One can apply the same theory to the choices facing Asante chiefs. With the military defeat of 1863 still fresh in his mind and aware that he risked more losses should there be a military showdown, the king's desire for a lower ransom fee may have been a ploy to forestall potential British attack. Another way of looking at the tension is that the king whose revenue came more from trade, taxes, and other royal benefits including annual stipends from the British, had more to lose from war with Britain.[62] For instance, despite his frustration with the loss of Elmina it was not lost on the Asantehene that Britain continued to pay his annual stipend of twenty-four ounces of gold (£80) and possibly double the amount on condition he abstained from any aggressive action against coastal states allied to Britain.[63] The king could also have remembered how in 1826, after the second war with Britain, the latter released elite Asante captives including his (king) grandmother and other princesses without ransom. Paradoxically, many of the king's subordinates were less concerned vowing to attack British territory on the coast and the king had no choice but to concede. The military whose power derived from warfare wanted opportunities for war. In a letter to the British administrator on 20 February 1872, the king wrote: "Tell the governor that I and my great men have decided that the treaty of peace shall be entered upon as soon as the ransom is paid to Adu Bofo, and not before."[64]

At the British colonial office in Cape Coast, Governor Hennessy, after consulting with his official messenger to Kumasi, Ansa, agreed to pay £1000 in addition to reopening trade, and releasing Adu Bofo's nephew, held by the government. But Hennessy also had a concern: he did not want the government to entertain the idea of exchanging Europeans for money. Specifically, Hennessy did not want to appear parsimonious in the matter of ransom for the Europeans though he also expressed fear his action could become a precedent either for Asante to detain Europeans in future and demand ransom or to give Europeans the impression that Britain would be there to defend them under all circumstances including paying ransom. Specifically he was concerned other European personnel could wander into the Gold Coast interior where they could be captured and yet expect diplomatic assistance from the government. With these prognoses Hennessy preferred not to call the payment to Asante "ransom" but to call it "compensation" for Bofo's expenses for caring for the captives and his wars.[65] Consciously or not the Asantehene shared the Governor's sentiment. He agreed to an arrangement that to the British the payment might look like a present, while his own Asante subjects would consider it a ransom. However, if Hennessy wanted to pay cash, the king, who also had his own political calculations including proving his mettle to the war party with plans to invade some southern states, wanted to be paid in arms.

When report reached Kumasi of the British government unwillingness, if not reluctance, to pay ransom, Bofo sent a letter to Salmon, stating that since he had "made great war expenses and caught [the captives]" he [Bofo] will not release them "without selling or asking a ransom." He reiterated that ransom payment for the Europeans was 800 *peregens* or 1800 ounces of gold.[66] Expectedly, by the end of 1872, three and a half years into the seizure Asantehene Karikari was ready to accept Britain's offer of £1000 in ransom provided it was paid in assortments of cash and goods: half in goods and the other half in gold dust or cash.[67]

There were other underlying reasons why Britain would not pay ransom. Apart from the fear that ransom payment could give the Africans the upper hand in their dealing with Europeans British officials claimed they had no ground for interfering since the prisoners were neither British subjects nor were they seized on British territory. They also added that the war resulting in the seizure of the four Europeans was fought between Asante and coastal states and not with Britain or its allies. Therefore, if on one hand Secretary of State Kimberly threatened to stop the stipend paid to the Asantehene (£80 per annum) he also warned Europeans operating in the region that if they venture beyond the coastal area "the government would not be responsible for their safety nor undertake to ransom them if taken captive by tribes in the interior."[68]

We do not know why Bofo set a huge price but there is one possibility. As the Treasurer, who, according to Ivor Wilks, "controlled the overall budgetary aspects of finance within the framework of general policy laid down by the Councils, and it was he who had to authorize all payments" it was also his duty to collect tributes.[69] Therefore since the seizure of the captives resulted in the course of affirming the tributary status of coastal states and European merchants and securing rent payment, British expansion was a direct assault on his [Bofo] office. For instance, he complained that some communities in the greater Asante region like "Asen, Akem, Akra, and Akuapem, which all formerly belonged to Ashantee, had been drawn over to serve the white men." When the king said this was an old complaint not worth reopening Bofo replied

> the right thing would be to regain our authority over these tribes. I have been to war, I have gained victories, used much powder, and lost more than a thousand men, and now am I to give up all that has been gained? No!...never, never will I let these prisoners go free! never, I say ...without a ransom.[70]

There was also the nationality of the captives. In economic terms, there was a popular assumption in Africa that Europeans be they merchants, diplomats, or missionaries possessed substantial wealth or had wealthy associates and could afford to make huge payments. As several chapters in this volume Europeans were often targeted because they or their families and employers could afford to pay huge ransom. This is certainly the case based on contemporary reports from Nigeria, the Sahel, the Middle East and Somali. This attitude ran deep in Africa. In a similar case, in 1862, a Yoruba chief had seized one Edward Roper, an agent of the Church Missionary Society whom he suspected of aiding a rival state. As a high-value captive, the chief, Ogunmola (Ibadan deputy chief) detained Roper vowing to sell him. When told no market existed for white captives he replied sarcastically that Roper would be a good poultry keeper.[71] But this was a ploy to wear the captive down emotionally. Before long Ogunmola set ransom at 200 bags of cowries (£200), 200 guns (c. £216), and 200 kegs of gunpowder at a time a prime slave cost around ten bags of cowries.[72] In Asante, the chiefs wanted to know if the captives were related to Queen Victoria of England; the implication being that Britain could afford to pay big ransom and that the captives were liable for the sins of the British government.[73]

Mistrust was an issue in Anglo-Asante ransom negotiations. Neither party trusted the other. In Asante some people believed the British governor could afford to pay huge ransom on the captives and that the reason he did not pay was stinginess. Others like Bofo's representative and the king's steward thought the governor had received from London the original sum of £6480, and only wanted to pay £1000 and take for himself the balance. The British and there Fante allies also viewed Asante chiefs negatively.[74] At a meeting of the Gold Coast Legislative Council on 12 October 1872, a member, Honorable George Blankson, a Fante merchant, doubted if the captives would be released after ransom payment for he viewed Asante people as "treacherous and not to be depended on." Another member, Colonel Forster, wanted Britain to send ransom to Prah under escort to exchange for the captives while the Chief Judge was concerned disagreements among Asante chiefs could sabotage discussions at the last minute.[75] These views by members of the Gold Coast Legislature previewed what Wilks later called "political polarization" between the "peace" and "war" parties forcing the king to be indecisive—a usual British accusation against African chiefs during imperialism.[76]

In late 1872, Britain and Kumasi reached a deal to send the captives to a half way station near Prah River where an Asante agent would release them and receive ransom sent from Cape Coast. On 9 November 1872, Karikari sent the captives to Fomena on the Prah River, and a message to the British administrator that £1000 should be paid to Asante agents in Cape Coast. A week later the captives reached Fomena. Before they left Kumasi they redeemed their two African helpers, Palmer and his wife, Kokoo by paying six *peregens* ($216) drawn on the Basel Mission account. The money was considered a loan to the Palmers who pledged their two houses in Accra and promised to repay the loan within a year.[77]

As soon as the captives left Kumasi the British administrator moved the negotiation post now demanding the captives must reach Cape Coast where ransom payment would also take place.[78] Why did Asante chiefs hurriedly release the captives after holding them for three years? Were the chiefs afraid of war with Britain and wanted the captives out of Kumasi as a preventive tactic? Did the hawks in Asante suddenly realize that ransom would not be paid if the captives remained in Kumasi? It is difficult to know which of these two or other factors made Asante to open the door to a peaceful resolution. The fact that one of the captives was very sick and reportedly near death could have convinced Kumasi that nothing would be gained from his death. Asante chiefs also could have acted in good faith since part of the discussion was that the release of the white captives would be accompanied by the release of more Asante captives in British prisons. In any case, Kumasi was outmaneuvered by releasing the captives prior to receiving cash payment or prisoner exchange. As the European captives journeyed toward the coast a British force headed in the opposite direction to face an advancing Asante army. The two armies clashed in 1873/74 when Britain defeated Asante, seized the captives, and led them as freed men to Cape Coast.

Conclusion

The stalled ransom negotiation between Britain and Asante officials harks to the debate on the commercial transition from slavery to "legitimate" commerce and the attendant "crisis of the monarchy" in nineteenth century West Africa popularized by Anthony Hopkins. The theory was that the transition weakened African kings as it transferred more power to their subordinates. But the "crisis," if any, in Asante was different from what Hopkins masterfully described for Yorubaland.[79] In Yorubaland, the crises derived from the lack of alternative trade products after the end of the Atlantic slave trade and the struggle for power by a new crop of elite composed of educated ex-slaves, soldiers, and merchants at the expense of old chiefs and aristocratic families.[80] In Asante, the gold and kolanut trade predated and coexisted with the slave trade, and when the latter ended these previous trades not only continued but expanded. The transition, thus, was less about what to sell in place of slaves but how to sustain a growing military power, supply slaves to the gold and kolanut fields, and maintain access to overseas trade. British intervention was antithetical to Asante political, commercial and cultural ambitions. Therefore, the seizure of European captives was symbolic of a state seeking to assert its autonomy and position itself as a regional power. British imperial expansion in the Gold Coast forced Asante into a defensive posture and this emboldened the military wing of Asante ruling elite. Asantehene Karikari was a candidate of the war party though his officers did not see him as forceful enough in his dealings with Britain and in maintaining the territorial integrity of the kingdom. By seizing the European captives Asante chiefs thought they could exert diplomatic pressure on the British Government to return Elmina. As Karikari watched the ransom negotiation dragged on he wanted a quick resolution to ward off possible British assault. The soldiers on the hand refused to budge. In a secret meeting with Plange, the Asantehene confessed it was his chiefs, not him, who wanted huge ransom and he could not stop them. Quoting the King, Plange writes, "I am willing to let these white men go…free, without any cent, but the chiefs stick upon the said money, and I beg the chiefs …that as I wish to have peace with the coast, the amount of £4000 you [chiefs] said to be reduced has to come to the amount of £2000."[81] The captives confirmed the king's powerlessness. Ramseyer reported the king "was in favor of peace, but his overbearing chiefs insisted on a ransom in gold."[82]

In furtherance of the research on the intricacies of ransoming operations, reasons why ransoming failed, and responses to unsuccessful ransom negotiations, this paper also explores the interface between ransoming practices and the decision making process in the era of commercial, political and social transition when perhaps as many people were held for ransom as for enslavement. The end of the Atlantic slave trade raised the need to generate more revenue from ransom. In Kumasi, the king could not impose himself on the society so he caved to his army's demand for ransom. It will be interesting to know, due to unsuccessful or prolonged ransoming negotiations, how many detainees became slaves or died in captivity.

Endnotes

1 Henry Plange, journal, September 1872, in Henry Brackenbury, *The Ashanti War: A Narrative*, 2 vols. (Edinburgh: William Blackwood, 1874), Vol. 1, 43-48.

2 Frederick Boyle, journal, 14 January 1874 in Frederick Boyle, *Through Fanteeland to Coomasie: A Diary of the Ashantee Expedition* (London: Chapman and Hall, 1874), 271-73.

3 Also see Cristina Barrios and Tobias Koepf, eds., *Re-mapping the Sahel: Transnational Security Challenges and international Responses* (Paris: EU Institute for Security Studies, 2014) and Jeremy Keenan, *The Dying Sahara: US Imperialism and Terror in Africa* (London: Pluto Press, 2012).

4 For a representative literature, see Mathew Carey, *A Short Account of Algiers* (Philadelphia: J. Parker, 1794); Robert Adams and S. Cock, *The Narrative of Robert Adams, an American Sailor* (London: John Murray, 1816); Paul Baepler, ed., *White Slaves, African Masters: An Anthology of American Barbary Captivity Narratives* (Chicago: University of Chicago Press, 1999); Ellen G. Friedman, "Christian Captives at 'Hard Labour' in Algiers 16th to 18th Centuries," *International Journal of African Historical Studies,* 13:4 (1980), 616–32; Friedman, *Spanish Captives in North Africa in the Early Modern Age* (Madison: University of Wisconsin Press, 1988); James Brodman, *Ransoming Captives in Crusader Spain: The Order of Merced on the Christian-Islamic Frontier* (Philadelphia: University of Pennsylvania Press, 1986); Kate Fleet, *European and Islamic Trade in the Early Ottoman State: The Merchants of Genoa and Turkey* (Cambridge: Cambridge University Press, 1999); Maria Garcés, *Cervantes in Algiers: A Captive's Tale* (Nashville: Vanderbilt University Press, 2002); Linda Colley, *Captives: Britain, Empire, and the World, 1600-1850* (London: Jonathan Cape, 2002); Jaques Heers, *The Barbary Corsairs: Warfare in the Mediterranean, 1480-1580* (Barnsley: Greenhill Books, 2003); Géza Dávid and Pál Fodor, eds., *Ransom Slavery along the Ottoman Borders: Early Fifteenth – Early Eighteenth Centuries* (Leiden: Brill, 2007); and François Moureau, *Captifs en Méditerranée (XVI-XVIIIe siècles), Histoires, Récits et Légendes* (Paris: Presses de l'Université Sorbonne, 2008) and Daniel Vitkus (ed.), *Piracy, Slavery, and Redemption: Barbary Captivity Narratives from Early Modern England* (New York: Columbia University Press, 2001).

5 Robin Law, "'Here is No Resisting the Country': The Realities of Power in Afro-European Relations on the West African 'Slave Coast,'" *Itinerário,* 10:2

(1994), 50-64; and David Eltis, *The Rise of African Slavery in the Americas* (Cambridge: Cambridge University Press, 2000), 145-50.

6 Richard F. Burton, *A Mission to Gelele King of Dahome* (London: Tinsley Brothers, 1864), II: 394, 405 and Law, "'Here is No Resisting the Country'."

7 Jennifer Lofkrantz, "Protecting Freeborn Muslims: The Sokoto Caliphates Attempts to Prevent Illegal Enslavement and its Acceptance of the Strategy of Ransoming," *Slavery and Abolition,* 31 (2011), 109-27.

8 Samuel Crowther to Thomas Hutchinson, September 10, 1856, CA2/031, Church Missionary Society Archives (CMS); Edward Alpers, "The Story of Swema: Female Vulnerability in 19th Century East Africa," in Claire Robertson and Martin Klein (eds.), *Women and Slavery in Africa* (Portsmouth: Heinemann, 1997), 185-219; Fred Morton, "Pawning and Slavery on the Kenya Coast: The Miji Kenda Case;" and James Giblin, "Pawning, Politics and Matriliny in Northeastern Tanzania," in Paul E. Lovejoy and Toyin Falola (eds.), *Pawnship, Slavery, and Colonialism in Africa* (Trenton: Africa World Press, 2003), 239-66.

9 Crowther to William Jowett, 22 February 1837, CA1/079/2, CMS.

10 See Minutes of the Church Missionary Conference on Slavery, Lagos, March 1880, CMS (Y) 2/2/3, Nigeria National Archives, Ibadan (NAI).

11 Phillip D. Curtin, "Ayuba Suleiman Diallo of Bondu," in Curtin (ed.), *Africa Remembered: Narratives by West Africans from the Era of the Slave Trade* (Madison: University of Wisconsin Press, 1967), 40.

12 William Bosman, *A New and Accurate Description of the coasts of Guinea, divided into the Gold, Slave, and the Ivory Coasts* (London: James Knapton, 1705), 363-65.

13 Sylviane Diouf, "The Last Resort: Redeeming Family and Friends," in Diouf (ed.), *Fighting the Slave Trade: West African Strategies* (Athens: Ohio University Press, 2003), 82-92; Olatunji Ojo, "'[I]n Search of their Relations, To Set at Liberty as Many as They Had the Means": Ransoming Captives in Nineteenth Century Yorubaland," *Nordic Journal of African Studies,* 19 (2010), 58-76; Lofkrantz, "Protecting Freeborn Muslims;" Lofkrantz, "Intellectual Discourse in the Sokoto Caliphate: The Triumvirate's Opinions on the Issue of Ransoming, ca.1810," *International Journal of African Historical Studies*, 45 (2012), 385-401; and Lofkrantz and Ojo, "Slavery, Freedom, and Failed Ransom Negotiations in West Africa, 1730-1900," *Journal of African History,* 53 (2012), 25-44.

14 Claude Meillassoux, *The Anthropology of Slavery: The Womb of Iron and Gold* (Chicago: University of Chicago Press, 1991), 103-109; and Ojo, "'[I]n Search of their Relations," 62.

15 Attila Ambrus, Eric Chaney, and Igor Salitskiy, "Pirates of the Mediterranean: An Empirical Investigation of Bargaining with Transaction Costs" (22 December 2011), *Economic Research Initiatives at Duke* (ERID) Working Paper No. 115. Available at SSRN: http://ssrn.com/abstract=1954149

16 Lofkrantz and Ojo, "Slavery, Freedom, and Failed Ransom Negotiations."

17 See Johannes M. Postma, *The Dutch in the Atlantic Slave Trade, 1600-1815*

(Cambridge: Cambridge University Press, 1990); and Robin Law (ed.), *The English in West Africa: The Local Correspondence of the Royal African Company of England*, 1681-1699, 3 vols. (Oxford: Oxford University Press, 1997-2007).

18 Willem de la Palma (Elmina) to Association of Ten, 5 September 1705, West Indies Company Papers, Wilberforce Institute, University of Hull.

19 Rebecca Shumway, *The Fante and the Transatlantic Slave Trade* (Rochester: University of Rochester Press, 2011), 25-52 and *Voyages: The Trans-Atlantic Slave Trade* Database, www.slavevoyages.org

20 Albert Van Dantzig, *Forts and Castles of Ghana* (Accra: Sedco Publishing, 1999).

21 John K. Fynn, *Asante and its Neighbors, 1700-1807* (London: Longman, 1971); Ray Kea, *Settlements, Trade and Politics in the Seventeenth-Century Gold Coast* (Baltimore: John Hopkins University, 1982); Harvey Feinberg, *Africans and Europeans in West Africa: Elminans and Dutchmen on the Gold Coast During the Eighteenth Century* (Philadelphia: American Philosophical Society, 1989); Postma, *Dutch in the Atlantic Slave Trade*; Law, *English in West Africa*; Shumway, *Fante*; and Randy Sparks, *Where the Negroes Are Masters* (Cambridge, MA: Harvard University Press, 2014).

22 T. C. McCaskie, "Denkyira in the Making of Asante," *Journal of African History,* 48 (2007), 1-25.

23 Edward Reynolds, *Trade and Economic Change on the Gold Coast*, 1807-1874 (London: Longman, 1974); and Schumway, Fante.

24 See Law, "'Here is No Resisting the Country.'"

25 D. Ryder's testimony, 5 August 1842 in "Report from The Select Committee on the West Coast of Africa," *British House of Commons Sessional Papers, 1842 XII [551-II]*.

26 Desp. #27, Benjamin Campbell to Earl of Clarendon, Dec. 1, 1854, British Parliamentary Papers (PP) 41, Class B.

27 Campbell to Clarendon, 1 December 1854, PP 41, Class B.

28 Paul E. Lovejoy and David Richardson, "The Initial 'Crisis of Adaptation': The Impact of British Abolition on the Atlantic Slave Trade in West Africa, 1808-1820," in Robin Law (ed.), *From Slave Trade to 'Legitimate' Commerce: The Commercial Transition in Nineteenth Century West Africa* (Cambridge: Cambridge University Press, 1995), 32-56.

29 Gareth Austin, "Between abolition and Jihad: the Asante response to the ending of the Atlantic slave trade, 1807-1896," in Law, *From Slave Trade to 'Legitimate' Commerce*, 93-118.

30 Ivor Wilks, *Asante in the Nineteenth Century: The Structure and Evolution of a Political Order* (Cambridge: Cambridge University Press, 1975), 170-72, 481-82

31 For details, see Freda Wolfson, "British Relations with the Gold Coast, 1843-1880," PhD dissertation, University of London, 1950, 237-39.

32 On the "Elmina note," see Feinberg, "There Was an Elmina Note, But...." *International Journal of African Historical Studies*, 9 (1976), 618-630; and Larry

Yarak, "The "Elmina Note:" Myth and Reality in Asante-Dutch Relations," *History in Africa,* 13 (1986), 363–382.

33 *Gold Coast Blue Books*, 1868, PP 49; "Transfer of the Dutch Forts" in "Correspondence relative to the cession of the Netherlands government to the British government of the Dutch settlements on the West Coast of Africa," PP 70, C.670 (1872); and Brackenbury, *Ashanti War*, I: 35.

34 Kofi Kakari to Herbert T. Ussher, Nov. 24, 1870, PP 70, 1872.

35 Desp. #71, Cornelis Nagtglas to Ussher, Governor of Cape Coast, Dec. 20, 1870, PP 70, 1872.

36 Wilks, *Asante in the Nineteenth Century*, 492-504; and Yarak, "Elmina and Greater Asante in the Nineteenth century," *Africa,* 56:1 (1986), 33-52.

37 Kennedy to Simpson, 26 July 1869 and Kennedy to Granville, 30 July 1869, CO96/80, TNA and Simpson to Kennedy, 7-8 August 1869, CO96/81, TNA; Foreign Office to Colonial Office, "Report of Seizure of German Missionaries by Asante King, 1872," Parliamentary Papers (PP) 50; Frederick Ramseyer and J. Kühne, *Four Years in Ashantee* (New York: Robert Carter & Brothers, 1875), 57-59, 133; and Jules Gros, *Voyages, Aventures et Captivité de J. Bonnat chez les Achantis* (Paris: Plon and Nourrit, 1884).

38 Francis C. Fuller, *A Vanished Dynasty: Ashanti* (London: Frank Cass, 1968 [1921]), 113-14.

39 Ramseyer and J. Kühne, *Four Years in Ashantee*, 127.

40 Ibid., 146.

41 Ibid., 8-15, 34-36, 48, 66,

42 Boyle, journal, 14 January 1874 in Boyle, *Through Fanteeland to Coomasie*, 271.

43 Ramseyer and Kühne, *Four Years in Ashantee,* 127-28, 140.

44 Ibid., 81-83, 93, 103-105, 135.

45 Wilks, *Asante in the Nineteenth Century*, 499-503, 675-76.

46 On negotiations to allow prisoner exchange between Asante and Fanti authorities, see Ussher to Kennedy, 11 and 27 July 1870, CO/96/85, The National Archives of United kingdom, Kew (TNA) and despatches 106,109 and 127 in PP 266.

47 Foreign Office to Colonial Office, 12 February 1872, "Report of Seizure of German Missionaries," PP 54, desp. #61 and "Affairs on the Gold Coast," *The Edinburgh Review or Critical Journal,* 138 (October 1873), 292-301; Ramseyer and Kühne, *Four Years in Ashantee*; and Henry M. Stanley, *Coomassie and Magdala: The Story of Two British Campaigns in Africa* (London: Sampson Low, 1874).

48 Ramseyer and Kühne, *Four Years in Ashantee*, 60, 68.

49 Ussher to Kennedy, 27 July 1870, CO96/85, TNA.

50 Hennessy to Kimberley, 1 June 1872, desp. #61, PP 58.

51 Protokoll der Kommittee, 3 June 1874, Basel Mission Archive, 46209. Cf. Adam Jones, "'Four Years in Asante': One Source or Several?," *History in Africa,* 18 (1991), 173.

52 Ramseyer and Kühne, *Four Years in Ashantee*, 69, 86, 155-56 and Ussher to Kennedy, 19 June 1871, CO96/88, TNA.

53 Ramseyer and Kühne, *Four Years in Ashantee*, 130, 137.

54 See Ojo, "In search of their Relations," 68-71.

55 Koffi Owusu-Mensa, "Prince Owusu-Ansa of Asante, 1823-1884," *Journal* of the *Historical Society of Nigeria,* 12:3/4 (1978), 9-22.

56 Ramseyer and Kühne, *Four Years in Ashantee*, 146.

57 Lofkrantz, "Intellectual Discourse in the Sokoto Caliphate."

58 Desp. #12, Foreign Office to Colonial Office, 12 February 1872 and desp. #61, Hennessy to Kimberley, June 1, 1872, PP 58.

59 Plange to Hennessy, 2 September 1872, PP 58.

60 Salmon to Hennessy, 20 September 1872, enclosure 4 in desp. #91, PP 58.

61 Lofkrantz and Ojo, "Slavery, Freedom, and Failed Ransom Negotiations."

62 Wilks, *Asante in the Nineteenth Century*, 414-45.

63 Kimberley to Hennessy, 19 February 1872, PP 44, 1873; Hennessy to King of Ashantee, 20 April 1872, PP 70 and Ramseyer and Kühne, *Four Years in Ashantee*, 176.

64 Ramseyer and Kühne, *Four Years in Ashantee*, 155-156, 160, 180-81.

65 Hennessy to Kimberley, 1 June 1872, PP 58 and Kimberley to Hennessy, 29 June 1872, PP 266.

66 See Charles Salmon to Hennessy, in enc. 2 in #61 Hennessy to Kimberley, 1 June 1872, PP 58.

67 Coffie Calcali to Hennessy, 24 September 1872, enc. 2 in dispatch #65, PP 58.

68 Kimberley to Hennessy, 5 July 1872, dispatch #68 PP 58

69 See Wilks, *Asante in the Nineteenth Century*, 414-444.

70 Ramseyer and Kühne, *Four Years in Ashantee*, 158.

71 This is a satire about Europeans love for eggs and poultry birds.

72 Samuel Johnson, *History of the Yorubas* (London: CSS, 1921), 353.

73 Ramseyer and Kühne, *Four Years in Ashantee*, 127.

74 Philip Curtin, *The Image of Africa: British Ideas and Action, 1780-1850* (Madison: University of Wisconsin Press, 1964); and David Northrup, *Africa's Discovery of Europe: 1450-1850* (Oxford: Oxford University Press, 2002).

75 "Minutes of Cape Coast Legislative Council, 12 October 1872," enc. 2 in #99, PP 50.

76 Wilks, *Asante in the Nineteenth Century*, 479-83, 544-45.

77 Ramseyer and Kühne, *Four Years in Ashantee*, 191.

78 Coffi Calcalli to Salmon, 9 November 1872, enc. 1 in #122, Kuhne, Ramseyer and Bonnat to Hennessy, 17 November 1872 and enc. 3 in #122, R. W. Harley (Acting Administrator) to Hennessy, 30 November 1872, PP 50.

79 A. G. Hopkins, "Economic Imperialism in West Africa: Lagos, 1880–1892," *Economic History Review*, 21 (1968), 580–606. For a revision of Hopkin's thesis, see Law, *From Slave Trade to 'Legitimate' Commerce.*

80 J. F. A. Ajayi, *Christian Missions in Nigeria: The Making of a New Elite, 1841-1891* (London: Longman, 1965); E. A. Oroge, "The Institution of Slavery in

Yorubaland with Particular Reference to the Nineteenth Century," PhD thesis, Birmingham, 1971; and Toyin Falola, *The Political Economy of a Pre-colonial African State: Ibadan, 1830-1900* (Ile-Ife: University of Ife Press, 1984).

81 Plange to Hennessy, 2 September 1872, PP 58 and Plange, journal, in Brackenbury, *Ashanti War*, I: 48.

82 Ramseyer and Kühne, *Four Years in Ashantee*, 182.

CHAPTER VII

West African Responses to Illegal Enslavement And Failed Ransom Negotiations[1]

Olatunji Ojo and Jennifer Lofkrantz

Introduction

In 1445, a group of Africans attacked a crew of Portuguese sailors off the coast of Mauritania "to avenge the capture of their relatives and friends."[2] While it was not unusual for Europeans and Africans to attack, take captive, and enslave each other, they both recognized the importance for some form of orderliness to make commerce, including the slave trade, profitable. That meant they had to operate within mutually accepted procedures which included provisions for the ransoming of captives by their relatives. In this particular instance, the Portuguese sailors violated accepted norms. The Portuguese ship was attacked because the crew enslaved the African captives without first giving their relatives an opportunity to ransom them. This case highlights among other things the ideology of slavery and the institutional underpinnings of ransoming. We define ransoming as the payment in cash or kind for the release of a captive prior to enslavement. In studying the institution of ransoming in West Africa, scholars have paid more attention to successful cases of ransoming rather than of cases of failed negotiations that often resulted in the enslavement of the captives.[3] Yet, as the Atlantic Sahara case and many others show, not all ransoming bids succeeded. Ransom negotiations could fail because of time constraints, disputes over price or with brokers, captor disinterest, state policies and legal complications. This chapter examines failed ransom cases in West Africa to explore why they failed and how West Africans reacted in the aftermath of unsuccessful negotiations.

Because occasionally ransoming bids failed and the captives enslaved, responses to unsuccessful negotiations contributed to the violence associated with slaving operations in Africa. By focusing on post-negotiation responses we maintain that in spite of the violence associated with enslavement processes, the initial reactions of communities whose members had been captured were in, many cases, peaceful. Kin and friends desired to negotiate with the captor and, if possible, offer huge payments, even if it meant indebtedness or parting with valuable possessions, in order to ensure the captive regained his or her freedom. Recourse to offensive strategies came when the captor's demands could not be met and when those whose ransom request had been rejected saw a correlation between such strategies and the attainment of freedom for their relative in captivity.

A focus on failed ransom negotiations permits us to revisit resistance to enslavement (not slavery) and to show that both slavers and their victims contributed to the violence associated with enslavement. The former did so by forcing people into bondage and the latter by fighting back. The fact that slavers and those seeking to secure the freedom of captives resorted to violence as they pushed their conflicting agendas reinforces the argument that slavery fuelled violence, and social, economic, and political instability in Africa. Moreover the study of failed ransom negotiations complicates the categorization of anti-slavery responses as strictly preventive, defensive, or offensive tactics. Put differently, violence or the threat of brute force could induce captors to permit the ransom of certain captives. The purpose of people paying ransom was to prevent the enslavement of certain captives who in their view, due to local ideologies of slavery, ought never to have faced the possibility of enslavement. Their purpose was not to reform slavery. We identify reasons why ransom negotiations failed and popular reactions to failed negotiations including road blockades, trade boycotts, retaliatory seizures, and warfare. This chapter is divided into three sections. It opens with an overview of the relationship between ransoming and the West African discourse on legal and illegal enslavement. Section two explores the reasons for the occasional failure of ransom negotiations and the final section addresses West African reactions to unsuccessful attempts at ransom negotiations.

Ransoming and the Laws of Enslavement

The study of ransoming in Africa highlights the relationship between captivity, enslavement, and societal debates on the rationalization and morality of slavery. Scholars have paid close attention to Africans' understandings of slavery, why they permitted it, and how they distinguished between legal and illegal enslavement. People had a vested interested in preventing what they viewed as illegal enslavement. Whether mandated by law or not, all African societies had clearly-defined ideas about who was enslavable and who was not. Similarly to European states, African states sought to regulate the slave trade, to prevent illegal enslavement, while facilitating culturally permitted modes of enslavement. Those involved in illegal slaving operations were punished for violating the law.[4]

In Muslim West Africa, the slavery debate centered on religious identity with recognized freeborn Muslims supposedly immune to enslavement.[5] Non-Muslim societies also banned the enslavement of their citizens, or "insiders," as defined by specific cultural constructions of ethnicity, class, religion, gender, age, and rights. As Robin Law, John Thornton, and Olatunji Ojo have shown, in general, Africans accepted the legitimacy of enslavement through warfare and raiding as long as the victims were foreigners. Under no circumstances was it legal to enslave members of the same community or citizens of friendly states except if they were criminals. In many West African societies, enslavement was a penalty for murder, treason, adultery with the wives of chiefs, witchcraft, and indebtedness. According to James Holman of the British navy, at Old Calabar in 1828, if captains were short the slaves they were owed as they were nearing their departure day, Duke Ephraim, the principal trader at the time, would order other Efik traders to send to him "every individual from the neighbouring villages, who have committed any crime or misdemeanor; and should he still continue unable to make up the specified demand, they sell their own servants to him."[6] Since Ephraim was a major trade financier one would assume people sold their servants to him as a form of debt payment. The sale could also be a disguised form of panyarring or seizure for debt. Thus, it was not that Africans rejected slavery. It was who and how individuals should be protected from enslavement, and the effectiveness of such protection that varied between African societies.[7]

Regardless of their socio-cultural make-up African societies were not fully closed to outsiders. Rather, the statuses of "insider" and "outsider" were flexible and situational. Within the context of slaving operations in West Africa, the boundary between "insider" and "outsider" was fluid. Hitherto, outsiders such as migrants, refugees, slaves, and foreign traders were frequently absorbed into host societies and became insiders while insiders who were major criminals or who rebelled against their home states lost the protection enjoyed by other citizens and thereby assumed the status of outsiders.[8] In his study of the cultural basis of commerce and slavery in the western Sudan, Claude Meillassoux alludes to the protection extended to foreigners and members of friendly neighboring states during war time. He notes that there was a better chance of successful ransom negotiations when rival states belonged to the "same society;" that is where hostile states had processes for ransoming and prisoner exchange.[9] European traders, with their complex socio-economic and political relationships with Africans could be considered, according to Meillassoux's definition, as belonging to this greater African society.[10] During peacetime, these societies usually banned attacks on each other and their citizens and had mechanisms to free individuals wrongly taken captive. To do otherwise amounted to breaking the law. Mutual protection across state borders formed part of African diplomatic strategies during the pre-colonial period and most likely accounted for some traditions of common origins among neighboring states. Moreover, while state expansion could initially lead to a greater number of captives who could be either ransomed or enslaved, eventually that expansion could also lead to the incorporation of former "foreign" populations as insiders. Thus on the Slave Coast, the number of slaves embarked from the port of Ouidah fell after the rise of Dahomey in the 1720s as Dahomey incorporated and enfranchised neighboring populations. According to David Eltis, slave exports from Ouidah fell from 374,400 on the eve of Dahomian conquest to about 178,000 during the first quarter century of its rule (1726-50), 130,000 over the next 25 years and barely 78,000 during the last quarter of the eighteenth century.[11] The variation in protective strategies against enslavement also permitted groups to shape the law to suit their purposes. Attacks on and enslavement of foreigners were legal while the victimization of allies was deemed illegal even in societies that permitted legal enslavement. Therefore, while we agree with the distinction between the notion of "legal" and "illegal" enslavement we also argue that there existed a third realm: the concept of immoral or unethical enslavement which led people to challenge aspects of legal enslavement. What was legal was not always appropriate or acceptable.[12] Even when an individual was captured under accepted norms, the failure to release the captive by rejecting an application to ransom could be deemed by the captive's family as immoral and illegal.

More often than not, enslavement involved "denial of kinship" and "de-socialization" or the rupturing of ties between captives and their homelands and their insertion into new societies as slaves.[13] In western Africa, many slaves destined for the Americas viewed the Atlantic crossing (middle passage) as a journey of no return because of the expectation they would die working on American plantations. Recollecting his enslavement in the 1820s, Joseph Wright, an Egba child slave wrote: "we were heavy and sorrowful in heart, because we were going to leave our land for another which we never knew."[14] Other Africans viewed white slavers and sailors as cannibals buying slaves to kill and "eat" them or use their blood as textile dye. William Bosman, a seventeenth century Dutch trader on the Gold Coast described how European slave traders were "sometime sufficiently plagued with a parcel of Slaves, which come from a far Inland Country, who very innocently perswade [sic] one another, that we buy them only to fatten and afterwards eat them as a Delicacy."[15] For others, enslavement was a mark of spiritual nakedness. In the case of Ayuba b. Sulayman Ibrahima Diallo (whom the English called Job ben Solomon) of Bundu and his friend/interpreter who were captured on the Gambia in February 1731, the Mandingo captors "shaved their Heads and Beards," which both men "resented as the highest Indignity; tho' the Mandingoes meant no more by it, than to make them appear like Slaves taken in War."[16]

If many captives and their allies considered slavery as the opposite of freedom it made sense that they struggled hard to avoid enslavement. Little wonder that some slaves sold into the trans-Atlantic slave trade jumped overboard during the middle passage choosing death over life in slavery, or mutilated themselves, and why families of captives employed tactics to try to prevent enslavement even when the outcome was unpredictable. According to George Brooks, drawing on contemporary reports from the Senegambia in the sixteenth century, "captured, the Bijago [of Guinea Bissau] would die rather than submit to slavery." Brooks also quoted from a Portuguese sailor, Almada: "There is no doubt about this: They simply hold their breath and die."[17]

To avoid captivity, which often led to enslavement, Africans utilized a myriad of defensive, protective, and offensive strategies including, if they had the means to do so, trying to ransom captives prior to their enslavement.[18] Only after attempts at ransoming had failed and the captive was transformed into a slave did kin consider more violent options to free their captive members or to seek revenge. Ransoming was not, therefore, an option of "last resort" but a strategy in a continuum of tactics against enslavement and demand for the restoration of freedom. Ransom negotiations and, in particular, responses to failed negotiations, highlight a link between protective and offensive strategies against enslavement. Ransoming was a protective tactic. When ransom negotiations failed families of the now enslaved captives went on the offensive to free their kin.

Why Ransom Negotiations Failed

In her study of ransoming in West Africa, Sylviane Diouf conflates the ransoming of captives with the redemption of slaves. Diouf lists a number of "obstacles to redemption" (appropriately ransoming) or reasons why many captives were not returned to freedom. These obstacles included failure to locate the captive, loss of family members, lack of knowledge about the captor, captors' unwillingness to wait until the completion of ransom negotiations or reluctance to release their captives; social distinctions between members of the elite and commoners and between freeborn and slaves; and enslavement being a symbolic form of exile for criminals and enemies.[19] The problem with some of these identified "obstacles" is that they do not fully account for the failure of ransom negotiations because they do not indicate whether negotiations had begun. For instance, families who could not contact or did not know those who had captured their members as well as captives cut off from their relatives or whose kin had all been captured hardly had any means of starting ransom negotiations.[20] We contend that contact had to have been established between the captor and those intending to effect the release of the detainee before a ransom negotiation could be deemed to have failed. This was the case for the already mentioned Diallo of Bundu.

In 1731, Diallo and his assistant were captured and sold to the English trader, Captain Stephen Pike of the slave ship *Arabella* (slave voyage #75094), a 90-ton British schooner, owned by Henry Hunt and William Hunt of London. Diallo contacted his father to arrange his ransom. This case, particularly the element of ransoming, has been cited by scholars as an example of Africans' protective strategies against enslavement.[21] Diallo, however, was not ransomed. He was sold alongside 169 other enslaved Africans to Annapolis, Maryland before ransom negotiations could be completed. We do not have information about how Diallo's family reacted to the enslavement of their son before the young man was located across the Atlantic in Maryland. While the sale of Diallo to Pike was not illegal, Pike's purchase of him raised a moral question. Pike and Diallo's family were commercial partners. Indeed, in the days immediately preceding his capture, Diallo and Pike had met and successfully concluded a commercial transaction involving the sale of slaves. Diallo would have expected that the familial and business relationships he had with Pike would protect him from enslavement and this he conveyed to his biographer, Thomas Bluett: "Soon after Job found means to acquaint Captain Pike that he was the same person that came to trade with him a few days before, and after what manner he had been taken."[22] Paradoxically, as a trader, Pike was within his legal rights to buy Diallo, but, in Bundu circles, his decision to buy and sail off with his ally, before Diallo could be ransomed was viewed as immoral. Pike's action, like that of the Portuguese in the 1445 case on the Saharan coast, contravened a widespread practice in West Africa whereby neighboring states, including those hostile to each other, and including European traders with their complex socioeconomic and political relationships with coastal states, had mechanisms to facilitate ransoming and prisoner exchange.

Diallo's case exemplifies the gulf that often occurred between what was perceived as moral versus legal slaving activities. This was also the case in the Sierra Leone region in the late eighteenth century where aggressive marketing and the quest for quick profit from slave trading, even if it meant attacks on and sale of allies and members of host communities, fuelled illegal slaving operations. European traders were buying slaves, many of whom were debtors and kidnapping victims, who had been seized and sold illegally by privateers. James Watt, of the Sierra Leone Colonization Company, reported such a case originating in Fuuta Jallon in 1794. While in Timbo, capital of the Fulbe kingdom of Fuuta Jallon, to negotiate trade and political relations between the Company and the Fuuta Jallon leadership, Watt met a father who begged him for help in locating his son who had been kidnapped along with six others by a Portuguese trader while they were returning from the Pongo River. The father had first complained to the Almamy (king) who, with the help of another British trader, discovered the names of the Portuguese kidnapper and the British trader to whom the captives were sold and confirmed that six of the captives had already been shipped to the West Indies. Watt promised the father that he would ask the Governor of Sierra Leone to enquire after his son.[23]

Other times European traders, especially those owed money by Africans, promoted the seizure and enslavement of local debtors.[24] Some of the victims included members of royal families of the Sierra Leone hinterland, free colonists from England, and pawns. Carl Bernhard Wadström, a Swedish abolitionist and employee of the Freetown Colonization Society, listed a number of instances of enslavement for debt in the early 1790s. In one case, nineteen freemen, including sons of chiefs, were sold. In another case three or four captives were sold in spite of protests from British administrators of Sierra Leone. In a third case three to four women being held as pawns on a trading vessel were carried away into slavery.[25] European slave traders blamed market forces for their participation in illegal enslavement. They argued that if they refused to buy illegally seized individuals their competitors would not do the same thus putting themselves at a commercial disadvantage.[26]

Illegal slaving operations in West Africa undermined the local inhabitants' trust in European and American traders. Consequently, in the 1790s, reports came from Sierra Leone of lack of local support for the nascent British colonial administration in Freetown, personal insecurity of colonial officials, and pillaging of the colony's property. Europeans knew that attacks on local people violated indigenous laws against arbitrary enslavement. This realization was evident in the furious discussions between lawful traders, officials of the Sierra Leone Company, and the British Crown condemning the acts which set in motion African efforts to free illegally enslaved Africans.[27] During the Atlantic slave trade, some African states like Old Calabar delayed the departure of slave vessels to verify if every bondsman and woman aboard a European ship had been legally enslaved. This is also why the kingdoms of Benin and Dahomey (after 1727) discouraged human pawning, especially if the creditor was a foreigner, in order to prevent the enslavement of pawns and the conflation of pawns with slaves.[28]

Why did European slavers risk infuriating African officials and trading partners by departing the African coast without negotiating or completing ransoms for captives that Africans wanted to set free? Until the large-scale use of quinine as a prophylaxis started around 1850, West Africa was considered a "white man's grave." It was the "horrid hole" where Europeans rarely survived the local diseases, especially the mosquito-borne malaria fever, and humid temperatures.[29] Therefore, European sailors did not want to stay long on the West African coast and seldom left their ships. Their goal was to embark slaves as quickly as possible and leave the coast. Hence, it would seem that Europeans disliked long ransom negotiations which, depending on the cost and distance between where captives were held and the location of their relatives, could take from a couple of days to several months. In Diallo's case, his family lived ten days away from the port so it would have taken at least three weeks to get a message to his family and for people bringing the ransom payment to arrive at the port town. Since Diallo was bought at the end of Pike's venture in the Gambia, Pike left for Maryland two days after he made the purchase, travel time and distance prevented Diallo's ransom.[30] In Sierra Leone and the Senegal River valley, the situation was different. As mentioned above, Europeans traders were not neutral in the violence that produced a number of captives. They took part in some of the kidnapping raids and panyarring or the seizure debtors or their associates to coerce payment. So it would have been imprudent on their part to wait for ransoming procedures to commence.

Disagreements over the cost of ransoming also led to failed negotiations. The goal of the captor was to maximize profit. In order to do so, they sometimes threatened the sale of captives to extract huge payments from the captives' relatives. Ransom prices were usually at least twice the price the captive would fetch on the slave market and often more.[31] Rich families could sometimes speed up the ransoming process by paying captors out of their surplus wealth. In certain extraordinary cases captors demanded and sometimes received more than 1000 per cent the value of their captives as slaves. For instance, in 1787, Barbier Borro, a Sierra Leonean man, arranged his own ransom by selling twenty-two of his slaves. His other slaves became so fearful that they might also be sold that they fled into the woods.[32] Northwest of Sierra Leone, in Fuuta Jallon, around 1828, a French trader, Theophilus Conneau (aka Theodore Canot), recorded that an eighteen year old woman was ransomed for ten slaves.[33] In the Aïr region of the Sahara, the Tuareg were willing to pay any demanded price for the return of a "white" member.[34]

Most African families, though, had limited resources for ransoming and could not satisfy the captors' demands. For example, in 1841, a boy who had been seized by Fulbe slavers near the confluence of the Niger River was sold into slavery because the ransom offered by his parents was not sufficient. According to William Allen, head of the British Expedition to the Niger Confluence in 1841

> A boy was lately carried off from Kinami by the Filatahs [i.e. Fulbe] to Egga, where he was exposed in the market-place for sale. His parents, poor, miserable, and heart-broken, resolved to make an attempt to redeem their child, and sold everything they possessed. With the cowries raised in this way, the father hurried off to Egga, hoping to be able to purchase his own child. His all was not enough for his rapacious foes. "Go back," said the Filatah, "you must get more cowries." "Yes," answered the half-distracted man, "I will endeavour to get more." Upon this the Filatah said, "You had better not come here; if you do, we will sell you" The mother, who was impatiently waiting the result, on being told that her child was not, on any terms, to be ransomed, wept long and bitterly.[35]

As we shall see shortly there is abundant evidence that not all of the families and communities whose ransoming applications were unsuccessful went home defeated. They expressed their bitterness by fighting back with all their power and in a variety of ways.

A third reason for the failure of ransom negotiations was disputes between the captive's family and the ransom brokers. The engagement of a mediator by the captive's family was essential since rarely did captors and payers of ransom have direct contact with each other.[36] The inability or unwillingness to pay a mediator after he had accomplished his task could result in the release of a captive from one captor only to be detained by the mediator. The mediator could detain a newly freed captive until payment was received, he could threaten to sell a newly released captive into slavery to force payment, or he could eventually sell the captive if payment was not forthcoming. One such case was reported at Igbobini in southeastern Yorubaland in 1885. Around March 1885, Ike, a Mahin trader from Oketoro, and two slaves went to Gbogun, an Ijebu town, to collect debts. At Gbogun, the party was attacked and the two slaves were seized in retaliation for an 1881 Mahin attack on the town. During the recurrent conflicts between Mahin and Ijebu, people seized in such frays were usually sold to the Lagos and Niger delta slave markets. This could have been the fate of the two slaves. Labite, owner of one of the slaves, begged Takuro, an influential ex-slave and trader, to help regain his slave through ransoming. Takuro sent messengers to Gbogun to negotiate the captives' release and Labite sent another slave to witness the negotiations. Rather than free the detainees, the captors seized the slave witness, giving the captors three captives in total and greater bargaining power. After long and tortuous negotiations the three captives were released to Takuro, who paid twenty bags of cowries of his own money in ransom for each of the detainees. When he did not receive payment for his expenses and efforts in ransoming the captives, Takuro detained the slaves until he received eighty bags of cowries including twenty bags as a brokerage fee.[37]

Although the victims in the Igbobini case were slaves and not freeborn citizens, the purpose of the negotiations was to prevent the re-enslavement and insertion into another society of the three detainees. This particular case challenges Diouf's view that ransoming involved only free individuals. She argues that slaves "were thus excluded from the benefit of a strategy designed as an alternative to the killing of prisoners" and that they (slaves) "seem to have been the only category that could not, as a matter of policy, be ransomed."[38] The implicit assumption by Diouf was that all slaves not only had the same status but they were always inferior to freeborn citizens. This is far from the truth. In reality, the status/rank of slaves varied depending on their sex, age, skill and length of time in bondage among other factors. Often times, slaves with military, mercantile, and medical experiences ranked above those employed on the farms just as slaves belonging to members of the nobility ranked above those owned by the commoners. These privileged or special slaves filled such offices as advisers, guards, traders and toll collectors enjoyed more power than lower class freeborn citizens and non-elite slaves. These elite slaves wore better clothes, supervised lower class slaves and often had their own slaves. In the Atlantic world they worked as guards, interpreters and cooks on slave ships and in the dungeons and as overseers on the plantations. The support and cooperation of these elite slaves was crucial to a chief in discharging their functions and in power. In turn, elite slaves leveraged their closeness to the source of power to the degree they became close allies and dependents who could not be easily disposed or punished unless for heinous crimes.[39] In the Mahin case, the three captives ransomed by Takuro were not new but assimilated slaves. Their status and the fact that they were ransomed supports Suzanne Miers and Igor Kopytoff's thesis that incorporated slaves ranked higher than new ones because they were not complete aliens and their status lay midway between enslaved and freeborn.[40] Due to their assimilation, incorporated slaves had masters who oftentimes were willing to fulfill the kinship role and defend their slaves if taken captive whereas many poor freeborn captives had no one to ransom them.

Sometimes, however, ransom negotiations failed simply because of captor disinterest.[41] For example, in 1793, in Sierra Leone, a slave-ship captain refused to permit a father to ransom his daughter stating that it was currently difficult to purchase slaves. Although the captain could have received more than the value of the girl in ransom, his refusal could be tied to eagerness to leave for the Americas rather than wait for possible prolonged ransom negotiations. Even after the intervention of the Governor at Freetown who persuaded the captain to accept a ransom payment, it is clear that captain was not inclined to release the girl because he sailed before the father had the chance to return with the agreed ransom price.[42]

Finally, there were also instances when ransoming was forbidden by the state. This could be the result of judicial sanction or political expediency. On the Gold Coast in the late seventeenth century high status captives such as senior military officers were sometimes denied access to ransom even when their families offered attractive ransom payments. According to William Bosman, "if the Person who occasioned [a] War be taken, they will not easily admit him to Ransom, though his weight in Gold Were offered, for fear he should for the future form some new design against their repose."[43] In the first half of the nineteenth century in the Sokoto Caliphate ransoming could be proscribed for political reasons. This was the case in Bauchi Emirate where the state had not yet fully consolidated its power. It was viewed as imprudent to return potential enemies to freedom especially when the state had not yet fully consolidated its power. If released, such enemies could lead future insurrections. The refusal to permit ransoming was despite the fact that according to the Mālikī *madh'hab* (school of law) practiced in the region, ransoming was a lawful means for dealing with prisoners of war. Forbidding ransoming, though, was also permissible under this law code since it was only one of several legitimate options for dealing with war prisoners. By the latter half of the century, when the Sokoto Caliphate was firmly established, including in Bauchi Emirate, it appears that the ransoming of prisoners held by Sokoto forces became permissible throughout the Caliphate.[44]

Confronting Failed Ransom Negotiations

The ability to actualize the release of a captive or respond to unsuccessful ransom negotiations depended on the combination of the captive or his/her community's power to act or to convince others to champion their cause, the opportunity cost of long ransom negotiations and the assessment that such actions would be successful. Therefore in societies with a relatively strong socioeconomic base, institutional support for ransoming, and the means to effect it, ransom negotiations were permitted to continue as long as there was hope for success. Examples of these societies include the early modern central European borderland regions, the Mediterranean basin, and a several nineteenth century Muslim West African states.[45] While the established ransoming procedures within these systems minimized the faltering of negotiations and their subsequent conflicts, they also prevented individuals from pursuing other options when those negotiations collapsed. In these systems it was the state or its agencies more than individual families of captives who moderated ransoming.

In these systems, those in charge of ransoming were aware that ransoming came with added costs beyond the actual financial costs of ransoming. These costs included, among others, physical dangers to ransom brokers, and the forgoing of other opportunities while bargaining for the captive. Therefore, a ransom broker would be eager to minimize losses by ending protracted negotiations if the cost was greater than the value of the captive. Applying the transactional economics model to ransom negotiations in the Maghrib, Attila Ambrus and Eric Chaney contend that ransom mediators factored these personal costs into their operations when bargaining for a captive.[46] The longer the mediator held out during negotiations, despite these personal costs, reflected the value he placed on the captive. From this perspective, it could be argued that in many cases in the Mediterranean world and central Europe, the dangers of taking action to redress failed ransom negotiations was greater than the value of the detainees, hence many captives were not rescued.

A change in the balance of power could enable one side to use other responses, besides ransoming, in its pursuit of freeing captives. For instance, beginning in the seventeenth century, in the Maghrib, if there were no other viable options for the release of a captive, Europeans continued to negotiate and pay ransoms. Yet, they no longer accepted all failed ransom negotiations as a *fait accompli*. According to Ellen Friedman, the presence of a Spanish garrison at Ceuta in the early seventeenth century helped ensure the fairness of negotiations between Spanish Trinitarian ransom brokers and Moroccan captors at Tetuán.[47] Similarly, Gillian Weiss demonstrates that after the seventeenth century, the French used its military superiority to alter the power structure in ransom negotiations with Morocco and Algiers. The French government was increasingly willing to use force to press for the release of French captives held in the Maghrib, and ultimately to stop corsair attacks on French interests.[48] The United States navy was established in 1798 to end attacks on American sailors in the Mediterranean.[49]

In 1962, Ronald Robinson identified two factors in African responses to European colonial penetration. First, he argued that because African societies were built around the "unity of equals, not in the unity imposed by a hierarchy" the continent failed to provide a united front against European imperial expansion. If the absence of a uniting authority to coordinate reactions to European conquest exposed Africa to defeat, the unique social structure of each state was crucial in shaping its options and responses. Upswing states with a strong army, central authority, and whose economy relied on slavery had more incentives to resist whereas downturn states with diminishing authority had limited options.[50] Robinson's thesis is applicable to the political economy of slavery in Africa whereby indigenous social structures underlined responses to slavery and enslavement and popular concepts of legal and illegal enslavement. John Thornton and Joseph Inikori stress the close link between the structure of African states and state involvement in the slave trade.[51] Powerful and expansive states more easily defended their citizens against enslavement than fragmented states with limited force or whose influence or that of its leaders, did not extend much beyond the city walls. Similarly, Eltis argues that after 1500 the evolution of European identity fuelled partly by shared Christian beliefs, and a sense of continental racial, geographical, and cultural unity obviated the enslavement of European citizens and explains why non-Europeans became the enslavable "cultural other."[52] Thus, in fragmented societies, mechanisms for negotiating ransoms across state lines may have been poorly developed and or even non-existent; hence members of these societies often lacked the means of pursuing other responses when ransom negotiations collapsed.

Yet, we caution not to overstate the parallels between a state system and a state's ability to defend against enslavement. While a strong centralized state structure in a balanced regional power system prevented individuals from pursuing their own interests over state interests, attempts at pursuing diplomatic finesse also sometimes delayed the state's ability to act quickly.

Records show that even if decentralized societies in West Africa lacked the military force to fight off foreign enemies, they were not "slave reservoirs" nor were their citizens readily available to be seized at will without resistance. Inhabitants of decentralized states resisted enslavement by relocating to less accessible locations such as hill tops, islands and swamps, constructing strong defense lines, forming close-knit defense-oriented kinship ties, using guerrilla tactics and carrying out preventive kidnappings (seizing potential slavers before they could attack) among other tactics.[53] A number of acephalous states might not have had the offensive power to pursue captors when ransom negotiations failed but their fragmentation offered other responses to failed ransom negotiations that were lacking in larger states.

Indeed in some places weak state institutions meant that captors, and sometimes relatives of captives, could neglect or ignore local laws without fear of sanctions. Under these circumstances private individuals had no incentive or need to convince their states to take further action when ransom negotiations failed. In West Africa this scenario is exemplified by nineteenth-century Yorubaland where political violence undermined and in some cases destroyed existing state power. This encouraged widespread lawlessness, leaving individual warlords and aristocrats to substitute for the state and to act as they deemed fit.[54] A comparison between states in Yorubaland and Igboland, on the one hand, and Europe on the other suffices. In Europe decision-makers lived far from where captives were held. Therefore, European leaders were usually physically detached from the problems associated with ransom negotiations in the Maghrib or Ottoman Europe. In contrast, rival Yoruba and Igbo state capitals were located in close proximity to each other and therefore military force could be more easily and quickly mobilized to pursue failed ransom cases.

Furthermore, in the Maghrib and central Europe, ransom payments were more central to state revenue than in fragmented societies in West Africa.[55] In Yorubaland the states relied more for their revenue on income derived from the slave trade and taxes than from ransom payments. This, coupled with the fear of letting loose potential rebels through ransoming meant that their authorities could more easily halt ransom negotiations and enslave or kill the captive. The urge to prevent enslavement and death meant a quick and often violent response to unsuccessful ransom negotiations. With the state system being central to ransom discussions, West African alternatives to failed negotiations ranged from attacks on captors, to road closures, trade boycotts, retaliatory seizures, collective punishment, and war. To the extent that many slaves died in bondage and many of those who survived could not reconnect with their families, West Africans generally regarded enslavement as a death sentence. Enslavement and deportation violated many Africans' worldview which stressed an unbroken connection to their place of birth. Mungo Park commented about western Sudanese peoples' attachment to their homelands while travelling in the upper Niger region from 1795-1797:

> notwithstanding this exterminating system [of warfare and displacement], it is surprising to behold how soon an African town is rebuilt and repeopled. The circumstance arises probably from this, that their pitched battles are few, the weakest know their own situation, and seek safety in flight. When their country has been desolated, and their ruined towns and villages deserted by the enemy, such of the inhabitants as have escaped the sword and the chain, generally return, though with cautious steps, to the place of their nativity; for it seems to be the universal wish of mankind to spend the evening of their days where they passed their infancy.[56]

With this worldview in mind, anyone who turned down a request to ransom or to otherwise free a captive can be compared to a murderer who had to atone for his crimes. Therefore, many relatives of captives whose ransom attempts were unsuccessful sought opportunities to kill the captor. This can be seen in Yorubaland in the aftermath of the Osogbo war of 1838 fought between Ilorin and Ibadan forces. In the war, Ibadan soldiers had captured some Ilorin military chiefs including the military commander, Lateju. While other captured army chiefs were released in compliance with the military etiquette that war chiefs protect one another, Lateju was not. Instead, he was found guilty of treason (waging war against his country) and also for preventing the ransoming of a Yoruba woman in 1833. For the last offense he was executed.[57]

Another potential response to the failure of ransom negotiations was a road blockade and trade boycott. Depending on geography this could be a particularly effective response. For example in 1861, Ayawo, the wife of the army chief of Abeokuta, Somoye, accompanied her husband to the Ijaye war (1860-1862) where she was captured by Ibadan forces. Considered a prime captive, the captors sent her to Ogunmola, the Ibadan deputy army chief. Egba chiefs responded to Ayawo's seizure by blocking the Abeokuta-Ibadan road; thus cutting off Ibadan's access to the sea. Without the access to this road, Ibadan citizens had limited access to European traders even though they relied solely on coastal trade for vital goods such as cowries, weapons, tobacco, and textiles. Four years later with the sanction hitting hard at home Ibadan chiefs released Ayawo as a peace gesture.[58]

The negative impact of trade embargoes was not limited to Africans. They also affected European traders including those not directly responsible for disrupting trade. We do not know how Diallo's father reacted to the failed attempt to restore his son's freedom. However we have glimpses of possible reactions against Europeans in Liberia, the Gold Coast, and at Old Calabar. In 1727 William Smith, an agent of the British Royal African Company trading around Cape Mount, west of Cape Mesurado, in modern Liberia , noted that local people refused to come on board his ship to trade because they suspected that Bristol and Liverpool privateers had recently seized some local debtors. Although this was a case of seizure for debt or panyarring, which allowed creditors to detain debtors or their associates to coerce payment, rather than a case of a person captured in warfare or a raid, victims of panyarring were technically captives because their return to freedom had to be bought without which they could be enslaved. Relatives of the Cape Mount debtors responded to the seizure by boycotting European trade vessels.[59] Responses were not limited to boycotting trade. They also involved violent attacks "when it is in [the] power" of the local people. For instance in another case recorded by Smith, in early January 1727, people from Cape Mount attacked a British vessel, *Expedition*, and seized the Third mate, Benjamin Cross, in retaliation for British sailors from another vessel panyarring local men. Cross was released after four weeks when another officer, Captain Creighton of the vessel *Elizabeth*, paid fifty pounds sterling in ransom. Such attacks on European traders engaged in illegal trade, according to eyewitnesses, hampered the activities of law abiding traders who described violence associated with privateering as "very pernicious to the slave trade" in the Cape Mount region.[60]

Seizures and counter-seizures were also used as responses to failed ransom transactions. Counter-seizures, depending on the number and status of captives involved, could sometimes tilt the balance against the original captor.[61] A number of West African societies viewed the refusal to ransom or otherwise release captives as a violation of codes of social engagement. Some relatives of captives resorted to retaliatory seizures in order to force captors back to the negotiating table. For example in November 1793 when Wadström, reported third-hand, an incident that took place in Sierra Leone around 1791 in which the Susu chief of Bowrah (Burara) attacked a neighboring village at Quiaport (Kabba, now Little Scarcies) River, in retaliation for a previous assault on his community and sale of his people to a British slave factory near Freetown. The chief used prisoners taken during the counter-attack to ransom his people from the factory.[62]

This tactic was also used by Africans against Europeans. As evidence from the Gold Coast shows early efforts made by Portuguese traders to operate outside local laws such as capturing and enslaving inhabitants of coastal towns failed. Rebecca Shumway notes that raids and destruction of Gold

Coast settlements often had the long-term effect of ruining trade around affected areas. Realizing this was a wrong-headed tactic "[t]hose with a long-term stake in the African trade learned to prevent such hostilities and, to retain good relations with potential African trade partners, even demanded that ships return goods and people that had been seized."[63] Societies on the Gold Coast, with a "highly developed maritime culture" and resources to defend their territories European traders ensured they followed local regulations and maintained peaceful relations with the Africans. Those who ignored these codes of conduct had themselves to blame for the consequences of their actions. Thus in 1709, at the port of Anomabo, a group of Fante men seized a British trader, Captain John Brethaver, in retaliation for his purchase and sale of a local man. The Fante men's action derived from the trader selling the victim into slavery and not permitting them to ransom him as expected under local slaving ethics.[64]

Another response to failed ransom negotiations was collective punishment including the total destruction of a captor's community. While a retaliatory attack was disruptive to trade it was both a tool for punishing illegal slavers and for deterring future law breakers. For instance, around 1833, a civil dispute erupted between two factions in the Yoruba town of Abemo. The winners captured some of their rivals and held them as captives. Neighboring Oyo chiefs intervened to settle the dispute and ordered the release of the captives, "contending that they cannot be regarded as prisoners of war but fellow townsmen and victims of a civil fight."[65] Many soldiers complied with the order and released their captives but others did not. For failing to release their victims, Oyo chiefs responded by ordering the destruction of Abemo.[66]

Warfare was another response to failed ransom negotiations. European travelers in Africa in the eighteenth and nineteenth century often made reference to the frequency of warfare associated with slavery in Africa. Some attributed the wars to armies seeking slaves and others viewed them as retaliations against slave traders. Matthew Winterbottom of the Freetown-based Sierra Leone Company, who travelled to the northern region of Sierra Leone to investigate potential trade relations between the region and the Company wrote that "wars were [often]...occasioned by some of their inhabitants having been kidnapped, or laid hold of and sold for debt."[67] One such war was launched by fugitive slaves who by escaping had regained their freedom but chose to fight to prevent their reenslavement. Around 1785/86, war broke out between some runaway slaves and their former Mandingo overlords. The former had seized upon conflicts between the Mandingo and the Susu to effect their escape and to live freely in a number of maroon villages like Yangekori, Kania and Funkoo. Unable to force the slaves to return, the Mandingo, operating out of Moria chiefdom, embarked on periodic raids and kidnappings against the maroons. The latter, joined by the Susu, retaliated by seizing several people including elite freeborn Mandingo citizens and held them for ransom and others as hostages to prevent future attacks from Moria.[68] In other areas the wars were between two states. For example, in 1862, a captor rejected Chief Ogundipe of Abeokuta's offer of two slaves for his wife and infant child held at Ile-Bioku, a small Oyo town. The source is silent on why the captor rejected the offer so it is unclear if he wanted a larger ransom or if he wanted to humiliate the chief by defying Egba power. Since the captives were not released, Ogundipe led an Egba army to sack Ile-Bioku in 1878. This case is significant because it shows that some negotiations were lengthy before they finally collapsed. It could be that Ogundipe could not easily mobilize the Egba to go to war without an assurance of victory. The timing of the revenge attack is particularly revealing since it took place in 1878 when Ibadan, Bioku's overlord, was engaged in another war and incapable of mounting a successful counter-assault on Egba.[69]

If negotiations failed or became complicated because relatives could not pay a mediator, the relatives could attack the broker or his community. To enjoy their right as a broker, a mediator must be seen as unbiased. The parties involved, though, usually wanted the broker to support their side and to force the other party to make concessions. This could put the broker in an awkward position, sometimes resulting in attacks. This was the case when Ketu acted as the mediator between Egba and Dahomey. In August 1851, following the breakdown of ransom negotiations between the parties over captives seized in a recent war, Dahomey planned to invade Ketu on market day knowing that the Egba were bringing Dahomian captives to the town. "On the eve of the market day," Thomas Bowen writes, "it was reported that a Dahomian army was coming to Ketu to free their countrymen by force."[70] Immediately, Ketu forces were put on alert and Dahomian traders already in town were expelled. It is unclear why Dahomey did not trust the neutrality of Ketu, which like Egba, was Yoruba-speaking, or why Dahomey believed it had the physical force to free the captives. The expulsion of Dahomian traders from Ketu disrupted trade relations between them. It appears that it took some time before Ketu again trusted that Dahomian traders were not combining commerce with espionage.

Sometimes, the threat of war instead of actual warfare was enough to restart ransom negotiations. For example, after the illegal shipment of captives taken in the Old Calabar civil war of 1767, pawns held on European ships for debt owed by the Efik were shipped to the Americas. In response

Efik authorities vowed to stop all trading activities with British traders and threatened to take revenge on English ship captains.[71] The seriousness of this threat was evident by the furious exchanges within the merchant community in which a number of European merchants condemned the enslavement of the pawns and set in motion efforts to return the illegally enslaved to freedom.[72]

On the part of a captive-turned-slave, responses to failed ransoming negotiations continued into the early days of enslavement though scholars have usually categorized these later actions as slave resistance. In reality, however, the various forms of resistance carried out by slaves in the first few days, weeks and sometimes months after their enslavement were against slavery and enslavement as well as reaction to failed ransom negotiations. This intervening period drove new slaves into desperation as they often found it difficult to accept their new fate. For this reason, sailors were known to reduce possible slave revolts by putting slaves in chains, reducing their movement on ships and in the barracoons and ensuring they had no access to weapons. Drawing on his experience as a surgeon on several slave ships in the 1780s, Alexander Falconbridge wrote:

> As very few of the Negroes can so far brook the loss of their liberty and the hardships they endure, they are ever on the watch to take advantage of the least negligence in their oppressors. Insurrections are frequently the consequence; which are seldom expressed without much bloodshed. Sometimes these are successful and the whole ship's company is cut off. They are likewise always ready to seize every opportunity for committing some acts of desperation to free themselves from their miserable state and notwithstanding the restraints which are laid.[73]

Conclusion

How did the indigenous social formation, ecology, and power relations in West Africa underpin reactions to unsuccessful attempts to ransom captives? How long did negotiations continue before they collapsed and were assumed to have failed? How did a captive's family and/or community calculate the social and economic cost of ransoming and who made the decision to call off ransom negotiations? The discourse on enslavement in West Africa has emphasized the disruptions and specifically the violence caused by slave raiders and slave revolts, and lately the success of ransom operations as well as discourses on legal and illegal enslavement. The cases examined in this chapter show how the issue of ransoming complicates our understanding of the legal aspects of slavery in West Africa and the necessity to rethink what constitutes legal and illegal enslavement. Moreover, these cases highlight the intriguingly procedural quality to not only enslavement but also to the reversal of captivity and enslavement. Slavery was a recognized and legal institution in Africa but very few people ever accepted their enslavement or that of their kin as legal or legitimate. During the nineteenth century Yoruba wars, a common refrain among Ekiti soldiers was to die in battle rather than be captured by Ibadan forces. A local proverb says '*iku ya j'esin. Kaka ka s'eru ka kuku ku*' (death is preferred to humiliation. It is better to die than become a slave).[74] The responses to unsuccessful ransom negotiations, and by extension illegal enslavement, further illuminates the cycle of violence associated with slaving operations, and the making of war and peace in West African societies.

That the allies of a captive would frequently try to negotiate and pay a ransom for the return of a captive indicates that, often, individuals, regardless of their status, sought peaceful means to ensure freedom because it was the best way to guarantee a captive's safety. However, the fact that families did not simply reconcile themselves to the loss through enslavement of their members in the aftermath of failed ransom negotiations but would resort to violent methods to ensure freedom or to seek revenge demonstrates the importance that Africans placed on freedom. Mungo Park captured this aspect of western Sudanese culture: for the African "no water is sweet but what is drawn from his own well, and no tree has so cool and pleasant a shade as the *tabba* tree of his native village." Often times, "he [African] turns his whole thoughts towards revenging some depredation or insult, which either he or his ancestors may have received from a neighbouring state."[75] Reactions to failed ransom negotiations highlight the issue of agency - how allies of slaves shaped the institution of slavery or "made" it in their own fashion. If shipboard revolts forced a reduction in the number of slaves taken to the Americas and impacted the regions/ports for slave embarkation in Africa, responses to failed ransom negotiations also mitigated enslavement.[76] They led to the release of many captives who would have become slaves and might have forced slave raiders to avoid areas prone to violent responses. Certainly slave raiders released captives who had powerful allies.

The study of failed ransom negotiations also opens up more avenues for historical exploration. Just as historians of Africa have modified the hitherto perception that Africans were divided between slave raiders and raided societies, and during colonialism between resistors and collaborators, this chapter also seeks to bridge the gulf between protective and offensive strategies against enslavement. Responses to failed ransom negotiations included both protective and offensive tactics against enslavement. Africans desired freedom for their relatives in captivity. Decisions about particular responses to failed ransom negotiations, though, were rarely made until people had adequately weighed the opportunity cost of various resolutions to captivity.

Endnotes

1 This is a revised version of an article that appeared in the *Journal of African History*, 52 (2012). We thank the publisher for allowing us to reprint a revised version in this edited volume.

2 Malyn Newitt (ed.), *The Portuguese in West Africa, 1415–1670: A Documentary History* (Cambridge: Cambridge University Press, 2010), 46-47.

3 See Sylvianne A. Diouf, "The Last Resort: Redeeming Family and Friends," in Sylvianne Diouf (ed.), *Fighting the Slave Trade, West African Strategies* (Athens: Ohio University Press, 2003), 82-92; Olatunji Ojo, "'[I]n Search of their Relations, To Set at Liberty as Many as They Had the Means': Ransoming Captives in Nineteenth Century Yorubaland," *Nordic Journal of African Studies*, 19:1 (2010), 58-76; Jennifer Lofkrantz, "Protecting Freeborn Muslims: The Sokoto Caliphate's Attempts to Prevent Illegal Enslavement and its Acceptance of the Strategy of Ransoming," *Slavery & Abolition*, 32:1 (2011), 109-117; Lofkrantz, "Intellectual Discourse in the Sokoto Caliphate: The Triumvirate's Opinions in the Issue of Ransoming, ca.1810," *International Journal of African Historical Studies*, 45:3 (2012), 385-401.

4 See for example John Hunwick, "Islamic Law and Polemics over Race and Slavery in North and West Africa (16th-19th Century)," in Shaun E. Marmon (ed.), *Slavery and Islamic Middle East* (Princeton: Markus Wiener, 1999), 43-68; Robin Law, "Legal and Illegal Enslavement in West Africa in the Context of the Trans-Atlantic Slave Trade," in Toyin Falola (ed.), *Ghana in Africa and the World: Essays in Honor of Adu Boahen* (Trenton: African World Press, 2003), 513-33; Jose C. Curto, "The Story of Nbena, 1817-1820: Unlawful Enslavement and the Concept of Original Freedom in Angola," in Paul E. Lovejoy and David Trotman (eds.), *Trans-Atlantic Dimensions of Ethnicity in the African Diaspora* (London: Continuum, 2003), 43-64; Paul E. Lovejoy and David Richardson, "Anglo-Efik Relations and Protection against the Illegal Enslavement at Old Calabar, 1740-1807," in Diouf, *Fighting the Slave Trade*, 101-23; John K. Thornton, "African Political Ethics and the Slave Trade," in Derek R. Peterson (ed.), *Abolitionism and Imperialism in Britain, Africa, and the Atlantic* (Athens: Ohio University Press, 2010), 38-62 and Ojo, "The Atlantic Slave Trade and Local Ethics of Slavery in Yorubaland," *African Economic History*, 41 (2013), 75-102.

5 Hunwick, "Al-Maghīlī and the Jews of Tuwāt: The Demise of a Community," *Studia Islamica*, 61 (1985): 155-83; Humphrey J. Fisher, "A Muslim William Wilberforce? The Sokoto Jihād as Anti-Slavery Crusade: An Enquiry into Historical Causes," in Serge Daget (ed.), *De la traite a l'esclavage du XV*[e] *au XVIII*[e] *siècle: Actes du Colloque Internationiale sur la traite des Noirs* (Nantes: CRHMA, 1985), Vol.2, 537-55; Lovejoy, "The Context of Enslavement in West

Africa: Ahmad Bābā and the Ethics of Slavery," in Jane Landers and Barry Robinson (eds.), *Slaves, Subjects and Subversives: Blacks in Colonial Latin America* (Albuquerque: University of New Mexico, 2006), 9-38. Also see John Hunwick and Fatima Harrak (eds.), *Mi'raj al-su'ud: Ahmad Baba's Replies on Slavery* (Rabat: Institut des Etudes Africaines, Université Mohamed V, 2000) and Hunwick, trans. and ed. *Shari'a in Songhay: The Replies of al-Maghīlī to the Questions of Askia al-hājj Muhammad* (Oxford: Oxford University Press, 1985).

6 James Holman, *Travels in Madeira, Sierra Leone, Teneriffe, St. Jago, Cape Coast, Fernando Po, Princes Island, Etc., Etc,* 2nd ed. (London: George Routledge, 1840), 396.

7 Law, "Legal," 518; Thornton, "African Political Ethics;" and Ojo, "Atlantic Slave Trade and Local Ethics."

8 Theophille Conneau noted that the Baga of the Upper Guinea Coast "neither sell nor buy each other, though they acquire children of both sexes from other tribes, and adopt them into their own, or dispose of them if not suitable." See Conneau, *A Slaver's Log Book or 20 Years' Residence in Africa: The Original Manuscript* (Englewood Cliffs, NJ: Prentice Hall, 1976 [1854]), 124.

9 Claude Meillassoux, *Anthropology of Slavery: The Womb of Iron and Gold* translated by Alide Dasnois (Chicago: University of Chicago Press, 1991), 103.

10 On the institutional basis of African trade, see Paul Lovejoy and David Richardson, "Trust, Pawnship, and Atlantic History: The Institutional Foundations of the Old Calabar Slave Trade," *American Historical Review,* 104:2 (1999), 333-55 and Machiko Nissanke and Alice Sindzingre, "Institutional Foundations for Shared Growth in Sub-Saharan Africa," *African Development Review*, 18:3 (2006), 353-91.

11 See David Eltis, "The Diaspora of Yoruba Speakers, 1650–1865: Dimensions and Implications," in Toyin Falola and Matt D. Childs (eds.), *The Yoruba Diaspora in the Atlantic World* (Indianapolis: Indiana University Press, 2004), 24; and Robin Law, *The Slave Coast of West Africa, 1550-1750: The Impact of the Atlantic Slave Trade on an African Society* (Oxford: Clarendon, 1991).

12 Thornton, "African Political Ethics," 44-45.

13 Meillassoux, *Anthropology of Slavery*, 33, 101-109.

14 Phillip Curtin, "Joseph Wright of the Egba" in Curtin (ed.), *Africa Remembered: Narratives by West Africans from the Era of the Slave Trade* (Madison: Wisconsin University Press, 1967), 317-34.

15 William Bosman, *A New and Accurate Description of the Coast of Guinea, Divided Into the Gold, the Slave, and the Ivory Coasts* (London: James Knapton, 1705), 365. European captives also thought their African captors would devour them. Cross-culturally cannibalism is a metaphor for hatred and ill-will towards the enemy. For details, see Gomes Eannes de Azurara, *The Chronicle of the Discovery and Conquest of Guinea*, trans. Charles Beazley and Edgar Prestage (London: Hakluyt Society, 1899), Vol. 2, 143-46; Newitt, *Portuguese in West Africa*, 47; Elizabeth Isichei, *Voices of the Poor in Africa* (Rochester, NY: Uni-

versity of Rochester Press, 2004), 36-38; Allan Rice, *Radical Narratives of the Black Atlantic* (London: Continuum, 2003), 120-46.

16 Thomas Bluett, *Some Memoirs of the Life of Job, the Son of Solomon the High Priest of Boonda in Africa* (London: Richard Ford, 1734), 16-18. Diallo was enslaved in 1731 and not 1730 as Bluett thought.

17 George E. Brooks, *Landlords and Strangers: Ecology, Society, and Trade in Western Africa, 1000-1630* (Boulder, CO: Westview Press, 1993), 262.

18 Eric R. Taylor, *If We Must Die: Shipboard Insurrections in the Era of the Atlantic Slave Trade* (Baton Rouge: Louisiana State University Press 2006); Bruce Mouser, "Rebellion, Marronage and Jihad: Strategies of Resistance to Slavery on the Sierra Leone Coast, c.1783-1796," *Journal of African History*, 48 (2007), 27-44; Richardson, "Shipboard Revolts, African Authority, and the African Slave Trade," *William & Mary Quarterly*, 58 (2001), 69-92; Richard Rathbone, "Some Thoughts on Resistance to Enslavement in Africa," *Slavery & Abolition,* 6 (1985), 11-22.

19 Diouf, "Last Resort," 84-89; and "Testimony of William Littleton," in Sheila Lambert (ed.), *House of Commons Sessional Papers* (Wilmington, DE: Scholarly Resources, 1975), 68: 286. However, some witnesses testified that the ransoming of convicts was permitted. See "Testimony of Richard Miles" and "Testimony of Jerome Bernard Weuves" in Lambert, *House of Commons Sessional Papers,* 68: 120, 124, 126, 218.

20 A good illustration of this phenomenon is Mahommah Baquaqua's two experiences with captivity. In the first instance in 1841, his brother was able to arrange for his freedom. The second time he was taken captive in 1846, he was quickly moved to the coast and out of the region where he knew that people could track him and ransom him. See Robin Law and Paul E. Lovejoy (eds.), *The Biography of Mahommah Gardo Baquaqua: His Passage from Slavery to Freedom in Africa and America* (Princeton: Markus Weiner, 2001), 130-31.

21 See voyage id. 75094 on the Atlantic Slave Trade Voyage database. See also Diouf, "Last," 89.

22 Bluett, *Some Memoirs*, 9-20.

23 Bruce Mouser (ed.), *Journal of James Watt, Expedition to Timbo Capital of the Fula Empire in 1794* (Madison: University of Wisconsin Press, 1994), 40.

24 Allan F. C. Ryder, *Benin and the Europeans 1485-1897* (London: Longman, 1969), 77-78, 130-33; Robin Law, "On Pawning and Enslavement for Debt in the Precolonial Slave Coast," in Paul E. Lovejoy and Toyin Falola (eds.), *Pawnship, Slavery and Colonialism in Africa* (Trenton: Africa World Press, 2003), 62-64; Lovejoy and Richardson, "Trust, Pawnship, and Atlantic History;" and Ojo, "*Èmú* (Àmúyá): The Yoruba Institution of Panyarring or Seizure for Debt," *African Economic History*, 35 (2007), 31-58.

25 Carl B. Wadström, *An Essay on Colonization, Particularly Applied to the Western Coast of Africa* (London: Darton and Harvey, 1795), Vol. 2, 90.

26 Ibid., Vol. II, 93-97.

27 Ibid., Vol. 2, 87-118.

28 See Ryder, *Benin*; Law, "On Pawning and Enslavement;" and Paul E. Lovejoy and David Richardson, "'Horrid Hole': Royal Authority, Commerce and Credit at Bonny, 1690-1840," *Journal of African History*, 45 (2004), 363-92.

29 James O. McWilliam, *Medical History of the Expedition to the Niger, During the Years 1841-1842* (London: John Churchill, 1843); Phillip D. Curtin, *The Image of Africa: British Ideas and Action, 1780-1850* (Madison: University of Wisconsin Press, 1964), 58-87, 483-87; Lovejoy and Richardson, "Horrid Hole."

30 Bluett, Some Memoirs, 18.

31 Diouf, "Last Resort;" Lofkrantz, "Protecting Freeborn Muslims;" Ojo, "In Search."

32 Wadström, *Essay*, Vol. 2, 17.

33 Conneau, *Slaver's Log Book*, 144-47.

34 Personal communication with Ibrahim Amouren, Director of the Archives d'Agadez, March 2007.

35 William Allen, journal, 25 Sept. 1841 in William Allen and T. R. H. Thomson, *A Narrative of the Expedition sent by Her Majesty's Government to the River Niger in 1841 under the Command of Captain H. D. Trotter* (London: Frank Cass, 1968 [1848]), Vol. 2, 92.

36 Lofkrantz, "Ransoming Captives in the Sokoto Caliphate" in Behnaz A. Mirzai, Ishmael M. Montana and Paul E. Lovejoy (eds.), *Slavery, Islam, and Diaspora* (Trenton: African World Press, 2009) 125-37; Ojo, "In Search."

37 National Archives, Ibadan (NAI), Bishop Charles Phillips Papers 3/1, Phillips diary, 11-23 Nov. 1885.

38 Diouf, "Last Resort," 87.

39 See Martin Klein, *Slavery and Colonial Rule in French West Africa* (Cambridge: Cambridge University Press, 1998), 7-15; Toru Miura and John E. Philips (eds.), *Slave Elites in the Middle East and Africa: A Comparative Study* (London: Kegan Paul, 2000); Sean Stilwell, *Paradoxes of Power: The Kano 'Mamluks' and Male Royal Slavery in the Sokoto Caliphate, 1804–1903* (Portsmouth, NH: Heinemann, 2004).

40 Igor Kopytoff and Suzanne Miers, "African 'Slavery' as an Institution of Marginality" in Miers and Kopytoff (eds.), *Slavery in Africa: Historical and Anthropological Perspectives* (Madison: University of Wisconsin Press, 1977), 3-81.

41 Bosman, *A New and Accurate Description*, 183; Lofkrantz, "Protecting."

42 Wadström, *Essay*, Vol. 2, 80.

43 Bosman, *New and Accurate Description*, 183.

44 Lofkrantz, "Intellectual Discourse."

45 Geza Pálffy, "Ransom Slavery along the Ottoman-Hungarian Frontier in the Sixteenth and Seventeenth Centuries," in Géza Dávid and Pál Fodor (eds.), *Ransom Slavery along the Ottoman Borders: Early Fifteenth – Early Eighteenth Centuries* (Leiden: Brill, 2007), 35-85; Robert Davis, *Christian Slaves, Muslim Masters* (New York: Palgrave Macmillan, 2003); Thomas Freller, "'The

Shining of the Moon' – The Mediterranean Tour of Muhammad ibn Uthmān, Envoy of Morocco, in 1782," *Journal of Mediterranean Studies (Malta)*, 12:2 (2002), 307-26; James Brodman, *Ransoming Captives in Crusader Spain: The Order of Merced on the Christian-Islamic Frontier* (Philadelphia: University of Pennsylvania Press, 1986); Diouf, "Last Resort;" Lofkrantz, "Protecting Free Born Muslims."

46 See Attilus Ambrus and Eric Chaney, "Pirates of the Mediterranean: An Empirical Investigation of Bargaining with Transaction Costs." http://www.economics.harvard.edu/faculty/ambrus/files/Barbary.pdf

47 Ellen G. Friedman, *Spanish Captives in North Africa in the Early Modern Age* (Madison: University of Wisconsin Press, 1983), 142.

48 Gillian Weiss, "Barbary Captivity and the French Idea of Freedom," *French Historical Studies*, 28:2 (2005), 231-64; and E. Nathalie Rothman, "Becoming Venetian: Conversion and Transformation in the Seventeenth-Century Mediterranean," *Mediterranean Historical Review*, 21:1 (2006), 39-75.

49 See also Lawrence A. Peskin, *Captives and Countrymen: Barbary Slaves and the American Public 1785-1816* (Baltimore: The Johns Hopkins University Press, 2009).

50 Ronald Robinson, "The Partition of Africa," in F. H. Hinsley (ed.), *The New Cambridge Modern History vol. 11: Material Progress and World-wide Problems 1870–1898* (Cambridge: Cambridge University Press, 1962), 617-20.

51 Thornton, *Africa and Africans in the Formation of the Atlantic World, 1400-1680* (New York: Cambridge University Press, 1992), 72-97; and Joseph Inikori, "The Struggle against the Transatlantic Slave Trade: the Role of the State," in Diouf, *Fighting the Slave Trade*, 170-98.

52 David Eltis, *The Rise of African Slavery in the Americas* (Cambridge: Cambridge University Press, 2000), 57-61, 224-34.

53 Diouf, *Fighting the Slave Trade*; Martin A. Klein, "The Slave Trade and Decentralized Societies," *Journal of African History*, 42:1 (2001), 49-65; Walter Hawthorne, "The Production of Slaves where there was no State: The Guinea-Bissau Region, 1450-1815," *Slavery & Abolition*, 20:2 (1999), 97-124.

54 Jacob Ajayi, "Professional Warriors in Nineteenth-Century Yoruba Politics," *Tarikh*, 1 (1965), 72-81.

55 Ellen Friedman, "Christian Captives at 'Hard Labour' in Algiers 16th to 18th Centuries," *International Journal of African Historical Studies*, 13 (1980), 616–32; Dávid and Fodor, *Ransom*; Ojo, "In Search," 66-67.

56 Mungo Park, *Travels in the Interior Districts of Africa: Performed Under the Direction and Patronage of the African Association, in the Years 1795, 1796, and 1797*, 5th ed. (London: W. Bulmer, 1807), 435.

57 Samuel Johnson, *The History of the Yorubas from the Earliest to the Beginning of the British Protectorate* (Lagos: CSS Books, 1976 [1921]), 287-88, 305.

58 Johnson, *History of the Yorubas*, 250.

59 William Smith, *A New Voyage to Guinea*, 2nd ed. (London: John Nourse, 1745), 101-102.

60 Smith, *New Voyage*, 102-104. The Expedition (voyage #21690) belonged to Jacob Jervois and Michael Pecheco de Silva of London. Under Captains William Malthus and Thomas Simpson it left London in Sept. 1726 and departed Africa with 322 slaves enroute Barbados in Aug. 1727. On the other hand, the Elizabeth (voyage #78283) owned by a consortium of the British South Sea Company, David Brahoult, Joseph Hayward and John Cleveland left Bristol in June 1826. After buying slaves in Sierra Leone and the Gold Coast she left Africa for Jamaica with 215 slaves in mid-1727.

61 While rare, counter-seizures were not unknown in the Mediterranean world and in New Mexico; see Friedman, *Spanish*, 136-37; and James F. Brooks, *Captives and Cousins: Slavery, Kinship, and Community in the Southwest Borderlands* (Chapel Hill: University of North Carolina Press, 2002), 52.

62 Wadström, *Essay*, Vol. 2, 77. The story previously appeared in the *Substance of the Report Delivered by the Court of Directors of the Sierra Leone Company, to the General Court of Proprietors, on Thursday, March 27th, 1794* (London: James Phillips, 1794), 76, 113.

63 Rebecca Shumway, *The Fante and the Transatlantic Slave Trade* (Rochester: University of Rochester Press, 2011), 34.

64 Dalby Thomas (Cape Coast Castle), 11 December 1709, T70/5, The National Archives, Kew (TNA). Perhaps Capt. John Brethaver of the British vessel Martin Gally (voyage #15193). The ship, owned by Richard Harris, Edward Searle, Richard Chauncey and Bill Chauncey embarked 295 slaves in Africa after which it was seized by the French and its cargo landed in the French Caribbean in March 1710.

65 Johnson, *History of the Yorubas*, 270.

66 Ibid., 270-271.

67 Thomas Winterbottom, *An Account of the Native Africans in the Neighbourhood of Sierra Leone* (London: C. Whittingham, 1803), Vol. 1, 153.

68 Ibid., Vol. 1, 155.

69 Johnson, *History of the Yorubas*, 455-457.

70 Thomas J. Bowen, *Adventures and Missionary Labours in Several Countries in the Interior of Africa from 1849 to 1856* (London: Frank Cass, 1968 [1857]), 148-49.

71 Gomer Williams, *History of the Liverpool Privateers and Letters of Marque, with an Account of the Liverpool Slave Trade* (London: William Heinemann, 1897), 541-48; Lovejoy and Richardson, "Anglo-Efik."

72 Williams, *History*, 541-48; and Randy Sparks, *The Two Princes of Calabar: An Eighteenth-Century Atlantic Odyssey* (Cambridge MA: Harvard University Press, 2004).

73 Alexander Falconbridge, *An Accounts of the Slave Trade on the Coast of Africa* (London: 1788),

74 Interview with Chief Joel Ige, 90 years, Omu-Ekiti, 9 June 2001.

75 Park, *Travels in the Interior*, 242-43.

76 Richardson, "Shipboard Revolts."

SECTION III
Contemporary Africa

Map 8.1: Republic of Biafra, May 1969

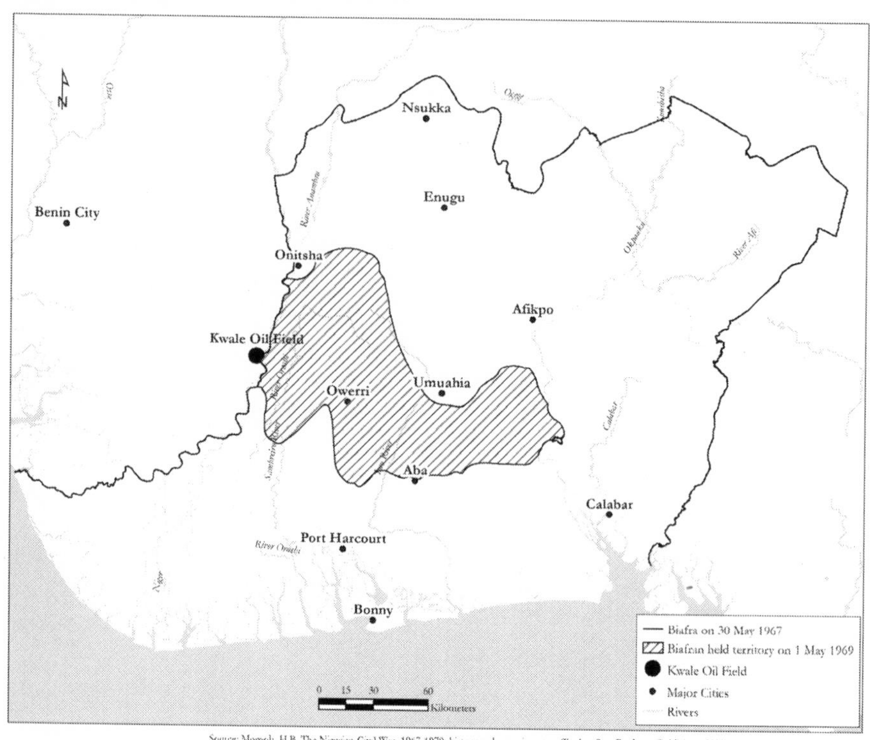

Source: Momoh, H.B. The Nigerian Civil War, 1967-1970: history and reminiscences. (Ibadan: Sam Bookman Publishers, 2000)
Projection: WGS 1984
Created by: Joseph Sloop & Pam Hurst

CHAPTER VIII

Biafra and the AGIP Oil Workers:

Ransoming and the Modern Nation State in Perspective

Roy Doron

Introduction

On 9 May 1969, in the midst of the Nigerian Civil War, a squad of Biafran commandoes attacked an oil facility belonging to the Italian oil company Azienda Generale Italiana Petroli (AGIP)[1] on the west bank of the River Niger, near the town of Kwale, some seventy kilometers south of Onitsha. In the assault, eleven oil workers were killed and a further eighteen were taken prisoner and ferried across the Niger into the secessionist enclave. After two weeks, when the Nigerian government and a team from AGIP found a mass grave with the eleven bodies, the Biafran government admitted to holding the surviving eighteen, which consisted of fourteen Italians, three Germans and a Jordanian. The Biafrans claimed the oil workers had taken up arms with their Nigerians guards during the raid and tried them for aiding the Nigerians in a genocidal war against Biafra, sentencing them to death on 2 June. Three days later the prisoners were released, after a Portuguese request for clemency. Unofficial reports, news interviews and declassified documents suggest that the Italian Foreign Ministry and AGIP paid a ransom of ITL 18,000,000,000, or USD 3,000,000, to secure their release. Biafra sought not only to hold the workers hostage, but to frighten the oil industry, which the Biafrans considered complicit in what they characterized as a genocidal war.[2]

Because public opinion in support of Biafra had begun to wane since early 1969, the Biafrans used this case to thrust their plight back into the global spotlight. Further, the Biafran Government used the affair to gain several material and political advantages. Not only did the Biafrans hold the oil workers until a ransom was allegedly paid, the Biafrans hoped to use the affair to establish de-facto recognition of their government by holding high level governmental talks and using Non-governmental organizations (NGOs) such as the International Committee of the Red Cross (ICRC) and other aid organizations. The affair proved an unmitigated disaster for the Biafrans and gave the Nigerians some authority in the propaganda war that the Biafrans had, until this moment, waged so effectively. Though the Biafrans received a substantial payment in exchange for the prisoners, the costs of taking hostages and holding them for ransom was so unpalatable to the international community that the monetary gains were far outstripped by the non-monetary costs associated with an act seen as criminal.

Biafra's attack on AGIP's facility and subsequent hostage crisis caused an international uproar and led to global public opinion, especially in Europe, turning against Biafra's cause. Biafra had hitherto cultivated an image of a modern state in the making and this affair tarnished the nascent republic's image. The decline in Biafra's standing came about because ransoming had, by the mid twentieth century, become an act associated with criminal behavior and not one that modern nation states engaged in. Biafra was actively engaging global public opinion to portray its cause as a just one and its image as a modern state worthy of joining the family of nations. This case showcases the shift in ransoming practices where the non-monetary costs associated with a state actor engaging in behavior now seen as a criminal far outweighed any gains made by the action.

Background to the Nigerian Civil War

Nigeria's civil war erupted in May 1967 as the culmination of the political crisis that had plagued the country since independence, and had its roots in the structure of the colonial and post-colonial state. Nigeria's politics had long been dominated by the three large ethnic groups, the predominantly Muslim Hausa in the Northern Region, the mainly Christian Igbo in the Eastern Region and the Yoruba in the Western Region, who comprised both Muslims and Christians. Together, these three groups comprised almost seventy percent of the country's population when Nigeria became independent on 1 October 1960.[3] Nigeria's crisis stemmed from the competition between the rival ethnic groups' over control of the country's power structure, which was the key to accessing Nigeria's natural resources, and the revenue derived from them. Several election crises in 1964 and 1965 and a disputed 1963 census, where figures were astronomically inflated to maximize the different regions' access to government positions, which were allocated according to population, stressed the instability of Nigeria's first republic.

On 15 January 1966, a group of mainly Igbo officers, commonly referred to as the Five Majors, staged a coup that toppled the first republic.[4] Though the coup was quickly defeated, the plotters managed to kill the Prime Minister, Abubakar Tafawa Balewa, a Northern Muslim along with Ahmadu Bello, the premier of the Northern Region and Samuel Akintola, the Yoruba Western Region's premier. Nigeria's President, Nnamdi Azikiwe, as well as the predominantly Igbo Eastern Region's leadership were spared. The ethnic composition of both the coup plotters and the carnage led many in the North to claim that this was an ethnic cleansing of Nigeria's leadership. On 28 July 1966, a group of Northern officers, led by Murtala Muhammad murdered the military head of state, Johnson Aguiyi-Ironsi, and installed Yakubu "Jack" Gowon as the country's new military leader. Accompanying this coup was a wave of unprecedented violence in Northern Nigeria directed mainly at the Igbo. By most estimates, over 50,000 Igbo were killed and more than two million fled their homes in Northern Nigeria to the Igbo heartland in the Eastern Region, creating a humanitarian catastrophe and caused the Igbo leaders to accuse Nigeria of genocide.

Seeking ways to unencumber Nigeria's political morass Gowon in May 1967 proposed a new Federal system that eliminated the four regions and replaced them with twelve states. However, the Eastern Region's military governor, Chukwuemeka Odumegwu Ojukwu objected to the new system, fearing this was just another step in Nigeria's campaign against the Igbo. In particular, the new Rivers State would sever the Igbo controlled Eastern Region's control over much of Nigeria's oil and, more importantly, the new Igbo East Central State would be completely surrounded by other Nigerian states, and dependent on the rest of Nigeria for its survival. Ojukwu stoked fears that this new federal structure would allow the Northern controlled government to continue its policy of violence and extermination against the Igbo. After several aborted attempts at compromise, Gowon implemented the twelve state federal structure. The next day, on 26 May 1967, Ojukwu's Eastern Region voted to secede from Nigeria and on 30 May, Ojuwku declared the Eastern Region the Republic of Biafra, igniting a thirty month civil war that would cost up to a million lives and end in January 1970 with Biafra's surrender.

Historiography

This case study occurs at a time when the legitimate monetization of human life turned from an acceptable practice into a criminal one. This process took its modern form beginning with the efforts of the abolitionists of the slave trade. Though the practice of ransoming foreign captives had a long history throughout the early modern period, by the mid nineteenth century, the practice came to be seen as increasingly illegitimate.[5] Olatunji Ojo highlights one instance during the Ashanti Wars in modern day Ghana where a group of European missionaries were captured and held for ransom. Despite a ransom being negotiated for their release, the British decided to free the captives by force rather than paying the agreed ransom to the Asantehene.[6] When European powers colonized the various African polities, they attempted to enforce their abolitionist policies on societies that had so far been immune to the growing demonetization of human life. In particular, Trevor Getz and Thaddeus Sunseri focus on cases where British and German colonial administrations developed hybrid strategies for dealing with the moral issues of slavery, captivity, redemption and ransoming without disturbing the commercial realities of their extractive economic models.[7]

More recent studies trace the evolution of the fight against slavery from its origins battling the transatlantic slave trade to the modern day struggle against human trafficking. Joel Quirk argues that the capability to shift the realm and the language of the debate gave governmental powers the ability change their responsibilities in ways that would protect their economic interests. In particular, the issue of bonded labor was once touted as an intermediary condition between slavery and freedom, but was in fact slavery in all but name. This practice, like many other forms of slavery, eventually became illegal. Thus, by the 1960s, most forms of holding humans for either labor or direct and overt monetary gain had been delegitimized as part of normal diplomatic relations.[8]

The case of the Biafrans and the ENI oil workers is a unique case of a state entity that engaged in a practice that the global community came to see as morally wrong and illegal in international law. Though not exclusive in the post-war period, the Biafran case differs significantly from other cases, such as the Iranian storming of the United States Embassy in Tehran in 1979 or the Black September hijacking of Air France Flight 139 to Uganda in

1976. Unlike Revolutionary Iran or Idi Amin's Uganda, Biafra was actively portraying its cause not only as just, but one of a modern nation in the making and using the image they constructed to actively court western public opinion.[9] However, by taking the oil workers hostage, the Biafrans engaged in a practice that was considered outside the norms for any state actor to openly engage in. This action, despite its nominal success proved a pyrrhic victory, even with the substantial monetary gains, both in the ransom and in frightening other oil companies from working in the region. This chapter shows that the damage to Biafra's global prestige and the undermining of their entire propaganda narrative abroad far overshadowed the substantial monetary gains they made by holding the Italians hostage.

Abduction of the Oil Workers

By the time the Biafran military attacked the AGIP installation on 9 May 1969; the Nigerian offensives that threatened to break Biafra had been successfully halted. The Biafrans suffered two severe military collapses in 1968, the first in May, which culminated in the fall of Port Harcourt, the last major entrepôt to the country. The second began in September of that year, and culminated in what Nigerian Colonel Benjamin Adekunle, nicknamed "The Black Scorpion", hoped would be his "OAU gift" to Nigeria, a reference to the Organization of African Unity, which was maligned by both Nigeria and Biafra. Adekunle meant that he would capture the last major urban areas in Biafra, namely Owerri, Aba and Umuahia.[10] Though initially successful, Adekunle's plan went terribly awry after capturing both Owerri and Aba. On 22 April 1969, the Biafrans succeeded in beating the 3rd Marine Commando Division out of Owerri and threatened to rout the entire division. However, while the Biafrans had considerable success against Adekunle's division, in the north, Muhammad Shuwa's 1st Division continually gained on the Biafrans.

The Biafran successes were due in no small part to French military and financial aid. The French funneled arms and money into Biafra by using Gabon and the Ivory Coast to donate weapons to the Biafrans. The French, in turn, resupplied the Ivoirians and Gabonese for their donated stores. French military aid, both in equipment and loans, totaled more than five million dollars, less than double the amount the Biafrans received from ransoming the oil workers.[11]

By May 1969, the Biafrans had stabilized the military situation and staved off collapse. Further, the Ojukwu regime began using more unconventional methods to pursue their aims rather than "by the book" military tactics that proved disastrous in the past.[12] Ojukwu, having studied tactics from the Vietnam War, began implementing the Biafran Organization of Freedom Fighters (BOFF) to fight behind enemy lines.[13] These forces committed hit and run raids across the Niger and, though they were not directly responsible for the assault on the AGIP installation, proved that the Biafrans could project their power deep into Nigerian held territory. Further, the Swedish Count Carl Gustav Von Rosen transferred smuggled light aircraft into the country, which he converted to guerilla-style combat planes that became known as the MINICONs or the Biafran Babies.[14]

The Biafran military resurgence, with French material assistance, allowed for a certain sense of optimism on the Biafran side, which just a year earlier was teetering on the verge of collapse. The Biafran attack on the Italian oil installation came at a point when the Biafrans were emboldened by their recent successes and cautiously optimistic that they could continue to reverse the war's course and rollback of the Nigerian forces that, in their estimation, began in Owerri. Biafran propaganda echoed this optimism, stating on Radio Biafra

> The times are now more auspicious than they ever were before. To our defense is now being added a new dimension: an operational air force. Our enemy has been shocked by the striking power of the Biafran Air Force.[15]

On the night of 9 May 1969, a Biafran commando force assaulted the AGIP installation near Kwale in modern day Delta State on the west bank of the River Niger, roughly seventy kilometers southwest of Onitsha. The raid on the installation came as the culmination of fighting between Nigerian troops and Biafran commandos, who were engaged in combat between Kwale and the town of Okpai, on the western bank of the River Niger, roughly thirty kilometers east of the installation. The Biafran forces opened fire on the installation, killing three workers, from Nigeria, Germany and Lebanon, respectively. They then opened fire on a caravan, where eleven other workers were hiding.[16] In total, eleven workers were killed in the attack, but the exact death toll could not be confirmed, as the only Italian survivor, a man named Alcide Poggi, escaped along with two Nigerian storekeepers by crawling for twenty kilometers in the swamp before securing a canoe to escape from the battle. He told reporters that as soon as he heard the gunshots, he jumped through a window and waited for the attack to end. He then crawled with his Nigerian co-workers until they found the canoe. At no point did he return to determine the fate of his fellow countrymen.[17] Though news of the attack made headlines in Italy, global media outlets paid the affair scant attention, with the *New York Times* burying the first mention of the matter at the bottom of page eleven, next to a giant advert for women's summer fashion.[18]

In the weeks that followed, the Nigerian government, along with the Italian government, the United Nations (UN) and the International Committee of the Red Cross (ICRC), attempted to ascertain the missing workers' fate. The Nigerian military did not fully regain control of the area until 30 May, when AGIP officials, along with Italian government and ICRC workers uncovered a mass grave with eleven bodies.[19] The Biafran government had previously acknowledged the raid and claimed to hold prisoners even before the bodies were discovered, but did not disclose the number of survivors.[20]

The Biafrans claimed that the captured eighteen oil workers, fourteen Italians, three West Germans and a Lebanese, engaged in combat alongside the Nigerian forces, and further claimed that they were captured with weapons. After a short trial, the eighteen workers were convicted of aiding the enemy in committing genocide and sentenced to death. Once the death sentences were publicized by Swiss public relations firm MarkPress,[21] frantic efforts began from many sides to secure the captives' release. Portugal and France, widely seen as Biafra's most important allies in Europe placed substantial pressure on the Biafrans to release the Italians. The French government went as far as to briefly suspend all civilian and military aid to the secessionists until the matter was settled. Portugal threatened to discontinue relief flights from São Tomé, the main departing point for flights into the Biafran enclave, unless the oilmen were freed.[22]

The reasoning behind the Biafran attempt to make an example of these captured oil workers is complex and includes economic necessity, political imperative, and moral posturing. Despite the optimism of early 1969, the Biafran situation remained grave. Biafra was reduced to an enclave surrounded by a Nigerian military that was slowly shrinking the territory Ojukwu controlled. This reality compounded the difficulties of obtaining war materials, demanding drastic, and sometimes desperate measures. The affair with the AGIP oil workers was both drastic and desperate, and ultimately a diplomatic failure. Perhaps most damaging, the affair seriously undercut the much cultivated Biafran moral superiority in global public opinion.

Despite the few Biafran successes in May and June of 1969, their situation was increasingly bleak. Politically, militarily, and financially, the Biafrans were near their breaking point. Even though they managed several successes against Adekunle's 3rd Marine Commando Division, notably the capture of Owerri, in the northern sector Muhammad Shuwa, proved a capable commander. While the Biafrans were busy ousting Federal troops from Owerri, Shuwa's men captured the Biafran capital at Umuahia.[23] Even though the Biafrans succeeded, for the only time in the war, in retaking a city from the Nigerians, they lost a much more important strategic location. Even more-so, their chain of command was disrupted to the extent that Ojukwu thought his second in command, Philip Efiong, had defected to the Nigerian side and briefly ordered the latter's summary execution.[24]

Because of their precarious situation, the Biafrans needed convertible currency to continue the war. Their financial situation was the more desperate because the Nigerians had been waging a very effective economic war since the beginning of the conflict. In late 1967, the Nigerian government issued the Central Bank Currency Conversion Decree 51, which had several effects. First, it decoupled the Nigerian Pound from the Pound Sterling, and set in place a series of controls, which made it more difficult to export Nigerian currency.[25] Second, an entire set of new banknotes, which had to be converted within nineteen days of the decree, made all previous banknotes, which formed the bulk of Biafra's currency reserves, obsolete.[26]

The Biafrans were also spending considerable resources on the ornamental aspects of sovereignty. Ojukwu created the Biafran Pound and issued the currency twice, once in January 1968 and a second time in February 1969.[27] Though the currency remained largely symbolic, as there was not enough circulated to make it the de facto currency of the region, Ojukwu devoted much effort to this type of symbolism of sovereignty. In his memoirs, Efiong stated that Ojukwu disregarded many essential elements of prosecuting the war and instead "concentrated more on the trappings and paraphernalia of office," including awarding medals to Efiong, who felt those awards "had nothing more than a nuisance value at the time."[28]

Thus the Biafrans were reduced to using a dwindling supply of foreign currency with little hope of generating sustainable income, even though theirs was a cause célèbre around the world. The many donations and fundraisers held around the world, which featured people like John Lennon, Jimi Hendrix and Joan Baez, went largely to humanitarian efforts. Private donations by Biafrans abroad, such as boxing champion Dick Tiger who donated his entire fortune to the Biafran cause, earning him an honorary commission in the Biafran army, were never enough to sustain a war.[29] As a result, the Biafran government constantly suffered from a lack of liquidity.

The Biafrans were further hampered by the fact that they no longer controlled the oil producing areas in Biafra. In addition to the areas west of the Niger, where the AGIP facility was located, by the end of 1968, the Nigerians controlled all of Biafra with the exception of the Igbo heartland. This loss of territory was especially devastating, as it included the vast majority of the oil reserves and the cities of Port Harcourt and Bonny, Biafra's main ports and oil production centers. Not only did this lack of control hamper the Biafran government's ability to raise the funds needed to prosecute the war, but the oil revenues supported the Nigerian side in the conflict. In fact, the Biafrans claimed that the royalties that foreign oil companies paid served to further the Nigerian war effort to such an extent that Biafran Information minister, Ifegwu Eke, said in an interview "the moment oil companies stop paying royalties to the federal government, at that moment the war will stop."[30]

Control of the oil producing areas was important for both sides because of the royalties from the large oil multinationals. In fact, the FMG timed many of its early military operations to coincide with royalty payments from the oil conglomerates. The capture of Bonny and later of Port Harcourt sent a message that Nigeria, and not Biafra, controlled the oil region, ensuring the payments to Nigeria. In fact, the FMG's early assault on Bonny in July 1967, though successful, led to a protracted counter attack. Control of the city was so important that the FMG did not firmly establish its control over the town until January of the following year. For both sides, the money was of utmost importance, but Biafra would have also touted receiving the oil royalties as de-facto recognition of sovereignty.[31]

Ojukwu used the oil workers' plight as a backdoor channel to gaining some form of international recognition. The Biafrans had long been using the crisis as a way to secure de facto recognition, or failing that, internationalize the conflict in a way that would give them a respite from the worst of the war's ravages. At one point, when asked how to best guarantee the oil workers' rights as prisoners, Louis Mbafeno, Biafra's Chief Justice, suggested that the only way to do so was to allow Biafra to sign the Geneva Convention. Throughout the war, the Biafrans attempted to secure this type of recognition by either negotiating for land corridors that would be protected by the United Nations or otherwise enshrined in a multilateral treaty of some sort. Mbafeno's suggestion amounted to another attempt to secure some kind of backdoor international recognition that would prove useful in any final status negotiations, should the war end through political rather than military means.[32]

The death sentences handed down to the Italian oil workers gave Ojukwu a global platform to decry what he considered the hypocritical attitude of the "Western" world, that placed a premium on the lives of the eighteen oil workers, while still allowing what the Biafrans increasingly claimed was a genocidal conflict against the Igbo.[33] Though Ojukwu's handling of the affair, which he insisted on handling personally, was increasingly damaging the Biafran public relations campaign, the affair nonetheless highlighted a perception of duality in the sanctity of life when comparing the lives of Europeans to those of Biafrans and Nigerians.[34]

The Biafrans came to view the fallout of their assault on the AGIP installation as unwelcome diversions to their war and propaganda efforts. First, as the Biafrans were increasingly optimistic that they were on the verge of turning the tide of the war, they sought to convey that message to the global media through MarkPress. However, the global media attention on the oil workers overshadowed the fact that the Biafrans could successfully penetrate Nigerian space, both on land and from the air. The story of the captured oil workers became what Ojukwu would later call "another 'human drama'."[35] Ojukwu went as far as to take to the airwaves to denounce the global furor, stating on Radio Biafra

> For eighteen white men, Europe is aroused! What have they said about our millions? Eighteen white men assisting in the crime of genocide. What do they say about our murdered innocents? How many black dead make one missing white? Mathematicians, please answer me. Is it infinity?[36]

Second, the raid on the installation came several weeks before Biafra's second Independence Day, on 30 May 1969, and the confirmation of the eleven dead oil workers became public at the end of May, with the *New York Times* reporting the discovery on 1 June. Ojukwu's plan was to use Biafra's Independence Day to unveil a new direction and model of self-sufficiency for the country in the Ahiara Declaration. The oil workers' fate overshadowed the Ahiara Declaration and indeed, the declaration received little attention around the world, despite Ojukwu's attempt to portray the new model of self-sufficiency for the republic.

The Biafrans were not alone in criticizing what they saw as a double standard in the value of Western lives compared to those of Africans. The *New Nigerian* published an editorial on 1 June 1969 titled "All Christians Equal?" In the editorial, the paper criticized the public outcry over the fate of the oil workers, explaining

> ...what Western people ought to realize is that we, too, care about our people. We lose hundreds every week on both sides of the firing line. The fact that thirty or so foreigners kidnapped can cause such uproar does not go down well with us.[37]

Ojukwu's protestations that the lives of two dozen foreigners meant more to the world than the lives of millions of Biafrans found a receptive audience on the other side of the lines, and the Nigerian press supported his assertion, ending this editorial by paraphrasing George Orwell, stating that "all Christians are equal – but white Christians are more equal."[38] Though Ojukwu's comment on the value of African lives versus those of foreigners raised an important point that found a receptive audience even in the newspapers of Biafra's enemies, Biafra largely depended on foreign aid, both to finance the war effort and to alleviate the humanitarian crisis. In addition to sparking the crisis, Ojukwu's fiery rhetoric further alienated his supporters abroad. In one conversation with Clarence Ferguson, American special coordinator for Biafran relief, Louis Mbafeno quipped, "all these governments which denied existence of Biafra now crawling on behalf of [eighteen] white lackeys."[39]

Despite the fact that Biafra's assault on the AGIP facility was almost universally condemned, Ojukwu's government decided to forge ahead with the death sentences. Ojukwu, however, agreed to negotiate with the Italian government regarding the release of the captives.[40] Even with diplomatic cables from the United States, the United Kingdom and Israel asserting that the Biafrans would only hold talks with the Italian government; it was a Portuguese appeal, requested by the Italians, which secured the release of the eighteen workers on 4 June.[41] The men arrived in Gabon on 5 June and returned to Rome on 7 June where they received an official welcome from Italian President Giuseppe Saragat and Pope Paul VI.[42] In his reception with the freed oil workers, and at Sunday mass the following day, Pope Paul VI declared that the Vatican's assistance to Biafra was apolitical and "only directed to bring the two opposing parties food and medicine, to save the innocent lives of the victims of the conflict [and] to suggest serene negotiations for some honorable solution to this tragic conflict."[43]

The global uproar over the captives and the intense efforts for their quick release gave credence to Ojukwu's assertions that Biafran lives were more expendable. The workers release came less than a month after they were captured, and only four days after the Biafrans passed sentence. The speed at which the negotiations took place is indicative of two very distinct realities that Biafra faced in the last year of the war. First and foremost, the Biafrans need the material support to continue the war as quickly as possible. Second, the Biafrans quickly realized the unwelcome distraction that the abduction caused around the world. They needed to end the brouhaha as quickly as possible and to minimize the damage to their now tarnished public relations campaign around the world.

One important clue as to Ojukwu's intentions comes from Lloyd Garrison, a *New York Times* correspondent who met with Biafran officials regarding the affair. In one instance, Garrison happened upon a chance meeting with one of the captives, who seemed rather bored with his ordeal and "was sunning himself in a reclining chair" outside one of the buildings of the Ministry of Foreign Affairs. When Garrison attempted to speak to him, the Italian replied "no speak English."[44] This encounter happened a few days before the death sentences were meted out, but shows that at least one of the Italian captives was rather unconcerned with his situation and not under guard as would be expected if he had indeed been actively fighting with the Nigerians. This account calls into question whether Ojukwu really planned to execute the Italians or if the sentence was a form of brinkmanship intended to hasten their release.

Because of the nature of the negotiations, details of any talks have never been made public, and only anecdotal evidence exists as to the nature of the discussions between the Biafran leadership and the Italian foreign ministry, AGIP and the Vatican. However, most unofficial sources confirmed that a ransom was paid, which was disguised as petroleum royalty payments from ENI, AGIP's parent company, to Biafra. The exact sum of the payment was never disclosed, but in two instances, very different sums were mentioned. In one instance, Mbafeno stated in an interview with Italian magazine *L'Europeo* a sum of three million dollars that were not paid as a ransom, but as "rightfully collected" royalties from AGIP. As soon as the interview was published, he quickly denied ever making the statement going as far as to deny that the interview itself ever took place. In addition, Biafran interior minister, Christopher Mojekwu, confirmed the official Biafran stance, stating that the oil workers' pardon and release stemmed not from any payment to Biafra, but "was inspired by [Ojukwu's] respect for human life."[45] John Stremlau, in his work *The International Politics of the Nigerian Civil War*, echoed the three million dollar sum, but also cited a conversation at a conference of Nigerian ambassadors which asserted that the ransom totaled twenty million dollars. However, the discrepancy could have because the sum of USD 3,000,000 was roughly equivalent to ITL 18,000,000,000 and the sums were then confused as they passed through the rumor and diplomatic pipelines.[46]

As Mbafeno's interview in *L'Europeo*, and other rumors, suggested that the Italians had paid a significant ransom to release the workers, the Pope's statement seemed a deliberate attempt to distance the Vatican's aid from the AGIP affair. Another highly developed tension was the conflict between the ICRC and the Nigerian Government that culminated in the downing of a Swedish ICRC plane, and the arrest and expulsion of ICRC chief relief coordinator Auguste Lindt from Lagos. Details of the tension between Nigeria and the ICRC are detailed below in the discussion of the effects of the AGIP affair on Nigerian and Biafran policy. However, the Pope's statements seemed to be a deliberate attempt to distance the Holy See's aid efforts from either of these volatile situations.

Consequences of the Affair

Ojukwu saw the importance of the oil industry in influencing Nigerian policy towards the war, but he underestimated Gowon's resolve to use military, rather than diplomatic and political means to secure the oil revenue. Though the Biafrans initially succeeded in diminishing the Nigerian Government's oil revenue, by the end of 1969, despite the attack on the oil installation and the use of the MINICONs, the Nigerians diverted enough military resources to protect the oil producing areas, especially west of the Niger. Thus, Gowon's government secured the oil industry's safety from future Biafran assaults and, in doing so, increased the oil revenue that Nigeria needed to counteract French assistance to Biafra.[47] However, the affair sufficiently frightened the oil industry that any word of further attacks was taken very seriously. Rumors even circulated that Shell-BP was secretly bribing the Biafrans to spare their installations.[48]

The Nigerian government used the crisis to redeploy their air force against targets all across Biafra. In March 1969, the Nigerian government came under scrutiny for a series of non-discriminatory air raids against Biafran targets. The raids, piloted mostly by ill-trained Egyptian pilots, led to increased civilian casualties and provided an advantage for Biafran propaganda, which portrayed the raids as evidence that their attacks against defenseless targets were but one aspect of the genocidal campaign that the Nigerians were perpetrating against the Igbo. However, after the raid on the AGIP installation, the Nigerians were able to renew their air attacks on Biafra, albeit with better trained pilots from East Germany and Czechoslovakia replacing the Egyptians.[49]

Closely related, the Nigerians used the AGIP affair to renew their opposition to the air corridor supplying Biafra. The nightly airlifts into Biafra were bringing in both humanitarian aid and large shipments of weapons and ammunition. Though many of the shipments came from private organizations such as the Joint Church Aid (JCA) and private citizens like the Israeli Abie Nathan, a large percentage of the humanitarian aid came from the ICRC. Unlike the private organizations and individuals, the ICRC was accountable to the governments and donors that funded its operations. After witnessing the global response to the Biafran raid, Gowon decided that his government could take a more hardline stance against the ICRC. First, on 27 May, the Nigerian government arrested Lindt on his arrival to Lagos.[50] Gowon's actions came as the culmination of a long standing feud between the two men over the nature of international aid to Biafra. Shortly thereafter, Lindt was deported from the country and declared persona non-grata.[51]

Lindt's arrest and deportation was the first step in Nigeria's escalation of their conflict with the ICRC. On the day that the Biafrans declared that the oil workers would be freed, a Nigerian MIG-17, flown by British pilot Mike Thompsett, shot down a Swedish Red Cross DC7 aircraft piloted by a crew consisting of two Swedes, a Norwegian and an American captain, killing all on board. The Nigerians initially stated that the incident was a case of misidentification, claiming that the plane was a Biafran DC6 engaged in a bombing run. However, shortly after the incident, Nigerian Air Force commander, Col. Shittu Alad, remarked "as far as we're concerned we are hitting at anything flying into Biafra, Red Cross or not."[52]

In reality, the attack on the ICRC aircraft was not a case of mistaken identity; rather it was a calculated event, meant to send a message to all parties the Nigerians claimed were assisting Biafra. In the years since the incident, details suggest that the incident was not meticulously planned in any way. However, the claim that the Swedish Red Cross plane was intentionally targeted emerged from several sources, as the Nigerians spotted at least one other plane, belonging to the JCA, which was allowed to continue. The fact that the ICRC plane belonged to the Swedish Red Cross proved fortuitous, as the incident was viewed as a Nigerian retaliation to von Rosen's role in implementing the MINICONs. One unnamed European officer stationed in Nigeria claimed that von Rosen and his aerial raids amounted to "the bee sting that made the horse go wild."[53]

Perhaps the most damaging aspect of the affair for Biafra was the humanitarian facet. Biafran propaganda, both at home and abroad, framed the humanitarian crisis not as a consequence of large scale siege warfare, but as a concerted Nigerian policy to exterminate the Igbo. As a result of Biafra's successful campaign both at home and abroad, many came to see the war as genocidal. In fact, Richard Nixon, in his 1968 Presidential campaign, categorized the war as such, stating

Until now efforts to relieve the Biafran people have been thwarted by the desire of the central government of Nigeria to pursue total and unconditional victory and by the fear of the Ibo people that surrender means wholesale atrocities and genocide. But genocide is what is taking place right now – and starvation is the grim reaper. This is not the time to stand on ceremony, or to 'go through channels' or to observe the diplomatic niceties… The destruction of an entire people is an immoral objective even in the most moral of wars…. While America is not the world's policeman, let us at least act as the world's conscience in this matter of life and death for millions.[54]

When news of the AGIP attack surfaced in the global media much of the moral persuasion that the Biafrans had worked so hard to garner during the war began to erode. This moral superiority was further challenged when the death sentences for the captured workers were announced. Chinua Achebe, referencing the abduction of the oil workers, stated in his memoir on the civil war,

> As a people proclaiming victimization at the hands of Nigeria, and rightfully so, we could not be seen as victimizers in any situation or setting, in order to continue receiving the widespread moral and humanitarian support we needed in order to survive. This failure to recognize this fundamental principle, I believe, contributed immensely to the downturn in Biafra's fortunes.[55]

The affair so harmed Biafra's standing in much of Europe that when the Nigerians resumed their air raids on Biafra, the raids were not met with the same universal condemnation that forced the Nigerians to halt them in March of that year. In fact, several papers compared Ojukwu's death sentences to that of the Nazi courts and others stated that Biafra's actions were "outside the pale of civilized society."[56] As a result, Biafra's fundraising efforts and those of the relief organizations collapsed in much of Europe. On 9 June 1969, Jacques Freymond, acting president of the ICRC, stated that fundraising efforts in the Netherlands and France had failed, citing the "murder of the Italians" and the "increasingly difficult attitude of Ojukwu who did not respond to single ICRC note re Italians [sic]" as separate reasons for this failure. He went even further, stating that in the climate created by the affair, it would be futile to attempt more fundraising efforts in Europe.[57]

Conclusion

Though the affair undoubtedly ended in a payment both in cash and increased aid to Biafra, the incident severely soured Biafra's standing in the war, especially in global public opinion, one of their most effective war fronts. Even though the USD 3,000,000 almost equaled the total sum of French aid to Biafra in 1969, the harm that the affair wreaked on Biafra's standing in the world far outweighed the financial benefits. Biafra's mishandling of the case allowed the FMG to resume some of the most egregious aspects of their war tactics, including indiscriminate bombing and attacks against the humanitarian relief efforts. Despite the fact that the Biafrans used the case to showcase racial bias in the world's reaction to both the affair and the war, that message was not well received outside of Nigeria. Humanitarian efforts ground to a standstill due, in large part, to global public perception of the Biafran regime which was no longer viewed as a just struggle, but now increasingly seen as criminal and illegitimate.

This case highlights the evolution of ransoming in Africa, especially when the captive takers are state actors. Even though Biafra existed for a short time as a state entity and was only recognized by five nations, Biafra must be seen as a state actor, as they actively portrayed themselves as a modern nation and courted public opinion for their cause as such. Biafra's entire existence depended on their being accepted as a state actor. The assault on the oil installation and subsequent ransoming undermined their legitimacy as a state, transforming their image into that of a criminal organization. As a result, their ability to maintain global support for their cause so severely battered that it became easy for global public opinion to turn against Biafra. Though this case did not in itself cause Biafra's destruction, it was a severe blow to the country's credibility as a nation, eroding the support that they had so successfully cultivated during the preceding two years, thus hastening Biafra's end.

Endnotes

1 AGIP was founded in 1928 as the Italian national oil company. In 1953, the Italian government created a new company, Ente Nazionale Idrocarburi (ENI), to consolidate the many state-run energy companies. AGIP became the largest component of ENI, and continued to operate under the AGIP name until 2003. The Nigerian subsidiary of ENI still uses the AGIP moniker and is called the Nigeria AGIP Oil Company (NAOC).

2 The USD 3,000,000 paid in 1969, counts for approximately USD 19,350,000 in 2014, adjusted for inflation. "Cpi Inflation Calculator," Bureau of Labor Statistics, http://data.bls.gov/cgi-bin/cpicalc.pl.

3 Pade Badru, *Imperialism and Ethnic Politics in Nigeria, 1960-1996* (Trenton, NJ: Africa World Press, 1998), 3.

4 They were called the Five Majors despite the fact that there were ten in total, of which seven were Majors in the Nigerian Army.

5 The literature on ransoming of captives is broad and extensive. It includes discussions of African captives in Africa, as well as internal captivity in the context of the slave trade in Africa. In particular, see Robert C. Davis, *Christian Slaves, Muslim Masters: White Slavery in the Mediterranean, the Barbary Coast, and Italy, 1500-1800* (Houndmills, Basingstoke, Hampshire; New York: Palgrave Macmillan, 2003); "The Geography of Slaving in the Early Modern Mediterranean, 1500 - 1800," *Journal of Medieval and Early Modern Studies,* 37:1 (2007); Jennifer Lofkrantz and Olatunji Ojo, "Slavery, Freedom and Failed Ransom Negotiations in West Africa, 1730-1900," *Journal of African History,* 53:1 (2012). For works that detail the mechanisms of non-African captive and slave ransoming and the global reach of these efforts, see Joachim Östlund, "Swedes in Barbary Captivity: The Political Culture Of "Human Security", Circa 1660-1760 / Schweden in Gefangenschaft Der Barbaresken: Die Politische Kultur Humaner Sicherheit, Circa 1660-1760," *Historical Social Research /*

Historische Sozialforschung, 35:4 (2010); Karen Melvin, "Charity without Borders: Alms-Giving in New Spain for Captives in North Africa," *Colonial Latin American Review,* 18:1 (2009). Scholars have also explored the issue in popular imagination of the time. See Paul Michel Baepler, *White Slaves, African Masters : An Anthology of American Barbary Captivity Narratives* (Chicago: University of Chicago Press, 1999); Paul Baepler, "White Slaves, African Masters," *Annals of the American Academy of Political and Social Science,* 588 (2003); Benilde Montgomery, "White Captives, African Slaves: A Drama of Abolition," *Eighteenth-Century Studies,* 27:4 (1994); and Lawrence A. Peskin, *Captives and Countrymen : Barbary Slavery and the American Public, 1785-1816* (Baltimore: Johns Hopkins University Press, 2009).

6 Olatunji Ojo, ""Matter of Money": Ransoming and the Crisis of the State in West Africa" (Paper presented at Perspectives on Historical and Contemporary Ransoming Practices conference at the Harriet Tubman Institute, York University, Toronto, ON, April 25-26, 2014)

7 Thaddeus Sunseri, "Slave Ransoming in German East Africa, 1885-1922," *International Journal of African Historical Studies,* 26:3 (1993); Trevor R. Getz and Clarke Liz, *Abina and the Important Men: A Graphic History* (New York: Oxford University Press, 2012).

8 Joel Quirk, *The Anti-Slavery Project : From the Slave Trade to Human Trafficking* (Philadelphia: University of Pennsylvania Press, 2011).

9 Douglas Anthony, "'Resourceful and Progressive Blackmen': Modernity and Race in Biafra, 1967-70," *Journal of African History,* 51:1 (2010).

10 H. B. Momoh, *The Nigerian Civil War, 1967-1970: History and Reminiscences* (Ibadan: Sam Bookman Publishers, 2000), 105.

11 John J. Stremlau, *The International Politics of the Nigerian Civil War, 1967-1970* (Princeton: Princeton University Press, 1977), 229-31.

12 One instance led to the expulsion of German mercenary Rolf Steiner who, at the end of November 1968, was ordered to perform a frontal assault against the city of Onitsha. Steiner's troops were massacred because they were drilled in guerilla tactics and untrained for a frontal assault against fortified positions with little air and artillery support. According to one Danish journalist, Steiner accused Ojukwu of massacring the former's troops and allegedly slapped the Biafran leader. Rather than kill Steiner, Ojukwu sent him out of the country the next day saying "it cuts across everything we believe here, to find our struggle for survival led by white mercenaries." For a full account of the incident, see Zdenek Cervenka, *The Nigerian War, 1967-1970. History of the War; Selected Bibliography and Documents* (Frankfurt am Main: Bernard & Graefe, 1971), 68.

13 R.W. Apple Jr., "Guerrillas Enter Nigeria," *New York Times*, 26 May 1969.

14 "How to Build an Instant Air Force," *Time*, 6 June 1969, 42-44. For a full history of the air campaign, including the civilian airlift, see Michael I. Draper, *Shadows : Airlift and Airwar in Biafra and Nigeria, 1967-1970* (Aldershot, Hants, UK; Charlottesville, Va.: Hikoki Publications, 1999).

15 Radio Biafra, cited in Stremlau, *International Politics of the Nigerian Civil War, 1967-1970*, 328.

16 Telegram from American Embassy, Lagos; "Unconfirmed Report on Missing Oil Men" 31 May 1969; National Archives and Records Administration (NARA), RG 0084, P 387, POL – Political Affairs and Rel.

17 "Incontro a Piadena Con Poggi: Il Racconto Della Sua Avventura," *La Provincia*, 20 May 1969.

18 "27 Europeans Are Missing after Attack by Biafrans," *New York Times*, 12 May 1969.

19 "11 Bodies Are Found after Biafran Raid," *New York Times*, 1 June 1969.

20 Telegram from Gardner Ackley, "Italians Missing in Nigeria," 21 May 1969; NARA, RG 0084, P 387, POL – Political Affairs and Rel.

21 The Biafrans were able to hire Swiss firm Markpress, whose owner, American H. Wm Bernhardt, supported the Biafran cause, stating "people all over the world are presently sending money to purchase food and medical supplies for the Biafrans. Our company is extending its services below costs as its contribution to this very worthy cause." Letter from H. Wm. Bernhardt to Editors receiving Markpress Releases. 25 June, 1968

22 Stremlau, *The International Politics of the Nigerian Civil War, 1967-1970*, 332.

23 The dates here are disputed, but the capture of Owerri and Umuahia seem to have been concurrent. Philip Efiong, *Nigeria and Biafra: My Story* (Princeton: Sungai Books, 2003), 272, 75. dates the capture of Umuahia on 22 April, and Owerri on 23 April. Momoh, *The Nigerian Civil War, 1967-1970: History and Reminiscences*, xvii. places Umuahia on 13 April in one instance and 22 April in another; while Owerri is dated to 23-24 April.

24 Efiong, *Nigeria and Biafra: My Story*, 274-75.

25 Yahaya Hashim and Kate Meagher, *Cross-Border Trade and the Parallel Currency Market : Trade and Finance in the Context of Structural Adjustment : A Case Study from Kano, Nigeria* (Uppsala; Stockholm; Somerset, NJ: Nordiska Afrikainstitutet, 1999), 33.

26 Festus O. Egwaikhide and Oyeranti O. Alabi, "Economics of the Nigerian Civil War: A Historical Analysis," in Eghosa E. Osaghae, Ebere Onwudiwe, and Rotimi T. Suberu (eds.), *The Nigerian Civil War and Its Aftermath* (Ibadan, Nigeria: Published by John Archers (Publishers) for Programme on Ethnic and Federal Studies, 2002), 180-81.

27 Olly Owen, "Biafran Pound Notes," *Africa (Edinburgh University Press)* 79:4 (2009), 570-71.

28 Efiong, *Nigeria and Biafra: My Story*, 334.

29 "Tiger's Thoughts Are in Biafra," *Chicago Daily Defender*, 28 October 1968.

30 David Mazzarella, "Biafra to Release Oilmen," *Nashua Telegraph*, 5 June 1969.

31 Ken Saro-Wiwa, *On a Darkling Plain: An Account of the Nigerian Civil War* (Port Harcourt: Saros, 1989), 92.

32 Department of State Telegram, "Ferguson called on Sir Louis Mbafeno," 3 June 1969; RG 59, P 387, POL 27-9

33 The issue of genocide in the Nigerian Civil War remains one of the most politically charged and controversial subjects. Though the issue of genocide was a central theme of Biafran propaganda, especially after May 1968, the issue of whether genocide actually occurred remains a thorny issue. For some scholarly treatments of the issue, see Axel Harneit-Sievers, Jones O. Ahazuem, and Sydney Emezue, *A Social History of the Nigerian Civil War : Perspectives from Below* (Enugu [Nigeria]; Hamburg: Jemezie, Lit, 1997); and Chima J. Korieh, *The Nigeria-Biafra War: Genocide and the Politics of Memory* (Amherst, NY: Cambria Press).

34 John De St. Jorre, *The Brothers' War; Biafra and Nigeria* (Boston: Houghton Mifflin, 1972), 343; Stremlau, *International Politics of the Nigerian Civil War,* 331-33.

35 Stremlau, *International Politics of the Nigerian Civil War,* 333.

36 "Reprieve for Eighteen," *Time*, 13 June 1969.

37 "All Christians Equal?," *New Nigerian*, 1 June 1969.

38 Ibid.

39 Department of State Telegram, "Ferguson called on Sir Louis Mbafeno."

40 Department of State Telegram 3 June 1969; RG 59, P 387, POL 27-9.

41 "Biafra Decides to Free 18 Doomed Oil Workers," *New York Times*, June 5 1969.

42 "18 Men, Freed by Biafra, Cheered on Arrival in Italy," *New York Times*, June 8 1969.

43 "Pope Declares Vatican Efforts in Nigeria War 'Non-Political'," *Sarasota Herald-Tribune*, June 9 1969.

44 Lloyd Garrison, "Ojukwu Faces Test," *New York Times*, 3 June 1969.

45 Department of State Telegram "Biafra" and "Reference ROME 3816"; NARA, RG 0084, P 387, POL – Political Affairs and Rel.

46 Stremlau, *International Politics of the Nigerian Civil War,* 333.

47 Said Adejumobi and Adewale Aderemi, "Oil and the Political Economy of the Nigerian Civil War and Its Aftermath," in Eghosa E. Osaghae, Ebere Onwudiwe, and Rotimi T. Suberu (eds.), *The Nigerian Civil War and Its Aftermath* (Ibadan: John Archers Limited, 2002), 197-99.

48 Department of State Telegram "Threat to Midwest Oil Installations" 10 June 1969; NARA RG 59, P 387, POL 27-9

49 During the Prague Spring of 1968, Czechoslovakian leader Alexander Dubček attempted to distinguish Czech foreign policy from that of the Warsaw Pact. One way the Czechs did so was to withdraw their support from Nigeria during the war. After the Soviet invasion the following August, Czech pilots were sent to fly in Nigeria as a statement signifying the return of Czechoslovakia to the Soviet fold. For a full discussion of the Nigerian Civil War as it pertained to Czech-Soviet relations during the Prague Spring and August Soviet invasion,

see S. E. Orobator, "The Nigerian Civil War and the Invasion of Czechoslovakia," *African Affairs,* 82:327 (1983).

50 "Relief Boss Arrested," *The Vancouver Sun*, 28 May 1969.

51 Dan Dimancescu, "Red Cross Loses Its Grasp on Biafran Relief Efforts," *The Boston Globe*, 10 August 1969.

52 "Red Cross Plane Downed," *The Windsor Star*, 7 June 1969.

53 R.W. Apple Jr., "Churchman Says Biafrans Face New Wave of Starvation Deaths," *New York Times*, 29 June 1969.

54 Richard Nixon Speech on 8 September 1968. Cited in George A. Obiozor, *The United States and the Nigerian Civil War : An American Dilemma in Africa, 1966-1970* (Lagos: Nigerian Institute of International Affairs, 1993), 23-24.

55 Chinua Achebe, *There Was a Country: A Personal History of Biafra* (New York: Penguin Press, 2012), 220.

56 Stremlau, *International Politics of the Nigerian Civil War,* 332-34.

57 Department of State Telegram "ICRC and Nigerian Relief" 9 June 1969; NARA RG 59, P 387, POL 27-9

CHAPTER IX

Deferred Reciprocity:

Historical and Theoretical Perspectives on Ransoming and the Ethics of Compensatory Justice

Amy Niang

Introduction

This chapter is part of larger project that is concerned with social, political, cultural and ideological processes that underpin ongoing transformations in the Sahel. It is particularly interested in the economic basis of violence, radicalized forms of militant engagement and shifting identities in the context of contested governance models. Specifically, it examines "ransoming" as a framework and a practice that articulates a particular view on the use, or threat of violence for political, ideological and economic aims. Since the end of the 1990s, there has been an increasingly powerful constellation of disparate and related groups that operate in the Sahelian region under a political economy of violence. Their claims for social justice or cultural particularism intersect with demands of essentialist variants of Islam, and these are couched in a militant language that obscures more than it reveals about the complexity of the motivations, the operating procedures, the actors and institutions involved. These claims are also about reviving fading modes of governance in a context whereby "traditional" trading structures and collective forms of resource management and distribution have been fundamentally disrupted.

The kidnapping and smuggling economy displays elements of banditry and insurgency that carry serious political repercussions and a potential for destabilization across the whole region. Between 2003 and 2013, al Qaeda in the Maghreb (AQIM) is said to have kidnapped between 50 and 100 Westerners. Unknown until the late 1990s, AQIM has become a formidable power with which Sahelian governments and societies now have to contend. If its radicalism and proselytizing methods have elicited a strong rejection from governments and civilians, it has succeeded in attracting scores of budding militants and idle youth from the Sahel and elsewhere. The successful kidnapping economy has inspired in turn the emergence of satellite militant groups across the Sahel, namely the Mouvement pour l'Unicité et le Jihad en Afrique de l'Ouest (MUJAO), Al Qaeda in the Sahel and Al Qaeda in Black Africa. Some of these groups have been able to bankroll their operations through ransom money.

My contention is that ransoming, like razzia, raiding, piracy and similar practices exists and operates within models of intelligibility that get easily flattened in the way we often frame our research questions.[1] This chapter thus seeks to examine ransoming practices in the Sahel in light of historical practices ranging from raiding, razzia, and piracy. These are examined in a broader framework of socio-political principles, modes, models of property, interchange and reciprocity that have shaped an ecological and historical region marked by scarcity, precariousness and instability.

Historically, raiding practices served many purposes. Firstly, they were deployed alongside many modalities of governance in an ecological context characterized by scarcity, the unpredictability of the elements, and the harshness of the climate. Secondly, they constituted a pivotal instrument to centralizing processes, territorial expansion, and to attempts to force scattered, rebellious groups under the fold of emerging states. Razzia in particular functioned as a vector of regulation and restoration of an ethic of interchange often subject to the vagaries of contingency and the effects of unequal material capacity. It was therefore a mechanism that produced both legal and illegal outcomes. Ultimately, in a context whereby theological interpretations of rights were entwined with political desires for autonomy and dissension, boundaries between the legal, the licit and the legitimate were historically contingent upon a conditional language. In fact, "legality" as a source of analytical certainty has long served to buttress state claims for violence while marginalizing often genuine political and economic claims. Raiding and ransoming strategies have thus been used as acts of defiance, as a form of adaptation to, and as a response to various social strains heightened by capitalism, the disruption of traditional trading and economic circuits, and ultimately as a political weapon.

Raiding, Ransoming, Razzia: Historical and Contemporary Iterations

Home to pastoralists, herders, agriculturalists, caravan traders, the Saharan-Sahelian region has historically been a zone of encounter, transition, cultural and commercial exchange, a place where Tuareg, Arab, Tubu, Songhay, Djerma, Kanuri, Berber etc have historically cohabited, traded and maintained a variety of relations. A long history of exchange reinforces the cohesiveness of the Sahara-Sahel zone as a distinct region bound together by historical ties and by contemporary events, as well as by linguistical, cultural, religious, and economic factors. The displacement of trans-Saharan trade by maritime trade in the nineteenth century, of the caravan by the caravel, motivated settlements around oases and the intensification of agricultural production. The nature of property relationships, dependency structures, political suzerainties and fragmented autonomies, slavery, servitude, *métayage* systems, and economic alliances were such however that any military pre-eminence could only be temporary.[2] The makers of centralized states had to contend with constant dissidence from within and outside of the polity. In the framework of reciprocity developed in this chapter, exchange models such as commercial transactions were never neutral or value-free acts; they were subject to restrictions and safeguards given the suspicion that clouded the legitimacy of commercial transactions. In fact, the disdain with which non-trading—particularly noble groups—approached the act of selling had very much to do with the idea that there was something degrading about committing to an economic ethos. Among the Bedouins, the pursuit of private interest, in the form of a purely commercial endeavor has little legitimacy unless conducted under special conditions lest they produced social inequalities. The restraints imposed upon commercial transactions were therefore ethical and institutional (e.g. the honor code).[3] Arguably, the common distinction between ethics and its application flattens the value of thinking about any political and social activity as fundamentally ethical. Furthermore, the principles that underline a violent activity, such as a reciprocal framework, make little room for a sound assessment of intent and purpose. The practice of ransoming, historically and in contemporary times, can therefore be variously interpreted as an economic necessity, a political instrument, an aspect of transnational crime, or a means of regulating resource distribution in a context of limited resources.

The principles that underline exchanges cannot be reduced to purely economic or anonymous transactions. For even transactions between strangers have to be turned into a social bond. Reciprocity thus could undermine the possibility of anonymity as well as the threat of accumulation and inequality. Marie Perinbam's study of the western Sahara shows the ways in which long-term trade was embedded into social organization.[4] This suggestion is all the more plausible when one considers the centrality of trust and promise in the economic transactions of non-industrialized societies. However, there was more to the fear of inequality than was apparent for trade could produce new "classes" of wealth-endowed individuals. On the other hand, the price paid for "protection" of trading caravans was nothing less than a ransom conceived in this instance as a toll. Conceived as a whole, raids, commercial exchanges, political uprisings, and systems of servitude were the many components of multi-layered and multi-directional networks defined by clientelist relationships of various kinds. What characterized these were cycles of alliances and breaks and ultimately a fundamental attachment and almost a necessity for a de-territorialized approach to social action and governance.[5] In the eighteenth and nineteenth centuries, but also in contemporary times, itinerant modes in the Sahara have always had a way of sidestepping the state logic.

Nomadic groups think of themselves as the rightful stewards of the desert, particularly as their lifestyle is inherently articulated around the possibility of mobility. In this regard, smuggling and other economic activities are in a way the continuation of a centuries-long tradition of trans-Saharan trans-Sahelian caravan trade in salt, slaves, gold, hides, feathers, and other goods between Africa and the Mediterranean. Interventions against smuggling are therefore seen as disruptive of activities crucial to preserving livelihoods. In parallel to smuggling, hostage liberation mediation has emerged as a lucrative field of practice in which government officials, private mediators and various kinds of intermediaries maintain a line of profit and a source of leverage. Equally, once the "legality" question has been destabilized, kidnapping, like piracy, closely mimics conventional trade by mobilizing its language, its forms, and its procedures. Indeed, there is nothing radical in viewing kidnapping and piracy as structured exchange models that rely on technology, intelligence, financiers and accountants, mediation and mediators, political facilitators and networks, communication strategies and outlets as well as other market modalities that regulate fluctuations.

Colonial stereotypes often presented nomads as backward, economically irrational and ignorant. These stereotypes have endured and have shaped colonial and postcolonial approaches to "development," particularly in the way they are used to berate pastoral practices and their complementary roles to agricultural practices. Thus conceived, rather than being economically, socially and environmentally enhancing, "development" has become destructive given its focus on the restriction of mobility and flexibility. Against the erosion of trans-Saharan trading circuits, disruptions wrought by colonial interventions extended to the imposition of boundaries, custom, the militarization of government, and the transformation of commons into private property.

Ernest Gellner describes a structural opposition between the Arab and Berber formulations of governance. For Gellner, there was no tribalism "prior to government" but a political and partial rejection of a particular government combined with some acceptance of a wider culture and its "ethical foundations": for a community that shared Islam and a wider common culture, political autonomy and opposition was always an explicit and deliberate choice. Gellner contends that until recently, Moroccan history could be written in terms of an opposition between the land of *makhazen* (the pale) and the land of *siba* (beyond the pale). In this configuration *siba* was a form of institutional dissidence (mistranslated as "anarchy"). *Siba* points to a space of autonomy and independence, in other words an ungoverned sphere not subordinated to the state.[6] Equally, the dismissal of western essentialisms, such as democracy, development, modernity, and secularism, can be seen as following in the rejection of the statist iron cage that can only apprehend a notion of *government* in formal, Weberian enactment.

In all of this, the role of raiding has been grossly misunderstood. For in the Sahel and places where livelihood models partly depend on mobility and seasonal circulation (such as transhumance), the modernization project was by and large an effort to mobilize and monetize resources, populations, and lands. In other words "modernization" was an enclosure project meant to turn the "ungoverned" into producers of taxes, currency, and national wealth while integrating them in international circuits, systems, structures and processes.[7] This followed a systematic effort to rationalize adversaries, their spaces, their culture and their beliefs all of which was characteristic of imperial expansion.[8] For example, colonial advance both in Mali and Niger in the early twentieth century greatly restricted the capacity for Tuareg to use pasture in the savannah or continue to tax sedentary famers.

The denial of the right for particularism or inhibition, whether cultural or religious, amounts to an impulse of contemporary forms of government to rationalize and erase *difference*. The combined infringement on pastoral mobility structures and the frequency of raids, often perpetrated at the expense of sedentary populations, can be seen as part of the same approach to tame difference.[9] The default response to Sahelian dissidences, in colonial and postcolonial times, has been systematic repression and militarization, control and trusteeship measures.[10]

Traditional raiding operated as one among many modalities of government in the Sahel. The violence involved in the razzia was often one way to enact the principles and values that weave relations among various groups. Gianni Albergoni for instance conceives of razzia among the Bedouin as "an honorable form of rapine" that cannot be dissociated from other mechanisms of adjustment, to climate, scarcity, the destruction of flock, the disintegration of families following famines, communal security frameworks such as clientelist relationships, cattle loan or mutual help among allied groups.[11] The political and transformative effects of violence can only be understood t in a framework of reciprocity where both razzia and clientalism play a similar redistributive role. If the values that circulate in this framework can be highly unequal, for instance where one group is required to pay a substantial tribute for protection, the positions of strength or weakness were equally unstable.

The bigger point is that in the enacting of subjectivities through acts of violent, there was an ontological commitment to a constant recreation of *self* and *other* which is cultivated in the "production, maintenance and reproduction of the virtuous self" towards an ideal subjectivity.[12] The very redemption of an individual's moral credentials depended on this dynamic. This instance points to an important aspect about Sahelian forms, which is that self-constitution and self-governance especially for non-sedentary groups are articulated not only around the possibility of movement, mobility, and certain kinds of interaction, but ultimately the possibility to become subjects outside the repressive forces of state, capital, and competing imperialisms, ultimately therefore the possibility of life as fits their particular ecology. The ecology of nomadic life is such that nomads cannot cohere in permanent, sedentarized institutions that are likely to curtail their capacity to move, to improvise and to experiment. There are obviously issues of "race," class and ideological differences that intersect and inflect the practice of raiding in a way that complicates a straightforward reading of its deployment as merely constitutive of subjectivities. However, the point is to stress that razzia, raids and ransoming were closely tied to the acquisition of certain rights through the use of violence and that they were, and to a degree still are informed by value systems and models of community.

I have discussed elsewhere the relevance of a modality of community engagement such as the *dina* in Sahelian conceptions of governance.[13] A system of coordinated management and enhancement of land, water resources, and grazing fields, the *dina* was designed to rationalize and facilitate access and use among communities involved in different activities requiring careful rotations so as to avoid conflict and promote co-governance. The *dina* was a system of collective ritual and political control but also social control since it was also a system for integrating strangers. The *dina* provided a basis for dealing with diversity, scarcity and an ethics of distribution among groups that were endowed unequally with different resources. Furthermore, a distinction between different categories of rights, of access, of usage, of political control or ritual rights did not prevent their juxtaposition depending on particular circumstances. Among herders for instance, this could mean the succession of different herding groups to the same pastures according to the species raised. The pasture reservation system ensured both rationalized productivity and environmental protection. As a modality of ecological, economic, social and political governance, the *dina* intersected with a variety of other modes such as taxation and conflict adjudication.

In contemporary times, raids have taken the form of kidnapping, mostly of westerners, and the forced recruitment of young Sahelians into militant, religious stakeholder groups. There was for instance the kidnapping in Niger in September 2010 of five employees of the French nuclear company AREVA and two employees of the engineering firm Satom, that of two Spanish in August the same year freed against a ransom and the liberation of an AQIM militant jailed in Mauritania. Taken in isolation, contemporary forms of piracy in the Gulf of Guinea, the Gulf of Aden, in the Sahel or the Niger Delta merely appear as acts of banditry unless one provides a context for their rise and their intensification. Equally, as discussed above, both raiding and ransoming can be interpreted as two among a variety of modalities of governance, a mode of self-government in the near absence of the state, the disappearance of networks of solidarity and the destruction of nomadic/sedentarian dynamics that had thus far sustained livelihoods.

Prescriptions and Proscriptions: Theological and Political Considerations on Raiding, Slavery and Ransoming

Raids conducted within the framework of the conjectural context of Islamic expansion finds a justification in the construction of the "infidel" as an abject category subject to different rules and treatments. One particular Islamic interpretation customarily speaks of the world as made of two spheres, the sphere of Islam (*dar al islam*) and the sphere of war (*dar al harb*). This conceptual field enables differentiation and its enforcement. According to the latter, the obligation to protect Muslims from captivity and enslavement does not systematically extent to non-Muslims even if they might enjoy a protected minority status. Slavery and enslavement in Islam are complex matters; they were once prohibited and regulated by texts; their practice helped expand the Muslim community but they also served to protect freeborn Muslims from being enslaved. The so-called jihad states of Fuuta Jallon, Fuuta Toro and the Sokoto Caliphate in particular sought to either restrict the sale of Muslims particularly to "Christians" including Europeans or to prevent their exportation outside of West Africa.[14] Slave trading and raiding were practices closely bound to state building and theological reform in nineteenth century Sahel, particularly under al-hadj Umar Taal and Almami Samori Ture, as modern weapons had to be sourced in fighting "jihads and wars of resistance that generated large number of enslaved Africans as currency to finance their revolutions" for also "the militarized resistance to European occupation contributed to increasing violence and enslavement."[15] Thus, political resistance and state building were very much part of the war economy and the broader economic order in which slavery occupied an important place.[16]

In the early days of Islamic history, razzia provided a justification for expansion to a nascent community. This was the case for seventh century Arabia when new converts raided Meccan caravans in a context of limited agricultural and trading opportunities since the exiled Muslims had a "guest" status in Medina. Given the context, trade was bound to put them in conflicts with Meccans and other groups. The universal mission to unify the world under a sharia rule was an idealized concept that nevertheless bore influence on the course of Islamic history. Already in the eleventh century, there were great discrepancies between the practice of plunder and various preoccupations, in the writing of theologians, scholars and various interpreters, interpretations of the Quran and the Sunnah that recognized jihad against pagans, apostates, and criminals. In fact, Islamic theorists elaborated in detail an ideal Islamic state which, while its historical reality bore no resemblance to the envisaged unitary state governed by Islamic principles, had limited practical relevance to the historical contexts in which Muslims found themselves. However, the idea of the ideal state had extended normative effects on the behavior of ordinary Muslims as well as warlords for it placed restraints on their conduct, hence their verbal adherence to Islamic norms. A result of this logic was that to declare a war against one's enemy as a jihad ensured that soldiers and followers were roused with religious fervor in their engagement. Although simplified to its principles, this conception of the relevance of Islamic rules with regards to practices such as raiding, plunder, jihad and enslavement points to a common quest for morality relentlessly pursued by various groups.[17]

Despite the possibilities and occurrences of arbitrary interpretations, theological elaborations on raiding transformed it into a practice that sought to govern and regulate diversity, divergence and dissidence in increasingly centralizing societies. Mechanisms ranged from the conduct of war, the integration of the newly converted into Muslim communities, the treatment of enemy military and civilian groups, social duties towards protected minorities, the management and distribution of collective resources, etc. In a careful engagement with nineteenth century private archives in Tishit (Mauritania), Ghislaine Lydon for instance shows the painstaking and duteous ways in which Saharans strove to subject transactions in slavery to Islamic, particularly Maliki jurisprudence and precepts. If these precepts had to be adapted to local Sahelian and Saharan contexts given their unstable, precarious nature, they regulated almost every aspect of the Trans-Saharan slave trade and the broader economic order including the sale, lease, manumission, bequeath, gift, transfer and the treatment of slaves.[18]

Producing and Governing Threats

Discourses of threat are meant to discipline subjectivities and spaces through the articulation of the conditions for necessary intervention. In the Sahel however, counterinsurgency and count-terrorist measures preceded the very manifestations of instability and threats (aggressions, kidnappings, skirmishes) much talked about in the media. Post- September 2001 Sahel is undoubtedly more unstable than it was before it became the object of American terror-obsessed attention.[19] However, in a context whereby "enemies [are determined] only in gross geopolitical terms," no consultation or form of deliberation precedes violent engagements with predetermined foes.[20] The language of counter-insurgency thus constitutes a preliminary validation for extraterritorial and extra-legal measures. The discourse on threats and emerging threats, as much as the idea of ungoverned spaces, is a discourse that is highly one-sided, it does not allow discussing the other side of the coin which is the production of uncertainties and disruptive intrusions ranging from insecurity to many social disruptions. Here, the common discourse on "shared temporalities" merely becomes a justification for the temporality produced by the GWoT is artificial, contingent and highly disruptive; it corresponds in no ways with Sahelian temporalities. It is animated by a desire to possess. The notion of shared temporalities is therefore a fiction, and a fantasy of imperial power. An examination of the experience of different temporalities demonstrates that dissident groups are gesturing beyond the compliance/resistance dichotomy. There are in fact procedures of survival and flight at work that might provide angles of analysis, which are more useful, for instance, than the material effects of "shared" temporalities. The justification practices alluded to above constitute counter -strategies against the deployment of external claims laid upon political subjects, land and resources. A fundamental question that emerges is "how are certain types of subjects produced in time and space?" One Somali pirate's response points to the implications of economic aggression: "If the world doesn't do anything about these fishing vessels [in Somali waters] then I'll fight them however I can whether I'm in jail or outside. We will not quit as long as there are fishing vessels in our seas."[21]

The renegotiation of fishing contracts between African states and the EU in the 1990s and 2000s caused much controversy and was taken on by civil society organizations which denounced their unequal and neocolonial character.[22] The fishing contracts depended on a system of compliance and monitoring for which African countries did not have the capacity to implement. Neither could they control their coasts and thus relied on the good faith of European ships for compliance. On the other hand, the European Union's (EU) relations with African regional bodies in general and the African Union (AU) in particular have largely become over-determined by a security agenda. An underlying thinking is that there are many security threats coming out of Africa with tremendous implications for Europe and these threats would need to be neutralized with the cooperation of African states and regional institutions. In contrast, very few people have questioned the extent to which policy choices, political, economic and military, in Europe affect the security of Africans. On the West African coast, the depletion of the Atlantic ocean of its nutritive sea life and resources, the competition for the resources of the Sahel and the Sahara are many sources of threat that produce mass migration, another perceived source of threat for Europe. This is as much a geopolitical as it is an ecological problem—in the sense of policies destroying eco-social and eco-cultural systems. As a "Somali pirate" again points out, "I'll tell the media and the international community, we went into this [piracy] because of unemployment after our livelihoods are destroyed. And now we request the international community to create jobs for us to quit this piracy and we will arrest anyone who remains in this business."[23]

There are multiple sources, layers, and effects of intrusions. They take benign and less benign forms, from technology (drones and other advanced weaponry, motorized transport) and the manning personnel, aid and humanitarian personnel and programs, extractive production by MNCs with detrimental effects to the environment and productive of pollution, sporting and tourist events that impose demands on lifestyles. The very encounter between Sahelians and the cluster of western missionaries of aid and humanitarian relief itself takes the form of raids for these agents storm the Sahel in their helicopters and their 4x4 cars to distribute food, medicine, etc and disappear as quickly like a desert storm. In parallel, land expropriation and the attendant monopolization of water resources constitute a form of capture that extends to a group's culture, livelihood, capacity for social progress and eventually a capacity to sustain a meaningful life.

Rarely however in our discussions of violence do we pay attention to the actual reality of the people who feel injured by security and development policies. We do not imagine in our reflections that they might have problems real enough, or serious enough to warrant more than a passing reference to the potential effects of state repression and external violence. In common discourses, Sahelians are subjects with no desires or needs, no will or self-governing capacity; they are merely mutes with a great capacity to suffer and resist. Little attention has been paid to the narratives, some would call them justificatory accounts, of pirates and hostage-takers even when these are stated in terms that rely heavily on the language of human rights, economic governance, self-determination and a politics of necessity. When the accounts of "Somali pirates" and "Sahelian terrorists" are juxtaposed, what emerges is the articulation of a subjective consciousness invested into a political purpose:

We used to work as fishermen until 1991. After the collapse of the central government we have faced attacks by international fishing vessels that used illegal fishing nets. They dumped toxic wastes and nuclear wastes in our seas. We have no central government to defend us and we took a responsibility to fight them and we defeated them. Then they came back and they brought with them weapons and that frightened us. They continued fishing in our seas armed with their weapons. We have an old saying in Somalia; it says 'if we can't find a thief, we can find his brother.[24]

There is more to this narrative than could possibly be said in the limited space available here. This statement is one of *responsibility* coming from a non-state actor who denounces at once a trading framework in its unequal deployment, the need for self-government in the face of unfair and illegal exploitation, the destruction of livelihoods and military aggression. It is a striking justificatory account of a "just war" frame of reference. The account makes every westerner and every individual seen as benefitting from illegal fishing, exploitation and military aggression liable because they are implicated in these harms. A similar line of argument was deployed in the kidnapping of AREVA employees in northern Niger in 2010. For both Sahelian and Somali populations, the effects of exploitation of natural resources without beneficiation and the effects of illegal fishing and environment destruction are hugely detrimental because experienced as a daily aggression.

Colonial Government and the Intrusion of Liberal Capitalism

As intimated above, the extent of external intrusions and interventions into Sahelian lives is not only underreported, their effects on livelihoods, life forms, and the preservation of the commons are often left untreated. The logic of capitalist violence is governed by a veneer of political correctness that characterizes a precise liberal morality, and where violence is distributed subtly, democratically, and consensually, in a way that makes subjects apparently consenting actors of their own subjugation for the end purpose of being enabled for "success," freedom and self-realization in a capitalist frame. The intrusion of liberal capitalism through the mediation of colonial government disrupted as much as it enhanced trading mobility patterns in the Sahelian-Saharan region. French occupation of the Sahel at times weakened the region's ties with the outside world rather than strengthening them first by disrupting trading routes ad configurations (for instance the Tripoli-Kano trade in tanned skins and feathers) and secondly through intensified hostility between the Tuareg and the French which "sapped the vitality of the desert economy."[25] Decline inevitably led to the reorganization of trade route and exchange circuits.[26] On one hand, the revolt of Senusiya and Tuareg in the Aïr region, which culminated in the siege of Agades in December 1916, recalibrated the frame in which the so-called pacification campaign evolved from an open war to razzia practiced by both colonizer and colonized, in a deadly fashion. Pacification was fraught with ambiguousness: it was at once designed to establish order, to repress revolts and contestations against the colonial campaign whose ultimate aim was to subdue future colonial subjects. Pacification was also a method of government, indispensable to colonization: far from seeking to *appease* (as in *pacify*), it sought to dominate by taming all sources of violence. In Algeria, it was a euphemism for war *tout court.* For the colonial order was never meant to share power, it could only dominate if it was to prevail. Pacification was therefore primarily a military endeavor: conquest was, in this context, a form of pacification, domination was a form of pacification, the divide-and-rule policy was also a form of pacification. Alexis de Tocqueville, a strong advocate of pacification saw in French repression of Algerian resistance, the only mean for the former to gain a firm entry and to fulfill its civilizational mission. It is worth quoting him *in extenso*:

In France, I have often heard men that I respect but do not approve of, deplore that crops should be burnt and granaries emptied and that unarmed men, women and children are seized. In my view these are unfortunate necessities that any people wishing to wage war against the Arabs must accept. In what sense is more odious to burn harvests and to make women and children prisonners, than to bomb the innocent population of a besieged city, or to seize the merchant vessels of an ennemy ? The one is in my view less harsh and less justifiable than the other. If we do not burn harvests in Europe, it is because in general we wage war on governments and not on populations. The second means in order of importance, after the prohibition of trade, is the destruction of the country. I personally believe that the laws of war allow us to ravage the country and that we must do so either by destroying the crops at harvest time or at all times by making fast forays also known as raids the aim of which is to get hold of men or flocks.[27]

In Algeria and in the Sahel more generally, the French resorted to insurgency tactics such as the poisoning of wells or stuffing them with rubbish in order to starve the enemy; they also burned villages in order to deter settlement. The progression of the Sadoux-led troops across the Azawak and the Tamesna was notoriously bloody. Sadoux' repression of the Kel Dinnik, despite the latter's offer to surrender and to pay a "tribute of submission," led to the near-extermination of the *Imageren* group in the early twentieth century.[28]

Tuareg opposition to French and Italian colonial forces was manifest at the very onset of their encounter. It intensified with the deterioration of the terms of their livelihood, namely the disruption of the caravan trade and new constraints on their capacity for a mobile and transhumant life. The 1910-1916 period was particularly tumultuous. On one hand, the 1913-4 famine greatly weakened Sahelian livelihood strategies. On another, aggressive French recruitment strategies in the form of requisition, forced conscription, auxiliarization of Tuareg leaders exacerbated a war context already marked by restricted economic opportunities.[29] The revolt in the Aïr followed the uprising of the western Ulliminden based around Gao led by a former French ally, the Amenokal Firhoun; this rebellion followed closely another Tuareg region in Dori in present day Burkina Faso. Even though in the end Tuareg rebellions against French authorities were not decisive, they spread across Aïr, Azawak, Tamesna and Tibesti, even extending into the Fezzan, thus greatly shaking the colonial authority in their attempt to restore freedoms (i.e. control). Of all these rebellions, the Aïr was by far the most detrimental and costly for the French for it cast serious doubt on the whole colonial enterprise in the Sahel.[30] Between 1914 and 1931, the French proceeded to subjugating Tuareg, Semori, Tubus, Senusiya and other groups while exploiting rivalries among these."[31]

The successive revolts in the Aïr (1914-1918), the Fezzan (1918-1920) and the Tibesti (1920-1923) and many other, less spectacular confrontations, revealed a fundamental truth about Sahelian modes of governance; the French deployed their military might and the power of modern weapons to repress Sahelian rebellions but they often found themselves in a circle of repetition as "pacified" zones were reignited when dissidence inevitably resumed. The practice of razzia in the context of colonial resistance must in this instance be seen as a reaction and response to colonial capitalism, using capitalist means. Ironically, there is a sort of intertextuality between the claims made by the dissident groups and the means of repression deployed by the state against these same groups.

What is shown above is that given the mobile, transhumant modes of life in most of the desert, attempts to derail traditional mobility patterns or to govern the movement of people have always come against strong resistance. In the nineteenth century, nomadic populations coped with colonial intrusions by oscillating between cooperation and conflict, through collaboration and resistance. The very harsh environmental and changing economic circumstances in the desert required high levels of flexibility, whether alliances had to be tied, preserved or unmade was a function of fluctuating conditions, so much so that categories of resistance or cooperation in themselves have limited explanatory import in accounting for the prevalence of loose and unstable political arrangements across the Sahel. The bigger point is that the desert was never the no-man's land or the empty space it is often portrayed to be in the literature for it was lined by caravan routes, networks and nodes of connection. In fact, the Sahara can be seen as nothing less than a connecting zone between the Maghreb and the Sahel. The idea of the Sahara as an obstacle to mobility and communication is in reality the result of the decline of the trans-Saharan trade and of prosperous markets such as Tishit, Shingiti, Walata, Timbuktu, Agadez, etc. The interdiction of slavery by the Ottoman sultanate after 1850 dealt a blow to trades routes running through Tripoli and Kano.[32]

The myth of "institutional void" has therefore historically served to mask the great ignorance of authorities, both colonial and postcolonial, that sought to lay claim on Sahelian peoples even while they were ill-informed about the region's networks, the identity of the emissaries, intermediaries and messengers, the nature, direction, the purpose, the importance of their message and the identity of their interlocutors. The myth of institutional void thus serves to negate the possibility of effective socio-political structures that have sustained Sahelian and Saharan populations for millenaries. It further justifies the use of predicates of order and security against "unruly" Sahelians and contemporary variants of the failed state thesis.

Many historians have noted the perplexing degree of the apparent inconsistencies in the production of local histories; where pacts and alliances shifted from one year to the next.[33] The seeming contradictions are resistant to easy categorization and ordering but can be made sense of when read as many coping mechanisms to both physical and external pressure brought to bear on carefully elaborated structures of adaptation by Sahelian populations. A famous example is that of Kaocen (Kaosen; Kawsan), a Targui from the Ikazkazan group of Damergou, often seen as the Tuareg Abd-el-Kader, who led the revolt in the Aïr region against the French garrison in Agades. Kaocen put together a free standing army made of disparate Tuareg (Ikazkaza and Imuzurag from Damergou, Kel Dinnik and Kel Owey etc) and other groups including European mercenaries. He placed his army successively at the disposition of Turks, Senusiya and other Sahelian groups for campaigns in the Fezzan, the Aïr, in Chad and northern Niger. Kaocen took siege of Agades for three months and ten days between 13 December 1916 and 3 March 1917 in one famous episode.[34] The siege mobilized over five thousands French troops from the North (Tamanrasett), the West (Menaka) and the South where French forces, made of *tirailleurs*[35] and Tuareg auxiliaries, had been stationed. Even in the midst of the punitive repression, the French were aware of the rules of reciprocity that governed the capturing of war prisoners. The Tuareg for instance captured, during the Agades and subsequent campaigns, the wives of *tirailleurs* who had been fighting at the side of the French. Whereas the French could and did agree to negotiate for the release of French troops, they were not deterred by the potential of death for auxiliary populations as they elected to mount punitive and retaliative operations against dissidents.

In fact, as the circumstances changed in favor of one party or the other, the distinction between resistance and disruption of order, collaboration or enmity became increasingly blurred and subject to precariousness. Among Tuareg and other Sahelian groups, if some were irreducibly attached to a principle of honor and were ready to sacrifice their lives for what they conceived as sacred, this was notably the case of dissidents in the Aïr and Tamesna, others, were happy to contract alliances with the French or act as auxiliaries in French punitive operations against other Sahelian groups. But like similar mechanisms, alliances and enmity were always temporary and susceptible to shift as circumstances and military positions evolved. In the deteriorating climate of the early twentieth century and the subsequent instability and torment that fell on the region, it would seem that the overarching principle that dictated the political conduct of dissident groups was a strong attachment to freedom, that is the possibility to engage in raiding, to impose tolls, to transact and to adapt to changing ecological requirements without an obligation of forced and restricted sedentarization, therefore the sedentarization of property, so as to preserve the characteristics of a nomadic life marked by a history of mobility, adaptation and flexibility in a context of permanent precariousness.[36] Since the end of the nineteenth century, nomadism had to be preserved against the successive effects of the decline of trans-Saharan trade, the colonial conquest, the 1914-1931 rebellions, and subsequent enforcements of sedentarization and modernization projects by the colonial and postcolonial states. Obviously, one should not assume the idealism or innocence of nomadism as opposed to sedentarianism for sedentarians have historically borne the brunt of raiding, being vulnerable prey to marauding, protection tax, razzia, capture, grain and livestock theft, from Tuareg and other nomadic groups.[37]

At any rate, alliances were tremendously crucial in the mediation of prerogatives, competence and conflict. In the trans-Saharan trade in salt and other goods, the Tubu and Tuareg were for instance associated with the transportation of salt and other goods on different routes, either Sokoto, Ghadames, Kano or Bornu. Within these groups, the roles of middlemen, brokers, service men etc might overlap as much as they could fall under the preserve of a specific family or clan.[38] Using the example of the trade in salt and focusing on trade volumes, fluctuations, trade networks, political and ideological configurations of production, the relative importance of salt in relation to the trade in ostrich feathers, ivory, tanned skins, slaves, etc, Lovejoy demonstrates the dynamism and vivacity of the trade in salt as an instance of a trans-Saharan regional trading world. In consequence, he tends to contest the idea of an early decline (of the trans-Saharan in relation to the trans-Atlantic trade) and therefore early capitalist penetration and rather focuses on intra-Saharan trade, thereby showing that it was more important than, and relatively autonomous from the international networks an links often invoked in the literature. He was able to do so by disaggregating the many aspects of the trade and by showing variations and commonalities across different routes, including Borno-Tripoli, Kano-Ghadames, Sokoto-Tripoli etc.[39]

Cooperation and Subversion

Richard Roberts and Lilian Kesteloot's studies of the Segu Bambara (c.1712-1761) provide an account of razzia in a context of precolonial state building and expansion, specifically in relation to the formation and the maintenance of a warrior class whose self-consciousness, desires and actions were indispensable to this endeavor. From their accounts, three types of military campaigns can be distinguished on the basis of the extent of state involvement and approbation. Firstly, the *kèlè* was a fully-fledged military campaign typically launched during the dry season. The state invested its full military power in the endeavor to ensure success in the defeat of enemies and the capturing of slaves and goods. Secondly, the *soboli* was made of relatively small groups with varied numbers of mounted cavalry that operated as *ton* (band) under the leadership of a *tontigi*. It was both a form of rebellion and predation for *tontigi* could acquire political power by dint of their physical prowess. Thus, *Biton* (Maamari Kulibali) emerged as a much feared *tontigi* in eighteenth century Mande. He eventually became *faama* and founded the Segu kingdom in 1720.[40]

Thirdly, the *jado* amounted to high banditry punishable under state law not because of its perceived immorality but rather because it constituted a source of disorder and instability for the state.[41] In reality, *jado* was a political strategy. Of all three forms of wars, *jado* was deemed the most predatory for it kept raiding bands busy in between military campaigns. Despite that it was a legal offense and an act of sabotage, the practice of *jado* had important political effects not least in the manner in which it could jolt a *faama* (king) to action. By disrupting the warring model normally sanctioned by the *faama*, *jado* had the effect of coercing the latter to restore order by creating new missions for a restless and entrepreneurial warrior class who only knew to fight wars. In that very sense, *jado* participated in the reproduction of *socio-political production*, if not of the state process, at least of particular groups and social processes that played a tremendous role in political reproduction. In fact, *jado* articulated the constant oscillation between cooperation and subversion between the *faama* and those groups that preserved the political coherence of his rule. As a result therefore, "a constant alternation between centralizing and decentralizing tendencies created the conditions which forced the *faama* to conduct successful wars or see the very structure and security of the state threatened by uncontrolled warriors."[42] As long as raiding was confined to "the fringes of the state," the latter could turn a blind eye or even facilitate the operations of its strategic allies. As the state came to be more entangled in ambiguous iterations of limited centralization, it was forced to enter a power-sharing framework with autonomous allies. During the reign of Monzon (1794-1808), Segu Bambara experienced administrative and political innovations that made it possible for the state to launch "punitive" campaigns against tax or tribute-incompliant regions within its very borders.[43] In all this, the state's toleration or facilitation of raids and razzias served to diffuse tensions in a context of competing interests from a variety of contingent allies. Thus, state allies were compensated in turn during times of peace through inaction, facilitation or policy reform.

Given the above discussion, it might be fair to say that Sahelian polities like other political formations have chiefly been concerned with two things, namely: (1) to keep power and (2) to accumulate resources while subversive groups have traditionally been less concerned with power in the narrow sense. However, in a raiding framework, both insurgency and resistance carry similar agential capacity to reshuffle a given order while effecting a repositioning of actors. Like elsewhere dissident groups typically cooperate with, or subvert the state as circumstances allow. They also resort to withdrawal strategies. Withdrawal takes many forms, namely (1)stepping outside (2) doing away with the logic, order, rules, laws that prevail in a particular system or order. I subscribe to Hard and Negri's use of 'exodus' to denote many forms of withdrawal.[44] One obviously must assume the possibility of choice here, without which even the most seemingly radical form of exodus has to be seen as merely a departure within.

During colonial times, the Kel Ewey of Niger first resisted French penetration before entering into an alliance with them against the Imezureg. They served as intermediaries whose economic power was to be gradually expanded through hunting expeditions in the name of colonial framings of order, a scenario presumably quite familiar for the French chose the Hausa and the Dagera, the Tuareg and the Dagera in turns in this position in the early 1900s. The alterations brought about on trading patterns partly resulted in the increased influence of outside actors. Most detrimental of all was the decreased ability of Tuareg and other nomadic populations to confront prolonged crises such as droughts and environmental change which in turn greatly affected the desert economy.[45] This was precisely the situation that prevailed in the Tibesti massif hard hit by the 1911-14 drought and intensified requisitions of camels by the French, both of which motivated intermittent rebellions and massive flights into northern Nigeria.[46]

Bugeaud's repressive policies in the Sahara were underpinned by a rationalization of the use of razzia as both a war instrument and a deterrence against dissidence. Razzia was a means to accumulate war resources by stealing cattle as well as a punitive measure. Its escalation however had a negative effect on his troops. In May 1842, the Ouled Hann welcomed over two dozen Legionnaires who had deserted to the enemy camp. As the practice became too destabilizing for Bugeaud to keep a harmonious front, the French general resorted to literally *grinding* Saharan groups. Thus Bugeaud contemptuously rejected ransom demands from the Sbeah in exchange for French hostages. In doing so, Bugeaud rejected the very principle of *sociality* which would be incurred by the payment of a ransom for according to him "the loss of Arab blood will never compensate for the spilling of the French blood."[47] Bugeaud's use of razzia amounted to a slash-and-burn mode of clearing obstacles first by instilling fear, burning villages, ambushing women and children to ensure death in a state of exposure to the elements, the destruction or seizure of cattle to weaken the enemy, then through occupation.[48] Bugeaud justified the use of unconventional, downright barbaric measures on account of a need to "adapt" to local practices. But even his troops found his methods rather disturbing. The year of 1842-43 was a particularly tumultuous year for the intensity of French repression caused much disillusion within the ranks of the Foreign Legion. Those troops that deserted were animated by ideological sentiments to do with the very principles that should govern the conduct of war, be it one fought against an irregular army. However, the Arab in Bugeaud's mind could not be an interlocutor, let alone a partner in a framework of exchange. Equally, the American government with its policy of no-ransom-payment does not recognize the agenciary claims of hostage-takers beyond that of surrounding "legitimate" forces.

In contemporary times, to define hostage-taking as an act of terrorism is to deny indirectly the fact of *war* the Sahel. What is happening in the Sahel is a war that involves non-state transnational actors, specific targets, recognizable claims and identifiable objectives. In fact, an abstract label of terrorism only obscures the very concrete manifestations of state and external actor interventionism in the region. Sahelian populations themselves bear the brunt of the violence, whether perpetrated by Islamist militants, their own governments or foreign forces.

What can be said to be common to both formal and informal types of criminality is an elite banditism that concentrates resources and proceeds of ransoming in the hands of political and economic opportunists. This is perhaps truer for militant radicalism of recent vintage. But the new sergeants of Islam such as AQIM, the *Mouvement des Nigériens pour la Justice* (MNJ) in northern Niger are caught up in the changing dynamics of the global economy in ways that allow them to develop an increasingly coherent political discourse. They articulate the latter in relation to questions that pertain both to environmental destruction (e.g. water contamination due to uranium exploitation and pending ecological disaster), beneficiation and self-determination but also to more distant issues that are less the doing of AREVA or the Nigerien government but are very much the consequence of broader, global economic configurations.

The birth of "terrorism"[49] in the Sahel is specifically linked to a peculiar story, that is, the alleged abduction of thirty two European tourists most of them German by the GSPC/AQIM in 2003 led by Saifi Amari aka El Para the fox.[50] As the story goes, the hostages were released six months later in North-eastern Mali against a payment of €5 million ransom to the GSPS of Abderazak el-Para with whom Belmokhtar had collaborated. Then there was a chase of El Para's group across Mali and Chad by joint Malian, American, Nigerien and Algerian forces. El Para lost 43 men in 2004 in the hands of Chadian forces. However, somebody like Keenan for instance shows how this specific example might be but a serious hoax mounted by U.S. secret services with the help of their Algerian collaborators as a way to up the bidding and as a prelude to laying claims on the Sahel. Keenan and others suspect that El Para might have been an agent of Algerian secret intelligence services, the infamous *Direction des Renseignements et de la Sécurite* (DRS) and that therefore the chase in question never actually happened. This story is often described as illustrative of a shift in dissident tactics in a region that was veering towards an inevitable "somalization." The U.S. suggested at the time a unilateral approach to the problem and saw the paying of ransom as making for a bad precedence. From the U.S. perspective, paying ransoms was a first great mistake made by the Europeans.[51] At any rate, the trigger event for the labeling of this part of the world a new al Qaeda hotbed could merely have been a fabricated story that enabled the U.S. to construct a new threat and therefore a new terrorist front. For all this, "the main ideological prop of the U.S.'s subsequent imperialist counter-terrorism strategies and militarization of the rest of the continent has been the threat presented by this false, over-hyped, US-constructed narrative of "terrorism in the Sahel."[52]

Although most of these groups, including AQIM, have a rather distant link to Al Qaeda, they have been able to use the veneer of Islamic ideology to embed themselves into local religious networks (this also applied to the Movement for Unity and Jihad in West Africa (MUJAO) and Ansar e-deen), some of which have recently gone through a radicalization phase. They are often structured around *qatiba* or battalions and they operate across the Sahel using guerilla strategies that allow them to escape state control quite successfully.[53] AQIM's form of ransoming is often seen as a scheme, a one-off opportunity that allows them to extract maximum resources; this precludes mutually beneficial relationship and future transfer while allowing them to bankroll their operations. Incidents of kidnapping thus tend to be violent, often leading to executions where payments are not forthcoming.

There are complex ways in which AQIM's activism in the Sahel is linked to global processes articulated around the war on terror, the militarization[54] of U.S. presence and support in North West Africa, and the widely perceived persecution of Muslims the world over. Kidnappings, like the killing of foreigners in the Sahel and North Arica, is part of a series of blowback responses to U.S. and Western interventions in Northern Africa among other things. The implications of these interventions are more damaging than apparent. The al Qaeda association gives a stamp, recognizable to outsiders, to free-floating and isolated agents seeking recognition, and to outside observers a legible framework and easy labels. The al Qaeda franchise thus becomes a blanket ideological mantle that attributes homogenous characteristics to a global jihad with many local faces. At any rate, two prominent ideas have been severally articulated in relation to the practice of kidnapping and the taking of ransom money in exchange for foreign captives, namely that (1) insurgency needs to be recognized as a legitimate response to aggression (2) that consultation among Muslims as a constitutional principle might be an analytically useful tool in understanding modes of decision-making among specific groups of transnational non-state actors. .

In this framework, the crusade of AQIM is as much about resuscitating Islam from a stultifying modernity than it is about fighting against political disenfranchisement, economic marginalization and cultural death. Political agency in the capture of Westerners and Western goods thus becomes a default *operant* made at once indispensable and enabling in the face of perceived *invasion*. AQIM's strategy, according to its own documents, was not to rule Northern Mali directly, at least not immediately, but to rely on local groups such as Ansar- el – Deen in order to rule by proxy in the region. AQIM also intended to abandon the jihadist rhetoric and the project to establish a sharia state. Instead, their idea was to support and accompany the establishment of an Emirate. In a document dated July 20, 2012, "discovered" by journalists from French RFI (radio) and Liberation (newspaper) in the rubble of the ORTM national television station in Timbuktu and entitled "Roadmap relating to Islamic Jihad in Azawad [northern Mali]" the leader of AQIM, Abou Moussab Abdelwadoud (aka Abdel Malek Droukdel) outlines the main points of a conceptual adaption of an ideal frame. The six chapter document provides some rare insight into the deliberations of AQIM's leadership on the one hand, and the articulation of the ethical and moral basis of their struggle on the other. The document indicates the centrality of AQIM's 33rd council meeting in the deployment of the strategy of conquest. In the first chapter, entitled "Global vision of the Islamic jihadist project in Azawad," Droukdel condemns the destruction of mausoleums and the stoning of "adulterers" carried out by some of his fellow jihadists: "you have made a serious mistake," he writes. "the population could turn against us, and we cannot fight against a whole people. You are in danger of destroying our experiment, of killing off our baby, our beautiful tree."

Competing Legitimacies

Two important points need to be raised at this point. The first one has to do with self-constitution as a basic principle of the realization of rights, governance, but also development. Self-constitution is a normative, often prescriptive endeavor in that it projects self-understandings of rights onto others unilaterally. The second one has to do with the different implications of the two aspects of state sovereignty, namely the internal aspect and the external aspect. Internally, the state is an institution that provides, organizes, regulates, but also oppresses, hence also the persistent tendencies from various groups, especially those at the periphery of centralized states, to rebel against or secede from it. Externally, its sovereignty depends on international recognition, complacency or protection. On the other hand, the conceptual and practical limits of Humanitarian law have come to naturalize one trend, which is *the normativity of violence*. The just war tradition provides a number of principles (many *justs*) that constitute a basis with which to partly think through the legitimacy of violence. Whereas these just principles apply to states in so far as they are recognized valid actors, their application becomes problematic when it comes to non-state actors. The requirement for a "just cause," a "just intent" etc in humanitarian law becomes a reason and an excuse in determining, a priori, the possibilities of life from the point of view of the state. Further, it also determines those whose worth is recognizable according to the just cause doctrine, hence those whose struggle is worthy of attention. The problem however with this outlook is that it is framed in a consensual imagery where heroes and villains can be clearly identified and located. As two authors put it, the dichotomized stories about pirates and kidnappers are inherently "raced, classed, geographically and historically located, and draw on older, larger stories of colonialism, capitalism and racism."[55]

In regard to this point, James Der Derian's perspective opens space for an extremely fertile engagement with the meaning of violence and its contemporary practices. When read along the lines of an ideological economy of political legitimation, the state-centered anti-terrorist discourse, in its ossified version depends on active procedures of denial of the problematic monopolization of violence made sacrosanct by Westphalia. For Der Derian therefore, anti-terrorist discourses essentially denote a crisis of legitimacy for "the state" as a contested actor.[56] At any rate, the anti-terrorist discourse does not necessarily reflect a rise in terrorism *per se* but rather an attempt, by the state, to protect a kind of "distinct" or exclusive sphere. What it has not succeeded in occulting, however, is the fact that the state does not have the moral upper hand when it comes to using violence. Consequently, violent dissidence that adopts the means, the resources and forms of state conduct express a concern that has broadly informed scholarly reflection on the problematic nature of *the sovereignty question* on the one hand and *the monopolization of violence by the state* on the other.[57] The nominal identity of the state as, historically, *the* anthropological standard has obscured a thorough reengagement of the ethics of rule and governance outside of, and beyond state politics.

There is nothing controversial in saying that Western, specifically American interventionism in the Sahel has "facilitated a terror diaspora, imperiling nations and endangering peoples across Africa."[58] The proxilization of war and the out-sourcing of state violence to ungoverned regions have facilitated the establishment of semi-permanent bases to serve as grounds of operation for American troops. Recent accounts have revealed the existence of bases in northern Mali (Tessalit), Eastern Mauritania (Nema), Southern Algeria (Tamanghasset), Northern Niger (Agadez).[59] In addition, multimillion-dollar counterterrorism program, such as the Pan-Sahel Initiative (PSI) and extended into the Trans-Saharan Counterterrorism Partnership (TSCTI) are instantiations of Operation Enduring Freedom on the Horn and the Sahel. The initiative sought to "bolster" the military apparatuses of Mali, Niger, Chad and Mauritania in a first offering before expanding to include Nigeria, Senegal, Morocco, Algeria and Tunisia. The various training and expert support initiatives were altogether in turn folded into AFRICOM from 2008.

Conclusion

If the semantic scope of the ransoming economy is perhaps broader than historical orthodoxy has been willing to recognize, the broader framework that produces raiding, ransoming and similar forms nonetheless needs to be conceived as a system of asymmetrical exchange often conducted between state and non-state actors. At a time when formidable pirate and kidnapping stories circulate freely in the public domain and are seared in the public consciousness as instances of revived barbarism in the twenty-first century, an analysis of modern articulations of raiding and ransoming practices can enable an engaged reassessment of old and new forms of political and economic violence. Two considerations weigh down on my assessment of contemporary forms of ransoming in the Sahel, namely that ransoming cannot be understood in isolation of parallel practices such as razzia, raiding and other structures of exchange in their historical and contemporary forms, and that it also needs to be read in conjunction with autonomous modes of governance in so far as the extent of violence often obscures a reciprocity principle.

Endnotes

1 Given the extremely varied contexts and purposes that govern their practice, I have chosen not to lock the concepts of razzia, ransoming, piracy in single definitions. Raiding practices can in fact range from one-off operations to large military campaigns, acts of brigandage, sedition or plunder. The tuareg *rezzou* (from Algerian *ġaziya*) is for instance used to refer to acts of pillage and raiding while *razzia* in the colonial context was a specific strategy of capture and plunder used by the French in Algeria and Morocco as a slash and burn strategy designed to both rationalize the costs of conquest and to demoralize the enemy . As far as the use of ransoming is concerned, if the payment of a fee or in kind in order to avoid an act of killing or the execution of a threat of violence is an obvious meaning, I use it also in this chapter to show how systems of deferred reciprocity operate, historically and in contemporary times, within broad frames of exchange. Specifically in the case of the Sahel, the effects of foreign extractive companies and military operations on livelihoods and their encroachments upon local governance arrangements are examined within a ransoming framework. The absence of the possibility of retrocession, reciprocation or exchange in this model therefore amounts to a denial or negation of the possibility of "exchange" broadly conceived.

2 Gianni Albergoni, "Les Bédouins et les Echanges: La Piste Introuvable" *Cahiers des Sciences Humaines*, 26:102 (1990), 198-9.

3 Albergoni, "Les Bédouins et les Echanges," 211 and 213.

4 B. Marie Perinbam, "Social Relations in the Trans-Saharan and western Sudanese trade: an overview," *Comparative Studies in Society and History*, 15:4 (1973), 416.

5 James L. A. Webb, *Desert Frontier: Ecological and Economic Change along the Western Sahel, 1600-1850* (Madison: University of Wisconsin Press, 1995).

6 Ernest Gellner, *Saints of the Atlas* (London: Weidenfeld and Nicolson, 1969).

7 James Scott, *The Art of Not Being Governed* (Princeton: Princeton University Press, 2009), 4.

8 Michael J. Shapiro, "That Obscure Object of Violence: Logistics, Desire, War," *Alternatives*, 17 (1992), 453.

9 Webb, *Desert Frontier*, 27 and 172.

10 Amy Niang, "Le « boom » des saisons dans l'espace sahélo-saharien : *Proto-révolution, désintégrations et reconfigurations sociopolitiques,*" *Afrique Contemporaine*, 245 (2013), 53-69.

11 Albergoni, "Les Bédouins et les Echanges," 196.

12 Shapiro, "That Obscure Object," 460.

13 This chapter draws on discussions on the *dina* and other modes developed in Amy Niang, "Ransoming, Compensatory Violence, and Humanitarianism in the Sahel," *Alternatives, Global, Local, Political,* 39:4 (2014), 231-251.

14 See Paul E. Lovejoy, "Islam, Slavery, and Political Transformation in West Africa: Constraints on the Trans-Atlantic Slave Trade," *Outre-Mers*, 89:336-337(2002), 251, 277, 279; also see Jennifer Lofkrantz, "Protecting Freeborn Muslims: The Sokoto Caliphate's Attempts to Prevent Illegal Enslavement and its Acceptance of the Strategy of Ransoming," *Slavery and Abolition,* 32:1 (2011), 109–127.

15 Ghislaine Lydon, "Islamic Legal Culture and Slave-Ownership Contests in Nineteenth-Century Sahara," *The International Journal of African Historical Studies*, 40:3 (2007), 402.

16 Richard Roberts, *Warriors, Merchants and Slaves: The State and the Economy in the Middle Niger Valley, 1700-1914* (Stanford: Stanford University Press, 1987).

17 Watt W. Montgomery, "Islamic Conceptions of the Holy War," in Thomas P. Murphy, ed., *The Holy War* (Columbus: Ohio State University Press, 1976), 141-56.

18 See Lydon "Islamic Legal Culture," 391-439. For a broader discussion of the nature, the conditions, the rules and the normative frameworks that governed the practice of slavery in the Sahara, see E. Ann McDougall, "In Search of a Desert-Edge Perspective: The Sahara-Sahel and the Atlantic Trade, c.1815-1890," in R. C. Law (ed.), *From Slave Trade to legitimate Commerce: The Commercial Transition in Nineteenth Century West Africa* (Cambridge: Cambridge University Press, 1995), 215-39.

19 In 2001, according to the global terrorism database of the National Consortium for the Study of Terrorism and Responses to Terrorism at the University of Maryland, there were 119 terror incidents in sub-Saharan Africa. By 2011, the last year for which numbers are available, there were close to 500.

A recent report from the International Centre for Terrorism Studies at the Potomac Institute for Policy Studies counted 21 terrorist attacks in the Maghreb and Sahel regions of northern Africa in 2001. During the Obama years, the figures have fluctuated between 144 and 204 annually."

20 Shapiro, "That Obscure Object of Violence," 456.

21 Interview with Abdirashid Muse Mohammed, nicknamed Juqraafi or "geography;" Mohammed Adow, *Meet the Pirate* (Al Jazeera, 2009), 15 June 2009. http://www.dailymotion.com/video/xq8w31_meet-the-pirates-abdirashid-muse-15-june-09_news

22 These were signed as early as 1979 starting with Guinea Bissau and Senegal. Between 1980 and 1990, the EU successfully negotiated most favorable fishing rights with Guinea (1980), Sao Tome and Equatorial Guinea (1983), The Seychelles and Mauritius (1984), Mozambique and Madagascar (1986) The Gam-

bia, Angola and Mauritania (1987), Morocco and Gabon (1988), Cape Verde and Cote d'Ivoire (1990).

23 Al Jazeera, *Meet the Pirate.*

24 Ibid.

25 Baier "Trans-Saharan Trade," 58-59.

26 Finn Fuglestad, "Révolte des Touareg du Niger (1916-17)," *Cahiers d'études africaines,* 13:49 (1973), 95; see also Martin Klein, *Slavery and Colonial Rule in French West Africa* (Cambridge: Cambridge University Press, 1998).

27 "[D'une autre part, j'ai souvent entendu en France des hommes que je respecte, mais que je n'approuve pas, trouver mauvais qu'on brûlât les moissons, qu'on vidât les silos et enfin qu'on s'emparât des hommes sans armes, des femmes et des enfants. Ce sont là, suivant moi, des nécessités fâcheuses, mais auxquelles tout peuple qui voudra faire la guerre aux Arabes sera obligé de se soumettre. Et, s'il faut dire ma pensée, ces actes ne me révoltent pas plus ni même autant que plusieurs autres que le droit de la guerre autorise évidemment et qui ont lieu dans toutes les guerres d'Europe. En quoi est-il plus odieux de brûler les moissons et de faire prisonniers les femmes et les enfants que de bombarder la population inoffensive d'une ville assiégée ou que de s'emparer en mer des vaisseaux marchands appartenant aux sujets d'une puissance ennemie ? L'un est, à mon avis, beaucoup plus dur et moins justifiable que l'autre. Si en Europe on ne brûle pas les moissons, c'est qu'en général on fait la guerre à des gouvernements et non à des peuples.... Le second moyen en importance, après l'interdiction du commerce, est le ravage du pays. Je crois que le droit de la guerre nous autorise à ravager le pays et que nous devons le faire soit en détruisant les moissons à l'époque de la récolte, soit dans tous les temps en faisant de ces incursions rapides qu'on nomme razzias et qui ont pour objet de s'emparer des hommes ou des troupeaux;" Alexis de Tocqueville, "Travail sur l'Algérie," in de Tocqueville (ed,), *De la colonie en Algérie* (Bruxelles: Complexe, 1841 [1988]) p. 77. John Stuart Mill was also a key ideologue of pacification; so was Gallieni, the initiator of the concept of *tache-d'huile*: according to him, pacification should be gradual, militarily as well as administratively. As both ideologue and practitioner, Bugeaud in turn popularized counter-insurgency tactics; he was convinced that pacification could ensure 'continuity' to the colonial endeavor. In contemporary history, Iraq and Afghanistan are two useful examples of experimental applications of the razzia approach; the American general Petraeus is said to be an avid reader of Gallieni.

28 Capitaine Tottier, "Rapport de Tournée Effectuée au Tibesti du 4 Mars au 18 Mai 1921," Bilma, 1-13, Archives Nationales du Niger, in Finn Funglestad, "Les Révoltes des Touaregs du Niger," *Cahiers d'Etudes Africaines,* 13:49 (1973), 118.

29 Ibid., 89.

30 Ibid., 96.

31 The power of the capitalist world system has not so much been its capacity to call into being new structures that maximize the extraction of commodities or

surpluses values as its global flexibility in finding alternative to areas it could not rigorously exploit and, ideologically, to marginalize and demean the people it could not incorporate," Frederick Cooper, "Africa in the World Economy," in Cooper et al., *Confronting Historical Paradigms: Peasants, Labor, and the Capitalist World* (Madison: University of Wisconsin Press, 1993), 84-204; see also Jean Louis Triaud, "Kawsan : Analyse d'un discours politique (1916-1917)," In Y. Poncet (ed.), *Hommage à Edmond Bernus. Les Temps du Sahel* (Paris: Institut de recherche pour le développement, 1999), 149-172.

32 Stephen Baier, "Trans-Saharan Trade and the Sahel: Damergu, 1870-1930," *Journal of African History*, 18:1 (1977), 43.

33 See D. B. C. O'Brien, J. Dunn and R. Rathbone (eds.), *Contemporary West African States* (Cambridge: Cambridge University Press, 1989).

34 Edmond Bernus, "Dates, Dromedaries, and Drought: Diversification in Tuareg Pastoral Systems," in J. G. Galaty and D. L. Johnson (eds.), *The World of Pastoralism: Herding Systems in Comparative Perspective* (New York: AWG Publishing, 1990), 159-160.

35 Generic name used for African conscripts who fought alongside the French in the two world wars and in French campaigns of colonization and repression in Indochina, Madagascar, etc.

36 See speech by Moktar Oul Daddah on historical immemorial nature of freedom for Moors and Sahelians; Discours 1 Juillet 1957, Archives Nationales d'Outre-Mer (ANOM), 14-AFFPOL/2210

37 Baier, "Trans-Saharan Trade," 49.

38 Paul E. Lovejoy, "Commercial Sectors in the Economy of the Nineteenth-Century Central Sudan: The Trans-Saharan Trade and the Desert-Side Salt Trade," *African Economic History,* 13 (1984), 109-110.

39 Lovejoy, "Commercial Sectors," 85-116.

40 Radical "*boli*" *to* gallop and *so* for horse; see Angelo Turco, "Sémantiques de la violence : territoire, guerre et pouvoir en Afrique mandingue," *Cahiers de Géographie du Québec,* 51:144 (2007), 307-332.

41 Richard L. Roberts, "Production and Reproduction of Warrior States: Segu Bambara and Segu Tokolor, c. 1912-1890," *International Journal of African Historical Studies*, 13:3 (1980), 407-10; Lilian Kesteloot, *Da Monzon de Segou: Epopee Bambara*, 4 Vols. (Paris : Fernand Nathan, 1972), 10

42 Richard L. Roberts "Production and Reproduction," 407, 409; see also Jean Bazin "Guerre et Servitude a Segou," in Claude Meillasoux (ed.), *L'Esclavage en Afrique précoloniale* (Paris: Maspero, 1975), 135-181.

43 Kesteloot *Da Monzon*, Vol. 1, 10-11, as cited in Roberts "Production and Reproduction," 410.

44 Michael Hard and Antonio Negri (eds.), *Commonwealth* (Cambridge: Belknap Press of Harvard University), 152-153.

45 Baier, "Trans-Saharan Trade," 54-55.

46 Baier, "Trans-Saharan Trade," 56.

47 Cited in William Gallois, *A History of Violence in the Early Algerian Colony* (New York: Palgrave Macmillan, 2013), 102.

48 Gallois, *A History of Violence,* 102-103.

49 The ongoing trend of labelling anti-state dissidents "terrorists" further renders them illegible to repressive regimes that only see disruptors and agitators. The "terrorist" has become merely another figure of the barbarian, the communist, the cannibal, in other words the decontextualised, demonized spectre of marginal figures within western conceptions; this includes those that are internally marginalised in western societies such as the homeless. See Eric Cheyfitz, *The Poetics of Imperialism: Translation and Colonization from The Tempest to Tarzan* (Philadelphia: University of Pennsylvania Press, 1997), 15

50 The Sahelian kidnapper and the Somali pirate have become the formidable characters of stories about dangerous criminals that stand against "liberal principles." There is for instance the portrait of Bel Moktar. Nicknamed "le borgne" (Laouer) or "Mister Malboro," Mokhtar Belmokhtar, aka Khaled Abul Abbas, is said to be the mastermind of the hostage taking of January 16, 2013 at The Algerians site of In Amenas. An Afghan war veteran in the 1980s, he joined the militantist movement at the young age of 19. He lost an eye after being injured by shrapnel. He joined the GSPS (AQIM) in the midst of the Algerian civil war in 1993 was credited with the murder of many border security guards and police officers; he was successively condemned to death twice in 2008 and again in 2012 for acts of terrorism. Married to a Tuareg of northern Mali, his extended Sahelian network and militant resilience owed him a "nomination" by the mother organization, Al Qaeda, as leader of the "Emirate of the Sahel." Malboro also gained a reputation across the Sahel as a transnational smuggler of cigarettes, drugs, weapons, and migrants. A comfortable financial independence would allow him to supply Al Qaeda with weapons and vehicles while recruiting Tuareg youth. His conversion into hostage-taker and prominence in the business of ransoming was inaugurated in 2003 with the kidnapping of German and Austrian tourists in the southern Sahel. He has been credited with the abduction of four French nationals in Mauritania in 2011 and two other young Frenchmen in Niamey in January 2011. The latter turned into a bloody chase by Nigerien and French forces across the Sahel and resulted in the execution of Antoine de Leocour and Vincent Delory. Given Malboro's excellent knowledge of, and years of experience in the Sahel with an extensive network of allies, he was in a strong position when he publicly announced, through a rare video footage, his rupture with Al Qaeda in December 2012. As a founder of a new battalion called Al Mutahalimin (those that sign with blood), he elected to operate principally in northern Mali and in Mauritania. His master campaign, most resounding by its unique violence, resulted in the death of 38 people following the kidnapping of 41 foreign nationals in Algeria's gas plant site of In Amenas and the intervention of Algerian army.

51 Interview of former US ambassador in Mali, Vicki Huddleston, on *Africa Past and Present* (Podcast), 26 March 2013, http://afripod.aodl.org/tag/vicki-huddleston/

52 Jeremy Keenan, "Uranium Goes Critical in Niger: Tuareg Rebellions Threaten Sahelian Conflagration," *Review of African Political Economy*, 31:117 (2008), 453.

53 Some call them "Signers in Blood." See Serge Daniel for a detailed and rich account of the mode of operation of AQIM in what he calls the "ransoming industry," *AQIM: L'Industrie de l'Enlèvement* (Paris: Fayard, 2012).

54 Not just the US but also France as first seller of weapons.

55 Muna Ali and Zahra Murad, "Unravelling Narratives of Piracy: Discourses of Somali Pirates," *Dark Matter*, 5 (2009), 91-102.

56 James Der Derian, *Antidiplomacy: Spies, Terror, Speed and War* (Oxford: Blackwell, 1992).

57 The [irruption] of non-state actors in spheres of action that traditionally were the preserve of conventional actors serves to problematize the distinction between "legal" and "illegal" actors. The global response to piracy in the Gulf of Aden is an instance of the sort of crispation and overlapping competencies among the various political, economic, private and military forces mobilised in fighting piracy for trade has to be protected from "illegal actors." Thus, the EU launched a Naval Task Force (EU NAVFOR), NATO launched the Combined Task Force 150 in 2002, the US the CTF151 gathered armed ships from a variety of trading allies including Japan, South Korea, China, Indonesia, Singapore, Malaysia, Saudi Arabia, Russia, Turkey, etc.

58 Nick Turse, "Obama's Scramble for Africa: US 'Stability' has Ripped Africa Apart," *Mail and Guardian,* 28 June 2013.

59 Baz Lecocq and Paul Schrijver, "The War on Terror in a Haze of Dust: Potholes and Pitfalls on the Saharan Front," *Journal of Contemporary African Studies*, 25:1 (2007), 143.

CHAPTER X

Evolution and Socio-Political Economy of Ransoming in Nigeria since the Late Twentieth Century

Akachi Odoemene

Introduction: Conceptualizing "Ransoming" in the Nigerian Context

The idea of "ransoming" is not completely strange to Nigerians; what seems quite novel is its new meaning. Indeed, the coalescence of the realities of this "new meaning" makes for a better understanding of why Nigeria was listed as the eighth among ten most affected countries by "economic kidnapping" in 1999.[1] Economic kidnapping are those with economic motivations, only realizable through ransoming. A decade later, as the spate of kidnapping for ransom intensified, the country became one of the "kidnapping capitals of the world."[2] It was also listed by the Control Risks Group, an independent, global risk consultancy, as the world's number one kidnapping hotspot in 2010.[3] Indeed, may be more than anywhere else in the world since the late twentieth century, the phenomenon of kidnapping for ransom has become a vibrantly lucrative industry in Nigeria. An important clarification about ransoming in modern Nigeria is that it goes hand-in-glove with kidnapping and hostage-taking. However, it is noteworthy that though this kind of relationship exists, these phenomena are not always directly related.

For the purposes of our present discussion, ransoming is defined as the demand of some payment of sort, either in cash or kind, in exchange for an abductee, either a person or something, often held in disadvantaged position. While it is habitually a further step of initial crime(s), usually kidnapping and hostage-taking, it is the act that often reveals the underlying motives behind the tripartite crime saga. Three factors are important in understanding the ransoming act: (1) abduction, often by force (2) making demand(s), and (3) payment for demand(s) made, if "successful." Correspondingly, three respective parties are involved: the abductee(s), the abductor(s), and the ransom payer(s). In addition, one or more of three motives, political, ideological or financial, often underlie ransoming. While in reality financial motives may be conveniently masked by other factors, the money from ransoms, if the ransom act is successful, may be used to fund political and/or ideological activities. Thus, all too often the lines between different motives are blurred and/or interlinked.[4]

Two contending perspectives exist regarding ransoming in Nigeria. On the one hand, it is perceived as an instrument for or a form of "coercive diplomacy" – something that is used to compel the other party/parties to accept or take a given course of action in a given political situation. It can be said to be a form of "legitimate behavior" especially where it is used as a last resort, that is, when all other diplomatic avenues and strategies have been explored without success. Indeed, this was the opinion of many sympathizers of the Niger Delta youth insurgency in Nigeria.[5] Another school of thought, on the other hand, sees it, in whatever guise, as a wholly criminal activity in which criminal perpetrators seek to gain undue advantage in a given circumstance. In other words, whether it is used as a form of coercive diplomacy or employed for pecuniary gains, this perspective considers it unacceptable and condemnable.[6] The purpose of this paper is two-fold. The first, on the one hand, is to critically examine and present the historical contexts out of which ransoming emerged and proliferated in late 20th century Nigeria. On the other hand, the second is to identify and examine the social, political and economic contingencies that affected it.

Background to the late Twentieth Century

Over the past fifty years since independence (1960), Nigeria has drawn over

$600 billion from its oil revenue.[7] It has also received over $400 billion in foreign aid.[8] These have, unfortunately, not translated into social and economic prosperity for millions of its citizens. Rather, the country, in spite of the immense human and mineral endowments, is in deep poverty, largely due to systemic corruption. The Structural Adjustment Programme (SAP) of the mid-1980s, based on stringent conditions that were dictated by the Bretton Woods institutions, also created serious social and economic crisis and exacerbated the conditions of poverty in Nigeria. Furthermore, the country was steeped in decades of corrupt military dictatorships that resulted in the alienation of many citizens. All these created the condition for conflicts and struggle over resource control to fester.[9]

Nigerian youths were born into these unfortunate conditions which affected them in highly complex ways.[10] As a historically constructed social category, as a relational concept, and as a group of actors, the youth form an especially sharp lens through which social forces have been focused in Nigeria. The youth was once seen as the hope of the continent.[11] They also appeared as agents in and of themselves, in their own diverse and often highly specific production.[12] However, this group of actors, the youth, became a "problematic category," trapped as it were in a tragic morass of crime, decadence and "given to sexuality that is unrestrained and threatening to the whole society." The youth was soon to be labelled as "dangerous," "criminal," and "decadent," and as "lumpen and/or "loose cannons," thus soon becoming a "social category in crisis."[13]

The questions arising from this unfortunate scenario are: how were the Nigerian youth organizing and making sense of their daily lives? How did they negotiate their private and public roles and envision their futures? How can we understand the youth in various contexts as both makers and breakers of society, while being simultaneously made and/or broken by that society? Undeniably, the future became rather grim for these young men and women, and within the context of their exclusion, it was only natural that they should become angry, bitter, disenchanted, frustrated and desperate.[14] Through their agency they began carving out a social space in a marginal geography and culture that was resistant to the mainstream or dominant culture.[15]

Emergence of Ransoming in Late Twentieth Century Nigeria

While these social, political and economic scenarios were virtually the same throughout Nigeria, the Niger Delta region, which began to experience another level of socio-economic and political oppression from the early 1990s, was hardest hit and popular agitations became rampant in the area. Their agitation was for greater inclusion into the scheme of things and they expressed discontent against the Nigerian government, petro-businesses in the area and their own "leaders." Despite the fact that the Niger Delta accounts for more than 23% of Nigeria's total population,[16] the region remained very "poor, backward, and neglected," even fifty-four years after the Willink's Commission described it thus.[17]

The region became the nerve-center of Nigeria's economy soon after the discovery of crude oil there in 1956 by Shell Darcy. However, due to irresponsible oil and gas exploration, the Niger Delta environment has been severely polluted and devastated. Both the Federal Government and the multinational oil corporations working in the region have been accused of working in cahoots to marginalize the people. Remarkably, for instance, poverty and unemployment in the area has consistently been higher than the national average. This is in spite of the region's privileged position as the economic honeypot of the nation in terms of crude oil and gas reserve, which account for more than 80% of the nation's Gross National Product.[18]

Dissatisfied with this situation, the region's youth intensified their agitations for adequate political representation, an increased and fair share of oil revenues, justice and equity in the management of their affairs and a repair of their degraded environment due to five decades of rapacious oil and gas exploration.[19] Intense agitations in the region began in the early 1990s and were particularly against the Nigerian state and the petrobusinesses operating in the region.[20] Led by the environmental activist and playwright, Kenule Saro-Wiwa, the agitations were characterized by non-violent protests, rallies, local and international campaigns against the excesses of oil companies and the Nigerian government, sensitization of communities to their rights, amongst others.[21] The official response of the government was, however, to initiate repressive policies and actions targeting the people through military invasions and occupations, often with mortal consequences. Things came to a head when on 10 November 1995 Saro-Wiwa and eight of his Ogoni kinsmen were hanged by the state after a flawed trial, despite several pleas by the international community. This marked a watershed in the Niger Delta struggles in Nigeria. The agitators resolved to employ new tactics to achieve their ultimate goal.

Following the execution of Saro-Wiwa, the struggles, activism and agitations in the Niger Delta by local *ethnies* and groups against perceived injustices began to intensify, and by 1999 two clear directions in these activities were discernable. The first was the demand of total resource control, political restructuring and self-determination for the Niger Delta region.[22] The tactics for realizing this demand degenerated into "militia-zation."[23] This was the second direction. With this, there was an eruption of various militant youth groups apparently manipulated by the region's power elite to actualize their demands. Tonwe *et al* have argued that the militant groups which emerged were a mix of ideologues purportedly representing the development aspirations of the people.[24] Popular among the militant groups were the Movement for the Emancipation of the Niger Delta (MEND), the Niger Delta People's Volunteer Force (NDPVF), the Niger Delta Vigilante Service (NDV), and Coalition of Militant Action of the Niger Delta (COMA), to mention but a few.[25] In 1999 and with these developments, full-scale armed rebellion, or what some termed "coercive diplomacy," directed against the Nigerian state and petrobusinesses, ensued, thus signaling a new phase in the history of the peoples' struggle.

Rebellion is seen as a form of organized crime because it thrives only through predatory activities. One of such activities is ransom kidnapping and which youths in the Niger Delta exploited to the fullest. Indeed, this development was expedient for two specific reasons. Firstly, as Bannon and Collier noted, there is always the need for "the organization" (in this case, the rebellion) to be "viable," that is, solvent fund wise.[26] As not just political organizations with a focus on pursuing social change, but also military and business organizations, rebel groups face enormous challenges, including "problems of recruitment, cohesion, equipment, and survival."[27] Thus, rebellions are faced with huge financing problems as several people (the rebels) would need to be fed, clothed and housed. Also, some operational activities would be financed, including arms purchase. So, as revenue does not accrue directly from military activities, rebel groups' survival as military and business organizations will have to depend on engaging in criminal activities.[28]

In the specific experience of youths in the Niger Delta, financing rebel activities came at the same "criminal cost." In addition to financial commitments by the local elite, as well as the imposition of illegal levies on road users, property developers and project contractors in the region, ransom kidnapping was a very notable tactic adopted by the groups. [29] Initially, it began as a local strategy by native communities in Bayelsa and Rivers states who captured oil workers to force the affected companies to either make redress or pay certain kinds of compensation(s) to aggrieved communities and/or persons before their abducted workers were released.[30] The tactic was eventually "hijacked" by the militant groups, whose members, I suspect, were also behind the same acts during the initial native communities' struggles. Essentially, ransom kidnapping became, as it were, an important means of "sustaining" the rebellion in the region.[31]

Secondly, ransom kidnapping became convenient as a coercive diplomacy tactic. It was an effort to voice out and/or publicize the grievances, frustrated emotions and unacceptable conditions of the region's peoples to the world; "a mechanism to draw attention to the unfair treatment of that area in respect of petroleum mining activities, fiscal federalism and low level development manifesting in poor livelihood conditions."[32] Thus, it was a way of "fighting back," of expressing displeasure, anger and disappointment in the Nigerian project, triggered by the socio-economic and political circumstances discussed earlier. Omotola aptly captures this expediency:

> Having exploited all peaceful avenues, including peaceful demonstrations and protests, media and publicity propagandas, direct dialogue and engagement with the State and/or the oil firms, etc but to no avail, the Niger Delta people felt as at that time the best option they had was to resort to "coercive diplomacy."[33]

Accordingly, persons were frequently kidnapped and ransomed by these groups in order to create international awareness concerning the region's plight, as well as to benefit sufficiently from what was going on in their land.

But there is a fundamental question about this course of action. For instance, if one claims to be fighting a liberation struggle, why kidnap people, keep them hostage and make ransoms out of such situations? To be sure, kidnapping and hostage taking are treated as criminal activities in international law. Neither are they condoned by any national legal framework. This remains a critical problematic for those who choose to advance the "liberation struggle" school of thought for the Niger Delta militant groups. However, because of the fluidities of the boundaries between crime and struggle, these militants were able to legitimize these criminal activities in the name of the struggle. They also were able to legitimize such activities in the name of trying to take what rightfully belonged to them. Noting the significance of their actions in this direction, a former member of one of the groups opined:

> We believed that the only language these oil companies, the government and the entire world would listen to and understand was "violence" and "force." These always get you the attention you want, demand and deserve. Can't you see it worked? Or did it not? That's simple.[34]

The petrobusinesses became the original targets of these groups' ransom kidnapping activities. However, it was not just "anybody" in these companies was kidnapped. As Alexander and Klein clearly indicated, these militants were not just well-organized, but were equally very selective in their "target" hostages due to the singular objective of their mission.[35] Thus, petrobusinesses were targeted not just because they were perceived as the main exploiters, but also because there was a preponderant of foreigners working in these companies. In other words, for the militants, it was not just that "only foreigners were worth more money."[36] But it was also because only such violent acts against them would send the urgent and desperate messages to the appropriate quarters the perpetrators wanted. Thus, foreigners were taken hostage and ransomed, either for money or for some other specific demand(s), from either the petrobusinesses or the government. This activity became very popular and viable within a short period. This was the "Type I" Niger Delta variant.

These groups operated a sophisticated network.[37] Thus, the rate of success, as well as the frequency and intensity of such events, was relatively high, despite the security measures put in place by both the government and petrobusinesses to check them. Over the next few years, the Niger Delta region was to witness an unprecedented prevalence of ransom kidnapping of foreigners. For instance, between January and December 2006 a total of 24 incidents, involving 118 hostages, were recorded.[38] Similarly, Shell Petroleum Development Corporation (SPDC) alone claimed that 133 of its staff were kidnapped between 2006 and 2008.[39] Interestingly, though these groups showed considerable dare-devilry in their action and were also courageous enough to claim responsibility for their criminality,[40] it was observed that it something of honour for them not to injure or mistreat their captives, at least in any way that would be considered "inhuman."[41] Nevertheless, a few victims were hurt and some lives were lost.

So, who were the youths – perpetrators of this ransoming crime? In official circles they were considered "criminal elements," as Nigeria's President Umaru Yar'Adua affirmed in an interview in which he challenged the militants' claim that their insurgency was a grievance-based protest and liberation movement.[42] They were "notably, able bodied young men usually armed with sophisticated weapons."[43] In other words, they were only a part of the abandoned, frustrated, and angry Nigerian youths described earlier in this paper. Apparently, the weapons used by these insurgents came from some political elite who clearly but covertly supported the insurgency. Thus, these insurgents can be said to be well connected politically and communally. We must make no mistakes about this: the insurgency was very popular in the region and to a large extent, had community sanction. Not only were the insurgents receiving critical assistance and protection, they also operated from amongst the region's communities.

For instance, the operational bases and hideouts of these groups included "isolated locations in rural communities, strongholds in thick forests and dangerous creeks, rough waterways and unfriendly tide of the high seas."[44] These strategic bases belonged to and were well known to the various communities. A typical case in point was in 2008, when Governor Rotimi Amaechi of Rivers state initiated moves designed to check the activities of the groups. He "ordered" the people of Okrika to give information on one of "their sons," Ateke Tom, the founder and leader of the notorious militant group, the Niger Delta Vigilante (NDV), a break-away faction of the infamous Niger Delta People's Volunteer Force (NDPVF) led by Alhaji Dokubo Asari.[45] Interestingly, no one from the community cooperated with such a directive.[46] The non-cooperation stemmed from three primary factors. Firstly, there was the fear of victimization and/or reprisals by the groups. Secondly, there was the lack of trust in a government controlled by compromised politicians.[47] Thirdly, there was communal solidarity for the insurgency – after all, as an indigene of the area noted, "their fight was for us all in the region; thus, it was equally our struggle."[48]

Changing Trends and Dispersal

Briggs had argued that there seemed very little scope for a "domestic ransom kidnapping business" in Nigeria, especially due to widespread poverty among the people.[49] However, this reality was to change significantly from about 2007. Two factors were responsible for this transition. The first was the security restructuring in petrobusinesses, which saw a drastic reduction of expatriate staff, the "tightening of security" for those remaining, and the employment of the "settlement culture" in order to get the militants on their side and reduce, if not totally eliminate, their harmful activities. "Settlement culture" involves petrobusinesses paying and arming some militant groups to guard oil wells and installations against vandalization by criminals or other militant groups.[50] Such security jobs often pitched the contracted group(s) against their less fortunate comrades-at-arms not so "settled" by the petrobusinesses.[51]

The second factor was the unfortunate "dividend of Nigerian democracy," especially towards the run-up to the 2003 general elections. The militias became hatchet men thugs for politicians in the delta region. Indeed, these militants had proven ties with political leaders who organized, mobilized, armed and used them during elections to harass and intimidate political opponents, rig votes and subvert the electoral process in their favor.[52] They were, however, often abandoned after the politicians had secured political offices.[53] Dropping one militant group also meant that another such group was "employed" and armed by the politicians for protection from the former, abandoned one. These also frequently led to violent clashes among groups and often presented an encouragement and viable opportunity for criminal elements and groups to enter the fray.

"Type II" Niger Delta Variant and its Multiplier Effects

It was the dynamics of the failed political system in addition to the tightening of security for expatriates and failure of the petrobusinesses' "settlement culture" that created the impetus for changes in ransoming. As a result of these developments, ransoming got transformed from a grievance-driven rebellion to a greed-driven venture.[54] The new form was essentially motivated by monetary profits. The transformation began, first in the Niger Delta, then spread to the South-east, and later, throughout the country. Its commencement in the delta was predictable, at least in view of the conditions of possibility already discussed.

As said above, the militants had connections with, and actually acted as thugs for, the political elite who also armed but never disarm them after the general elections were held, won and/or lost.[55] Thus, when these politicians "dumped" or abandoned them after the elections, they became in effect standing armies of their own with new political allegiances, agendas and motivations. With the arms, huge ammunition and training at their disposal, they took advantage of the prevalent culture of violence in the region, quickly turning to crime, particularly ransoming. This time, however, they turned their violence against the wealthy local political elite.[56] This strategy, in the militants' calculations, was considered right, reckoning that their new target must have acquired a lot of wealth largely through fraud and/or at the expense of the masses.[57] Thus, they were seen as part of society's problem. Indeed, due to the complicity of the political elite in such sinister dealings, and with the constant threat of blackmail should things turn around, these militants enjoyed extensive protection from prosecution.[58] This situation led to further mushrooming of militant youth groups in the region through the mid-2000s. In other words, though foreign nationals were still perceived as prize assets by the militants, this new brand of ransoming targeted high placed authority and society, especially their relatives, including aged people, youths and children, male and female alike. These political elite were considered "ransomable" by virtue of their social statuses. Indeed, it was this rather radical change in context and content that effectively initiated the domestication of ransoming in other Nigerian communities.

Rise of the "South-East Variant"

A few years later, the new ransoming trend began to spread, moving inward, specifically to the South-eastern parts of the country, the Igbo heartland, and from about 2009 it became a major part of the crime dynamics in the area.[59] It was in this area that the trend first got truly "localized" and effectively "domesticated."[60] Indeed, these reasons made it to be defined as the "South-east variant." The motive for this variant of the ransom trend, like the Type II Niger Delta variant, was squarely financial gain or profit; nothing more, nothing less.[61] This is very popular among other scholars. For instance, since its localization in this area it has become "a mercantile enterprise," or "a lucrative business," or as Osumah and Aghedo referred to it, the "commodification of kidnapping."[62] In other words, the eventual "transition" of the dynamics of ransoming in the South-east area undoubtedly underlined it as "a form of investment from which investors expect[ed] optimal returns."[63] The relevant question here is: why was the south-east eventually disproportionately represented in Nigeria's ransom business, after the initial Niger Delta Experience? Could the reason(s) be found in the sociology of the people? Or perhaps, could it be an unfortunate socio-political and economic fall-out of its people's civil war experiences? I would axiomatically argue that it is both.

One underlining and indispensable factor for the success of ransoming is the presence of "domestic wealth and prosperity" capable of supporting the business. Indeed, many societies in Africa met this singular demand. Like all businesses and with entrepreneurial flair, the "new" ransom kidnappers adapted their business models and the way they operated in response to, and to fit prevailing market conditions.[64] According to Nwajiuba, the Igbo, who overwhelmingly dominated the South-eastern part of the country,

> learn quickly any successful trade or vocation. When those who went to school emerged the first owners of bicycles and metal roofed houses, they quickly seized the schooling culture and …exceeded the literacy levels of compatriots on the coast who had several decades of start in access to Western education. When acquaintances became successful in road transport, then everyone around sought to become transporters [sic]. When one became successful in fake and real drugs, that emerged the dream of all around, the same for shoe making, cloth trading, import and export, restaurant and hoteliers, supermarket, etc. …When it also became fashionable to run away from school and engage in *Otokoto*[65] activities, *Yahoo*,[66] *419*,[67] etc, the boys moved over. So has it become with the new trade of kidnapping for ransom.[68]

Of course, Nwajiuba's position is in agreement with Osuntokun's thinking that "since people in the South-east are traditionally mercantilist and business people, ransoming seemed to be for them just another business; a quick business through which to make money."[69]

I would also argue that this was partly a fall-out of the exigencies of post-civil war socio-political economy and realities of the erstwhile secessionist South-east region. With a near-total destruction of the South-east local economy during the war, continued marginalization of the area in the post-war period and "lack of promise" in terms of government socio-economic development, there was necessarily a dissolution and abandonment of the once famed spirit and lofty philosophy of collective brotherhood, epitomized in the *onye aghala nwanneya* (no relative should be left behind) dictum. In its stead, there was the gradual development of the *Ike keta O rie* ("survival of the fittest") philosophy as a survival strategy, with "every man on his own." Therefore, even one's blood brother could prey on one.

One may ask: what exactly could make someone a victim of this new variant? The answer is straightforward, and ultimately linked to the perception of the perpetrators that their victims had "rich people" who would "bail them out" of the situation.

> If your children are defined as successful, then you are a target. It is not a vendetta or you do not need to have offended anybody, you just have to be perceived as being capable of paying or having friends and associates who can contribute the money requested. What are the parameters seen as evidence that you can pay? The house you live in, the car you ride, and most painful is that you donate handsomely at community and village events. These are the indices of your "kidnap value" which can be translated into monetary terms.[70]

In addition to this list was ownership of thriving business outfits, or working in establishments known to pay their staff "handsomely well," like the petro-businesses, the banking sector, or the telecommunications. In other words, anyone whom the perpetrators believed will be able to attract a "reasonable ransom" could become a victim.[71] Even family members of the perpetrators could become victims too if they met such conditions. Thus, in this new development, the victims expanded to include not just the wealthy and their family members, but just any one, including even toddlers.[72] Indeed, it was at this stage that the ransoming phenomenon was perfected as a 'productive tactics' for money-seeking.

Apart from the lesser cases of self-ransoming and petty "family politics" and intrigues involved in some of these dynamics, as we shall show later, the core criminal perpetrators and conspirators of this South-east variant were also significantly different. The perpetrators included dubious elements from different walks of life – student cultists, artisans, robbers, the unemployed, "professional fraudsters" and, at least in one instance, an ordained clergy.[73] In some instances, these criminals had patrons to whom they made returns, and who, on their own part, gave the culprits the needed protection to operate with impunity.[74] Indeed, some perpetrators who were arrested had named some of their patrons, which included notable traditional rulers who covertly supported the criminals for protection and pecuniary benefits.[75] This informed the Abia government's decision to sack the affected "royal fathers" for alleged complicity in the crime.[76] Their perpetrators' networks involved multiple independent but well-organized syndicates.

These perpetrators wielded different kinds of dangerous weapons, which they often threatened to use at the slightest provocation. Due to its violence, the new South-east variant often facilitated other crimes. For example, victims were often robbed, humiliated, assaulted, gagged and/or assailed.[77] Similarly, female abductees were "frequently subjected to sexual assault or rape."[78] This was unlike what was experienced in the Type I Niger Delta variant. Though ransoms demanded were often on a modest scale to ensure the victim's relatives and friends paid promptly, a strategy referred to as "express kidnapping," the perpetrators often utilized threats of harm or death to elicit maximum cooperation and to ensure compliance with their demands. If demands were either not paid or not paid in time, or directives given not strictly adhered to, the perpetrators sometimes carried their threats to the shock of all.[79] As time went on, it was also noted that there was an exponential increase in the level of desperation and ruthlessness exhibited by the perpetrators.[80]

The nature of some ransoming acts in this later development was, however, no more than ludicrous. For instance, in some towns in both Anambra and Abia states, everybody had a "kidnap value," which could actually be haggled openly on the streets in broad daylight with the perpetrators. In the city of Aba, for instance,

> a "house boy" or "house girl" could attract as low as recharge card money which in some cases are #1,500. The kidnappers could then declare that there are ten of them and each needs a card which you should purchase and send them. That amounts to a kidnap value of #15,000 Naira.[81]

Without a doubt, these instances clearly underline the upsurge of this crime as desperate acts of survival prompted by poverty and frustration. There was a case of two young men who ransomed their mother in order to get "good money" out of their elder brother based in the United States of America.[82] Again, interesting tales of people who ransomed themselves also abound. In one such example, the objective of the young man was to extract from his family members enough money for his personal purposes. He thus arranged with his friends for his kidnap, after which he was ransomed.[83] Another equally popular case was that of a man in Lagos who ransomed himself to get huge sums of money from his wife. He was arrested by the police when he attempted to withdraw the funds from the bank.[84]

This later South-east variant accounted for 97% of ransom incidents recorded around the country between mid-2000s and 2012.[85] I am also strongly convinced that a lot of ransom kidnapping took place at village levels, in which case they were not made public through the media. The reason being, I suspect, that in the case of many families, if the kidnapped persons were not politically exposed and connected, it made no sense for the affected families to publicize such incidents. It made sense, however, for friends and family members to listen carefully to the terms of the ransom, haggle and agree with the culprits on a payable amount soonest, meet those terms as quickly as possible and to keep mute about the incident. Indeed, this was largely the case in the rural areas where this ransom menace was equally frustratingly endemic.[86]

Was this new variant limited only to the South-east? No, it was not; the trend has become widespread throughout the country, though with different prevalence rates. For instance, ransom kidnappings have been widely reported in Lagos, where it has even become an "established business," and in Ondo, Ekiti, and Oyo states, as well as in Edo, Kano, Kaduna and Abuja.[87] It has also been reported in the northern parts, especially since 2009 with the upsurge of the *Boko Haram* Islamic insurgency.[88] However, as Lofkrantz and also Ojo have shown, ransoming is a historical phenomenon in both Northern Nigeria and Yorubaland.[89] Therefore, this phenomenon has clearly become a nation-wide criminal malaise, the very reason why Abati argued that the entire country had become "a kidnappers' den."[90] In other words, the South-east only became significant within the context of a fledging Nigerian-wide experience, because the variant originated there and the trend became endemic there. This is corroborated by CLEEN 2010 statistics which indicated that the South-east had the highest level of kidnapping in Nigeria.[91] Again, Chukwuma argued that between 2009 and 2010 there was hardly a day passed without cases of kidnapping being reported in the South-east area.[92]

There was also the belief in some quarters that the crime was being championed and "exported" by "South-easterners" (the Igbo) to other parts of the country. This is, however, evidently not the case. The identities of many members of ransom kidnapping syndicates that were arrested and exposed by the police around the country show that such claims of Igbo dominance of the "trade" across the country were rather fictional, and at best, a figment of some people's imagination. Indeed, each dominant ethnic group in each state across the country must have likely dominated the business in that state, as they would have a better idea and knowledge of the terrain, workings and cultures of the area. However, each of such group may have acted sometimes in conjunction with othr criminals from diverse backgrounds.

Table 10.1: "Kidnapping Incidents" in Six Geopolitical Zones in Nigeria between 2008 and 2010

Zone	States	Incidence by Year			Total
		2008	2009	2010	
North-Central	Benue, Kogi, Kwara, Nassarawa, Niger, Plateau, and Abuja	3	43	41	87
Northeast	Adamawa, Bauchi, Borno, Gombe, Taraba and Yobe	1	101	19	121
Northwest	Jigawa, Katsina, Kano, Kaduna, Kebbi, Sokoto, and Zamfara	2	13	17	32
Southeast	Abia, Anambra, Ebonyi, Enugu, and Imo	40	307	122	469
South-South	Akwa Ibom, Bayelsa, Cross River, Delta, Edo, and Rivers	128	362	137	627
Southwest	Ekiti, Lagos, Ogun, Osun, Ondo and Oyo	16	113	42	171
Total for all six zones		**190**	**939**	**378**	**1,507**

Source: Adapted from Statistics on Kidnapping, Force Headquarters, Nigeria Police Force, Abuja.[93]

The table above shows the summary of "kidnapping incidents" in six Geo-political zones in Nigeria between 2008 and 2010, as compiled by the Nigerian Police. A point to note is that this is certainly not an exhaustive list. Without a doubt, so many incidences were not publicized or brought to the knowledge of the police. Be that as it may, some critical deductions could be made from the table. Firstly, it is obvious that these incidences were equally for ransom purposes. Second, the table confirms ransom kidnaping as a widespread crime in Nigeria, although the phenomenon is more endemic in some sections than the others. Thirdly, it further shows that during the period, while the South-east was generally believed to have been most affected by the incidence, the Niger Delta region actually recorded the highest occurrence of the crime. Finally, it shows a persistent progression in the incidence. Indeed, this was a reflection of how prevalent, common and rife the crime was becoming in the society.

With this South-east variant, – strictly greed-driven ransoming acts, that is, motivated by and undertaken squarely for financial gains or profits – ransoming became commonplace but it was rarely reported by the Western news media, ostensibly for two reasons: firstly, it became largely a "local" or domestic economic practice in Nigerian communities, and secondly, it concerned or affected foreigners less. One is of the opinion and would argue that it was the very rampant and callous nature of this variant in the country that eventually transformed ransoming into a "popular criminal social culture" of sort – one in which many deprived, frustrated and idle youths, as well as some privileged elite, as evidence suggest, took solace and made a source of livelihood.

Other Motives for Ransoming

Ransoming sometimes may be a politically motivated criminal tactic. With Nigeria's return to civil rule in 1999, a new form of ransoming equally emerged. This is what I refer to as "political ransoming," which comes in diverse arrangements. Firstly, it involved the kidnapping and ransoming of a politician by his/her political rival(s) for the political office he/she was occupying or vying for. As Adegbulu explains, the idea was to intimidate and force such kidnapped rivals to resign their positions, or step down and not run for the office. Of course it is someone who is "free" and "available" that can contest or run for an office.[94] Rejecting such pressures could be fatal, as outright assassination could be the next option. Indeed, assassination of politicians is not new and has been all too frequent. A good case in point is that of Chief Funsho Williams, who was assassinated because of his unwavering ambition to run for the Lagos state gubernatorial seat. Indeed, his assassination, as well as those of Chiefs Marshal Harry and Bola Ige, to mention but a few, continued to serve as a warning to many politicians who were lucky to be so "ransomed."

Secondly, "godfatherism" was another form of political ransoming. Godfatherism – a common feature of Nigerian politics – is neo-patrimonial clientelism of symbiotic relationship between a "godfather" (powerful political patron) and "godson" (upstart political office aspirant or holder). Godfathers manipulated entire democratic process – from rigging votes and influencing results during electoral exercises and securing political offices for their "Godsons" to actually running the government in order to service their private socio-economic interests.[95] It was necessarily an economic investment that must yield profits at all cost. This phenomenon created a gun-point, "do-or-die" and naked violence democracy. Two prominent godfatherism cases in point in Nigeria's fourth republic were those of Dr. Chris Ngige of Anambra state and Alhaji Rashidi Ladoja of Oyo state respectively.

On 10 July 2003, Ngige, then serving governor of Anambra state, was abducted, taken hostage and then forced to resign his political office because he refused to make adequate monthly financial returns to his Godfather, Mr. Chris Uba, as hitherto agreed. Ngige argued that he reneged because making such payments would jeopardize development in the state. Ngige was, however, reinstated as his resignation was deemed illegal and unconstitutional since it was done under duress.[96] A similar incident took place in the case of Ladoja who was ousted on 12 January 2006 through the political intrigues of his Godfather, Alhaji Lamidi Adedibu, for similar reasons as in Ngige's case. Ladoja's removal from office was eventually voided by Nigeria's Supreme Court as it was unconstitutional.[97]

In other words, with this phenomenon taking root in the country since the 1999, it was the wealthy elite of power that oppressed and ransomed the masses through acts of electoral manipulation, political violence, personal gratification and fraud. In a sense, this was the exact opposite of the economic variant, where it was the poor that waged a war against "the wealthy and powerful" in society, utilizing the instrumentality of ransom kidnapping.

Ransoming: Society-specific Reasons for Prevalence

As we have noted earlier, the primary factor underlining the emergence and spread of this social ill in the Nigerian society was the unacceptable and deplorable conditions of the youth which exploded into acts of criminality, one of which was ransoming. However, beyond these stated conditions, some other factors notably explain the prevalence of this crime in the society. The first is what may be referred to as transitions in the political economy of criminality in the country. From the early 1970s, after the civil war, armed robbery emerged as a notable organized crime in Nigeria, thriving through the 1980s and 1990s. But the tide began to change and several of the criminals shifted to other means of criminal gains. The country began to witness a rise in a new wave of crime known as "advance fee fraud," or "419" in Nigerian parlance. This kind of crime emerged in the early 1990s and thrived throughout that decade and beyond. Instructively, there were elements of both armed robbery and ransoming within the framework of the "419" crime,[98] such that the former was gradually phasing out while the later was almost a novelty. Therefore, one can construe the eventual emergence and prevalence of ransoming as a sort of paradigm shift in the political economy of criminality in Nigeria, such that new forms of organized crimes and criminal opportunities emerged from time to time in the country.

In the second instance, it is pertinent to look closely at the evolution of ransoming from the perspective of crime and punishment. This emphasizes the natural shift, among criminals, to "safer crimes," that is, those crimes with seemingly lesser risks for the criminals. For instance, in relation to our first point here, one of the measures put in place by government to tackle the rising incidents of armed robbery in the country was the establishment of the Armed Robbery and Firearms Tribunals. This resulted in the prosecution and public execution of thousands of poor, deprived and frustrated youth who perpetrated this crime. In contrast, and unlike armed robbery, the "419" crime did not involve the use of arms nor did it attract capital punishment. It involved far lesser penalty of imprisonment for a few years. This made it far more preferable to armed robbery.

When one looks at the punishment for the crime of kidnapping and hostage-taking – not ransoming, as it is not considered a crime in itself – until recently they carried far more lenient punishments, the maximum of which is between five to ten years jail term, even when such act was perpetrated with arms. But more than that, when the culprits were "connected," or actually colluded with politicians or state security forces, they often got away with such crimes. Hence, perpetrators understood that ransoming did not attract the capital punishment, had minimal risks and paid well.[99] This is especially so as there was almost a certainty that families and friends of the victims will pay the ransom without involving the police. These shifts in criminality were necessarily engendered by the need for self-preservation.

Militarization and the proliferation of arms constituted the third factor, especially in the context of the Niger Delta case with its culture of impunity. This primarily came about due to the State's incessant engagements with delta peoples' agitations through acts of military brutalizations in the last twenty years, which eventually militarized and engrained militancy in the youths of the region.[100] The next was the proliferation of sophisticated (small arms and light) weapons in the Niger Delta region by its political elite. Of course, the escalation of crises in the region led to such proliferation – a fact acknowledged by a serving Minister of State for Defense, Dr. Rowland Oritsejafor.[101]

A fourth factor has to do with changes in societal worldview and values due to growing materialism, especially among the youth. A good number of the young held nothing sacred any more, not even the time-honored tradition of respect.[102] The Nigerian youth was in his/her own world, seemingly uncontrollable and an agent in his/her own right, taking and enforcing critical decisions. There is also the desire for "quick money" or what many have called the "get rich quick" syndrome, which made the desire for a decent occupation, hardwork, discipline and legitimate earnings become rather the exception, especially amongst the youth.[103] Religious organizations which used to be bastion of and bases for morality and discipline equally lost it to materialism; even the so-called Ministers of God themselves flaunted excessive wealth in the face of unacceptable societal poverty and destitution.[104]

Finally, the pervasive wave and prevalence of ransoming was a symptom of a larger malaise – a failing state – a designate for a state "which has shattered social and political structures," and whose governments have weakened to such an extent that they are unable to provide basic public goods.[105] Thus, it represents a state in transition, one that was becoming a "failed state." Most accounts of such states center on "erosion of state capacity" especially in ensuring peace and stability (adequate security of life and property), effective governance, territorial control, and economic sustainability.[106] Without a doubt, this was what Nigeria truly epitomized. Briggs noted that under such conditions as one finds in Nigeria, "the state's ability to put forward risks to deter kidnappers is severely hampered." Indeed, it was such lawless conditions and institutional weaknesses that allowed ransom kidnapping to grow and thrive in the country.[107] Consequent upon these facts, Nigeria was ranked 54th position in the 2005 Failed States Index,[108] as well as in 17th and 18th positions in 2007[109] and 2008[110] respectively. This was a statement on the progressive decline of its socio-political and economic situation and descent into a failed state.

Implications for the Nigerian State

The issues and trends of ransoming are an insalubrious phenomenon of the Nigerian society. They have significant dire implications for the county's overall development trajectory. The main fallouts are the concern about insecurity among the general populace and the stalling of democratic development in virtually all parts of the country. These, of course, have many facets, ranging from the local to the global. It is in this light that I would articulate the consequences to the Nigerian society. Ransoming created a palpable fear amongst the people of the country, especially in the areas where the crime was endemic. This was especially so as just anyone could become a victim – if not as the abducted, then as a payer of or contributor to the ransom. In other words, the crime drastically undermined the public's sense of security and put citizens in a state of fear, and the country in a state of terror.[111] Indeed, it created a "culture of fear" in society, with the result that it was difficult for people to express their potentials to the fullest because of uncertainties of that moment.[112] As Añurunwa appropriately noted:

> We all lived in real fear. It could be anyone's turn the next day and the outcome of the whole saga could eventually be fatal. People went to bed early. Children were not free anymore to walk around the streets and even the elderly ones were subjected to a life of 'hide and seek', literarily sneaking in and out of their homes.... It was quite bad.[113]

The situation warranted a good number of the wealthy who lived in the rather endemic regions to seek safer abodes, relocating their families elsewhere within or outside the country. Similarly, many victims also relocated due to the same security reason.[114] One such endemic place was Aba, the once bustling commercial "*Enyimba* City" that attracted merchants from across West Africa. Aba became a ghost of itself as its new image repulsed both visitors and its rich residents who relocated to safer places.[115]

Ransoming dramatically changed the social lives of the people. Most elite kept off from social outings, ceremonies, public gatherings and relaxation centers because they saw themselves as potential victims.[116] Such "forced ostracism" impacted negatively on society. For instance, the famed spirit of and drive for "self-help" rural community development among the Igbo was weakened if not destroyed as the wealthy and well-meaning members of society began to keep away from public gatherings or making public donations towards "self-help" projects. Indeed, such donations could be the basis for singling them or their relatives out for ransoming. As this is a region where most public projects – school, hospitals, water and electricity schemes, community halls, churches, etc – are all financed by the popular self-help culture, what then becomes of the area if the financially endowed stops donating to community projects, especially in the face of a very weak formal structure of governance? [117] The ransoming phenomenon, thus, led to what I term "arrested development" in many rural communities. Many people who started any projects in rural communities, whether for personal or industrial purposes, abandoned such projects as they were often strong basis for ransoming.

The prevalence of this crime also impacted negatively on the efforts of many Nigerian entrepreneurs to give the economy a boost. As Fyanka argued:

> Nigeria's economy was growing fast, especially before the upsurge of this criminal trend, largely because of the tenacity of Nigerians to build the economy. Many entrepreneurs in the country took initiative and the lead in bolstering the economy...But the emergence of this trend worked seriously against these efforts; the cohesion that we saw in the Nigerian economy to move forward was seriously hampered.... Ransoming was rather an attack on the root and foundation of the economic growth of the country.[118]

The attack was primarily against members of the business class. As these people were at the forefront of the economic growth in the country, and their resource base happened to be the targets of this particular criminal phenomenon, it goes without saying that it was also an attack on the economic growth of the country. The impact was thus remarkable.[119]

Ransoming led to disruptions in the oil industry which caused a significant reduction in Nigeria's oil production. This negatively affected the country's foreign exchange and developmental objectives, especially in the face of global financial and economic meltdown.[120] With such genuine threats to the lives of their staff, some petrobusinesses were forced to declare a *force majeure*. Such trends hurt the industry and constituted a major setback for the economy. For example, it was estimated that in 2009 alone ransom kidnapping acts drastically cut oil production in the country by about 25% and a revenue loss of over $44 billion.[121] In other words, if this was the estimated loss to the oil sector for one year during the "lull period" of the incidents, one can reasonably project that the overall loss (between 1999 and 2012) could be anything between $740 billion to $1 trillion.

In addition, "ransom cost" was introduced into the cost of production by many companies, especially those working with expatriates. This raised the cost of production as companies hired more security personnel.[122] They also earmarked huge "kidnap funds" for their staff.[123] Amusan explains the context and dynamic of this development in petrobusinesses:

> [W]ith the inclusion of ransom cost in the cost of production in their joint ventures with the federal government through the NNPC, with the help of their parent states' diplomatic missions and the traditional chiefs in the oil bearing region, negotiation would be organized without direct involvement of the Nigerian government where huge sum ... would be paid to the militants in exchange for the release of expatriates. Eventually, it is the government that would pay for this cost.[124]

As a result of this security threat, many foreign multinational companies in different sectors abandoned developmental projects, closed offices and/or relocated to other parts of the country, or abroad. For instance, Julius Berger, a German construction giant in Nigeria, abandoned many of its road construction and civil engineering work in the region. Similarly, such high level of insecurity led to the closure of such notable companies as Lever Brothers, Nigerian Breweries, Aba Textile Mills and Dana Motors (all in Aba, Abia state).[125]

Criminal acts like ransom kidnapping also portrayed Nigeria as an investment-unfriendly destination.[126] For instance, in 2009 the Russian Ambassador to Nigeria, Mr. Alexander D. Polyakov, reiterated the need for the Nigerian government to tackle kidnapping problems and other security challenges to enable business activities to thrive.[127] Indeed, with the spread of this crime to other parts of the country, reluctance to invest in troubled regions became a country-wide problem. In this light, Mrs. Helen Clark, the Prime Minister of New Zealand, characterized Nigeria as "particularly dangerous from a personal security point of view."[128] Thus, like many other foreign leaders, she asked her country's nationals resident or working in Nigeria to leave as their security was no longer guaranteed. Nigeria was, therefore, seen as a country in which insecurity loomed large and where the ransoming criminality had assumed significant notoriety.[129]

Since Nigeria relies heavily on foreign direct investments (FDIs) to boost its domestic economy, a socio-political crisis like ransoming was a real bad news. Meaningful economic investments that could affect the lives of the people and the fortunes of the country were lost as foreign investors "don't invest in risky climate, particularly in the context of global economic recession.[130] The insecurity also created a vicious cycle in the society, which led to massive unemployment arising from the lack or withdrawal of investment. Without a doubt, the adverse effects of these to the development of the domestic economy, as well as to the developmental strides in and of the country cannot be over emphasized.

Lastly, when such crimes as ransoming continued unabated, it "sustained" an international image crisis for Nigeria. Indeed, one cannot put a cost on the image of the country. From the late 1970s Nigeria began to slide into ignobility due to the activities of its citizens both at home and abroad, especially due to a steady increase in corruption and organized crimes. These began to tarnish its image on the international scene. Therefore, the upsurge in the rate of ransoming in the country further hurt the country's already flawed image, especially as it (the country) assumed the status of "the kidnapping center of the world."[131]

Conclusion

Ransoming became endemic due to a critical nexus of social, political and economic factors in Nigeria. A section of the youth initially took to this crime as a tool of coercion or as a form of militant diplomacy in their ideological struggles in the Niger Delta region where violent militancy and criminality largely became notable instruments. Their targets were originally expatriate oil workers. The phenomenon then quickly got transformed, shifting in context, location and content. In other words, it became commercialized and a booming "cottage industry" – a major source of livelihood for so many deprived, abused and frustrated youths across the country. This was the outcome of the lack of economic development and opportunity for a majority of Nigerians which led many to crime as a means of supporting themselves and their families. In this context, the typical victim profile also changed, shifting to include wealthy political and business elite, and eventually just anyone in the society. It did not just become a multi-million-naira business venture, but also a popular criminal "social culture" in different parts of the country.

Our discourse underlines an important dynamic of the ransoming debate: the notion of "competing victimhoods." On the one hand, the poor, oppressed, abused and frustrated youth in society claimed ransoming was a means of survival and "payback" for a ruthless and oppressive system in which the power elite governed mainly in their own interest and at the expense of the overall interest of the majority of the people. On the other hand, the elite and society itself claimed they were targeted victims of wicked, heinous and gruesome acts by common criminals and dangerous youths. In such competing narratives a salient point is clear: ransoming was actually a product of the mismanagement of the enormous human and natural resources subsisting in the Nigerian society. This was squarely a very sad misadventure of governance. Moreover, it became a "big, productive and lucrative business" due to inept governance, a predatory elite, and weak institutional frameworks. Indeed, bad governance increased the rate of crimes. This has had debilitating developmental implications for Nigeria.

Endnotes

1 Rachel Briggs, *The Kidnapping Business* (London: The Foreign Policy Centre, 2001), 13.

2 Jideofor Adibe, "Pervasive Kidnapping in Nigeria: Symptom of a Failing State," Holler Africa website, June 2009, http://www.hollerafrica.com/showArticle.php?artId=304&catId=1,&page=1 (accessed: 21 December 2011).

3 Control Risks Group, "Energy Industry", *Kidnapping and Ransoming* (K&R) *Bulletin* (April 2012), 1.

4 Control Risks Group, "Energy Industry,"1.

5 Justus Ofili Omiloli, 35 years, Ijaw (Izon)/Niger Delta youth and university postgraduate student, Yenagoa, Bayelsa state, Nigeria. Personal communication; interviewed on 29 July 2012; Martin Alfred-Smith, 32 years, former member of MEND, a notorious militant group in the Niger Delta (currently undergoing a government-sponsored Amnesty Programme); Port-Harcourt city, Rivers state, Nigeria. Personal communication; interviewed on 23 July 2012; Dr. Shola Omotola, 38 years, Political Scientist, Lecturer and Researcher; Lagos, Nigeria. Personal Communication; interviewed on Monday, 17 September 2012.

6 Akinjide Osuntokun, 73 years, Emeritus Professor of Diplomatic History and Renowned Diplomat; Mowe, Nigeria. Personal communication; interviewed on 17 September 2012.

7 Michael Watts, "Has Globalization failed Nigeria?" Site title, April 2009, http://insights.som.yale.edu/insights/has-globalization-failed-nigeria (accessed: 28 October 2013).

8 Michael Burleigh, "A Country so Corrupt it would be Better to Burn Our Aid Money", *Daily Mail Online*, (9 August, 2013, http://www.dailymail.co.uk/debate/article-2387359/Nigeria-country-corrupt-better-burn-aid-money.html (accessed: 28 October 2013).

9 Daniel. A. Tonwe, Godwin U. Ojo and Iro Aghedo, "Spoils Politics and Environmental Struggle in the Niger Delta Region of Nigeria," *Inkanyiso: Journal of Humanities and Social Sciences,* 4:1 (2012), 40.

10 Deborah Durham, "Youth and the Social Imagination in Africa: Introduction to Parts 1 and 2," *Anthropological Quarterly*, 73:3 (July 2000), 1.

11 Oarhe Osumah and Iro Aghedo, "Who wants to be a Millionaire? Nigerian Youths and the Commodification of Kidnapping," *Review of African Political Economy,* 38:128 (June 2011), 278.

12 Sarah Gibbs, "Post-War Reconstruction in Mozambique: Reframing Children's Experience of War and Healing," *Disasters,* 18:3 (1994); Pamela Reynolds, *Traditional Healers and Childhood in Zimbabwe* (Athens, OH: Ohio University Press, 1996); Alcinda Honwana, "Okusiakala Ondalo Yokalye, Let's Light a New Fire: Local Knowledge in the Post-War Reintegration of War Affected Children in Angola," *Consultancy Report* for the Christian Children's Fund (1998).

13 Mamadou Diouf, "Engaging Postcolonial Cultures: African Youth and Public Space," *African Studies Review,* 46:2 (2003), 4; Ibrahim Abdullah, "Bush Path to Destruction: the Origin and Character of the Revolutionary United Front/ Sierra Leone," *Journal of Modern African Studies,* 36:2 (1998); Robert D. Kaplan, "The Coming of Anarchy," in Gearóid Ó Tuathail, Simon Dalby and Paul Routledge (eds.), *The Geopolitics Reader* (London: Routledge, 2006); Osumah and Aghedo, "Who wants to be a Millionaire?," 278; Eghosa Osaghae, Augustine Ikelegbe, Omobolaji Olarinmoye and Steven Okhonmina, *Youth Militia, Self-determination and Resource Control Struggles in the Niger Delta Region*

of Nigeria (CODESRIA and ASC Leiden Consortium for Development Partnership Research Report No. 5, Modules 5 and 6, 2007), 5.

14 Henrik E. Vigh, *Navigating Terrains of War: Youth and Soldiering in Guinea* (Oxford: Berghahn, 2006); Henrik E. Vigh, "Social Death and Violent Life Changes," in Catrine Christiansen, Mats Utas and Henrik E. Vigh (eds.), *Navigating Youth, Generating Adulthood: Social Belonging in an African Context* (Uppsala: Nordiska Afrikainstitutet, 2006); Osaghae et al, *Youth Militia, Self-determination and Resource Control Struggles*, 5; Osumah and Aghedo, "Who wants to be a Millionaire?," 278.

15 Diouf, "Engaging Postcolonial Cultures," 5-7; Osumah and Aghedo, "Who Wants to be a Millionaire?" 278.

16 National Population Commission, *Nigeria's National Census Figures* (Abuja: NPC, 2006).

17 Akachi Odoemene, "Social Consequences of Environmental Change in the Niger Delta of Nigeria," *Journal of Sustainable Development,* 4:2 (2011); Willinks Commission Report, *Report of the Commission Appointed to Inquire into the Fears of Minorities and the Means of Allaying Them* (London: Her Majesty's Stationery Office, 1957), 5.

18 Tonwe, Ojo and Aghedo, "Spoils Politics and Environmental Struggle," 37-48; Robert O. Dode. "The Political Economy of Resource Curse and the Niger Delta Crisis in Nigeria: Matters Arising," *Afro-Asian Journal of Social Sciences,* 2:1 (2011), 1-15.

19 William Ehwarieme, "Fishers of Men: The Political Economy of Kidnapping in the Niger Delta," in Victor Ojakorotu (ed.), *Contending Issues in the Niger Delta Crisis of Nigeria* (Delray Beach, FL: JAPSS Press Inc., 2009), 95-122.

20 Tonwe, Ojo and Aghedo, "Spoils Politics and Environmental Struggle."

21 O.J. Agbonifo, *Development as Conflict: Ogoni Movement, the State and Oil Resources in the Niger Delta, Nigeria* (The Hague: Shaker Publishing Press, 2009); B. Naanen, "The Niger Delta and the National Question," in Eghosa E. Osaghae and Ebere Onwudiwe (eds.), *The Management of the National Question in Nigeria* (Okada: Igbinedion University Press, 2007).

22 Ehwarieme, "Fishers of Men", 95-122.

23 Augustine Ikelegbe, "Beyond the Threshold of Civil Struggle: Youth Militancy and the Militia-ization of the Resource Conflict in the Niger Delta Region of Nigeria," *African Study Monographs,* 27:3 (2006), 87-122.

24 Tonwe, Ojo and Aghedo, "Spoils Politics and Environmental Struggle."

25 Felix Tuodolo, "Generation," in Michael Watts (ed.), *Curse of the Black Gold: 50 Years of Oil in the Niger Delta* (Brooklyn, NY: Power House Books, 2008).

26 Ian Bannon and Paul Collier (eds.), *Natural Resources and Violent Conflict: Options and Actions* (Washington D.C: World Bank, 2003).

27 Paul Collier, V.L. Elliot, Hegre Havard, H. Anke, M. Reynal-Querol, and N. Sambanis, *Breaking the Conflict Trap: Civil War and Development Policy* (Washington DC: World Bank and Oxford University Press, 2003), 67.

28 Tonwe, Ojo and Aghedo, "Spoils Politics and Environmental Struggle."

29 AOAV and NWGAV, "The Violent Road: Nigeria's South East," Action of Warmed Violence Website, 12 December 2013, http://aoav.org.uk/2013/the-violent-road-nigeria-south-east/ (accessed: 20 December 2013); D. Onojowo, "Of Hoodlums, North and South," *Punch Newspaper*, 21 October, 2001, 12.

30 Dr. Harry Olufunwa, Literary Scholar and Social Critic; Redeemer's University, Nigeria. Personal communication; interviewed on Monday, 17 September 2012; Justus Omiloli; Shola Omotola, Personal Communication.

31 Paul Okumagba, "Ethnic Militias and Criminality in the Niger-Delta," *African Research Review,* 3:3 (April 2009), 315-330.

32 Chinedum Nwajiuba, "The Socioeconomics of the Kidnapping Industry in Southeast Nigeria (1)," *The Leader Newspaper*, 29 November – 6 December 2009, 8.

33 Shola Omotola, Personal Communication.

34 Martin Alfred-Smith, personal communication.

35 Alexander and Klein. "Kidnapping and Hostage-taking."

36 Alfred-Smith, Personal Communication.

37 Aniedi J. Ikpang, "Kidnapping: Exacerbating the Corridors of Criminality in Nigeria," 13, http://www.docstoc.com/docs/16881285/kidnapping (accessed: 11 December, 2012).

38 Ibaba S. Ibaba, "Alienation and Militancy in the Niger Delta: Hostage Taking and the Dilemma of the Nigerian State," *African Journal on Conflict Resolution,* 8:2 (2008), 14.

39 Arinze Ngwube, "Threats to Security in Nigeria," *Review of Public Administration and Management,* 3 (2013), 79-80.

40 Ikpang, "Kidnapping: Exacerbating the Corridors," 13.

41 Justus Omiloli; Shola Omotola, Personal Communications.

42 Anonymous, "Yar'Adua: Between Me, My Friends and the Fight against Corruption," *The Guardian,* 30 April 2009, 9.

43 Ikpang, "Kidnapping: Exacerbating the Corridors," 13.

44 Ibid., 13.

45 Judith B. Asuni, "Blood Oil in the Niger Delta," *USIP Special Report* 229 (August) (Washington D.C.: United States Institute of Peace, 2009), 13.

46 M.K. Obiyo, "On Rotimi Amaechi's Stewardship in Rivers State, 1999-2010," *Horizon*, 10 January 2011, 8-9.

47 Akachi Odoemene, "'Agony in the Garden': Incongruity of Governance and the Travails of Port Harcourt city, Niger Delta, Nigeria, 1912-2010," *Africana: A Journal of Ideas on Africa and the African Diaspora,* 5:1 (2011), 126.

48 Justus Omiloli, Personal Communication.

49 Briggs, *The Kidnapping Business*, 20.

50 Martin Alfred-Smith; Shola Omotola; 'Jide Osuntokun; and Kenneth Nwoko, Personal Communication.

51 Martin Alfred-Smith; Justus Omiloli, Personal Communication.

52 Odoemene, "'Agony in the Garden';" Judith B. Asuni, "Understanding the Armed Groups of the Niger Delta," *Council on Foreign Relations* Working Pa-

per (September 2009); Asuni, "Blood Oil in the Niger Delta;" Lydia Polgreen, "Nigerian Gangs Turn their Guns on Their Own," *International Herald Tribune*, 8 November 2007, http://www.iht.com/bin/printfriendly.php?id=8252160 (accessed: 2 December 2007).

53 Odoemene, "'Agony in the Garden'."

54 Cyril Obi, Personal communication; adult, Social Scholar and Researcher, Nairobi, Kenya. Personal communication; interviewed on, 24 January 2013.

55 Asuni, "Understanding the Armed Groups of the Niger Delta," 13.

56 ASI Global, "Kidnapping and Insecurity in Nigeria," title of website, (2012), http://www.asiglobalresponse.com (accessed: 17 February 2013); Osumah and Aghedo, "Who Wants to be a Millionaire?"; O. Onovo, "Combating the Crimes of Armed Robbery and Kidnapping in the South-East and South-South Zones of Nigeria: Strategies, Challenges and Prospects," *Igbinedion Journal of Diplomacy and Strategy*, 1:1 (2009), 12-21.

57 Alfred-Smith, Personal Communication; Justus Omiloli, Personal Communication.

58 Augustine Ikelegbe, "Popular and Criminal Violence as Instruments of the Struggle: The Case of Youth Militias in the Niger Delta Region," a paper presented at the International workshop on "Violent Conflict in the Niger Delta" organized by the Nordic Africa Institute (NAI) and the International Peace and Research Institute, Oslo (PRIO), Norway (2008), 18-19; Ibiba DonPedro, *Oil in the Water: Crude Power and Militancy in the Niger Delta* (Lagos: Forward Communications, 2006).

59 Cyril Obi, Personal Communication.

60 'Jide Osuntokun; Kenneth Nwoko, Personal Communication; Editorial, "Enugu/Death Penalty for Kidnappers," *The News Magazine*, 29 December 2008, 8.

61 Shola Omotola, Personal Communication; Alexander and Klein. "Kidnapping and Hostage-taking," 11; Nwajiuba, "The Socioeconomics of the Kidnapping Industry," 8.

62 'Jide Osuntokun, Personal Communication; Ikpang, "Kidnapping: Exacerbating the Corridors," 4; Osumah and Aghedo, "Who Wants to be a Millionaire?"

63 Nwajiuba, "The Socioeconomics of the Kidnapping Industry," 8.

64 Briggs, *The Kidnapping Business*, 19.

65 "*Otokoto*" has become the name given to the clandestine act of ritual murder in this part of Nigeria. For some in-depth discussion on the dynamics of the *Otokoto* incident in Owerri, from where the name was adopted, see: Akachi Odoemene, "Fighting Corruption without the State: Civil Society Agency and the 'Otokoto Saga'," *Journal of Historical Sociology*, 25:3 (2012).

66 "Yahoo-yahoo" was the name given to a kind of "Advance Fee Fraud" in which some criminal-minded young Nigerian youth (*Yahoo Boys*) duped foreigners of huge sums of money using the Internet as a medium. These *Yahoo Boys* send tens of thousands of deceptive, but convincing and attractive e-mails, particularly through the Yahoo domain, to foreigners in which they offered bogus deals. A good number of these foreigners fall for and are duped due to their greed.

67 "419" is the number of the criminal code that deals with "Advance Fee Fraud" (Nigerian Criminal Code 419). However, it is a popularly notorious and common parlance in the country used to qualify most of those who take to such clandestine activities, or those whose sources of wealth are questionable.

68 Nwajiuba, "The Socioeconomics of the Kidnapping Industry," 8.

69 'Jide Osuntokun, Personal Communication.

70 Nwajiuba, "The Socioeconomics of the Kidnapping Industry," 8.

71 This is the whole idea behind the determination of "kidnap value" or "ransom value" of people. Thus, anyone whose kidnap value was high due to the wealth of his relatives, friends and associates was in the danger of being kidnapped for ransom.

72 Abati, "Ransom Kidnapping."

73 Robert Chiedo Ezebuiro, adult, businessman; kidnap and ransoming victim, Owerri, Imo state, Nigeria. Personal communication; interviewed on Sunday, 29 July 2012; Adibe, "Pervasive Kidnapping in Nigeria;" Ernest Ibhaze, "General Security Awareness for Organization: a Case Study of Kidnapping and Terrorism" (paper presented at a one-day Zonal Police Security Awareness Seminar, Shehu Musa Yar'Adua Centre Abuja, 2 June 2011).

74 Shola Omotola; Femi Adegbulu, adult, Diplomatic Historian and Security Expert, Lagos, Nigeria. Personal communication; interviewed on 18 September 2012; Philip Akobundu, 34 years, Social critic, commentator and writer, Port-Harcourt city, Rivers State, Nigeria. Personal Communication; interviewed on 26 July 2012.

75 Defence Headquarters, *First Quarter Report on Security in the Niger Delta* (Abuja: DHQ, 2009); Ukoha Ukiwo, Ada Henri-Ukoha and Magdalene O. Emole, "Governance and Security in Abia State," in Ukoha Ukiwo and Innocent Chukwuma (eds.), *Governance and Insecurity in Southeastern Nigeria* (Lagos, Abuja, Owerri: CLEEN Foundation, 2012), 50-51

76 Ukiwo, Henri-Ukoha and Emole, "Governance and Security in Abia State," 50-51.

77 Robert Ezebuiro; Philip Akobundu; Kenneth Nwoko; Olumide Ekanade, 40 years, Economic Historian and lecturer, Redeemer's University of Nigeria (RUN), Mowe, Ogun state, Nigeria. Personal communication; interviewed on 19 September 2012; Chukwudi Nduka, 48 years, Pastor and businessman, Aba, Abia State, Nigeria. Personal communication; interviewed on 22 July 2012.

78 AOAV and NWGAV, "The Violent Road;" Femi Adegbulu; Chukwudi Nduka; Philip Akobundu; Kenneth Nwoko; Olumide Ekanade, Personal Communications.

79 Alexander and Klein, "Kidnapping and Hostage-taking;" Femi Adegbulu; Robert Ezebuiro; Philip Akobundu, Personal Communications.

80 AOAV and NWGAV, "The Violent Road;" B.O. Okaba and Ngboawaji Daniel Nte, "Youth, Conflict and Urban Africa: A Review of some Niger Delta Cities," *Commonwealth Youth Development,* 6:2 (2008), 41-54.

81 Nwajiuba, "The Socioeconomics of the Kidnapping Industry," 8.
82 Chukwudi Nduka, Personal Communication.
83 Chukwudi Nduka, Personal Communication.
84 Philip Akobundu, Personal Communication.
85 Control Risks Group, "Energy Industry," *Kidnapping and Ransoming*, 1.
86 Nwajiuba, "The Socioeconomics of the Kidnapping Industry;" D. Onojowo, "Of Hoodlums, North and South," *Punch Newspaper,* 21 October 2001.
87 Kunle Falayi, "Terrified Lagosians Groan as Kidnappers Prowl Metropolis," *Saturday Punch Newspaper,* 27 April 2013, 2; 37; Robinson Osarumwense Owenvbiugie and H.A. Olumese, "Kidnapping: A Threat to Entrepreneurship in Nigeria," *Journal of Education, Health and Technology Research (JEHERT)* 1:1 (2011), 67-73; Abati, "Ransom Kidnapping."
88 "Boko Haram Members Kidnap Wives, Children of Soldiers in Borno," *Kidnap and Ransom Magazine*, 22 December 2013, http://www.krmagazine.com/tag/boko-haram/ (accessed: 25 December 2013); Ola' Audu, "How Boko Haram Turned to Kidnapping to Raise Funds in Borno," *Premium Times*, 20 May 2013, http://premiumtimesng.com/news/135082-how-boko-haram-turned-to-kidnapping-to-raise-funds-in-borno.html (accessed: 5 October 2013); Michael Olugbode, "JTF: Boko Haram Resorts to Kidnapping to Raise Funds," *ThisDay Newspaper*, 29 April 2013, http://www.thisdaylive.com/articles/jtf-boko-haram-resorts-to-kidnapping-to-raise-funds/146240/ (accessed: 19 November 2013); Reuters News Agency, "Nigeria's Boko Haram 'got $3m Ransom' to Free Hostages," *BBC News*, 27 April 2013, http://www.bbc.co.uk/news/world-africa-22320077 (accessed: 6 December 2013).
89 Jennifer Lofkrantz, "Ransoming Captives in the Sokoto Caliphate," in Behnaz Mirzai, Ismael Montana and Paul E. Lovejoy (eds.), *Islam, Slave and Diaspora* (Trenton, NJ: Africa World Press, 2009), 125-37; Olatunji Ojo, "'[I]n Search of their Relations, To Set at Liberty as Many as They Had the Means': Ransoming Captives in Nineteenth Century Yorubaland," *Nordic Journal of African Studies,* 19:1 (2010).
90 Abati, "Ransom Kidnapping."
91 CLEEN Foundation, *National Crime and Victimization Survey* (*NCVS*) (Lagos: CLEEN Foundation, 2010).
92 Innocent Chukwuma, "Preface," in Ukoha Ukiwo and Innocent Chukwuma (eds.) *Governance and Insecurity in Southeastern Nigeria* (Lagos, Abuja, Owerri: CLEEN Foundation, 2012), viii.
93 Ibhaze, "General Security Awareness for Organization," 8-9.
94 Femi Adegbulu, Personal Communication.
95 For some discussion on Godfatherism, see Isaac Olawale Albert, "Explaining 'Godfatherism' in Nigerian Politics," *African Sociological Review,* 9:2 (2005), 79-105; L.U. Edigin, "Political Conflicts and Godfatherism in Nigeria: A Focus on the Fourth Republic," *African Research Review* 4:4 (October 2010), 174-186; Chimaroke Nnamani, "The Godfather Phenomenon in Democratic Nigeria: Silicon or Real?," *The Source* Magazine (2 June 2003), 5-6; Jibrin Ibrahim,

"The Rise of Nigeria's Godfathers," *BBC News* Online, 10 November 2003, http://news.bbc.co.uk/2/hi/africa/3156540.stm (accessed: 9 March 2010).

96 Albert, "Explaining 'Godfatherism'."

97 Edigin, "Political Conflicts and Godfatherism in Nigeria."

98 Odoemene, "Fighting Corruption without the State."

99 H. Eso, "Incessant Kidnappings and the *Beirutization* of Nigeria," (2009), www.kwenu.com (accessed: 13 February 2013).

100 John Iyene Owubokiri, "Kidnapping – A Crime against Humanity: What is the Way Out?" (Fourth Dr. Martin Luther King (Jr) Memorial Lecture, Nigeria Institute of International Affairs (NIIA), Lagos, 27 May 2009, http://www.vanguardngr.com/2009/06/kidnapping-a-crime-against-humanitywhat-is-the-way-out/ (accessed: 8 February 2011).

101 Owubokiri, "Kidnapping – A Crime against Humanity: What is the Way Out?"

102 Nwajiuba, "The Socioeconomics of the Kidnapping Industry," 8.

103 Dr. Anthony Ali, adult, Economic historian and researcher, Benson Idahosa University, Benin city, Edo state, Nigeria. Personal communication; interviewed on 1 July 2012; 'Jide Osuntokun; Chukwudi Nduka; Olumide Ekanade, Personal Communications.

104 Anthony Ali, Personal Communication.

105 Anonymous, "Failed State" *Source Watch*, http://www.sourcewatch.org/index.php?title=Failed_state (accessed: 3 December 2013).

106 Adibe, "Pervasive Kidnapping in Nigeria;" Liana Sun Wyler, "Weak and Failing States: Evolving Security Threats and US Policy," *CRS Report for Congress* (2007), 3.

107 Briggs, *The Kidnapping Business*, 2.

108 Anonymous, "The Failed States Index 2005," http://ffp.statesindex.org/rankings-2005-sortable (accessed: 3 August 2013).

109 Pax Christi Netherlands, *Kidnapping is Booming Business* (July) (Utrecht: IKV Pax Christi, 2008), 12.

110 "2011 Failed State Index-Interactive Maps and Ranking," http://www.foreignpolicy.com/articles/2011/06/17/2011_failed_states_index_interactive_map_and_rankings#sthash.YVOL5ui3.dpbs (accessed: 20 December 2013).

111 Pax Christi Netherlands, *Kidnapping is Booming*; Anthony Ali, Personal Communication.

112 J. Shola Omotola, Personal Communication.

113 Chukwudi Añurunwa, 40 years, Architect and ransoming victim, Aba, Abia state, Nigeria. Personal communication; interviewed on 22 July 2012.

114 Nwajiuba, "The Socioeconomics of the Kidnapping Industry," 8; Ukiwo, Henri-Ukoha and Emole, "Governance and Security in Abia State," 50.

115 Ukoha Ukiwo, Ada Henri-Ukoha and Magdalene O. Emole, "Governance and Security in Abia State," in Ukoha Ukiwo and Innocent Chukwuma (eds.), *Governance and Insecurity in Southeastern Nigeria* (Lagos, Abuja, Owerri: CLEEN Foundation, 2012), 24.

116 Ikpang, "Kidnapping: Exacerbating the Corridors," 5.

117 Nwajiuba, “The Socioeconomics of the Kidnapping Industry,” 8.
118 Bernard Fyanka, Personal Communication.
119 Bernard Fyanka, Personal Communication.
120 Ikpang, “Kidnapping: Exacerbating the Corridors,” 6.
121 Nte, “Kidnapping, Hostage Taking,” 64.
122 Cyril Obi, Personal Communication.
123 Femi Adegbulu; Justus Omiloli, Personal Communications.
124 Lere Amusan, “The Political Economy of Fossil Fuels in Nigeria,” in Victor Ojakorotu (ed.) *Contending Issues in the Niger Delta Crisis of Nigeria* (Delray Beach, FL: JAPSS Press, Inc., 2009), 20-53.
125 Anonymous, “Anarchic Aba is Our Kidnap Capital” (2010), http://news2.onlinenigeria.com/news/general/49001-anarchic-aba-is-our-kidnap-capital.html?print (accessed: 25 September 2013).
126 Ikpang, “Kidnapping: Exacerbating the Corridors.”
127 Editorial, “Federal Government Woos Russia to Invest in Niger Delta” *Midweek Pioneer* Newspaper, 1 April 2009, 2.
128 *The News Magazine*, 11 August 2008, 22.
129 Ikpang, “Kidnapping: Exacerbating the Corridors,” 6.
130 Cyril Obi, Personal Communication.
131 Adibe, “Pervasive Kidnapping in Nigeria.”

CHAPTER XI

Contemporary Piracy and Ransoming off The Coast of Somalia

Abdi M. Kusow

Introduction

Over the past decade, international maritime piracy and ransoming, particularly along the Indian Ocean coast of Somalia, have become important global security and trade issues. In 2011 alone, Somali pirates attacked 237 ships and hijacked 28. The reported global financial cost of piracy is even more staggering, estimated to be between $6.6 and $6.9 billion in 2011.[1] More importantly, piracy off the Red Sea and the Western Indian Ocean region has set off a global security and trade alarm and has led to multiple international and United Nations Security Council resolutions, increased use of private armed security, and the deployment of navy vessels, maritime patrol/reconnaissance aircraft, and the deployment of military teams from over 30 countries for vessel protection. According to Major General Buster Howes, the former operation commander of the European Union Naval Force Somalia (EU NAVFOR), "There are anywhere between ten and sixteen vessels deployed on any given day in the Gulf of Aden and Indian Ocean."[2]

Beyond the security concerns, however, international piracy and ransoming has increasingly become an important research focus for scholars, maritime policy experts, and journalists alike.[3] The current literature on international piracy and ransoming includes works that treat piracy and ransoming as a transnational crime and/or maritime terrorism and others that assume piracy and ransoming to be the result of failed or diminished state structures, a lack of economic opportunity, and resistance to the economically exploitative nature of global capitalism, which Anderson has referred to as an "expropriation of the expropriators."[4]

The "transnational crime" argument operates from the assumption that piracy and ransoming are essentially international crimes and pirates are sea robbers and outlaws.[5] National courts and international organizations treat piracy as a criminal activity to be prosecuted. A German court recently found one of the hijackers of the Marshall Islands–flagged ship *Marida Marguerite* off the coast of Oman in 2010 guilty of kidnapping and extortion charges.[6] The International Maritime Organization (IMO) primarily describes pirates as robbers. In its 2014 report, the IMO routinely characterized pirates as in the following example: "Two robbers boarded an anchored chemical tanker. They caught the duty watch keeper, threatened him with a knife and stole ship's stores."[7] In another instance in East Africa, the report writes, "While berthed, robbers boarded the ship unnoticed, stole ship's stores and escaped."[8] Consequently, the "piracy as a crime" argument concentrates on ways of controlling and suppressing piracy through legal, military, and technological means.

The "state failure" argument is primarily based on the assumption that piracy and ransoming occur as a result of conditions in which the state does not have the assumed legitimacy or military and economic means to protect, patrol, and control its territorial waters. However, the research in this area remains inconclusive. According to Samatar, Lindberg, and Mahayni, the absence of a Somali national government along with increased conflict over resources is the principal factor in creating opportunities for piracy.[9] Others suggest that an understanding of the geography and nature of state failure is more relevant in conceptualizing piracy than attributing it solely to a generic state failure. In his *Geographies of State Failure and Sophistication in Maritime Piracy Hijackings*, Hastings compares piracy in the several regions that experienced different levels of state failure from weak failure to total failure. He concludes that, in some situations, weak states may be more prone to piracy and therefore more problematic to international security than failed states.[10]

The "demographic and economic opportunities" argument suggests that a lack of economic and educational opportunities in general and youth unemployment in particular provide a fertile environment for piracy and other violent crimes to flourish. This is particularly true in the case of Somalia. According to the 2012 UNDP Human Development Report, more than 70 percent of Somalia's population is under the age of 30, and has one of the highest unemployment rates, 67 percent for youth aged 14-29.[11]

My purpose in this chapter is to extend the conceptual and analytical parameters of piracy and ransoming to include wider socio-historical, political, and economic processes. I am specifically interested in providing a conceptual framework for understanding Somali piracy and maritime ransoming. The chapter is divided into three sections. The first section expands on the existing definition of piracy to place it within a larger socio-political context. The second section attempts to sketch the sociological forces that contribute to the source, natures, and dynamics of piracy and ransoming along the Red Sea and Indian Ocean coasts of Somalia. In the third section, I provide a brief conclusion and preliminary comments about the future direction of international piracy and ransoming and a suggestion for further research on piracy and ransoming.

Conceptualizing Contemporary Piracy and Ransoming

Broadly speaking, two grand narratives, one institutional and the other counterinstitutional, inform the idea and meaning of Somali piracy and maritime ransoming. The institutional narrative sponsored by the global capitalist structure simply defines piracy and ransoming as a transnational crime. This definition is institutionalized in Article 101 of the 1982 United Nations Convention on the Law of the Sea and defines piracy as consisting of the following acts:

a. any illegal acts of violence or detention, or any act of depredation, committed for private ends by the crew or the passengers of a private ship or a private aircraft, and directed:

   (i) on the high seas, against another ship or aircraft, or against persons or property on board such ship or aircraft;

   (ii) against a ship, aircraft, persons or property in a place outside the jurisdiction of any State;

b. any act of voluntary participation in the operation of a ship or of an aircraft with knowledge of facts making it a pirate ship or aircraft;

c. any act inciting or intentionally facilitating an act described in sub-paragraph (a) or (b).[12]

As clearly stipulated piracy is institutionally defined as a violent, acquisitive crime, one that involves robbery or hijacking where the motive is to rob/loot an internationally sanctioned maritime vessel or kidnap its crew in international waters for profit. It is defined as simple theft, illegally taking the property of another person or group, and therefore an act punishable by international law.

The counter-institutional narrative, on the other hand, defines piracy as an expropriation of the capitalist expropriators or the protection of property in one's territorial waters from illegal expropriation.[13] This is illustrated in the responses of several individuals interviewed by Ali and Murad (2009) with regard to the justifiability of Somali piracy and ransom taking. One of the interviewees, Ali Farah, said, "I don't agree with piracy by itself. But, in this case, to go against the illegal dumping and fishing . . . they have the right to do that, they have the right to protect the country and water."[14] Another interviewee, Farah Adam, describes pirates as "a bunch of thieves, but some, as far as Somalis are concerned, are heroes because they are defending our natural and marine resources."[15]

These comments parallel what Christian Bueger referred to as Somali coast guard narratives.[16] "Coast Guard" is what Somali pirates call themselves to create a positive identity and, more importantly, to "produce legitimacy and recognition for piracy as a practice that has socio-political objectives."[17] In fact, the Somali coast guard narrative is designed not only to provide legitimacy for piracy and ransoming but also to reverse the criminal identity label and place it on the owners of the ships and the international community in general. In this regard, the spokesperson for the 2008 hijackers of the MV *Faina*, a Ukrainian ship loaded with weapons, responded to an interview by saying, "We do not consider ourselves sea bandits. [*Sea bandit* is one way Somalis translate the English word *pirate*.] We consider sea bandits those who illegally fish in our seas and dump waste in our seas and bury in our seas. We are simply patrolling our seas. Think of us like coast guard."[18] He went on to say, "I, as do most pirates, consider myself as having been performing the duties of a coast guard. . . . We had to defend ourselves. We became watchmen of our coasts and took up our duty to protect our country. Don't call us pirates. We are protectors."[19] From this point of view, ransom becomes a sort of taxation. According to one pirate interviewed by *IRIN News*, "The ransom they pay is somehow a punishment for their illegal activity in the Somali water, especially in the area without government."[20]

That some international maritime companies are themselves engaged in some sort of illegal trade was revealed in the MV *Faina* incident in 2008, where it became apparent that the ship was delivering illegal military equipment to South Sudan. The Financial Action Task Force (FATF), an independent European inter-governmental body, gave the following details:

> Approximately 50 Somali pirates calling themselves the Central Regional Coast Guard hijacked the Ukrainian-operated *Faina* on 25 December 2008, off the coast of Kenya. The ship was heading to Mombasa, Kenya, from Ukraine laden with 33 Soviet-made T-72 tanks, stocks of weapons, including rocket-propelled grenades, antiaircraft guns, and quantities of ammunition on board when it was seized. The pirates denied having information about the ship's cargo, but claimed that documents found onboard indicated the arms were destined for Jubba, South Sudan.... The MV *Faina*'s mysterious owners paid a ransom of USD 3.2 million on 4 February 2009. The pirates left the vessel early the next day, releasing the *Faina* and her crew after five months.[21]

It is clear from this incident that both the pirates and the mysterious owners of the MV *Faina* were engaged in some form of international maritime violation, a condition that complicates the definition of international maritime piracy.

While the Somali coast guard story seems a convincing counternarrative to the transnational crime narrative, scholars should avoid falling into an apologist's trap for Somali pirates. There is no empirical indication that they are working on behalf of Somalia, the Somali people, or the Somali coast. Rather, they are not any different from the organizations they accuse of illegal fishing or toxic-waste dumping. The same may be said of the capitalist owners of the ships that frequent Somali waters for illegal activities. The real victims are the everyday Somali people who suffer from the negative impact of the activities of both the Somali pirates and those engaged in illegal activities in Somali waters.

To place international maritime piracy and ransoming within a wider socio-political context, it is important to move beyond both the criminal-based definition and the Somali pirates' counter-narrative. It is important to underline the socio-historical, political, and economic processes that form the nature of international maritime piracy and ransoming. Such an understanding conceptualizes piracy as part of a general behavior whose primary motive may range from purely securing financial ransom to larger socio-political objectives. Here, I proceed from Jennifer Lofkrantz's definition of ransoming as "the practice of paying for the release of a captive at the time of capture or soon afterwards."[22] However, since maritime piracy is not just a matter of paying for the release of a captive but also a system of value exchange, I borrow from Tzanelli's conceptualization of kidnapping as a rational system of value exchange. According to Tzanelli, kidnapping, and therefore ransoming, refers to a condition in which "captors hold someone of political/economic significance (i.e., persons who have the ability to negotiate their way back to freedom)." At the center of this process, according to Tzanelli, is "a single factor: the victim himself/herself, and the political, economic, or the social value they possess," such that kidnappers threaten to take the lives of their captives with a full certainty that the victim's family or the organizations and authorities that sponsor them will try to save their lives.[23]

However, the idea of piracy as a system of value exchange is not confined to the potential financial ransom derivable from the value of certain human lives. It may also include the value of the goods involved: in the case of piracy, what is on the ship. The extent to which the lives of human individuals or the goods on a particular ship become the target of piracy is simply a matter of the opportunity and/or infrastructure available to the pirates involved. If pirates have the organizational ability to offload, transport, store, and sell the goods from the ship, they will do that and release the crew with an empty ship, perhaps injuring or killing them if they resist. On the other hand, if pirates do not have the organizational structure to handle the goods from the ship, their best bet is to hold the crew hostage. In other words, pirates use different business models, depending on their organizational abilities and the infrastructural opportunities available to them. Both scenarios can be illustrated with a comparison between West and East African piracy aptly articulated by Birdger:

> Regionally distinct pirate "business models" partially explain this phenomenon. When Somali pirates hijack a vessel, they must ensure that the hostages are kept alive so that ransom negotiations for the return of the entire crew and ship can proceed smoothly. West African hijackings, by comparison, are usually "extended duration robberies," in which the crew and vessel are only held hostage until the ship can be pumped of its petroleum cargo. When maritime kidnappings occur, pirates take only the most valuable (usually Western or Asian) officers for ransom while leaving the rest of the crew and vessel behind. Under both scenarios, the majority of the crew holds no value for the pirates and is thus considered disposable assets.[24]

In essence then, piracy, kidnapping, and hostage taking constitute types of ransoming or systems of value exchange and thus belong to the global political economy. Moreover, the process of ransoming is neither spatially nor historically specific. Historically, references to maritime ransoming (piracy) were found in the *Justinian Digest*, the body of civil law issued under

Justinian I of the Roman Empire in the sixth century (AD 530–533), and they continue to the present day.[25] Spatially, ransoming occurs in all kinds of spaces both on the high seas and on land. Ultimately, however, ransoming is a process of (1) converting human individuals into objects by way of the political, economic, or social value they possess—a matter of "collecting people for profit"[26]—and/or (2) collecting the value of the goods and objects they possess. In other words, depending on organizational ability and the nature of the goods on the ship, pirates may ransom the individuals on the ship, as in the case of Somali pirates, or offload the goods on the ship and let the crew and their ship go, as in the case of West African pirates.

Figure 11.1: Piracy and Ransoming Cycle

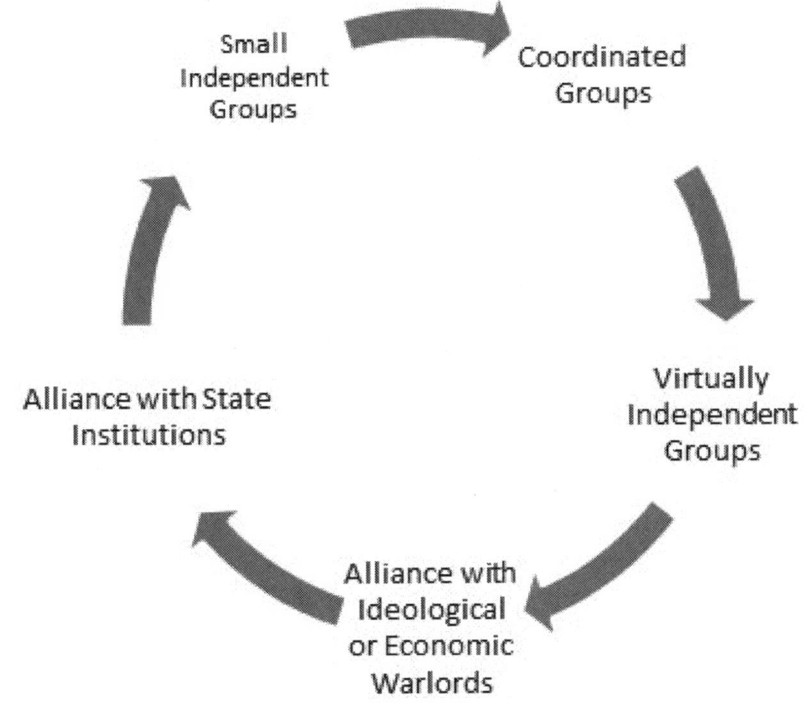

Source: Kusow, 2015 (expanded version of Philip Grosse's orginal rendition of the "piracy cycle," *The History of Piracy* (New York: Burt Franklin, 1932).

Analytically, I borrow from Philip Grosse's "piracy cycle" to explore the nature of the dynamics of ransoming along the Indian Ocean coast of Somalia. According to Grosse, piracy progresses through three distinct stages or cycles. In the first stage, piracy is conducted by small and independent groups using small boats against the easiest and most vulnerable ships so as to secure subsistence. Once successful at the small-group subsistence level, pirates accumulate capital, gain experience, and become larger and more organized such that they develop the capability to attack and hijack larger and more secured ships. At this stage, pirates are also able to maintain an underground network to move capital around and to buy the necessary equipment to facilitate their expanding operation. Further success at this level leads to a condition in which pirates "become a virtually independent power, where they may or may not choose to enter into alliance with some recognized state. At that point, the pirates have become in effect a mercenary navy, paid by plunder."[27]

The cycle of piracy and ransoming should not, however, be understood as a simple linear phenomenon. Pirate organizations may disintegrate at any stage. Some may disband before reaching the second stage in the cycle while others may disintegrate after completing the full cycle, at which point they may hibernate for a while, reorganize, and start the process again. In other words, piracy may be parasitic in its form or expression, depending on the extent of seaborne trade or the economic conditions of littorals. It may be episodic due to disruption of normal trading patterns or political stability, or it may be intrinsic to the basic economic functioning of the society concerned.[28] More significantly, as we will discuss later, piracy is not spatially specific in that it can start on territorial land and move to the high seas or vice versa. The following analysis applies some of the above ideas and concepts to the nature and dynamics of international maritime piracy and ransoming off the coasts of Somalia.

Figure 11.2: Forms of Ransoming

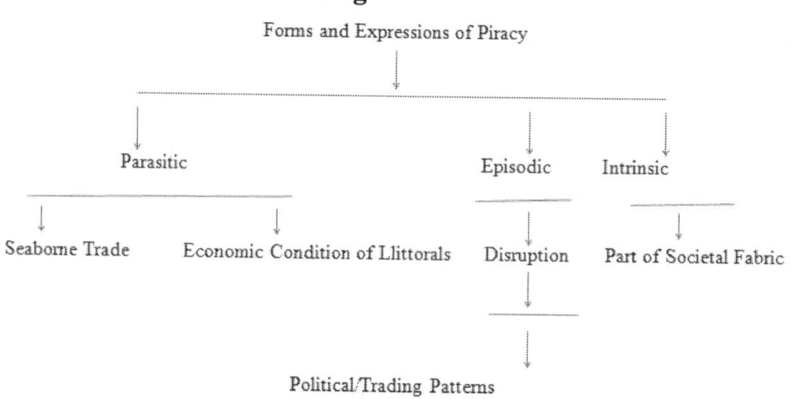

Source: Kusow, 2016 (expanded version of J. L. Anderson's forms and expression of piracy ("Piracy and World History: An Economic Prespective on Martime Predation," *Journal of World History,* 6, no. 3 (1995): 175–199).

In Somali vernacular, piracy and ransoming are defined as *burcad* and *rahan*, respectively. Burcad refers to bandits organized for the purpose of wholesale looting by force in daylight. The idea of burcad can be heuristically divided into two categories: *burcad badeed*, that which occurs on the high seas, and *burcad berri*, that which occurs on land. *Rahan*, on the other hand, refers to the process of holding people or goods for profit, a system of value exchange. *Burcad* and *rahan* may or may not occur together, depending on the motive and/or the object of ransom. If it is valuable goods, ransom may not be the primary object; the profit is inherent in the goods. However, if the object is the value inherent in a human being, then ransoming becomes the primary objective.

Piracy (*burcad)* and ransoming (rahan) are not new phenomena in Somalia. *Burcad Badeed*, or sea piracy, may have started as part of the trans-oceanic trade along the Red Sea and Indian Ocean regions. The waters of the Red Sea and western Indian Ocean were important for global trade long before the advent of colonialism and the construction of the Suez Canal. Societies from both the eastern and western shores of the Red Sea and the Indian Ocean have historically engaged in looting and plundering *dhows* (Arab sailing ships) and small commercial boats between the northern Somali coasts, Yemen, Oman, southern Arabia, and south India. Increased international trade and unreliable currents increased the number of shipwrecks along the Red Sea and the western Indian Ocean and may have been the key to the development of piracy in the region. At this stage, however, Somali groups did not go out of their way to hijack ships except in the case of wrecked ships or boats that drifted into their immediate shores.[29] Somali Red Sea and Indian Ocean piracy slowed down and ultimately disappeared as a result of British and Italian colonial intervention and later the Somali post-colonial government.

The Source of Piracy and Ransoming in Somalia

The modern version of ransoming along the Somali coasts is the result of a number of sociological factors, including demographic and economic factors, as well as the nature of state structures. An important aspect of contemporary ransoming in Somalia is related to the weakness of Somali government institutions and regional administration. The Somali Republic came into being as an independent country in 1960. A military coup led by General Mohamed Siyad Barre toppled the third democratically elected government in 1969 and formed a military junta. This regime ruled the country until civil war forced Barre to leave the country in 1991. Within the first two years, the war resulted in the death of several hundred thousand people, mainly women, the elderly, and children. The war also forced hundreds of thousands of people to flee the country and seek refuge in several neighboring African countries as well as the Middle East, Europe, Canada, and the United States. To this day, Somali political institutions remain weak and unable to provide economic opportunities for the Somali people or protect the legal territory under Somali sovereignty.

Figure 11.3: Underlying Social and Economic Forces of Piracy and Ransoming

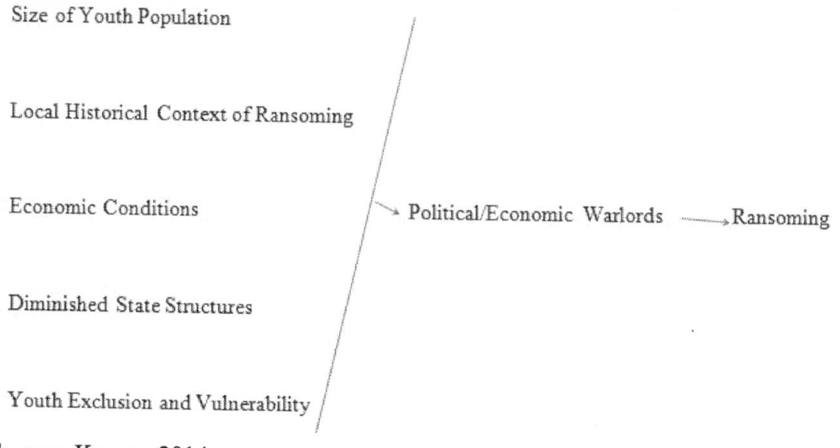

Source: Kusow, 2014.

Specifically, the modern signs of *burcad berri*, land piracy, started to appear during the 1977 Somali-Ethiopian war. A few months into the war, disaffected and greed-driven military officers started a highly organized scheme to randomly capture and recruit scores of youth and put them into military camps with the assumption that parents with the means to do so would pay ransom to avoid the drafting of their children. In a matter a few months, military draft ransoming became a full-fledged industry such that parents with financial means paid military middlemen to take their children back. Mostly, it was children from a poor economic background who ended up fighting on the frontlines.

After the civil war, and particularly on the eve of the now-infamous 1992 conflict-induced Somali famine, ransoming took a different and a more sinister form: food aid piracy. A report by Oxfam America states, "The absence of any order in southern Somalia in 1992 posed therefore unusual operational problems. International agencies could operate only under the protection of armed guards, and then only after a substantial portion of the food aid was given to the gun-toting juvenile bandits answering to one of a dozen different warlords."[30] The food aid pirates also used various tactics, including forcing relief agencies to hire trucks owned by their own militia for transport of the food to rural towns. Moreover, food aid pirates created *isbaaro*, road blocks, and methodically looted trucks carrying aid to rural towns. Finally, when the United Nations started to airlift aid, armed militia groups captured Baidoa Airport and imposed a fee per flight of $5,000 and a percentage of the food load before it could be delivered to those in need.[31] *Burcad Berri* still continues where organized militia have erected hundreds of permanent road blocks between cities and towns to collect ransom from all cars or trucks on the main roads in southern Somalia. These bandits implicitly operate under the banner of their clans such that they cannot be targeted as individuals by members of the clans they stole from.

Another important factor that has contributed to the recent increase in ransoming in Somalia is the nature of the intersection between the large youth population and economic vulnerability. Broadly speaking, the size and age distribution of population is one of the most important variables in structuring the political and economic stability of any given society. According to UNICEF, more than 50 percent of the total Somali population is under 18.[32] Of course, the mere number of youth as a percentage of population is not necessarily influential in one way or another, but coupled with a lack of economic opportunities, it provides a significant pool of young, unemployed, restless, and disaffected youth. This phenomenon, known as the "youth bulge," may, according to some social scientists, serve as a demographic dividend, a situation in which a falling birth rate changes the age structure of society such that "fewer investments are needed to meet the needs of the youngest age groups and resources are released for investment in development."[33] More likely, however, and particularly in the case of Somalia, the existence of such a large pool of disenfranchised and disaffected youth may lead to a greater susceptibility to recruitment by sinister politically or economically motivated groups. The problem of disenfranchised Somali youth joining pirate organizations has recently become a significant problem among Somali Kenyans. Recently, a Somali youth group, Youth United for Social Mobilization, organized an antipiracy conference designed to discourage Somali youth from joining up with pirates. One aspect of the conference included teaching youth about the problems of piracy by way of entertainment and staged drama. A 24-year-old Somali man who participated in this conference said, "As we hear from the news that the pirates have captured a ship and therefore the ransom is, let me say $35 million, that is a lot of money in my head. As a youth, I can't see getting that millions of dollars at my age. That is a long time that I am going to serve to get this amount of money, so therefore, if I join the pirates, I can get it easily."[34]

According to another youth, "I became a pirate because I realized it was the only way a Somali like me can make good money. I can afford to buy a new car and home, and when we are back on shore we have big parties, with girls, lots to drink, and plenty of *qhat* [the narcotic leaf chewed by Somalis]."[35]

The relatively large number of the Somali youth as a percentage of the total population, coupled with the total collapse of state structures and extremely difficult economic conditions, leads to youth exclusion form society and increased vulnerability. Youth exclusion, according to a recent report, refers to the relative distance of youth from the epicenter of educational and economic structures and processes that shape their daily lives. Vulnerability refers to the relative risk youth run of experiencing a lower living standard, often for a great length of time or even permanently. It refers to the "subjective feeling and/or objective state of insecurity and to the fears and dangers of a decline in the well-being of youth."[36]

Therefore, given that Somalia has a significant youth population, extremely high youth unemployment, and a long standing civil war and political instabi8lity it is safe to assume that youth exclusion and vulnerability are very high. The extent of youth vulnerability in Somalia buttressed by high levels of unemployment and political instability generally leads to one of two outcomes.

The first is to leave the country, which Somalis call *Tahriib*, or join a violent political, economic, or religious organization. If they leave the country, they end up in a refugee camp in Kenya or Ethiopia, or take to the Red Sea or the Mediterranean Sea in hopes of getting to Yemen or Italy with, in some situations, a 50/50 chance of survival. According to IRIN, a service of the UN office for the Coordination of Humanitarian Affairs, "In 2011 alone, some 89 people drowned or went missing while crossing the Gulf of Aden from Somalia to Yemen. The worst single incident took place in late February when 57 refugees died after their boat capsized, according to UN Refugee Agency (UNHCR). Since 2008, well over 1,000 people have failed to survive the crossing."[37]

In the Somali regions along the Red Sea and the western Indian Ocean coast, youth who are recruited into the piracy industry suffer from the same exclusion and vulnerability as those who risk crossing the Red Sea. In other words, the recruitment of Somali youth as a result of their vulnerability is usually achieved by appealing to clan or Islamic sentiments or through monetary enticements. Consequently, politically and economically motivated middlemen, using any necessary combination of these recruiting strategies, have mobilized to bring Somali youth into either armed conflicts or piracy.

The history of recruiting Somali youth and exposing them to criminal activities and armed conflict may have started as early as the Barre regime, but the public appeal and mass recruitment of Somali youth into criminal activities, armed conflict, and piracy started during the warlord era in the late 1990s. During the height of the Somali civil war, they were known as *Mooryaan.* According to Ahmed, *Mooryaan* are the product of long-unresolved social and class inequalities that characterized Mogadishu in the 1980s. Ahmed predicted this in a poem: "a homeless woman with three kids on the curb-side of *Croce Del Sud* [a fancy part of pre-war Mogadishu] vowed that her kids will one day avenge her humiliation." According to Ahmed, "the *Mooryaan* thugs could perhaps represent generically the protagonist's embittered kids."[38] In a news article titled "Confessions of a Reformed Mooryaan," Abukar Hassan narrates the confession of a former Somali *Mooryaan* who currently lives in a large city in the West. He talks about his upbringing, characterized by the absence of a father figure, and the harsh life of a herdsman as a child in the central regions of Somalia, for whom Mogadishu was "a place full of excitements; cars, tall buildings, good food, wealth, etc."[39] This experience is probably typical of most of the youth who continue to be manipulated into piracy.

The intersection between youth exclusion, economic vulnerability, and participation in piracy and ransoming activities among Somali youth is not unlike Paul Collier's recent articulation of political violence resulting from the intersection between greed and grievance on the one hand and the size of the uneducated youth population on the other. According to Collier, the level of recruitment or the willingness of young men to join piracy groups is based on the intersection between the size of the youth population and the availability of other income-generating opportunities.[40]

The theoretical implications are obvious. All necessary conditions that may lead to participation in piracy are not only present in Somalia but look attractive to idle youth neglected by society due to a harsh economy and broken socio-political systems. What makes Somali youth even more susceptible to recruitment is the fact that the youth population has no knowledge of a world beyond a permanent civil war and weak state structure. The combination of these factors makes Somali youth very receptive to all forms of indoctrination.

Conclusion

I set out to provide a preliminary framework for understanding contemporary piracy and ransoming off the coast of Somalia. I specifically argued that, unlike the criminological understanding common in current literature, piracy and ransoming must be understood as a rational system of value exchange. As a system of value exchange, therefore, the process and dynamics of piracy and ransoming depend on a number of factors: the organizational ability of pirates; the social, economic, and political value of the captives as opposed to the goods on the ship; and ultimately the socio-political context in which it occurs. The pirates might be a small number of individuals with no specific organizational structure whose primary motive is to sneak into small and vulnerable ships and rob or steal whatever goods they can carry without arousing the attention of the crew. They might be a highly organized group whose motive is to turn piracy and ransoming into an organized and durable business project. Whether the target of piracy is the individual crew members or the goods on the ship depends on the value of the individuals versus that of the goods. If the cargo on the ship is more valuable than the crew and the pirates have the organizational ability to offload, transport, store, and bring the goods to market, then the crew members become of less value to the pirates. If, however, the pirates do not have the infrastructure to process the cargo, then the ability of the crew to negotiate their way back to freedom becomes the primary factor.

Beyond organizational abilities, however, the nature of piracy depends on two external sociological factors. The first relates to the interaction between the demographic composition and the macro-economic condition of a given community near the shore. Seconds, lack of economic opportunity coupled with a large pool of unemployed youth provides fertile grounds for piracy and other violent crimes to flourish. This condition is exacerbated in situations where the state is weak and does not have the necessary legitimacy or military and economic means to protect, patrol, and control its territorial waters.

Endnotes

1 Jonathan Bellish, "The Economic Cost of Somali Piracy" (working paper, Oceans Beyond Piracy, 2012).

2 Anna Bowden and Shikha Basnet, "The Economics of Somali Piracy" (working paper, Oceans Beyond Piracy, 2011).

3 See for example, Peter Chalk, "Piracy Off the Horn of Africa: Scope, Dimensions, Causes and Reponses," *The Brown Journal of World Affairs,* 16: 2 (2010),

89–108; Edward Lucas, "Somalia's 'Pirate Cycle': The Three Phases of Somali Piracy," *Journal of Strategic Security,* 6:1 (2013), 55–63; Roland Marchal, "Somali Piracy: The Local Contexts of an International Obsession," *Humanity: An International Journal of Human Rights, Humanitarianism, and Development,* 2:1 (2011), 31–50.

4 J. L. Anderson, "Piracy and World History: An Economic Perspective on Maritime Predation," *Journal of World History,* 6:2 (1995), 175–199.

5 Hua-Lun Huang, "Who are Seacutthroats? A Typological Analysis of Pirates," *Criminal Law Social Change,* 53 (2010), 277–298; J. S. Barnett, *Dangerous Waters: Modern Piracy and Terror on the High Seas* (New York: Dutton, 2002); Gerhard O. W. Mueller, *Outlaws of the Ocean: The Complete Book of Contemporary Crime on the High Seas* (New York: Hurst, 1985); Martin N. Murphy, *Small Boats, Weak States, Dirty Money: Piracy and Maritime Terrorism in the Modern World* (New York: Columbia University Press, 2009).

6 Reuters, "German Court Sentences Somali Pirate to 12 Years in Prison," news release, April 17 Day, 2014, http://www.reuters.com/article/2014/04/17/us-germany-piracy-trial-idUSBREA3G17Q20140417.

7 Financial Action Task Force (FAFTA), "Organized Maritime Piracy and Related Kidnapping for Ransom" (July 2011).

8 IMO, International Maritime Organization, "Reports on Acts of Piracy and Armed Robbery against Ships" (2014), 1-3.

9 Abdi Ismail Samatar, Mark Lindberg, and Basil Mahayni, "The Dialectics of Piracy in Somalia: The Rich Versus the Poor," *Third World Quarterly,* 31:8 (2010), 1381.

10 Justin Hastings, "Geographies of State Failure and Sophistication in Maritime Piracy," *Political Geography* 28 (2009), 213–223.

11 UNDP, Somalia Human development Report 2012: Empowering Youth for Peace and Development, http://www.so.undp.org. Accessed June 24, 2015.

12 United Nations Convention on the Law of the Sea, December 10, 1982, http://www.un.org/depts/los/convention agreements/texts/unclos/unclos_e.pdf.

13 Anderson, "Piracy and World History," 176.

14 Muna Ali and Zahra Murad, "Unraveling Narratives of Piracy," *Darkmatter Journal,* 5 (2009), 98.

15 Ali and Murad, "Unraveling Narratives of Piracy," 98.

16 Christian Bueger, "Practice, Pirates, and Coast Guards: The Grand Narrative of Somali Piracy," *Third World Quarterly,* 32:10 (2013), 1811–1827.

17 Bueger, "Practice, Pirates, and Coast Guards," 1812.

18 Ibid., 1811-1812.

19 Ibid., 1818.

20 "Somalia: Inside a Pirate Network," *IRIN News*, January 13, 2009. Accessed, August 11, 2014.

21 FATF), "Organized Maritime Piracy," July 2011.

22 Jennifer Lofkrantz, "Protecting Freeborn Muslims: The Sokoto Caliphate's Attempts to Prevent Illegal Enslavement and Its Acceptance of the Strategy of Ransoming," *Slavery and Abolition,* 32:1 (2011), 109–27.

23 Rodanthi Tzanelli, "Capitalizing on Value: Towards a Sociological Understanding of Kidnapping," *Sociology,* 40:5 (2006), 929–47.

24 James Bidger, "The Most Violent Pirates," *USNI News*, May 12, 2014.

25 P. W. Bernie, "Piracy: Past, Present, and Future," *Marine Policy,* 11:3 (1987), 163-193.

26 Gregory Warner, "In Somalia, Collecting People for Profit," *Title of Program*, National Public Radio, May 14, 2014. Accessed June 24, 2015.

27 Philip Grosse, *The History of Piracy* (New York: Burt Franklin, 1932), quoted in Anderson, "Piracy and World History," 183.

28 For a good discussion of the forms of piracy, see Anderson, "Piracy and World History."

29 For a good discussion of the historical roots of Somalia's Red Sea piracy, see David Anderson, "Somali Piracy: Historical Context and Political Contingency," in *Somalia and the Pirates*, Working Paper No. 33, European Security Forum (2009); see also, Mohamed Haji (Ingiriis), "The History of Somali Piracy: From Classical Piracy to Contemporary Piracy, c. 1801–2011," *The Northern Mariner,* 23:3 (2013), 239–66.

30 Innovation Growth, "Oxfam America, Oxfam America and 1992 Somali Famine."

31 M. H. Mukhtar and Abdi M Kusow, "The Bottom-Up Approach in Reconciliation in the Inter-river Region of Somalia—A Visiting Mission Report" (18 August–23 September 1994), unpublished paper.

32 UNICEF Humanitarian Action Somalia, 2009, http://www.unicef.org/har09/files/HAR_2009_FULL_Report_English.pdf. Accessed, June 24, 2015.

33 Nabil Kronfal, "The Youth Bulge and the Changing Demographics in the MENA Region: Challenges and Opportunities," The WAD-HSG Discussion Paper Series on Demographic Issues, 2011, WDA Forum, University of St. Gallen.

34 "Somali Youth Warned Not to Become Pirates," BBC World Service, February 16, 2012.

35 Colin Freeman, "Piracy and Terrorism: Why Somalia?" *The Telegraph*, July 16, 2014.

36 Wale Ismail, Funmi Olonisakin, Bob Piccatto, and Dave Wybrow, "Youth Vulnerability and Exclusion in West Africa: Synthesis Report," CSDG Report, Africa Peace and Security (Kings College, London, 2009).

37 "Yemen-Somalia: Deadly Sea Migrant Now Flows Both Ways," *IRIN News*, March 2011.

38 Ali J. Ahmed *The Invention of Somalia* (Trenton, NJ: Red Sea Press, 1995), x.

39 Hassan Abukar, "The Confessions of a Reformed Mooryaan," *Wardheernews*, March 9, 2011.

40 Paul Collier, "Doing Well Out of War" (paper prepared for Conference on Economic Agendas in Civil Wars, London, April 26–27, 1999); see also Korf Benedikt, "Rethinking the Greed-Grievance Nexus: Property Rights and the Political Economy of War in Sri Lanka," *Journal of Peace Research* 42:2 (2005), 201–217.

CHAPTER XII

From Hostage Taking to (Ab)use of Ransoming in 21st Century North-east Africa: The Lifecycle of Piracy in Somalia

Awet T. Weldemichael[1]

Introduction

Ransoming is an age-old phenomenon dating at least as far back as the mid-first century BC when pirates kidnapped Julius Caesar near the Greek island of Pharmacusa and demanded "twenty talents" for his release. According to the Greek historian Plutarch, Caesar "laughed at them for not knowing who their captive was, and of his own accord agreed to give them fifty [talents]."[2] This chain of events has an eerie resemblance to the alacrity of hijacked foreign illegal fishers in Somali waters in the early 2000s, who offered their captors irresistible sums of money to secure their speedy release.

When local Somali vigilantes captured illegal foreign fishing vessels, the former demanded "fines" and the latter readily paid – sometimes offering more money than they would be asked to – in order to avoid drawn-out legal altercations and embarrassment.[3] With more than 20,000 vessels crisscrossing this pirate prone area, such alacrity to pay rising fines helped usher in predatory ransom piracy. This criminal enterprise became as much a contributory factor to the vicious cycle of insecurity and political-economic deterioration as it is a symptom and consequence of it.

Although ransoming in Africa is also an old practice of paying for the freedom of captives, contemporary piracy and ransoming off the Horn of African coast are both recent and unique. The two emerged and thrived in the wake of complete breakdown of any semblance of law and order. Unlike other historic cases of piracy and ransoming, defensive Somali piracy emerged in the late 1990s against the plundering of Somalia's marine environment by resource pirates since the collapse of the central government in 1991.[4] By mid-2000s, it metastasized into a predatory enterprise when criminal elements – also taking advantage of the collapse of the state – hijacked the impromptu grassroots response of the coastal communities.[5] The lawlessness was so unbridled that pirates, unsupported by the state like the historic North African piracy, commandeered their captive vessels to – and held them and their crew hostage in – coastal waters of inhabited territories and went inland to celebrate their "catch" while ransom was being negotiated.

The regional and global effects of Somali ransom piracy are understood in their broad contours but the economics and inner dynamics of ransoming on the ground in Somalia continue to elude scrutiny as do its local consequences. Efforts to investigate the multitude of questions that arise often lead to treacherous, and even risky, dead ends and vicious cycles. This paper examines the dynamics and economic aspects of ransoming foreign hostage sailors out of pirate captivity in twenty-first century Somalia. In establishing the general framework of the entire practice, from the start of negotiations to the aftermath of receiving ransoms, this paper addresses the following questions: How did ransom negotiations take place? How were ransoms paid to and split among all the stakeholders? And finally what are the effects of the practice itself on the local communities and the infusion of large unearned sums into the local economies? In answering these questions, the paper contends that while presenting extremely few, very lucrative and equally dangerous criminal prospects for the daring, jobless and/or greedy few, ransom piracy deteriorated the security of local communities and wrecked their weak and vulnerable economies.

Minding the Inauspicious Victim-Beneficiary Binary

Without tackling the morality, legitimacy, and/or legality of the means and circumstances in which sailors are taken and held hostage and freed, this paper documents from the field in Puntland how the majority of ransom money was ab/used, and examines the effects of the injection of large sums of ill-gotten cash into weak economies and vulnerable communities. Besides the practical hardship and security threats that make fieldwork difficult, doing so is muddied by scholarly works, policy analyses and media coverage that have fanned widely-held but inaccurate views that regard the majority, if not all, Somalis as beneficiaries of pirate-generated ransom money.

A January 2012 Chatham House report authored by Anja Shortland is but one example. Arguing that a land based solution needs to replace the income that piracy generates, Shortland posits that piracy "has a large interest group behind its continuation" because "pirate incomes have widespread and significant positive impacts on the Somali economy."[6] Among the benefits that Shortland claims Somalis, and especially Putlanders, got from piracy is that the criminal enterprise "offset the loss of purchasing power of local wages after the 2007/2008 food price shocks."[7] That is the case, she claimed, because pirates reportedly provided "local governance and stability, the side-effect of which has been to help other entrepreneurs to trade more easily."[8]

Preceding reports and this paper show how Shortland's sweeping claims in the Chatham House document could not have been further from the reality on the ground, its innovative methodology notwithstanding. A year earlier in January 2011 Jack Lang, the United Nations Secretary General's legal advisor on piracy, warned that "piracy-driven economy [was] gradually overtaking the traditional economy, owing to the development of activities on land in support of the pirates, the lack of job-creating investments in a context of widespread insecurity, and the destructive effect of piracy on Somali society which creates a vicious circle."[9] In a more pointed reference to Puntland, Lang reported how "growing insecurity caused by piracy is depriving the north of Somalia of possible job-creating investments (port operations, fishing and development of public infrastructure)."[10]

Six month later, in a rare case of notable exception, Kaija Hurlburt drew attention to the lot of innocent Somalis caught in between a rock and a hard place. In a report on the human costs of piracy that she authored for Oceans Beyond Piracy project of One Earth Future Foundation, a conflict-related policy think tank, Hurlburt argued that pirates exacerbated food insecurity, hampered trade and targeted fishermen's equipment and catch.[11] In spite of her incisive observations and balanced recommendations, however, the lack of field-based research and direct observation led her to conclude that "it cannot be assumed that … negative impact of piracy on Somalis … are large enough to incentivize Somalis to root out piracy independently."[12] This wrongly comes across as accurate when taken in with the astronomical figures that Somali piracy has reportedly cost the global economy.

According to a working paper of the Oceans Beyond Piracy project, piracy off the Somali coast in 2010 drained the international economy of some US$7-12 billion.[13] Soon afterwards, Geopolicity, another consulting firm, reported a different figure for the same year. It claimed that the cost of Somali piracy ranged between $4.9 and $8.3 billion.[14] Although, it remained in the billions of US dollars, the estimated figures have since been steadily declining. One Earth Future's 2011 estimates range between $6.6 and $6.9 billion.[15] Its 2012 estimates dropped further to $5.7 to 6.1 billion, of which 1 percent went to "ransom and recovery."[16]

While useful, such statistical analyses of global economic costs of piracy neither tell us how the ransom payers and payees reached an agreement nor do they give an accurate picture of how much of the purported ransoms actually found their way into Somalia and how they were ab/used. This paper documents the dynamics of ransom negotiations in Somalia based on fieldtrips in the one time notorious pirate den Puntland between 2011 and 2014, consisting of participant observations as well as open-ended interviews with pirates, pirate financiers/organizers, counter-piracy officials and grassroots community activities. It shows how large quantities of ransom money were misspent with detrimental consequences to the local communities. In doing so, it will take to task claims that Somalis benefited from ransom piracy and argue that the local communities took a firm stand against the pirates because of the grave danger that piracy posed to them.

The Process and Some of the Actors in Ransom Negotiations

Once pirates, in teams of 5-15 members, board a vessel, there is little that an external rescue operation can do, and much less the sailors themselves without facing the real prospect of serious physical harm. In a rush to consolidate their control, the pirates try, often times successfully, to cut off the ship's communications and gather all the sailors-turned-hostages. The ship's distress signal is the final communication of the hijacked vessel with its owner/manager; the latter's communications on the satellite phone are either unanswered or are only answered to confirm the hijack.[17] Not until they felt secure enough onboard the vessel and reroute it to, and often times even arrive at, their desired pirate hub does the captive ship's communication system go alive again as do the communications to shore in Somalia. Whereas the contacts to Somalia are done either on Thuraya satellite phone and/or mobile phones (where there is coverage) to share the news and make security and logistical arrangements, those made to individuals or organizations believed to be capable of paying the desired ransom is done under strict instructions and monitoring of the pirate leader(s). In rare cases where one of the pirates spoke English and either he or another pirate onboard the captured vessel had the power to call the shots, ransom negotiations started from the moment the pirates took full control of the vessel.[18] Generally, however, and especially in the later phase of piracy, around 2009 and after, the pirate kingpins and capable translators stayed onshore and so ransom negotiations did not begin until the ship docked at the desired pirate hub and the pirate boss and translator-cum-negotiator came onboard to take charge.

Three broad schematic breakdowns of the phases and actors in the ransom negotiations emerge from the available aggregate data and they by and large determined the duration of negotiations and their outcomes. Broadly outlined below, these phases and intermediaries were not clearly delineated by time, geography or pirate groups. They sometimes overlapped especially in the second half of the 2000s when diverse and highly professionalized pirate groups emerged and their leaders led the boarding teams in the high seas.

During the first phase of ransom piracy between 2005 and 2008, Somali pirates went through practically anyone who they felt could deliver them the ransom: from well-placed individuals in, as well as out, of the successive central and regional governments in Somalia to individuals and groups across the region. It is possible that the Mombasa-based East Africa Seafarers Assistance Program (SAP) entered the ransom negotiations terrain during the earliest cases of ransom piracy. SAP was founded in 1996 to monitor maritime activities in the Indian Ocean and offer seafarers assistance at sea and on land. In that capacity, it grew to become frontline hub of information gathering and dissemination on troubled vessels and sailors and maritime events.[19] The initial contacts between the captive sailors and pirates, on the one hand, and SAP, on the other, is still shrouded in secrecy. But SAP started to serve as go-between the pirates in Somalia and the owners/managers of the captive vessels/sailors around the world. Whereas individual intermediaries lacked the wherewithal to keep a pace with the increasingly complex and prolonged process with professional negotiators that the companies started to hire, some pirates started to complain that SAP was either not being an honest broker or charging them a hefty percentage for the services it rendered. While corroborating such pirate claims and related conspiracy theories has proven extremely difficult, SAP founder and director Andrew Mwangura does not divulge any detail beyond insisting that his organization got involved and remains so for "humanitarian reasons and not monetary gain."[20]

By 2008, there then emerged a motley group of Somali and non-Somali intermediaries as go-betweens for the pirates in Somalia and the shipping companies wherever they were. Conveniently placed in some Middle Eastern or East African cities, they briefly displaced SAP only to see their favored position to quickly deteriorate in its turn. On numerous occasions, the pirates felt cheated and even double-crossed by the Somali middlemen (and at least one middlewoman) who lived far from the pirates' reach. Besides the deaths of several negotiators-cum-translators in the hands of paranoid pirate linchpins, the case of three Thai fishing vessels that were seajacked in mid-August 2010 epitomizes the breakdown of trust between pirates and their negotiators.[21] Between the fishing company that owned the boats claiming that it delivered the agreed upon $1.2 million ransom and the pirates insisting that they did not receive it, the 77 captive fishermen remained in limbo. The Indian navy rescued some of them in early 2011 when its warships attacked the pirates who had commandeered two of the fishing vessels to serve as motherships.[22] More than a dozen of them (those hailing from Myanmar) were handed to the regional government after a few died onshore due to lack of basic necessities.[23] The whereabouts of the rest remained unknown until four of them were release on ransom in late February 2015.[24]

As a result of such double-crossing or breakdown of trust, the pirates started to introduce their own negotiators on the ground – often times English speaking Somalis, some of whom were returned Diasporas from the West. With at least one notable exception of the February 2010-hijacking of MV Rim by a multi-lingual pirate linchpin who led the boarding team, the pirate leaders and capable translators-cum-negotiators stayed onshore. That meant that ransom negotiations did not begin until the ship docked at the desired pirate den and the pirate leader and translator-cum-negotiator came onboard to take charge.[25]

Ransoms were delivered in either of three ways. Initially, the money was delivered to the local intermediaries either in person or through wire transfer to Somali (often Mogadishu-based) bank accounts. In their turn, the in-person deliveries of ransoms took two forms. First, tugboats, often times sailing from Kenyan waters, and according to some sources, under the aegis of the Mombasa-based SAP, did the delivery. Second, cash was flown in small, chartered planes, and then transported overland under close protection of foreign private security companies. The Canada-registered, Kenya-based private security and risk management company Salama Fikira International was involved in such ransom negotiations and deliveries. It is unknown how long its operations went on before one of its attempted deliveries was exposed and its personnel arrested at Mogadishu's Aden Adde International Airport with US$3.6 million in late May 2011.[26] But Salama Fikira continued ransom deliveries at least until late March 2012 when it flew in over a million US dollars to pirates in Galmudug region of Somalia and flew out their British hostage, a tourist kidnapped from Kenya and held in pirate captivity for six months between September 2011 and March 2012.[27]

As tugboat deliveries took a long time and chartered plane deliveries were exposed after the Salama Fikira's fiasco, airdropping of ransoms started to rise as a preferred method. It is believed that notorious pirate leader Aden Abdirizak Hussein "Aden Sanjab" (whose final prey was the MV Iceberg I, held between March 2010 and December 2012) was the first to demand that the ransom for one of his earlier preys be delivered by plane. Typically, a small aircraft buzzed past the hijacked ship to first get the sign of life of the captive sailors, only then did it parachute the bag of cash into the nearby water whereupon the pirates dispatch a skiff to fetch it.

However delivered, the entire ransom amount is brought in front of all the pirates (those who hijacked the vessel at sea and those who guarded it in the onshore waters) and pirate financiers for splitting according to the pre-arranged formula. Language experts or translators-cum-negotiators were either paid a negotiated figure regardless of the total ransom or accepted stock shares that the pirates called *saami*. Whereas negotiators in the former category received a single lump sum ranging between $5,000 and $50,000 (a few are reported to have collected as much as $150,000), the pay for those in the latter category was determined by how much each share ended up being worth. That in turn was determined by the gross amount of ransom, cost of the pirate mission, expenses incurred, and the size of pirate personnel (from investors to security guards on land and their weapons and equipment).

Ab/Use of Ransom Proceeds and its Consequences

In the wake of the 2004 tsunami, three seasoned fishermen from Eyl and former members of coastal community vigilantes against foreign trawlers decided to attack commercial vessels passing by because the majority of fishing vessels were either armed or had retreated deeper into the ocean. Considering what Abshir Abdullahi Abdule "Boyah," one of the earliest ransom pirates, called their local peers' aversion to the inherent risks and the resistance of their community, they searched for harbors where they could take captured ships. New developments in local conditions further south along the coast offered them an option.[28]

A bloody intra-clan feud among branches of the Habar Gidir (Hawiye clan) in South Mudug, where the coastal town of Hobyo and its inland counterpart of Haradere are located, had just subsided.[29] The cessation of the conflict granted the pioneer ransom pirates from Puntland an ideal natural harbor at Hobyo and an inaccessible inland hideout in Haradere. With a local forerunner in the person of Mohammed Abdi Hassan "Afweyne," and many enthusiastic volunteers, ransom piracy got off the ground with the capture in April 2005 of the Hong Kong LPG carrier, MV Feisty Gas.[30]

Some of the ransoms that pirates collected either stayed outside of Somalia from the get go or immediately left Somalia after the partners in the crime split their shares. Often times those who took their money out of Somalia did so by injecting it in legitimate, overt businesses. In July 2011, for example, the UN Security Council mandated Monitoring Group on Somalia and Eritrea reported that a

> large proportion of the ransom money is invested by pirate leaders in the 'qaad or 'miraa' [the mildly narcotic drug] trade through Somali businessmen in Nairobi. Aircraft that fly qaad from Kenya into Somalia often return to Nairobi with cash – an important channel for piracy proceeds to leave the country. Pirate leader Mohammed Abdi Hassan "Afweyne," for example, is said to run such a business for the piracy network in Harardheere/Hobyo.[31]

Claims also abound that piracy money flooded into Kenya and created construction and real estate boom in a Somali-dominated Nairobi neighborhood. While that claim remains to be substantiated, it is difficult, if not impossible, to establish the exact ransom figures paid in the first place as the cases below demonstrate. Moreover, the amount of ransom money that flowed out of Somalia was inherently limited because a minimum of two-thirds of the ransom was shared among locals in quantities that are too small to cross the border and have a consequential investment. At least a third of the ransom was split among piracy's smaller stakeholders and regular foot soldiers, the majority of whom squandered it on khat, alcohol, prostitution, luxury sports vehicles and latterly (in a few occasions) on more potent drugs that had devastating impact on the local communities.

On their first case of ransom piracy in 2005, Boyah and his partners in crime demanded half a million to release the MV Feisty Gas but received $300,000 that was divided according to a pre-agreed upon formula: 30 percent to the investor, 40 percent to the hijacking team; the remaining were split among the local area, the translator and donations. This formula remained by and large unchanged except that as the hijacking pirates got increasingly emboldened, they insisted and raised their share to 50 percent in many cases. When split among the seven pirates, Boyah's share bordered $20,000 but he recalls going broke a few weeks later: "people [shahat] took everything!"[32]

In one of his purportedly final hands-on piracy operations, Boyah joined six other pirates and, on 28 October 2007, succeeded to hijack the MV Golden Nori, a Panamian-flagged Japanese chemical tanker. Different sources give different figures paid as ransom to free this ship and its crew. Whereas some media outlets reported that the ransom ranged between $1 million and $1.5 million, others said that it was $1 million.[33] Local sources give different figures and vary among themselves. A self-declared accountant for that pirate group said that the final ransom was dropped to $500,000.[34] Boyah, for his part, said that they collected $700,000 for Golden Nori.[35] These conflicting figures reflect the difficulty of establishing how much ransom money found its way into Somali hands inside Somalia. Whatever the total ransom figures, the way the majority of it was spent on harmful, addictive practices and non-productive vocations had a devastating impact on the local communities.

Around the same time in 2007, a group of 14 pirates onboard two boats captured a ship (most likely the Danish MV Danica White) and held it and its crew hostage for just under three months when they received a disputed figure in ransom. While Lloyd's List put the ransom at $1.5 million, one of the pirates put the figure at $1.7 million.[36] This group of pirates, like the other pirate groups before and after them, allocated shares or *saami* to individual members and to weapons and equipment. Individual pirates received a *saami* each and the first one to board the captive ship received an additional share. AK-47 and RPG (without rockets) were allocated half a *saami* each, whereas an RPG with its rockets weighted a *saami.*

The monetary value of a *saami* varied depending on a number of factors listed above. In the particular case of the aforementioned ship, a share was worth about $40,000. A pirate, who joined this group with his own AK-47, "earned" $60,000.[37] But he had incurred a $10,000 debt (in khat, alcohol and women) during the ten weeks that they had held the vessel and its crew hostage. Although he got off the ship with $50,000, he arrived in the nearest urban center of Galkacyo with only $38,000. Around mid-2008, he was left penniless with no one to borrow from. By then, he said, he had already become a "bemboweyne" (the pirates' word for insatiable guzzler) and was gripped by the urge to go out to sea again.[38] This is the most common of pirate stories in Somalia. One-time captors, many pirates found themselves held captive by their addiction to excesses or in some cases of foot soldiers, held hostage by their small-scale lenders.

In yet another case of risky venture typical among many pirates, a former fisherman-turned-pirate put in the final $13,000 left from his fishing business into a piracy mission of seven pirates. His investment equaled to nearly a quarter of that mission's stock and was used to buy a bazooka and 6 AK 47s, a ladder, fuel, food and a Thuraya phone. They captured a German vessel, possibly the MV BBC Trinidad that was sailing under the Antigua and Barbuda flag and was captured by pirates on 21 August 2008.[39] Although Andrew Mwangura of the Seafarers Assistance Program (SAP) reported then that the ship was released after the delivery of a ransom in the order of $1.1 million, the main pirate investor said they actually extorted $1.3 million from its owners. His personal share of the ransom totaled $300,000, a whopping 2,307 percent return on his investment.[40] Like many pirates before and after him, he bought a "new" SUV and drove it without any prior driving experience (and possibly while under the influence of alcohol and khat) until it flipped over and he narrowly escaped with his life – but sustained a permanent leg injury.

In spite of the astronomical ransom figures that pirates collected and contrary to widespread claims that Somalis benefited as a result, the vast majority of Somalis suffered the consequences of similar commonplace stories of dangerous wastage in pirate safe havens across Somalia. The advent of pirates among previously peaceful coastal communities, thus, had the immediate effect of deteriorating their security as the sudden injection of the ransom money destabilized their already precarious economies. The excessive consumption of alcohol and drugs lubricated the fast and costly downward spiral. A typical day in pirate dens involved, in the words of a former pirate, getting high on khat during the day, getting drunk in the evening, and shooting at night.

Excessive Consumption of Alcohol and Khat[41]

Although fierce Islamic prohibition drives the illicit trade of alcohol deep underground, consultations with some retailers in Puntland offer an estimate of how much alcohol was consumed during the heyday of piracy in that region. Accordingly, an estimated 500 bottles were consumed daily during the piracy season between 2008 and 2009. That figure jumped to over 840 bottles per day in 2009-2010; and increased by an additional 100 bottles the following year at 945 per day.[42] The exorbitant prices that traders and retailers charged did not deter the pirates; nor did the strict Islamic prohibition of alcohol among an entirely Muslim population. *Baro's Dry Gin*, the Ethiopian gin popular among Somali pirates in coastal areas and towns alike, is retailed in the Ethiopian capital, Addis Ababa, at no more than $10. One would be considered lucky to get a bottle in Garowe and Galkacyo for less than $100. That price doubled in the coastal areas and it was traded as openly as it was consumed publicly. There were times when a 75cl bottle of gin cost as much as $500 in the Galkacyo – Garacad corridor.

The explosion of piracy saw a parallel increase in the consumption, hence sale, of the mildly narcotic leaf, *khat*, across Somalia and quadrupling of prices, hence absorbing considerable sums of the ransom that pirates collected. From the 1990s to the first half of the 2000s, a *fer* (a pack of five bundles) of Kenyan *khat* or *mirah* cost between $1 and $5 in the urban centers.[43] By the mid-2000s, the price jumped to $10 on average, and the latter price doubled by 2009. While it was not uncommon to see a *fer* of *mirah* going for up to $25 in the towns, it is hard to find it for less than $40 along the coast between Eyl and Garacad in Puntland. There were times between 2009 and 2012 when a *fer* of Kenyan khat cost $50. These skyrocketing of prices did not reduce or contain consumption levels.

According to estimates of Puntland's Ministry of Planning and International Cooperation (MOPIC), import of Kenyan *meeru* and Ethiopian *hareeri* khat into Puntland was consistently on the rise and had reached an annual import of 142,944 tons in 2007, when piracy exploded.[44] Many dispute this figure allegedly because imports are not accurately reported in order to evade taxation. But this estimate gives a picture of what was to come. In the years that followed, when Galkacyo became a major pirate town, its imports of the Kenyan variety alone nearly equaled the rest of region's total. According to confidential data collection from some of the fifteen, or so, khat importers (the bulk traders), small cargo airplanes flew in from Kenya with a total of 84,320 tons of khat in 2008; 96,425 in 2009; 108,780 tons in 2010; and 111,410 tons in 2011.

A closer look into the trends of these traders corroborates the exponential increase in consumption of khat in spite of parallel skyrocketing of the price. According to one of them, for well over a decade before the advent of ransom piracy, his sales ranged between ten and twenty *fer*s during the fishing season. But after piracy, his sales exceeded 300 bundles (i.e. six sacks and more) per day and business ran year round.[45] Similarly, as a lucrative business venture that one can start without capital, women became easily attracted to khat retailing in spite of the attendant physical and financial dangers, especially worsened by the kind of their clientele base. In a random survey conducted in February 2012 among khat vendors in Galkacyo and Garowe, only six of the 51 respondents in Galkacyo and five out of 34 respondents in Garowe entered that business between 2005 and 2006, but 50 percent in

Galkacyo and 64 percent in Garowe started in 2007 and after. In 2009 and after, Garowe saw a 44 percent increase in khat retailers while Galkacyo's retailers increased by 29 percent.

Such pouring in of unearned cash and attendant substance abuse led to the deterioration of security, worsening erosion of the social and family fabric, and destabilization of the traditional order that had preserved itself through the years of conflict. The safety and security of previously peaceful communities suddenly deteriorated immediately after the advent of pirates on the scene because, amidst least armed communities, the pirates came heavily armed and did not hesitate to use them for fun, against each other and against non-pirate local residents. The attendant insecurity affected everyone. But the exact statistics of security incidents involving pirates are hard to come by because, among other factors, pirates choose to settle disputes outside the justice system as represented by state authorities.[46] The combined effects of their activities are, however, inescapable to the naked eye. Referencing such insecurity, the advisor to the Secretary General of the United Nations concluded that northern Somalia (Puntland in particular) had lost job creating investment opportunities due to the piracy-caused deterioration of security.[47]

Collapse of the Fishing Sector

More specifically, ransom piracy became the proverbial last straw that broke the back of the lucrative export-oriented Somali artisanal fishing. Ransom piracy worsened the vicious cycle of diminishing catch, declining income, dwindling capital (to be reinvest in equipment), and dissipating employment opportunities. This downward spiral of the Somali fishing sector pushed many to illegal migration and others were either cajoled into piracy or joined in of their own volition, depriving fishing companies of manpower – both skilled and unskilled. Many companies went bankrupt as a result. The few that survived in Puntland started to bring laborers from south and central Somalia to make up for their loss of manpower to piracy. But they could not retain their newly arrived workers because they too were drawn into piracy.[48]

Assisted by other factors, like illegal, unreported and unregulated (IUU) fishing, artisanal over-fishing, and natural disasters, ransom piracy thus caused the collapse of the fishing sector. Based on statistics from three companies with complete data sets, the following table best demonstrates the dire predicament of the fishing sector in the hands of foreign resource pirates and Somali ransom pirates. After a steady decade-long rise, the stocks and export of the Somali fishing companies started to decline in 2003/2004 and dramatically accelerated from 2005 onwards.

Figure 12.1: Lobster exports (in tons) by private Somali fishing companies

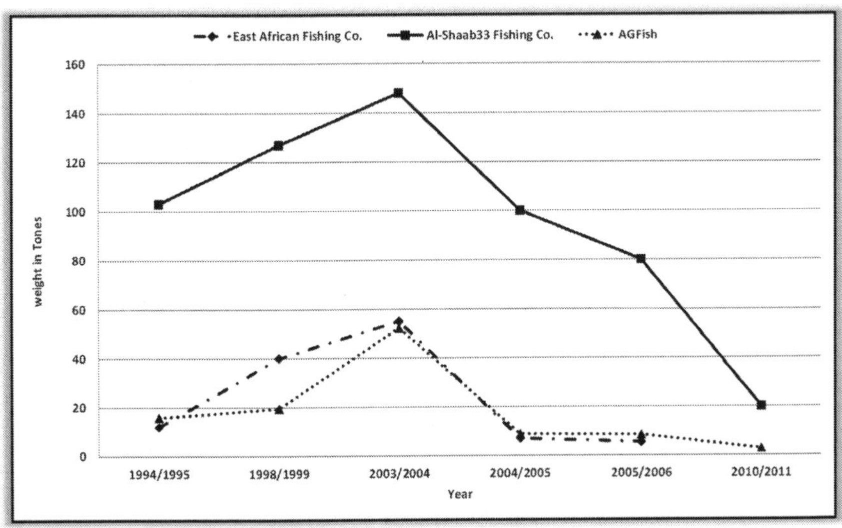

Moreover, pirates affected the individual fishermen directly and indirectly. Indirectly, pirates compromised the safety of the small-scale local fishermen because international navies could not tell the two apart and innocent fishermen became victims of anti-piracy forces. After many such incidents, fishermen feared to venture out to sea and many completely stopped doing so. More directly, Somali fishermen have consistently complained about pirates stealing their fishing boats and catch, fighting and injuring or killing them in the process.[49] Ransom piracy and fishing have thus developed an inversely proportional relationship.

Inflation and Price Hikes

While thus starving the local economies of job-creating opportunities, the piracy-borne insecurity caused the skyrocketing of prices of basic consumer goods from 2007 onwards. In October 2012, the Puntland Ministry of Planning and International Cooperation (MOPIC) released a price index for basic consumer goods in the regional capital Garowe and its commercial capital, the port city of Bosaso, in the preceding three years with 2005 as a base year. Accordingly, the retail prices of basic necessities like foodstuffs, medicines and clothing rose by an average of 47.6 percent per year in both Garowe and Bosaso.[50] Compiled from the 2012 MOPIC data, Figure 2 illustrates the percentage increase in price for basic consumer goods in Puntland, which happened in at least two easily identifiable ways: spendthrift pirates' massive borrowing on exorbitant interest rates and skyrocketing insurance premiums that also impeded trade.

Figure 12.2: Percentage increase in price index for basic consumer goods in Puntland towns*

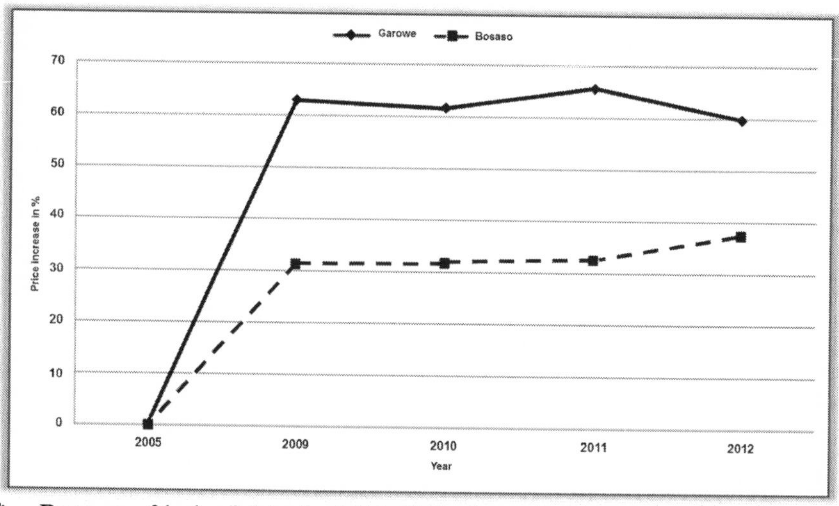

* Because of lack of data for 2006-2008, the period between 2005 and 2009 is truncated into a single interval, making the increase in prices of consumer goods look sharper on the graph than it was in reality. It does, however, demonstrate the skyrocketing of prices from 2005, which MOPIC took as a reference point. I am grateful to the anonymous reviewer who pointed this out.

Exorbitant insurance premiums exacted a heavy toll on Somalia. According to The former Somali prime minister and current president of the semi-autonomous state of Puntland, Abdiweli Mohamed Ali Gaas, of the more than 20,000 vessels that sail past the Gulf of Aden, less than 5 percent came under attack by Somali pirates, and at the height of pirate success, 3 percent of the attacked were actually hijacked and their crew taken hostage. But insurance costs increased for all those buying coverage when sailing past the piracy prone waters – in some cases insurance premiums tripled or quadrupled.[51] Industry sources in fact show far more dramatic increase in insurance premiums since Lloyd's classified Somali coastline as "a war risk area" in mid 2008. Maritime London, a British promotional maritime company, cited "insurance broker Marsh & McLennan" as saying that "the cost of insuring ships against piracy has increased 1,900 percent since [January 2009]." In other words, "shipping firms that were paying 0.05% of the value of their goods for insurance premiums are now paying as much as 0.1%."[52] In 2010 Oceans Beyond Piracy reported that while not all vessels purchase insurance premiums in the four categories that they are offered, war risk premiums alone "have increased 300 fold, from $500 per ship, per voyage; to up to $150,000 per ship, per voyage, in 2010."[53]

As a result, many foreign vessels simply refused to transport goods to/from Somalia and the ones that continued to operate did so at a significantly increased transportation charge (as much as 30 percent across the board) for the same cargo because of the increased insurance premiums for sailing in piracy-infested waters.[54] The increased insurance premiums and transportation costs had a direct bearing on prices of basic consumer goods in at least two ways: first, the increased costs trickled down to retail prices and the end consumers absorbed them, and second, the consequent reduction of competing suppliers gave the remaining few significant pricing leverage.[55] All these increases in prices of basic consumer goods happened without new or additional sources of legitimate income. In fact besides the plummeting of the fishing sector, the livestock business also suffered. The export of livestock generates substantial revenue for Somalia and supports the livelihoods of many Somali families.[56] In the case of Puntland, the region's export of livestock averaged at 1.8 million heads of livestock between 2005 and 2008, with 2008 witnessing the summit figure of 1,926,062 heads.[57] But that dropped to an average of 1.4 million heads of livestock between 2009 and 2011, and the year 2012 was expected to end with a further drop in livestock export at about 1.3 million heads.[58]

Figure 12.3: Puntland's livestock export

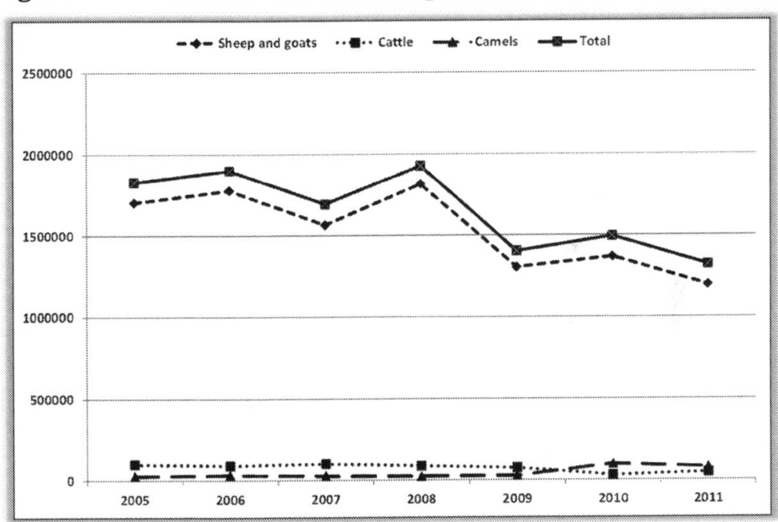

Massive Pirate Borrowing on High Interest Rates

Finally, pirates played a more direct role in influencing the prices of basic consumer goods. Average pirates hardly retained fluid cash before, or long after, the delivery of ransoms. Wherever they went, they either bought supplies on credit from local businesses or borrowed massively. Given the pirates' desperation at the moment and their alacrity to pay hefty interest afterwards, and given the overall level of risk involved for the legitimate retail businesses, the latter demanded, and in many cases were offered without demanding, as much as 100 percent interest rates. Generally negotiations to free captured ships during the first two years (between 2007 and 2009) did not drag on for long and ransoms were quickly delivered.[59] During those years, pirates also paid back their debts as quickly as the ransoms were received. The speed with which those debts were settled had the immediate effect of doubling the prices of commodities for everyone in the pirate dens.

This increase in prices was not restricted to coastal villages, as those in the town also showed commensurate rise. Businesses in inland towns gave out credits to their partners in the coast and faced as much risks as they charged interests that were as quickly paid as the ransoms were delivered and pirate debts in the coast settled. Meanwhile, immediately after the capture of the ship(s), the attack team(s) (no more than 20 pirates per ship) descended on the nearby towns and went on their own spending sprees on credit secured by the captured ship along the coast. Immediately after the ransom was paid and split, the ground/security teams also went to the towns to spend their smaller share of the ill-gotten fortunes. Even when they were paying for their purchases up front, pirates were too willing to continue paying twice the value of the items. The risk in such lending was not a hypothetical one. After amassing so much debt for food (for the hostages and hostage takers alike), and for the pirates' khat, alcohol and other luxuries like cars and women, the hostage takers themselves become hostages of their creditors, perpetuating at least at the individual level the cycle of piracy and its consequences.[60]

The cumulative effect of these dynamics was the parallel rise in commodity prices across the board in Puntland, which made it increasingly difficult for the non-pirates to afford the rising living costs. More and more people sunk deeper into poverty and piracy or illegal migration became the only option available for increasing number of the able bodied willing to undertake either of the risky ventures. Whereas the need for quick money is an undeniable incentive for many of those who joined piracy, claims that it was the relatively well-off who did so is not borne out of the reality on the ground in Puntland.[61] Piracy's foot soldiers needed quick money because they lived in abject poverty. As discussed above, a lion's share of these borrowings was, unfortunately, spent on alcohol and khat, among other excesses in which the pirates indulged.

Conclusion

Prompted by external factors, piracy and ransoming off the coast of Northeast Africa thrived in the vacuum of authority in post-Siyad Barre Somalia, making it unique in its origins, dynamics and consequences. More field research is likely to reveal more details about the dynamics of ransom negotiations on the ground in Somalia and fill in the gaps in the current account. This paper has established that a subsidiary industry developed around the criminal enterprise of ransoming in the Horn of Africa and ascertained that this subsidiary business involved an army of local negotiators-cum-language experts and foreign intermediaries assigning themselves sanguine names and accolades. Similarly, without serious investigations into the dire predicament of those Somalis who were trapped between armed pirates on the one hand and the private and multinational counter-piracy forces on the other, statistics on global consequences of piracy are incomplete. So is aerial imaging methodologically unsound to ascertain the benefits of ransom piracy on the ground. Both lead to the misdiagnosis of the problem. By presenting, or making look, the majority of Somalis, who suffered because of piracy, as beneficiaries of the criminal enterprise, they contribute to alienating local victims of piracy from their international counterparts, hence local anti-piracy endeavors from international counter-piracy operations.

Ransom piracy, like other criminal activities, benefited from the initial problem of unemployment across Somalia. Rampant joblessness supplied the exploding piracy industry with a seemingly endless reservoir of manpower that contributed to make Somalia uninviting to job-creating investments. Piracy then grew to become the biggest impediment for solutions based on job-creation. The cascade of economic difficulties that piracy caused directly affected the creation of local jobs, which in turn made jobless young men available in abundance for recruitment into piracy. It became a vicious cycle.

The thriving of piracy contributed to the dramatic deterioration of security and safety among previously peaceful coastal communities. The onetime profitable Somali artisanal fishing ceased to exist. Maritime trade to/from Somalia decreased and imported goods became significantly more expensive for the average person to afford. Pirates borrowed on very high interest rates that contributed to increase prices of consumer goods even more. To make matters even worse, the majority of pirates splurged nearly all of their "earnings" in unproductive addictive practices with dire economic and security consequences to the average Somalis, in general. That was why the ordinary people waged a sustained campaign and even launched armed operations against piracy with remarkable success that is yet to be recognized and supported.

Endnotes

1 The author would like to thank Jennifer Lofkrantz for her hard work to bring this volume to fruition, in general, and, more particularly, for her useful feedback on an earlier draft of this chapter.

2 Plutarch, *The Parallel Lives*, volume IV, trans. Bernadotte Perrin (Cambridge, MA and London: Loeb Classical Library edition, 1919) 447, available online at: http://penelope.uchicago.edu/Thayer/E/Roman/Texts/Plutarch/Lives/Caesar*.html#1. Relevant excerpts are also reproduced in *The Best Pirate Stories ever Told*, ed. Stephen Brennan (New York: Skyhorse Publishing, 2011), 29-30.

3 Mayor Musa Osman Yusuf, personal interview, February 24, 2012 (Eyl, Puntland) and Mohamud Abdulkadir ("John"), personal interview, February 27, 2012 (Galkacyo, Puntland). See also Stig Jarle Hansen, *Piracy in the Greater Gulf of Aden: Myths, Misconceptions and Remedies* (Norwegian Institute for Urban and Regional Research, NIBR Report 29, 2009), http://www.nibr.no/filer/2009-29-ny.pdf; Martin N. Murphy, *Somalia: The New Barbary? Piracy and Islam in the Horn of Africa* (New York: Columbia University Press, 2011).

4 Abdirahman Jama Kulmiye, "Militia vs Trawlers: Who is the Villain?" *The East African Magazine*, July 9, 2001, http://www.ecop.info/e-news/e-news-01-07-9.htm; and Mohamed Abshir Waldo, "The Two Piracies in Somalia: Why the World Ignores the Other?" wardheernews.com, January 8, 2009, http://wardheernews.com/Articles_09/Jan/Waldo/08_The_two_piracies_in_Somalia.html.

5 There now are numerous accounts on this topic, but the most reliable remain Hansen's, *Piracy in the Greater Gulf of Aden* and Murphy's *Somalia: The New Barbary?* Also see Weldemichael, "Maritime Corporate Terrorism and its Consequences in the Western Indian Ocean Region: Waste Dumping, Illegal Fishing and Piracy in 21st Century Somalia," *Journal of the Indian Ocean Region*, 8:2 (2012), 110-126.

6 Anja Shortland, "Treasure Mapped: Using Satellite Imagery to Track the Developmental Effects of Somalia Piracy" (Chatham House Africa Programme Paper: AFP PP 2012/01), 3, 9.

7 Ibid., 3.

8 Ibid., 7.

9 Jack Lang, *Report of the Special Adviser to the Secretary-General on Legal Issues Related to Piracy off the Coast of Somalia* (January 2011), 14.

10 Lang, *Report of the Special Adviser to the Secretary-General*, 14.

11 Kaija Hurlburt, *The Human Cost of Somali Piracy*, One Earth Future Foundation, June 2011, 24-26, http://oceansbeyondpiracy.org/sites/default/files/human_cost_of_somali_piracy.pdf (accessed August 15, 2011).

12 Hurlburt, *The Human Cost of Somali Piracy*.

13 Anna Bowden et al., *The Economic Cost of Maritime Piracy, 2010*, One Earth Future Working Paper, December 2010, http://oceansbeyondpiracy.org/documents/The_Economic_Cost_of_Piracy_Full_Report.pdf (accessed on March 11, 2011).

14 Geopolicity, "The Economics of Piracy: Pirates Ransoms and Livelihoods off the Coast of Somalia," May 2011: http://www.geopolicity.com/upload/content/pub_1305229189_regular.pdf (accessed May 18, 2011).

15 Anna Bowden and Shikha Basnet, *The Economic Cost of Somali Piracy 2011*, One Earth Future Foundation Working Paper: http://oceansbeyondpiracy.org/sites/default/files/economic_cost_of_piracy_2011.pdf

16 Jonathan Bellish, *The Economic Cost of Somali Piracy 2012*, One Earth Future Foundation Working Paper: http://oceansbeyondpiracy.org/sites/default/files/attachments/View%20Full%20Report_1.pdf

17 While the specifics of each case were likely to be different, this general framework is confirmed by the earliest pirate Abshir Abdullahi Abdule "Boyah," personal interview, June 8 and 15, 2014, (Garowe, Puntland) and numerous latecomers to ransom piracy.

18 This, for example, was the case of MV Rim that was hijacked by pirates in early February 2010.

19 See its webpage: http://www.ecop.info/english/e-sap-net.htm

20 Andrew Mwangura, personal interview, January 8, 2012 (Mombasa, Kenya).

21 These are Prantalay 11, 12, and 14.

22 "Navy, Coast Guard destroy Somali pirate vessel," *Deccan Herald*, January 29, 2011, http://www.deccanherald.com/content/133143/navy-coast-guard-destroy-somali.html; Sanjoy Majumder, "Indian navy seizes pirates' Indian Ocean mothership," BBC News, February 6, 2011, http://www.bbc.co.uk/news/world-south-asia-12376695.

23 Confidential Interviews, October 2012 (Galkacyo, Puntland) and June 2014 (Garowe, Puntland).

24 "Somali pirates release fishermen held for five years," Al-Jazeera, February 27, 2015, http://www.aljazeera.com/news/2015/02/somali-pirates-release-fishermen-held-years-150227094729606.html; "Somali pirates free Thai fishermen held for four years," BBC News, February 27, 2015, http://www.bbc.com/news/world-asia-31664266. While some reports indicate that the ransom paid was US$150,000, others say that it was US$ 1 million.

25 Another partial example is that of notorious pirate kingpin Garad Mohamed's abortive April 2012 hijacking of Panamanian-flagged, Chinese cargo vessel Xiang Hua Men that culminated in the Iranian navy capturing Garad and his men. Partial because the pirates did not speak English and, had they been suc-

cessful, they would have been unlikely to start negotiations before arriving in their desired pirate hub.

See "XIANG HUA MEN Freed By Iranian Naval Commandos. High Profile Pirate Leader Garaad Captured In The Operation," *SomaliaReport*, April 6, 2012, http://somaliareport.com/index.php/post/3219/XIANG_HUA_MEN_Freed_By_Iranian_Naval_Commandos

26 "Brits Arrested in Somalia with '£2.2 million ransom for pirates'," *The Telegraph*, May 26, 2011, http://www.telegraph.co.uk/news/worldnews/piracy/8539542/Brits-arrested-in-Somalia-with-2.2-million-ransom-for-pirates.html. Also see S/2011/433, Report of the UN Monitoring Group on Somalia and Eritrea, July 18, 2011, Annex 6.1: "Private security companies operating in Somalia," paragraphs 20-23.

27 Dominic Wabala, "Ex-UK Soldiers Based in Nairobi Carried Tebbutt Ransom to Adado," *The Star*, March 23, 2012, http://www.the-star.co.ke/news/article-25134/ex-uk-soldiers-based-nairobi-carried-tebbutt-ransom-adado

28 These were Boyah himself [personal interview, June 8 and 15, 2014 (Garowe, Puntland)], Garad Mohamed and Farah Abdullahi. Also see Hansen, *Piracy in the Greater Gulf of Aden*, 25.

29 Unrelated to piracy, this conflict erupted between the 'Ayr and Saleebaan families of Habar Gidir sub-clan of the Hawiye and has to be looked within the broader intra-clan and inter-clan conflicts over meager resources, power (local and regional), and revenge killings that particularly ravaged post-Siyad Barre Somalia.

30 The timing that Boyah gave me is off by at least one year from the timing that Norwegian scholar Stig Jarle Hansen attributed to him in 2008. Boya, personal interview, June 8 and 15, 2014 (Garowe, Puntland). For Hansen's rendition of what happened when, see *Piracy in the Greater Gulf of Aden*, 23 ff.

31 S/2011/433, Report of the UN Monitoring Group on Somalia and Eritrea, 18 July 2011, Annex 4.3: "Case study: pirates and finances – the Hobyo-Harardheere 'business model'," paragraph 5.

32 Boyah, personal interview, June 8 and 15, 2014 (Garowe, Puntland).

33 Rob Crilly, "Somali Pirates on 'Benzene Bomb' Threaten to Kill Hostages," *The Times,* December 12, 2007, http://www.thetimes.co.uk/tto/news/world/africa/article2593380.ece (accessed June 10, 2014).

Mari Yamaguchi, "Seized Crew of Japan Tanker Believed Safe," *The Associated Press*, December 11, 2007, http://www.washingtonpost.com/wp-dyn/content/article/2007/12/11/AR2007121100098.html (accessed June 10, 2014); "Somali pirates free Japan tanker," BBC News, December 12, 2007, http://news.bbc.co.uk/2/hi/africa/7139897.stm (accessed June 10, 2014).

34 Confidential interview, February 23, 2012 (Eyl, Puntland).

35 Abshir Abdullahi Abdule "Boyah," personal interview, June 8 and 15, 2014 (Garowe, Puntland).

36 One of the pirates who captured this vessel was very specific of the number of days that they held the ship captive, which is an important clue when compared

to other ships captured around the same time: "For 2 months and 20 days [that we held the ship], I had no knowledge of my family." Captured on 1 June 1m 2007, MV Danica White was released on 23 August 23, 2007 upon the payment of ransom a day or two earlier. Confidential interview (February 8, 2012, (Garowe, Puntland); David Osler, "Svitzer tug hijacked off Somali coast," Lloydslist, February 4, 2008: http://www.lloydslist.com/ll/news/viewArticle.htm?articleId=20017501599&src=ticker.

37 Confidential interview, February 8, 2012 (Garowe, Puntland).

38 Ibid.

39 The main features that lead me to assume that the pirate was talking about MV BBC Trinidad are the fact that it was a German vessel, the general timing being in the second half of 2008, and the proximity of the ransom figure reported by third party sources to the figure given by the pirate himself. Confidential interview, February 7, 2012, (Garowe, Puntland).

40 "German-owned ship paid 1.1. mln USD ransom to Somali pirates," *Xinhua*, September 12, 2008: http://news.xinhuanet.com/english/2008-09/12/content_9944030.htm (accessed June 10, 2014), Confidential interview, February 7, 2012, (Garowe, Puntland).

41 A version of this and the subsequent sections on the domestic consequences of piracy have appeared in *Dalhousie Marine Piracy Project: When Elephants Fight, the Grass Suffers: A report on the Local Consequences of Piracy in Puntland* (Dalhousie University: Marine Affairs Program Technical Report #12, 2014), http://www.dal.ca/content/dam/dalhousie/images/faculty/science/marine-affairs-program/Technical_series/Dalhousie-Marine-Affairs-Program-Technical-Report-%2312.pdf

42 Noticing my shock about what seemed unlikely figures, one informant continued: "have you seen pirates drink this poisonous drink? I have!" This makes perfect sense in light of the fact that pirates hardly did anything leisurely. The concept of recreational drinking is unknown to them and they reached the climax of their consumptive capacity as fast they were introduced to the drink. Confidential interview, October 20, 2012 (Galkacyo, Puntland).

43 Prices for khat almost always doubled – or just about – in remote coastal villages in Puntland like Eyl and Garacad.

44 Ministry of Planning and International Cooperation, *Puntland Facts and Figures*, 4th edition (Puntland State of Somalia, 2008), 18.

45 As with most other commodities, khat was sold on credit with exorbitant interest rates, which is partially responsible for the price hikes. "I know a single pirate borrowing as much as $40,000 in khat within a period of 5 – 6 months," related one trader and continued, "but you have to know that one person takes care of many [*shahat*]."

46 According to a one time investor and pirate organizer in Mudug, the elders whom the pirates corrupted were important in resolving intra-pirate disputes as well as the pirates' disputes with the host communities. Confidential interview, October 24, 2012 (Galkacyo, Puntland).

47 Lang, *Report of the Special Adviser to the Secretary-General*, 14.

48 Within days of coming to the fishing villages, the fishermen would make contact with pirates, who actively recruit them or provided handouts of cash, food, drinks or chew – as they do to *shahat* (literally beggar). Even as shahat, the laborers ended up making more money (in cash and in kind) than they otherwise would as laborers or even divers for the fishing companies that brought them there.

49 Whereas executives of a fishing company in Bosaso related the injuries and deaths their smaller-scale fishermen suffered in the hands of the pirates, a fisherwoman from Eyl lost one of her boats to pirates, but intercepted another daring group of pirates pulling her other boat behind their truck and driving fast through Bedey, the coastal half of Eyl. For more of similar stories, see Mohamed Beerdhige, "Pirates Hijack Vessel Despite Gov Security Team. Iranian Dhow Fishing Legally with Support of Puntland Government," January 25, 2012, http://somaliareport.com/index.php/post/2618/Pirates_Hijack_Vessel_Despite_Gov_Security_Team

50 Galkacyo was not included because MOPIC did not start to compile data on its prices for consumer goods until 2008. Nevertheless, even Galkacyo's already high price index witnessed an additional average increase of 15.3 percent per year during the same time frame.

51 Interview with former TFG Prime Minister Abdiweli Mohamed Ali (21 October 2012, Galkacyo). Industry sources in fact show far more dramatic increase in insurance premiums since Lloyds classified Somali coastline as "a war risk area" in mid 2008. Londonmaritime.com cited "insurance broker Marsh & McLennan," that reported "the cost of insuring ships against piracy has increased 1,900% since [January 2009]." In other words, "shipping firms that were paying 0.05% of the value of their goods for insurance premiums are now paying as much as 0.1%." See "Piracy: a tax for shipping?", Maritime London, June 29, 2009, http://www.maritimelondon.com/london_matters29june09.htm#1
In 2010 Oceans Beyond Piracy reported that while not all vessels purchase insurance premiums in the four categories that they are offered, war risk premiums alone "have increased 300 fold, from $500 per ship, per voyage; to up to $150,000 per ship, per voyage, in 2010." See Bowden, *The Economic Cost of Maritime Piracy*, 10.

52 See "Piracy: a tax for shipping?" *Maritime London*, June 29, 2009, http://www.maritimelondon.com/london_matters29june09.htm#1

53 See Bowden, *The Economic Cost of Maritime Piracy*, 10.

54 Confidential interviews, August 8, 2011 (Nairobi, Kenya) and February 15, 2012 (Bosaso, Puntland).

55 Confidential interview, February 15, 2012 (Bosaso, Puntland).

56 Peter D. Little, *Somalia: Economy without State* (Oxford: James Currey, 2003) offers a reliable account on livestock trading of southern Somalia with Kenya that also gives the general picture of livestock industry across Somalia.

57 Statistics from the Puntland Ministry of Livestock and Animal Husbandry.

58 Although protracted clan conflicts contribute to the decline of livestock export when either traders or herders have to traverse the territory of a rival clan, none of such conflicts have taken place since 2007 to significantly affect trade routes.

59 On average, ransoms were delivered in less than three months of captivity and retailers in coastal pirate dens generally procured supplies on monthly or bi-monthly basis. In cases when the local retailers did not have cash to pay for their supplies right away, they bought their goods on credit from the suppliers.

60 The latest such case is that of MV Iceberg I. After more than two-and-half years of captivity and accruing an estimated $2.5 million in debt, the Puntland Marine Police Force (PMPF) defeated the pirates, took control of the ship and freed its surviving 22 sailors in December 2012. According to confidential sources on the ground, the amount of debt that the pirates owed their diverse creditors was one of the factors that kept complicating ransom negotiations.

61 The key proponent of this argument is the Norwegian scholar Stig Jarle Hansen who is the earliest to have conducted fieldwork among the pirates in Puntland and Galmudug regions.

Bibliography

Abdullah, Ibrahim. "Bush Path to Destruction: the Origin and Character of the Revolutionary United Front/Sierra Leone." *Journal of Modern African Studies* 36 (1998): 203-235.

Adams, Charles Hansford, ed. *The Narrative of Robert Adams, A Barbary Captive.* Cambridge: Cambridge University Press, 2005.

Adams, Robert and S. Cock. *The Narrative of Robert Adams, an American Sailor.* London: John Murray, 1816.

Adeleye, R. A. *Power and Diplomacy in Northern Nigeria 1804–1806.* London: Longman, 1971.

"Affairs on the Gold Coast." *The Edinburgh Review or Critical Journal* 138 (1873): 292-301.

Africanus, Leo. *The History and Description of Africa,* trans. John Pory. London: Hakluyt Society, 1896.

Ajayi, J. F. A. *Christian Missions in Nigeria: The Making of a New Elite, 1841-1891.* London: Longman, 1965.

--------. "Professional Warriors in Nineteenth-Century Yoruba Politics." *Tarikh* 1 (1965): 72-81.

Albergoni, Gianni. "Les Bédouins et les Echanges: La Piste Introuvable." *Cahiers des Sciences Humaines* 26 (1990): 195-215.

Albert, Isaac Olawale. "Explaining 'Godfatherism' in Nigerian Politics." *African Sociological Review* 9 (2005): 79-105.

Ali, Muna and Zahra Murad. "Unravelling Narratives of Piracy: Discourses of Somali Pirates." *Dark Matter* 5 (2009): 91-102.

Allen, William and T. R. H. Thomson. *A Narrative of the Expedition sent by Her Majesty's Government to the River Niger in 1841 under the command of Captain H. D. Trotter.* London: Frank Cass, 1968 [1848].

Al-Naqar, Umar. *The Pilgrimage Tradition in West Africa.* Khartoum: Khartoum University Press, 1972.

Alonso Acero, Beatriz. *Orán-Mazalquivir, 1589-1639: una sociedad española en la frontera de Berbería.* Madrid: CSIC, 2000.

Alpers, Edward. "The Story of Swema: Female Vulnerability in 19th Century East Africa." In *Women and Slavery in Africa,* edited by Claire Robertson and Martin Klein, 185-219. Portsmouth: Heinemann, 1997.

Ambrus, Attila, Eric Chaney, and Igor Salitskiy. "Pirates of the Mediterranean: An Empirical Investigation of Bargaining with Transaction Costs." *Economic Research Initiatives at Duke* 115 (2011). Available at SSRN: http://ssrn.com/abstract=1954149

Amusan, Lere. "The Political Economy of Fossil Fuels in Nigeria." In *Contending Issues in the Niger Delta Crisis of Nigeria,* edited by Victor Ojakorotu, 20-53. Delray Beach, FL: JAPSS Press, Inc., 2009.

Anderson, Elliot A. "It's a Pirate's Life for Some: The Development of An Illegal Industry in Response to an Unjust Global Power Dynamic." *Indiana Journal of Global Legal* Studies 17 (2010): 319-339.

Anderson, John. "Piracy and World History: An Economic Perspective on Maritime Predation." *Journal of World History* 6 (1995): 175-199.

Arribas Palau, Mariano. "De nuevo sobre la embajada de al-Gassani, 1690-1691." *Al-Qantara* 6 (1985): 199-289.

----------. "Argelinos cautivos en España, rescatados por el sultán de Marruecos." *Boletín de la Asociación Española de Orientalistas* 26 (1990): 23-54.

Asad, Talal. *The Idea of an Anthropology of Islam.* Washington DC: Center for Contemporary Arab Studies Georgetown University, 1986.

Austen, Ralph and Jan Jansen. "History, Oral Transmission, and Structure in Ibn Khaldun's Chronology of Mali Rulers." *History in Africa* 23 (1996): 17-28

Austin, Gareth. "Between Abolition and Jihad: the Asante Response to the Ending of the Atlantic Slave Trade, 1807-1896." In *From Slave Trade to 'Legitimate' Commerce,* edited by Robin Law, 93-118.

Baier, Stephen. "Trans-Saharan Trade and the Sahel: Damergu, 1870-1930." *The Journal of African History* 18 (1977): 37-60.

Baepler, Paul, ed. *White Slaves, African Master: An Anthology of American Barbary Captivity Narratives*. Chicago: University of Chicago Press, 1999.

Bamford, Paul. *Fighting Ships and Prisons: The Mediterranean Galleys of France in the Age of Louis XIV*. Minneapolis: University of Minnesota Press, 1973.

Bannon, Ian and Paul Collier, eds. *Natural Resources and Violent Conflict: Options and Actions*. Washington D.C: World Bank, 2003.

Barrio Gozalo, Maximiliano. *Esclavos y cautivos: conflicto entre la cristiandad y el islam en el siglo XVIII*. Valladolid: Junta de Castilla y León, 2006.

Barrios, Cristina and Tobias Koepf, eds. *Re-mapping the Sahel: Transnational Security Challenges and international Responses*. Paris: EU Institute for Security Studies, 2014.

Bazin, Jean. "Guerre et Servitude a Segou." In *L'Esclavage en Afrique Précoloniale*, edited by Claude Meillasoux, 135-181. Paris: Maspero, 1975.

Beach, Adam R. "African Slaves, English Slave Narratives, and Early Modern Morocco." *Eighteenth-Century Studies* 46 (2013): 333-48.

Behrendt, Stephen D. "The British Slave Trade, 1785-1807: Volume, Profitability, and Mortality." Ph.D. dissertation, University of Wisconsin-Madison, 1993.

Belhamissi, Moulay. *Les Captifs Algériens et l'Europe Chrétienne (1518-1830)*. Alger: L'Entreprise Nationale du Livre, 1988.

Bernus, Edmund. "Dates, Dromedaries, and Drought: Diversification in Tuareg Pastoral Systems." in *World of Pastoralism: Herding Systems in Comparative Perspective*, edited by J. G. Galaty and D. L. Johnson, 149-76. New York: AWG Publishing, 1990.

Bertrand, Régis, "Les Cimetières des 'esclaves turcs' des arsenaux de Marseille et de Toulon au XVIIIe siècle." *Revue des mondes musulmans et de la Méditerranée* 99-100 (2002): 205–217.

Bivar, A. D. H. and M. Hiskett. "The Arabic Literature of Nigeria to 1804: A Provisional Account." *Bulletin of the School of Oriental and African Studies University of London* 25 (1962): 104-148.

Blanes Andrés, Roberto. *Valencia y el Magreb. Las Relaciones comerciales marítimas (1600-1703)*. Barcelona: Bellaterra, 2010.

Bluett, Thomas. *Some Memoirs of the Life of Job, the Son of Solomon the High Priest of Boonda in Africa.* London: Richard Ford, 1734.

Bono, Salvatore. "Slave Histories and Memoirs in the Mediterranean World: A Study of the Sources. Sixteenth-Eighteenth Centuries." In *Trade and Cultural Exchange in the Early Modern Mediterranean, Braudel's Maritime Legacy*, edited by Maria Fusaro, Colin Heywood and Mohamed-Salah Omro, 97-116. New York: I. B. Tauris, 2010.

--------. "Forniture dall'Italia di schiavi musulmani per le galere francesi (1685-1693)." *Annali delle facoltà di scienze politiche dell'Università di Cagliari* 9 (1983): 83–97.

Bosman, William. *A New and Accurate Description of the Coasts of Guinea, Divided into the Gold, Slave, and the Ivory Coasts*. London: James Knapton, 1705.

Boubaker, Sadok. "Réseaux et techniques de rachat des captifs de la course à Tunis au XVIIIe siècle." In *Le commerce des captifs: les intermédiaires dans l'échange et le rachat des prisonniers en Méditerranée, XVe-XVIIIe siècle*, edited by Wolfgang Kaiser, 25-46. Rome: École Française de Rome, 2008.

Bowen, Thomas J. *Adventures and Missionary Labours in Several Countries in the Interior of Africa from 1849 to 1856*. London: Frank Cass, 1968 [1857].

Boyer, Pierre. "La Chiourme turque des galères de France de 1685 à 1687." *Revue de l'Occident musulman et de la Méditerranée* 6 (1969): 53-74.

Boyle, Frederick. *Through Fanteeland to Coomasie: A Diary of the Ashantee Expedition*. London: Chapman and Hall, 1874.

Brackenbury, Henry. *The Ashanti War: A Narrative*, 2 vols. Edinburgh: William Blackwood, 1874.

Braudel, Fernand. *The Mediterranean and the Mediterranean World in the Age of Philip II.* New York: Harper & Row, 1972.

Brenner, Louis. "The Jihad Debate between Sokoto and Borno: An Historical Analysis of Islamic Political Discourse in Nigeria." In *People and Empires in African History: Essays in Memory of Michael Crowder*, edited by J. F. A. Ajayi and J. D. Y. Peel, 21-45. London: Longman, 1992.

--------. "Muhammad al-Amin al-Kanimi and Religion and Politics in Bornu." In *Studies in West African Islamic History,* vol. 1: *Cultivators of Islam*, edited by John Ralph Willis, 160-176. London: Frank Cass, 1979.

Briggs, Rachel. *The Kidnapping Business*. London: The Foreign Policy Centre, 2001.

Brockopp, Jonathan E. *Early Mālikī Law, Ibn 'Abd al-Ḥakkam and his Major Copendium of Jurisprudence*. Leiden: Brill, 2000.

Brodman, James. *Ransoming Captives in Crusader Spain: The Order of Merced on the Christian-Islamic Frontier*. Philadelphia: University of Pennsylvania Press, 1986.

--------. "Municipal Ransoming Law on the Medieval Spanish Frontier." *Speculum* 60 (1985): 318-30.

Brooks, George E. *Landlords and Strangers: Ecology, Society, and Trade in Western Africa, 1000-1630*. Boulder, CO: Westview Press, 1993.

Brooks, James F. *Captives and Cousins: Slavery, Kinship, and Community in the Southwest Borderlands*. Chapel Hill: University of North Carolina Press, 2002.

Brown, Christopher Leslie. *Moral Capital. Foundations of British Abolitionism.* Chapel Hill: University of North Carolina Press, 2006.

Brown, James A. O. C. *Crossing the Strait Morocco, Gibraltar and Great Britain in the 18th and 19th Centuries*. Leiden: Brill, 2012.

Bruce Lockhart, Jamie and Paul E. Lovejoy, eds. *Hugh Clapperton into the Interior of Africa. Records of the Second Expedition, 1825-1827*. Leiden: Brill, 2005.

Buchanan, Thomas C. "Rascals on the Antebellum Mississippi: African American Steamboat Workers and the St. Louis Hanging of 1841." *Journal of Social History* 34 (2001): 797-816.

Burlet, René, André Zysberg, and Jean Carrière. "Mais comment pouvait-on ramer sur les galères du Roi-Soleil." *Histoire et Mesure* 1.3–4 (1986): 147–208.

Burnham, Philip and Murray Last, "From Pastoralist to Politician: The Problem of a Fulbe 'Aristocracy,'" *Cahiers d'Études Africaines* 34.133/135 (1994): 313–57.

Burton, Richard F. *A Mission to Gelele King of Dahome* 2 vols. London: Tinsley Brothers, 1864.

Carey, Mathew. *A Short Account of Algiers*. Philadelphia: J. Parker, 1794.

Casanova y Todolí, Ubaldo de. "Algunas anotaciones sobre el comportamiento de los esclavos moros en Mallorca durante el siglo XVII y un ejemplo de intercambio con cautivos cristianos." *Bolletí de la Societat Arqueològica Lul·liana: Revista d'estudis històrics* 41 (1985): 323-332.

Cheyfitz, Eric. *The Poetics of Imperialism: Translation and Colonization from the Tempest to Tarzan.* Philadelphia: University of Pennsylvania Press, 1997.

Clarence-Smith, William G. and David Eltis, "White Servitude." In *The Cambridge World History of Slavery, Volume 3, AD 1420-AD 1804,* edited by David Eltis and Stanley L. Engerman, 132-59. Cambridge: Cambridge University Press, 2011.

CLEEN Foundation. *National Crime and Victimization Survey*. Lagos: CLEEN Foundation, 2010.

Cochelet, Charles, *Narrative of the Shipwreck of the Sophia.* London: Richard Philips, 1822.

Cohen, Ralph, ed. *The Essential Works of David Hume*. New York: Bantam Books, 1965.

Colley, Linda. *Captives: Britain, Empire, and the World, 1600-1850.* London: Jonathan Cape, 2002.

Collier, Paul, V.L. Elliot, Hegre Havard, H. Anke, M. Reynal-Querol, and N. Sambanis. *Breaking the Conflict Trap: Civil War and Development Policy*. Washington DC: World Bank and Oxford University Press, 2003.

Conneau, Theophille. *A Slaver's Log Book or 20 Years' Residence in Africa: The Original Manuscript*. Englewood Cliffs, NJ: Prentice Hall, 1976 [1854].

Cooper, Frederick. "The Problem of Slavery in African Studies." *Journal of African History* 20 (1979): 103-125.

--------. "Africa in the World Economy." In *Confronting Historical Paradigms: Peasants, Labor, and the Capitalist World*, edited by Frederick Cooper, Allen F. Isaacman, Florencia C. Mallon, William Roseberry, and Steve J. Stern, 84-204. Madison: University of Wisconsin Press, 1993.

Cornell, Vincent J. "Ibn Battuta's Opportunism: The Networks and Loyalties of a Medieval Muslim Scholar." In *Muslim Networks from Hajj to Hip Hop*, edited by Miriam Cooke and Bruce B. Lawrence, 31-50. Chapel Hill: The University of North Carolina Press, 2005.

Corrales Eloy, Martín. *Comercio de Cataluña con el Mediterráneo musulmán (siglos XVI-XVIII): el Comercio con los 'enemigos de la fe'*. Barcelona: Bellaterra, 2001.

Curtin, Phillip D. "Jihad in West Africa: Early Phases and Inter-Relations in Mauritania and Senegal." *Journal of African History* 12 (1971): 11-24.

--------. "Ayuba Suleiman Diallo of Bondu." In *Africa Remembered: Narratives by West Africans from the Era of the Slave Trade*, edited by Phillip D. Curtin, 17-59. Madison: University of Wisconsin Press, 1967.

--------. "Joseph Wright of the Egba." In Curtin, *Africa Remembered*, 317-33.

--------. *The Image of Africa: British Ideas and Action, 1780-1850*. Madison: University of Wisconsin Press, 1964.

Curto, Jose C. "The Story of Nbena, 1817-1820: Unlawful Enslavement and the Concept of Original Freedom in Angola." In *Trans-Atlantic Dimensions of Ethnicity in the African Diaspora*, edited by Paul E. Lovejoy and David Trotman, 43-64. London: Continuum, 2003.

Dakhlia, Jocelyne. "Musulmans en France et en Grande-Bretagne à l'époque moderne: exemplaires et invisibles." In *Les Musulmans dans l'histoire de l'Europe*, vol. 1: *Une integration invisible*, edited by Jocelyne Dakhlia, Bernard Vincent, and Wolfgang Kaiser, 231-407. Paris: Albin Michel, 2011.

Daniels, Christopher L. *Somali Piracy and Terrorism in the Horn of Africa*. Lanham, MD.: Scarecrow Press, 2012.

Daniel, Serge. *AQIM: L'Industrie de l'Enlèvement*. Paris: Fayard, 2012.

Dávid, Géza and Pál Fodor, eds. *Ransom Slavery along the Ottoman Borders (Early Fifteenth-Early Eighteenth Centuries*). Leiden: Brill, 2007.

Davis, Robert. "Counting European Slaves on the Barbary Coast." *Past and Present* 172 (2001): 87-124

--------. "Slave Redemption in Venice, 1585-1797." In *Venice Reconsidered: The History and Civilization of an Italian City-State, 1297–1797*, edited by John Martin and Dennis Romano, 454-90. Baltimore: Johns Hopkins University Press, 2000.

--------. *Christian Slaves, Muslim Masters: White Slavery in the Mediterranean, the Barbary Coast and Italy, 1500-1800*. New York: Palgrave Macmillan, 2004.

De Azurara, Gomes Eannes. *The Chronicle of the Discovery and Conquest of Guinea*, trans. Charles Beazley and Edgar Prestage. London: Hakluyt Society, 1899.

De Brisson, *Account of the Shipwreck and Captivity of Mr. De Brisson with A Description of the Desert of Africa, from Senegal to Morocco and his own Observation, While Harassed from Place to Place by the Wandering Arabs*. London: Robert Barker, 1790.

Demaio, Andrew. "Upping the Stakes to Win the War Against Somali Piracy: Justifications for a New Strategy Based on International Humanitarian Law." *George Mason Law Review* 22 (2015): 387-437.

Derian, James Der. *Antidiplomacy: Spies, Terror, Speed and War.* Oxford: Blackwell, 1992.

Diallo, Thierno. *Institutions politiques du Fouta Dyalon*. Dakar: IFAN, 1972.

Díaz Borrás, Andrés. *El miedo al Mediterráneo: la caridad popular valenciana y la redención de cautivos bajo poder musulmán 1323-1539*. Barcelona: CSIC, Instituto Milá Fontanals, 2001.

Diouf, Mamadou. "Engaging Postcolonial Cultures: African Youth and Public Space." *African Studies Review* 46, 2 (2003): 1-12.

Diouf, Sylviane A., ed. *Fighting the Slave Trade: West African Strategies*, Athens: Ohio University Press, 2003.

Diouf, Sylviane A. "The Last Resort: Redeeming Family and Friends." In Diouf, *Fighting the Slave Trade*, 82-92.

Dode, Robert. "The Political Economy of Resource Curse and the Niger Delta Crisis in Nigeria: Matters Arising." *Afro-Asian Journal of Social Sciences* 2 (2011): 1-15.

Don Pedro, Ibiba. *Oil in the Water: Crude Power and Militancy in the Niger Delta*. Lagos: Forward Communications, 2006.

Dottain, Ernest. "Un Chapitre de l'histoire de la Marine sous Louis XIV: La Justice et les galères." *Revue Contemporaine* 29 (1862): 464-496.

Drescher, Seymour. "The Slaving Capital of the World: Liverpool and National Opinion in the Age of Abolition." *Slavery and Abolition* 9 (1988): 128-43.

Durham, Deborah. "Youth and the Social Imagination in Africa: Introduction to Parts 1 and 2." *Anthropological Quarterly* 73, 3 (2000): 113-120.

Edigin, Uyi. “Political Conflicts and Godfatherism in Nigeria: A Focus on the Fourth Republic.” *African Research Review* 4, 4 (2010): 174-86.

Ehwarieme, William. “Fishers of Men: The Political Economy of Kidnapping in the Niger Delta.” In *Contending Issues in the Niger Delta Crisis of Nigeria*, edited by Victor Ojakorotu, 95-122. Delray Beach, FL: JAPSS Press Inc., 2009.

El Hamel, Chouki. *Black Morocco: A History of Slavery, Race, and Islam*. New York: Cambridge University Press, 2013.

--------. “The Register of the Slaves of Sultan Mawlay Isma’il of Morocco at the Turn of the Eighteenth Century.” *Journal of African History* 51 (2010): 89-98.

-------. “‘Race, Slavery and Islam in Maghribi Mediterranean Thought: The Question of the Haratin in Morocco.” *Journal of North African Studies* 7, 3 (2002): 29-52.

Eltis, David. *The Rise of African Slavery in the Americas*. Cambridge: Cambridge University Press, 2000.

--------. “The Diaspora of Yoruba Speakers, 1650–1865: Dimensions and Implications.” In *The Yoruba Diaspora in the Atlantic World*, edited by Toyin Falola and Matt D. Childs, 17-39. Indianapolis: Indiana University Press, 2004.

Einzig, Paul. *Primitive Money in Its Ethnological, Historical and Economic Aspects*. London: Eyre & Spottiswoode, 1948.

Ennaji, Mohammed and Paul Pascon. *Le makhzen et le Souss al-Aqsa, la correspondence politique de la maison d’Illigh, 1821-1894*. Paris-Casablanca: C.N.R.S et Toubkal, 1988.

Epalza, Míkel. “Moriscos y andalusíes en Túnez durante el siglo XVII.” *Al-Andalus* 34 (1969): 247-327.

Falconbridge, Alexander. *An Account of the Slave Trade on the Coast of Africa.* London: J. Phillips, 1788.

Falola, Toyin. *The Political Economy of a Pre-colonial African State: Ibadan, 1830-1900*. Ile-Ife: University of Ife Press, 1984.

Feinberg, Harvey. *Africans and Europeans in West Africa: Elminans and Dutchmen on the Gold Coast During the Eighteenth Century*. Philadelphia: American Philosophical Society, 1989.

--------. “There Was an Elmina Note, But...” *International Journal of African Historical Studies* 9 (1976): 618–630.

Fisher, Humphrey J. *Slavery in the History of Muslim Black Africa*. New York: New York University Press, 2001.

--------. "A Muslim William Wilberforce? The Sokoto Jihad as Anti-Slavery Crusade: An Enquiry into Historical Causes." In *De la traite a l'esclavage du XV au XIXe siècle: Actes du Colloque Internationiale sur la traite des Noirs*, volume II, edited by Serge Daget, 537-55. Nantes: CRHMA, 1985.

Fleet, Kate. *European and Islamic Trade in the Early Ottoman State: The Merchants of Genoa and Turkey*. Cambridge: Cambridge University Press, 1999.

Fontenay, Michel. "Il mercato maltese degli schiavi al tempo dei Cavalieri di San Giovanni." *Quaderni Storici* 107 (2001): 391-414.

--------. "L'esclave galérien dans la Méditerranée des Temps Modernes." In *Figures de l'esclave au Moyen-Age et dans le monde moderne: actes de la table ronde*, edited by Henri Bresc, 115-142. Paris: Éditions L'Harmattan, 1996.

--------. "Esclaves et/ou captifs: préciser les concepts." In *Le commerce des captifs*, 15-24.

--------. "Le Maghreb barbaresque et l'esclavage méditerranéen aux XVIe et XVIIe siècles." *Cahiers de Tunisie* 44, 3–4 (1991): 17-43.

Freller, Thomas. "'The Shining of the Moon' – The Mediterranean Tour of Muhammad ibn Uthman, Envoy of Morocco, in 1782." *Journal of Mediterranean Studies (Malta)* 12 (2002): 307-26.

Friedman, Ellen G. "Christian Captives at 'Hard Labour' in Algiers, 16th to 18th Centuries." *International Journal of African Historical Studies* 13 (1980): 616-32.

--------. *Spanish Captives in North Africa in the Early Modern Age*. Madison: University of Wisconsin Press, 1983.

Fuglestad, Finn. "Révolte des Touareg du Niger (1916-17)." *Cahiers d'Études Africaines* 13, 49 (1973): 82-120.

Fuller, Francis C. *A Vanished Dynasty: Ashanti*. London: Frank Cass, 1968 [1921].

Fynn, John K. *Asante and its Neighbors, 1700-1807*. London: Longman, 1971.

Gallois, William. *A History of Violence in the Early Algerian Colony*. New York: Palgrave Macmillan, 2013.

Garcés, Maria A. *Cervantes in Algiers: A Captive's Tale*. Nashville: Vanderbilt University Press, 2002.

García, Arenal M. *Ahmad al-Mansur: The Beginning of Modern Morocco*. Oxford: Oneworld Publications, 2009.

García Figueras, Tomás and Carlos Rodríguez, Joulia Saint-Cy. *Larache: datos para su historia en el siglo XVII.* Madrid: Instituto de Estudios Africanos, 1972.

Gellner, Ernest. *Saints of the Atlas*. London: Weidenfeld and Nicolson, 1969.

Gibbs, Sarah. "Post-War Reconstruction in Mozambique: Reframing Children's Experience of War and Healing." *Disasters* 18 (1994): 268-300.

Gibling, James. "Pawning, Politics and Matriliny in Northeastern Tanzania." In *Pawnship, Slavery, and Colonialism in Africa,* edited by Paul E. Lovejoy and Toyin Falola, 239-266. Trenton: Africa World Press, 2003.

Gomez, Michael. *Pragmatism in the Age of Jihad*. New York: Cambridge University Press, 1992.

Gourdin, Philippe. *Tabarka: histoire et archéologie d'un préside espagnol et d'un comptoir génois en terre africaine. XVe-XVIIIe siècle.* Rome: École Française de Rome, 2008.

Graham IV, Franklin. "Abductions, Kidnappings and Killings in the Sahel and Sahara." *Review of African Political Economy* 38, 130 (2011): 587-604.

"Great Britain and the Barbary States in the Eighteenth Century." *Historical Research* 29,79 (1956): 87-107.

Gros, Jules. *Voyages, Aventures et Captivité de J. Bonnat chez les Achantis*. Paris: Plon and Nourrit, 1884.

Guilfoyle, Douglas, ed. *Modern Piracy: Legal Challenges and Responses*. Northampton, MA: Edward Elgar, 2013.

--------. "Piracy off Somalia: UN Security Resolution 1816 and IMO Regional Counter-Piracy Efforts." *International and Comparative Law Quarterly* 57 (2008): 690-695.

Hajji, Mohamed and M. al-Akhdar, ed. trans. *Wasf afriqiya li al-Hasan Ibn Muhammad al-Wazan al-ma'ruf bi Jan Leon al-afriqi*, 3 vols. Rabat: al-sharika al-maghribya li-dur al-nashr, 1980.

Hall, Bruce S. *A History of Race in Muslim West Africa 1600-1960*. Cambridge: Cambridge University Press, 2011.

--------. "The Question of 'Race' in Pre-colonial Southern Sahara." *Journal of North African Studies* 10 (2005): 339-367.

-------- and Charles C. Stewart. "The Historic 'Core Curriculum' and the Book Market in Islamic West Africa." In *Trans-Saharan Book Trade, The Trans-Saharan Book Trade, Manuscript Culture, Arabic Literacy and Intellectual History in Muslim Africa*, edited by Graziano Krätli and Ghislaine Lydon, 109-74. Leiden: Brill, 2011.

Hallaq, Wael B. *The Origins and Evolution of Islamic Law*. Cambridge: Cambridge University Press, 2005.

Hansen, Stig J. "The Dynamics of Somali Piracy." *Studies in Conflict & Terrorism* 35 (2012): 523-30.

Hanson, John. *Migration, Jihad, and Muslim Authority in West Africa*. Bloomington: Indiana University Press, 1996.

Hardt, Michael and Antonio Negri. *Commonwealth*. Cambridge: Belknap Press of Harvard University, 2009.

Hashim, Allice Bettis. *The Fallen State: Dissonance, Dictatorship and Death in Somalia*. Lanham: University Press of America, 1997.

Hawthorne, Walter. "The Production of Slaves where there was no State: The Guinea-Bissau Region, 1450-1815." *Slavery and Abolition* 20 (1999): 97-124.

Heers, Jaques. *The Barbary Corsairs: Warfare in the Mediterranean, 1480-1580*. Barnsley: Greenhill Books, 2003.

Hershenzon, Daniel. "Plaintes et menaces réciproques: captivité et violence religieuses dans la Méditerranée du XVIIe siècle." In *Les Musulmans dans l'histoire de l'Europe. Tome 2. Passages et contacts en Méditerranée*, edited by Jocelyne Dakhlia and Wolfgang Kaiser, 441-460. Paris: Albin Michel, 2013.

Hiskett, Mervyn. *The Sword of Truth: The Life and Times of the Shehu Usuman dan Fodio*. New York: Oxford University Press, 1973.

Hoexter, Miriam. *Endowments, Rulers and Community, Waqf al Haramayn in Ottoman Algiers*. Leiden: Brill, 1998.

Hobsbawm, Eric. *Social Bandits and Primitive Rebels*. Glencoe, Ill.: Free Press, 1960)

Hogendorn, Jan. "Slaves as Money in the Sokoto Caliphate." In *Credit, Currencies and Culture: African Financial Institutions in Historical Per-*

spective, edited by Endre Stiansen and Jane Guyer, 56-71. Stockholm: Nordiska Afrikainstitutet, 1999.

Holman, James. *Travels in Madeira, Sierra Leone, Teneriffe, St. Jago, Cape Coast, Fernando Po, Princes Island, Etc., Etc*, 2nd ed. London: George Routledge, 1840.

Hopley, Russell. "The Ransoming of Prisoners in Medieval North Africa and Andalusia: An Analysis of the Legal Framework." *Medieval Encounters* 15 (2009): 337-54.

Hopkins, A. G. "Economic Imperialism in West Africa: Lagos, 1880–1892." *Economic History Review* 21 (1968): 580–606.

Hunwick, John, trans. and ed. *Shari'a in Songhay: The Replies of al-Maghili to the Questions of Askia al-hājj Muhammad.* Oxford: Oxford University Press, 1985.

--------. "Islamic Law and Polemics over Race and Slavery in North and West Africa. 16th-19th Century)." In *Slavery and Islamic Middle East*, edited by Shaun E. Marmon, 43-68. Princeton: Markus Wiener, 1999.

--------. "Al-Maghili and the Jews of Tuwat: The Demise of a Community." *Studia Islamica* 61 (1985): 155-83.

-------- and Fatima Harrak, eds. *Mi'raj al-su'ud: Ahmad Baba's Replies on Slavery*. Rabat: Institut des Etudes Africaines, Université Mohamed V, 2000.

Ibaba, S. Ibaba. "Alienation and Militancy in the Niger Delta: Hostage Taking and the Dilemma of the Nigerian State." *African Journal on Conflict Resolution* 8,2 (2008): 11-34

Ikelegbe, Augustine. "Beyond the Threshold of Civil Struggle: Youth Militancy and the Militiaization of the Resource Conflict in the Niger Delta Region of Nigeria." *African Study Monographs* 27, 3 (2006): 87-122.

Ingriis, Mohammed H. "The History of Somali Piracy: From Classical Piracy to Contemporary Piracy, c.1801-2011." *The Northern Mariner* 23 (2013): 239-66.

Inikori, Joseph. "The Struggle against the Transatlantic Slave Trade: the Role of the State." In Diouf, *Fighting the Slave Trade*, 170-98.

Isichei, Elizabeth. *Voices of the Poor in Africa*. Rochester: University of Rochester Press, 2004.

Jablonski, Ryan S. and Steven Oliver, "The Political Economy of Plunder: Economic Opportunity and Modern Piracy." *Journal of Conflict Resolution* 54 (2012): 682-708.

Jackson, James G. *An Account of the Empire of Morocco and the Districts of Suse and Tafilelt*. London: Frank Cass, 1968 [1814].

James, Alan. *The Navy and Government in Early Modern France, 1572-1661*. Suffolk, UK: Royal Historical Society, 2004.

Johnson, Samuel. *The History of the Yorubas from the Earliest to the Beginning of the British Protectorate*. Lagos: CSS Book, 1976 [1921].

Johnston, H.A.S. *The Fulani Empire of Sokoto*. London: Oxford University Press, 1967.

Juan Ginés, Vernet. "La embajada de al-Ghassani. 1690-1691." *Al-Andalus* 18 (1953): 109-131.

Kaiser, Wolfgang. "L'économie de la rançon en Méditerranée occidentale. XVIe-XVIIe siècle)." In *Ricchezza dal mare, secc. XIII-XVIII*, Vol. 2, edited by Simonetta Cavaciocchi, 689-701. Florence: Le Monnier, 2006.

----------. "La excepción permanente. Actores, visibilidad y asimetrías en los intercambios comerciales entre los países europeos y el Magreb (siglos XVI-XVII)." In *Circulación de personas e intercambios en el Mediterráneo y en el Atlántico (siglos XVI, XVII, XVIII):* edited by José Antonio Martínez Torres, 171-189. Madrid: CSIC, 2008.

---------, ed. *Le commerce des captifs: les intermédiaires dans l'échange et le rachat des prisonniers en Méditerranée, XVe-XVIIIe siècle*. Rome: École Française de Rome, 2008.

----------. "Zones de transit. Lieux, temps, modalités du rachat de captifs en Méditerranée." In *Les Musulmans dans l'histoire de l'Europe. Tome 2. Passages et contacts en Méditerranée*, edited by Jocelyne Dakhlia and Wolfgang Kaiser, 251-272. Paris: Albin Michel, 2013.

---------. "Asymétries méditerranéens: présence et circulation de marchands entre Alger, Tunis et Marseille." In *Les Musulmans dans l'histoire de l'Europe*, vol. 1: *Une integration invisible*, edited by Jocelyne Dakhlia and Bernard Vincent, 417–442. Paris: Albin Michel, 2011.

Kaplan, Robert D. "The Coming of Anarchy." In *The Geopolitics Reader*, edited by Gearóid Ó Tuathail, Simon Dalby and Paul Routledge, 188-196. London: Routledge, 2006.

Kea, Ray. *Settlements, Trade and Politics in the Seventeenth-Century Gold Coast*. Baltimore: John Hopkins University, 1982.

Keating, Thomas. "The Political Economy of Somali Piracy." *SAIS Review of International Affairs* 33 (2013): 85-91.

Keenan, Jeremy. *The Dying Sahara: US Imperialism and Terror in Africa*. London: Pluto, 2012.

--------."Uranium Goes Critical in Niger: Tuareg Rebellions Threaten Sahelian Conflagration." *Review of African Political Economy* 31, 117 (2008): 449-66.

Kesteloot, Lillian. *Da Monzon de Segou: Epopee Bambara*, 4 Vols. Paris: Fernand Nathan, 1972.

Klein, Martin. "The Slave Trade and Decentralized Societies." *Journal of African History* 42 (2001): 49-65.

--------. *Slavery and Colonial Rule in French West Africa*. Cambridge: Cambridge University Press, 1998.

--------. "Social and Economic Factors in the Muslim Revolution in Senegambia." *Journal of African History* 13 (1972): 419–441.

--------. *Islam and Imperialism in Senegal*. Stanford: Stanford University Press, 1968.

Kopytoff, Igor and Suzanne Miers. "African 'Slavery' as an Institution of Marginality." In *Slavery in Africa: Historical and Anthropological Perspectives*, edited by Miers and Kopytoff, 3-81. Madison: University of Wisconsin Press, 1977.

Lambert, Sheila, ed. *House of Commons Sessional Papers*. Wilmington, DE: Scholarly Resources, 1975.

Larquié, Claude. "Captifs chrétiens et esclaves maghrébins au XVIIIe siècle: Une tentative de comparaison." In *Captius i esclaus a l'antiguitat i al món modern. XIXe colloque du GIREA, Palma de Mallorca 1991*, edited by Gonçal López Nadal and María Luisa Sánchez León, 347-364. Naples: Jovene Editore, 1996.

Last, Murray. "Reform in West Africa: The Jihad Movements of the Nineteenth Century." In *History of West Africa*, vol. 2, edited by J. F. Ajayi and Michael Crowder, 1-15. London: Longman, 1974.

--------. *The Sokoto Caliphate*. London: Longmans, 1967.

-------- and M.A. Al-Hajj, "Attempts at Defining a Muslim in 19th Century

Hausaland and Bornu." *Journal of the Historical Society of Nigeria* 3 (1965): 231–49.

Lavisse, Ernest. "Sur les galères du roi." *Revue de Paris* 4, 22 (1897): 225-262.

Law, Robin, ed. *The English in West Africa: The Local Correspondence of the Royal African Company of England, 1681-1699*, 3 vols. Oxford: Oxford University Press, 1997-2007.

--------. "Legal and Illegal Enslavement in West Africa in the Context of the Trans-Atlantic Slave Trade." in *Ghana in Africa and the World: Essays in Honor of Adu Boahen*, edited by Toyin Falola, 513-33. Trenton: Africa World Press, 2003.

--------, ed. *From Slave Trade to 'Legitimate' Commerce: The Commercial Transition in Nineteenth Century West Africa.* Cambridge: Cambridge University Press, 1995.

--------. "'Here is No Resisting the Country': The Realities of Power in Afro-European Relations on the West African 'Slave Coast,'" *Itinerário* 10, 2 (1994): 50-64.

--------. *The Slave Coast of West Africa, 1550-1750: The Impact of the Atlantic Slave Trade on an African Society.* Oxford: Clarendon, 1991.

-------- and Paul E. Lovejoy, eds. *The Biography of Mahommah Gardo Baquaqua: His Passage from Slavery to Freedom in Africa and America.* Princeton: Markus Weiner, 2001.

Lebrun, François. "Turcs, barbaresques, musulmans, vus par les français du XVIIe siècles, d'après le 'Dictionnaire' de Furetière." *Cahiers de Tunisie* 44, 3–4 (1991): 69–74.

Lecocq, Baz and Paul Schrijver. "The War on Terror in a Haze of Dust: Potholes and Pitfalls onthe Saharan Front." *Journal of Contemporary African Studies* 25 (2007): 141-66.

Leiner, Frederic. *The End of Barbary Terror: America's 1815 War Against the Pirates of North Africa.* Oxford: Oxford University Press, 2007.

Little, Peter D. *Somalia: Economy without State.* Oxford: James Currey, 2003.

Lofkrantz, Jennifer. "Intellectual Discourse in the Sokoto Caliphate: The Triumvirate's Opinions on the Issue of Ransoming, ca.1810." *International Journal of African Historical Studies* 45 (2012): 385-401.

--------. "Protecting Freeborn Muslims: The Sokoto Caliphate's Attempts to Prevent Illegal Enslavement and its Acceptance of the Strategy of Ransoming." *Slavery & Abolition* 32 (2011): 109-127.

--------. "Ransoming Captives in the Sokoto Caliphate." In *Islam, Slave and Diaspora,* edited by Behnaz Mirzai, Ismael Montana and Paul E. Lovejoy, 125-37. Trenton: Africa World Press, 2009.

-------- and Paul Lovejoy, "Maintaining Network Boundaries: Islamic Law and Commerce from Sahara to Guinea Shores." *Slavery & Abolition* 36 (2015): 211-232.

-------- and Olatunji Ojo. "Slavery, Freedom, and Failed Ransom Negotiations in West Africa, 1730-1900." *Journal of African History* 53 (2012): 25-44.

Loimeier, Roman. *Between Social Skills and Marketable Skills: The Politics of Islamic Education in 20th Century Zanzibar*. Leiden: Brill, 2009.

Lomas Cortés, Manuel. "Les galériens du Roi Catholique: esclaves, forçats et rameurs salariés dans les escadres de Philippe III. 1598-1621." *Cahiers des Annales de Normandie* 36 (2011): 111-124.

Loualich, Fatiha. "In the Regency of Algiers: The human Side of the Algerine Corso." in *Trade and Cultural Exchange in the Early Modern Mediterranean, Braudel's Maritime Legacy*, edited by Maria Fusaro, Colin Heywood and Mohamed-Salah Omro, 69-96. New York: I. B. Tauris: 2010.

Lourido Díaz, Ramón. "La obra redentora del sultán marroquí Sīdī Muḥammad b. 'Abd Allāh entre los cautivos musulmanes en Europa siglo XVIII." *Cuadernos de Historia del Islam* 11 (1984): 138-183.

Lovejoy, Paul E. *Jihad in West Africa during the Age of Revolutions*. Athens: Ohio University Press, 2016.

--------. *Transformations in Slavery. A History of Slavery in Africa,* 3rd ed. Cambridge: Cambridge University Press, 2012.

--------. "The Context of Enslavement in West Africa: Ahmad Baba and the Ethics of Slavery." In *Slaves, Subjects and Subversives: Blacks in Colonial Latin America,* edited by Jane Landers and Barry Robinson, 9-38. Albuquerque: University of New Mexico, 2006.

--------. "Autobiography and Memory: Gustavus Vassa, alias Olaudah Equiano, the African." *Slavery and Abolition* 27 (2006): 317-47

--------. "Islam, Slavery, and Political Transformation in West Africa: Constraints on the Trans-Atlantic Slave Trade," *Outre-Mers* 89, 336/37 (2002): 247-282.

--------. "The Bello-Clapperton Exchange: The Sokoto Jihad and the Trans-Atlantic Slave Trade." In *The Desert Shore: Literatures of the Sahel*, edited by Christopher Wise, 201-28. Boulder CO: Lynne Reiner Publishers, 2001.

--------. "Murgu: The Wages of Slavery in the Sokoto Caliphate." *Slavery and Abolition* 14 (1993): 168-85.

--------. "Commercial Sectors in the Economy of the Nineteenth-Century Central Sudan: The TransSaharan Trade and the Desert-Side Salt Trade." *African Economic History* 13 (1984): 85-116.

-------- and David Richardson, "African Agency and the Liverpool Slave Trade." In *Liverpool and Transatlantic Slavery,* edited by David Richardson, Suzanne Schwarz and Anthony Tibbles, 43-65. Liverpool: Liverpool University Press, 2007.

--------. "'Horrid Hole': Royal Authority, Commerce and Credit at Bonny, 1690-1840." *Journal of African History* 45 (2004): 363-92.

--------. "Anglo-Efik Relations and Protection against the Illegal Enslavement at Old Calabar, 1740-1807." In Diouf, *Fighting the Slave Trade*, 101-23

--------. "Trust, Pawnship, and Atlantic History: The Institutional Foundations of the Old Calabar Slave Trade." *American Historical Review* 104 (1999): 333–55.

--------. "The Initial 'Crisis of Adaptation': The Impact of the British Abolition on the Atlantic Slave Trade in West Africa, 1808-1820." In Law, *From Slave Trade to 'Legitimate' Commerce*, 32-56.

Lydon, Ghislaine. "Islamic Legal Culture and Slave-Ownership Contests in Nineteenth-Century Sahara." *International Journal of African Historical Studies* 40 (2007): 391-439.

Martin, Meredith and Gillian Weiss. "'Turks' on Display during the Reign of Louis XIV." *L'Esprit Créateur* 53, 4 (2013): 98–112.

Martínez Torres, José Antonio. *Prisioneros de los infieles: vida y rescate de los cautivos cristianos en el Mediterráneo musulmán (siglos XVI-XVII).* Barcelona: Ediciones Bellaterra, 2004.

Masson, Paul. *Les Galères de France, 1481-1781: Marseille, port de guerre*. Paris: Hachette, 1938.

Masquelier, Adeline. *Women and Islamic Revival in a West African Town*. Bloomington: Indiana University Press, 2009.

Matar, Nabil. *Turks, Moors and Englishmen in the Age of Discovery*. New York: Columbia University Press, 1999.

--------. "English Accounts of Captivity in North Africa and the Middle East: 1577-1625." *Renaissance Quarterly* 54 (2001): 553-572.

----------. *Britain and Barbary, 1589-1689*. Gainesville: University Press of Florida, 2005.

----------. "Piracy and Captivity in the Early Modern Mediterranean: The Perspective from Barbary." in *Pirates? The Politics of Plunder, 1550-1650*, edited by Claire Jowett, 56-73. Basingstoke: Palgrave Macmillan, 2007.

--------. *British Captives from the Mediterranean to the Atlantic*, 1563-1760. Leiden: Brill, 2014.

Mathiex, Jean. "Trafic et Prix de l'Homme en Méditerranée aux XVIIe et XVIIIe siècles." *Annales E.S.C.* 9 (1954): 157-64.

Mazur, Peter A. "Combating 'Mohammedan Indecency': The Baptism of Muslim Slaves in Spanish Naples, 1563-1667." *Journal of Early Modern History* 13 (2009): 25-48.

McCaskie, T.C. "Denkyira in the Making of Asante." *Journal of African History* 48 (2007): 1-25.

McDougall, E. Ann. "In Search of a Desert-Edge Perspective: The Sahara-Sahel and the Atlantic Trade, c.1815-1890." In Law, *From Slave Trade to Legitimate Commerce*, 215-39.

McGowan, Winston. "The Development of European Relations with Futa Jallon and the Foundation of French Colonial Rule 1794-1897." Ph.D. dissertation, University of London, 1978.

McWilliam, James O. *Medical History of the Expedition to the Niger, During the Years 1841-1842.* London: John Churchill, 1843.

Meillassoux, Claude. *The Anthropology of Slavery: The Womb of Iron and Gold.* trans. Alide Dasnois. University of Chicago Press, 1991.

Miura, Toru and John E. Philips, eds. *Slave Elites in the Middle East and Africa: A Comparative Study*. London: Kegan Paul, 2000.

Mohamed, H. Mohamed. *Between Caravan and Sultan: The Bayruk of Southern Morocco--A Study in History and Identity.* Leiden-Boston: Brill, 2012.

--------. "Africanists and Africans of the Maghrib II: Casualties of Secularity." *Journal of North African Studies* 17 (2012): 409-431.

Montgomery, Watt W. "Islamic Conceptions of the Holy War." In *Holy War*, edited by Thomas P. Murphy, 141-56. Columbus: Ohio State University Press, 1976.

Morton, Fred. "Pawning and Slavery on the Kenya Coast: The Miji Kenda Case." In Lovejoy and Falola, *Pawnship, Slavery, and Colonialism in Africa,* 239-66.

Moureau, François. *Captifs en Méditerranée. XVI-XVIIIe siècles): Histoires, Récits et Légendes*. Paris: Presses de l'Universite Sorbonne, 2008.

Mouser, Bruce. "'Walking Caravans' of Nineteenth Century Fuuta Jaloo, Western Africa." *Mande Studies* 12 (2010): 19-104.

--------. "Rebellion, Marronage and Jihad: Strategies of Resistance to Slavery on the Sierra Leone Coast, c.1783-1796." *Journal of African History* 48 (2007): 27-44.

--------, ed. *Journal of James Watt, Expedition to Timbo Capital of the Fula Empire in 1794*. Madison: University of Wisconsin Press, 1994.

Mudimbe, V.Y. *The Invention of Africa: Gnosis, Philosophy and the Order of Knowledge.* Bloomington: Indiana University Press, 1988.

Murphy, Martin. *Somalia: The New Barbary? Piracy and Islam in the Horn of Africa.* New York: Columbia University Press, 2011.

Naanen, B. "The Niger Delta and the National Question." In *The Management of the National Question in Nigeria*, edited by Eghosa Osaghae and Ebere Onwudiwe, 197-206. Okada: Igbinedion University Press, 2007.

Newitt, Malyn, ed. *The Portuguese in West Africa, 1415–1670: A Documentary History.* Cambridge: Cambridge University Press, 2010.

Newson, Linda A. "The Slave-Trading Accounts of Manoel Batista Peres, 1613–1619: Double-Entry Bookkeeping in Cloth Money." *Accounting History* 18 (2013): 343–365.

Niang, Amy. "Le 'boom' des saisons dans l'espace sahélo-saharien: Proto-révolution, désintégrations et reconfigurations sociopolitiques." *Afrique Contemporaine* 245 (2013): 53-69.

--------. “Ransoming, Compensatory Violence, and Humanitarianism in the Sahel,” *Alternatives, Global, Local, Political* 39 (2014): 231-251.

Nicolas, Guy. “Détours d’une conversion collective. Ouverture à l’Islam d’un bastion soudanais de résistance à une guerre sainte.” *Archives de sciences sociales des religions* 48 (1979): 83–105.

Nissanke, Machiko and Alice Sindzingre. “Institutional Foundations for Shared Growth in Sub-Saharan Africa.” *African Development Review* 18 (2006): 353-91.

Norris, H.T. *The Arab Conquest of the Western Sahara, Studies of the Historical Events, Religious Beliefs and Social Customs which Made the Remotest Sahara a Part of the Arab World*. London: Longman, 1986.

Northrup, David. *Africa's Discovery of Europe: 1450-1850*. Oxford: Oxford University Press, 2002.

O’Brien, D. B. C., J. Dunn and R. Rathbone, eds. *Contemporary West African States*. Cambridge: Cambridge University Press, 1989.

Odoemene, Akachi. “‘Agony in the Garden’: Incongruity of Governance and the Travails of Port Harcourt city, Niger Delta, Nigeria, 1912-2010.” *Africana: A Journal of Ideas on Africa and the African Diaspora* 5 (2011): 108-139.

--------. “Fighting Corruption without the State: Civil Society Agency and the ‘Otokoto Saga’” *Journal of Historical Sociology* 25 (2012): 475-503.

--------. “Social Consequences of Environmental Change in the Niger Delta of Nigeria.” *Journal of Sustainable Development* 4 (2011): 123-135.

Ojo, Olatunji. “Amazing Struggle: Dasalu, Global Yoruba Networks, and the Fight against Slavery.” *Atlantic Studies* 12 (2015): 5-25.

--------. “The Atlantic Slave Trade and Local Ethics of Slavery in Yoruba-land.” *African Economic History* 41 (2013): 75-102.

--------. “‘[I]n Search of their Relations, To Set at Liberty as Many as They Had the Means”: Ransoming Captives in Nineteenth Century Yorubaland.” *Nordic Journal of African Studies* 19 (2010): 58-76.

--------. “*Èmú* (Àmúyá): The Yoruba Institution of Panyarring or Seizure for Debt.” *African Economic History* 35 (2007): 31-58.

Onovo, Ogbonna. “Combating the Crimes of Armed Robbery and Kidnapping in the South-East and South-South Zones of Nigeria: Strategies, Challenges and Prospects.” *Igbinedion Journal of Diplomacy and Strategy* 1 (2009): 12-21.

Oroge, E. A. "The Institution of Slavery in Yorubaland with Particular Reference to the Nineteenth Century." Ph.D. thesis, Birmingham, 1971.

Osumah, Oarhe and Iro Aghedo. "Who Wants to be a Millionaire? Nigerian Youths and the Commodification of Kidnapping." *Review of African Political Economy* 38, 128 (2011): 277-87.

Owenvbiugie, R.O. and Olumese, H.A. "Kidnapping: A Threat to Entrepreneurship in Nigeria." *Journal of Education, Health and Technology Research* 1 (2011): 67-73.

Owusu-Mensa, Koffi. "Prince Owusu-Ansa of Asante, 1823-1884." *Journal of the Historical Society of Nigeria* 12, 3-4 (1978): 9-22.

Pálffy, Geza. "Ransom Slavery along the Ottoman-Hungarian Frontier in the Sixteenth and Seventeenth Centuries." In *Ransom Slavery along the Ottoman Borders (Early Fifteenth-Early Eighteenth Centuries)*, edited by Dávid, Géza and Pál Fodor, 35-85. Leiden: Brill, 2007.

Park, Mungo. *Travels in the Interior Districts of Africa: Performed Under the Direction and Patronage of the African Association, in the Years 1795, 1796, and 1797*, 5th ed. London: W. Bulmer, 1807.

Peabody, Sue. *"There Are No Slaves in France": The Political Culture of Race and Slavery in the Ancien Régime*. New York: Oxford University Press, 1996.

Penz, Charles. *Les Captifs français du Maroc au XVIIe siècle, 1577-1699.* Rabat: Imprimerie Officielle, 1944.

Percy, Sarah and Anja Shortland. "The Business of Piracy in Somalia." *Journal of Strategic Studies* 36 (2013): 541-78.

Perinbam, B. Marie. "Social Relations in the Trans-Saharan and Western Sudanese trade: An Overview." *Comparative Studies in Society and History* 15 (1973): 416-36.

Peskin, Lawrence A. *Captives and Countrymen: Barbary Slaves and the American Public 1785-1816*. Baltimore: The Johns Hopkins University Press, 2009.

Planas, Natividad. "La frontière franchissable: normes et pratiques dans les échanges entre le royaume de Majorque et les terres d'Islam au XVIIe siècle." *Revue d'histoire moderne et contemporaine* 48, 2 (2001): 123-47.

----------. "Conflits de compétence aux frontières. Le contrôle de la circulation des homes et des marchandises dans le royaume de Majorque au XVIIe siècle." *Cromohs* 8 (2003): 1-14.

Pope, David. "The Wealth and Social Aspirations of Liverpool's Slave Merchants of the Second Half of the Eighteenth Century." In *Liverpool and Transatlantic Slavery*, edited by David Richardson, Suzanne Schwarz and Anthony Tibbles, 164-226. Liverpool: Liverpool University Press, 2007.

Postma, Johannes M. *The Dutch in the Atlantic Slave Trade, 1600-1815.* Cambridge: Cambridge University Press, 1990.

Ramseyer, Frederick and J. Kühne. *Four Years in Ashantee*. New York: Robert Carter, 1875.

Rathbone, Richard. "Some Thoughts on Resistance to Enslavement in Africa." *Slavery & Abolition* 6 (1985): 11-22.

Reese, Scott. "Islam in Africa/Africans and Islam." *Journal of African History* 55 (2014): 17-26.

Ressel, Marcus. "Conflicts Between Early Modern European States about Rescuing their Own Subjects from Barbary Captivity." *Scandinavian Journal of History* 36 (2011): 1-22.

Reynolds, Edward. *Trade and Economic Change on the Gold Coast, 1807-1874*. London: Longman, 1974.

Reynolds, Pamela. *Traditional Healers and Childhood in Zimbabwe*. Athens: Ohio University Press, 1996.

Rice, Allan. *Radical Narratives of the Black Atlantic*. London: Continuum, 2003.

Richardson, David. "Shipboard Revolts, African Authority, and the African Slave Trade." *William & Mary Quarterly* 58 (2001): 69-92.

Riley, James. *An Authentic Narrative of the Loss of the American Brig Commerce*. London: Richard Philips, 1822.

Riley, James. *Suffering in Africa: Captain Riley's Narrative*, edited by Gordon Evans. New York: Clarkson N. Potters Publishers, 1965.

Roach, J. Ashley. "Countering Piracy off Somalia: International Law and International Institutions." *American Journal of International Law* 104 (2010): 397-416.

Roberts, Richard. *Warriors, Merchants and Slaves: The State and the Economy in the Middle Niger Valley, 1700-1914*. Stanford: Stanford University Press, 1987.

-------. "Production and Reproduction of Warrior States: Segu Bambara and Segu Tokolor, c.1712-1890." *The International Journal of African Historical Studies* 13 (1980): 389-419.

Robinson, Ronald. "The Partition of Africa." In *The New Cambridge Modern History vol. 11: Material Progress and World-wide Problems 1870–1898*, edited by F. H. Hinsley, 593-640. Cambridge: Cambridge University Press, 1962.

Rothman, E. Nathalie. "Becoming Venetian: Conversion and Transformation in the Seventeenth-Century Mediterranean." *Mediterranean Historical Review* 21 (2006): 39-75.

Rushforth, Brett. *Bonds of Alliance: Indigenous and Atlantic Slaveries in New France*. Chapel Hill, NC: UNC Press Books, 2012.

Ryder, Allan F.C. *Benin and the Europeans 1485-1897*. London: Longman, 1969.

Sanderson, F.E. "The Liverpool Delegates and Sir William Dolben's Bill." *Transactions of the Historic Society of Lancashire and Cheshire* 124 (1972): 57-84

Sarti, Raffaella. "Bolognesi schiavi dei 'Turchi' e schiavi 'turchi' a Bologna tra Cinque e Settecento: alterità etnico-religiosa e riduzione in schiavitù." *Quaderni Storici* 107 (2001): 437-473.

Schaub, Jean-Frédéric. *Les juifs du roi d'Espagne*. Paris: Hachette Littératures, 1999.

Schroeter, Daniel J. *The Sultan's Jew, Morocco and the Sephardi World*. Stanford: Stanford University Press, 2002.

--------. *Merchants of Essaouira: Urban Society and Imperialism in Southern Morocco, 1844-1866*. Cambridge: Cambridge University Press, 1988.

Schwarz, Suzanne, ed., *Slave Captain: the Career of James Irving in the Liverpool Slave Trade*. Liverpool: Liverpool University Press, 2008.

Scott, James. *The Art of Not Being Governed*. Princeton: Princeton University Press, 2009.

Shapiro, Michael J. "That Obscure Object of Violence: Logistics, Desire, War." *Alternatives* 17 (1992): 453-77.

Shumway, Rebecca. *The Fante and the Transatlantic Slave Trade*. Rochester: University of Rochester Press, 2011.

Smaldone, Joseph. *Warfare in the Sokoto Caliphate: Historical and Sociological Perspectives*. Cambridge: Cambridge University Press, 1977.

Smith, M. G. *Government in Kano*. Boulder CO: Westview Press, 1997.

Smith, William. *A New Voyage to Guinea*, 2nd ed. London: John Nourse, 1745.

Sparks, Randy. *Where the Negroes Are Masters*. Cambridge, MA: Harvard University Press, 2014.

--------. *The Two Princes of Calabar: An Eighteenth-Century Atlantic Odyssey.* Cambridge MA: Harvard University Press, 2004.

Stanley, Henry M. *Coomassie and Magdala: The Story of Two British Campaigns in Africa*. London: Sampson Low, 1874.

Stella, Alessandro. *Histoires d'esclaves dans la Péninsule Ibérique*. Paris: Éditions EHESS, 2000.

Stillman, Norman. *The Jews of Arab Lands: A History and Sourcebook.* Philadephia: The Jewish Publication Society, 1998):

Stilwell, Sean. *Paradoxes of Power: The Kano 'Mamluks' and Male Royal Slavery in the Sokoto Caliphate, 1804–1903.* Portsmouth, NH: Heinemann, 2004.

Subrahmanyam, Sanjay. "Par-delà l'incommensurabilité: pour une histoire connectée des empires aux temps modernes." *Revue d'histoire moderne et contemporaine* 54.4 (2007): 34–53.

Substance of the Report Delivered by the Court of Directors of the Sierra Leone Company, to the General Court of Proprietors, on Thursday, March 27th, 1794. London: James Phillips, 1794.

Sunseri, Thaddeus. "Slave Ransoming in German East Africa, 1885-1922." *International Journal of African Historical Studies* 26 (1993): 481-511.

Taylor, Eric R. *If We Must Die: Shipboard Insurrections in the Era of the Atlantic Slave Trade.* Baton Rouge: Louisiana State University Press 2006.

Taylor, Raymond. "Of Disciples and Sultans: Power, Authority and Society in the Nineteenth-Century Mauritania Gebla." Ph.D. dissertation, University of Illinois, Urbana-Champaign, 1996.

Tayob, Abdulkader. *Islam in South Africa: Mosques, Imams and Sermons*. Gainesville: University of Florida Press, 1999.

Thompson, Ann. *Barbary and Enlightenment: European Attitudes Towards the Maghreb in the Eighteenth Century*. Leiden: Brill, 1987.

Thornton, John K. *Africa and Africans in the Formation of the Atlantic World, 1400-1680*. New York: Cambridge University Press, 1992.

Tocqueville, Alexis, ed. *De la colonie en Algérie*. Bruxelles: Complexe, 1841 [1988].

Tonwe, Daniel A., Godwin Uyi Ojo, and Iro Aghedo. "Spoils, Politics and Environmental Struggle in the Niger Delta Region of Nigeria." *Inkanyiso: Journal of Humanities and Social Sciences* 4 (2012): 37-48.

Tournier, Gaston. *Les Galères de France et les galériens protestants des XVIIe et XVIIIe siècles*, 3 vols. Cévennes: Musée du Désert, 1943.

Triaud, Jean Louis. "Kawsan: Analyse d'un discours politique (1916-1917)." In *Hommage à Edmond Bernus: Les Temps du Sahel*, edited by Y. Poncet, 149-172. Paris: Institut de recherche pour le développement, 1999.

Turco, Angeolo. "Sémantiques de la violence: Territoire, guerre et pouvoir en Afrique Mandingue." *Cahiers de Géographie du Québec* 51 (2007): 307-332.

Tzanelli, Rodanthi. "Capitalizing on Value: Towards a Sociological Understanding of Kidnapping." *Sociology* 40 (2006): 929-947.

Van Koningsveld, Pieter Sjoerd. "Muslim Slaves and Captives in Western Europe During the Late Middle Ages." *Islam & Christian Muslim Relations* 6 (1995): 5-23.

Varga, János J. "Ransoming Ottoman Slaves from Munich, 1688." In *Ransom Slavery along the Ottoman Borders (Early Fifteenth-Early Eighteenth Centuries*), edited by Dávid, Géza and Pál Fodor, 169-182. Leiden: Brill, 2007.

Veinstein, Gilles. "Les Capitulations franco-ottomanes de 1536: sont-elles encore controversables." In *Living in the Ottoman Ecumenical Community: Essays in Honour of Suraiya Faroqhi*, edited by Vera Costantini and Markus Koller, 71–88. Leidens: Brill, 2008.

Vitkus, Daniel J., ed. *Piracy, Slavery and Redemption: Barbary Captivity Narratives from Early Modern England*. New York: Columbia University Press, 2001.

Wadström, Carl B. *An Essay on Colonization, Particularly Applied to the Western Coast of Africa*. London: Darton and Harvey, 1795.

Walvin, James. "The Public Campaign in England against Slavery, 1787-1834." In *The Abolition of the Atlantic Slave Trade: Origins and Effects in Europe, Africa, and the Americas,* edited by David Eltis and James Walvin, 63-79. Madison: University of Wisconsin Press, 1981.

Ware III, Rudolph T. *The Walking Qu'ran, Islamic Education, Embodied Knowledge and History in West Africa*. Chapel Hill: University of North Carolina Press, 2014.

Watts, Michael. "Petro-Insurgency or Criminal Syndicate? Conflict & Violence in the Niger Delta." *Review of African Political Economy* 34,114 (2007): 637-60.

Watts, Michael, ed. *Curse of the Black Gold: 50 Years of Oil in the Niger Delta.* Brooklyn: Power House Books, 2008.

Webb, James L. A., Jr. *Desert Frontier: Ecological and Economic Change along the Western Sahel, 1600-1850***.** Madison: University of Wisconsin Press, 1995.

Weldemichael, Awet T. "Maritime Corporate Terrorism and its Consequences in the Western Indian Ocean Region: Waste Dumping, Illegal Fishing and Piracy in 21st Century Somalia." *Journal of the Indian Ocean Region* 8 (2012): 110-126.

Weiss, Gillian Lee. *Captives and Corsairs, France and Slavery in the Early Modern Mediterranean*. Stanford: Stanford University Press, 2011.

--------. "Infidels at the Oar: A Mediterranean Exception to France's Free Soil Principle." *Slavery and Abolition* 32 (2011): 397–412.

--------. "Barbary Captivity and the French Idea of Freedom." *French Historical Studies* 28 (2005): 231-64

Wilks, Ivor. *Asante in the Nineteenth Century: The Structure and Evolution of a Political Order*. Cambridge: Cambridge University Press, 1975.

Williams, Gomer. *History of the Liverpool Privateers and Letters of Marque, with an Account of the Liverpool Slave Trade*. London: William Heinemann, 1897.

Willis, John Ralph. *In the Path of Allah: The Passion of Al-Hajj 'Umar.* London: Frank Cass, 1989.

Winterbottom, Thomas. *An Account of the Native Africans in the Neighbourhood of Sierra Leone*. London: C. Whittingham, 1803.

Wolfson, Freda. "British Relations with the Gold Coast, 1843-1880." Ph.D. dissertation, University of London, 1950.

Wright, Richard. *Kidnap for Ransom: Resolving the Unthinkable*. Boca Raton, FL: Taylor & Francis, 2009.

Yarak, Larry. "The 'Elmina Note:' Myth and Reality in Asante-Dutch Relations." *History in Africa* 13 (1986): 363–382.

--------. "Elmina and Greater Asante in the Nineteenth century." *Africa* 56 (1986): 33-52.

Zenn, Jacob. "Boko Haram: Recruitment, Financing, and Arms Trafficking in the Lake Chad Region." *Combating Terrorism Center Sentinel* 7, 10 (2014): 5-9.

--------. "Boko Haram and the Kidnapping of the Chibok Schoolgirls." *Combating Terrorism Center Sentinel* 7, 6 (2014): 1-8.

Zysberg, André. "Un Audit rétrospectif: analyse du budget des galères de France entre 1669 et 1716." In *Histoire des familles, de la démographie et des comportements*, edited by Jean-Pierre Poussou and Isabelle Robin-Romero, 1063-1070. Paris: Presses de l'Université de Paris-Sorbonne, 2007.

--------. "Un Esclavage d'Etat: le recrutement des rameurs sur les galères de Louis XIV." In *Contraintes et libertés dans les sociétés méditerranées aux époque modernes et contemporanéennes, XVI*[e]*-XX*[e] *siècles*, edited by Andre Zysberg and Sadok Boubaker, 69-82. Tunis: Faculté des sciences humaines et sociales, Université de Caen, 2007.

--------. *Les Galériens: vies et destins de 60,000 forçats sur les galères de France, 1680-1748*. Paris: Editions du Seuil, 1987.

Notes on Contributors

Roy Doron is an Assistant Professor of History at Winston-Salem State University, where he examines the intersection of war, ethnicity and identity formation in post-colonial Africa, focusing on the Nigerian Civil War. His work has appeared in edited volumes, as well as the *Journal of Genocide Research* and *African Economic History*. He is a founding Managing Editor of the new *Journal of African Military History* as well as editor for H-Net's H-West Africa network. He is currently completing a comprehensive history of the Nigerian Civil War. He also works on heavy metal music in Africa. doronrs@wssu.edu

Daniel Hershenzon is an Assistant Professor in the Department of Literatures, Cultures, and Languages at the University of Connecticut. He is completing a book manuscript titled *Early Modern Spain and the Mediterranean: Captivity, Commerce, and Communication*. The book explores the entangled histories of Spain, Morocco and Ottoman Algiers, arguing that piracy, captivity, and redemption shaped the Mediterranean as a socially, politically, and economically integrated region. He has published articles on Arabic manuscripts and knowledge in early modern Spain in the *Journal of Early Modern History* and *Philological Encounters* and he has a forthcoming article in *Past and Present* on the early modern Mediterranean political economy of ransoming. daniel.hershenszon@uconn.edu

Abdi M. Kusow is Associate Professor of Sociology at Iowa State University. His research is primarily concerned with international migration, ethnic and racial inequality, social stigma, methodology, and African societies and the African diaspora. His research appeared in *Symbolic Interaction, Ethnic and Racial Studies, Journal of Migration and Ethnic Studies, Interna-*

tional Journal of Migration and Integration, and *Journal of Somali Studies*, among other peer-reviewed journals and book chapters. He is the editor of *Putting the Cart before the Horse: Contested Nationalism and the Crisis of the Nation-state in Somalia*, and with Stephanie Bjork, *From Mogadishu to Dixon: The Somali Diaspora in a Global Context*. His article "Contesting Stigma: On Goffman's Assumptions of Normative Order," *Symbolic Interaction* 27:179–97, 2004 appeared in the top 20 most read articles in *Symbolic Interaction* from 2005 to 2009. His most recent article, "Formula Narratives and the Making of Social Stratification," *Sociology of Race and Ethnicity* 1: 3: 409-423, 2015 won the 2015 David Maines Narrative Research Award. kusow@iastate.edu

Jennifer Lofkrantz is Visiting Associate Professor in the Department of History and the Program of Global and Regional Studies at St. Mary's College of California. She is a co-editor of this edited volume. She is the author of several articles and book chapters on ransoming in precolonial West Africa and is currently writing a book on ransoming in West Africa entitled *Scholars, Captives and Slaves: Ransoming Prisoners in Muslim West Africa*. She is also co-editor of *African Economic History*. She holds a Ph.D in African History from York University, Toronto. jal21@stmarys-ca.edu.

Mohamed Hassan Mohamed received his BA and MA in history from the Department of History, the University of Khartoum, Sudan (1984, 1988). He completed his Ph.D at the Department of History and Classics, the University of Alberta, Edmonton Canada (2004). Currently, he is an Associate Professor of African History at the University of Windsor, Windsor, Ontario, Canada. mmohamed@windsor.ca

Amy Niang is an Assistant Professor in International Relations at the University of the Witwatersrand in Johannesburg and a Visiting Research Fellow at the Princeton Institute for International and Regional Studies (PIIRS). Her research is a theoretical investigation into notions of sovereignty, order and community and an empirical and historical investigation in state and social processes in the West African region, particularly in the Sahel. amy.niang@wits.ac.za

Akachi Odoemene holds a PhD in African History from the University of Ibadan, Nigeria. His current research focuses on African Social and Cultural History, Urban History, Ethnic Studies, and Peace and Conflict Studies. He was an Oxford-Princeton Global Leaders Post-doctoral Fellow (2013-2015), a Hewlett Visiting Scholar at Brown University, Providence, USA (2012), and an African Humanities Program (AHP) Fellow of the American Council of Learned Societies (ACLS) in 2009. Dr. Odoemene is a Senior Lecturer in the Department of History and International Relations, Federal University, Otuoke, Nigeria. akaigolo@yahoo.com

Olatunji Ojo is Associate Professor of History at Brock University, Canada where he has taught since 2007. He is co-editor of this editor volume. He is also co-editor with Nadine Hunt *Slavery in Africa and the Caribbean: A History of Enslavement and Identity Since the 18th Century*(London: I. B. Tauris, 2012). He is currently writing about Yoruba Warfare, Economy and Identity in the Age of Empire. His research and teaching are in the fields of modern African economic and social history, slavery, African diaspora, and gender. His essays on these topics has appeared in numerous journals and book chapters.oojo@brocku.ca

Suzanne Schwarz is Professor of History at the University of Worcester, and an Honorary Fellow of the Wilberforce Institute for the study of Slavery and Emancipation at the University of Hull. Her recent publications include: Paul E. Lovejoy and Suzanne Schwarz, eds., *Slavery, Abolition and the Transition to Colonialism in Sierra Leone* (Trenton, NJ: Africa World Press, 2015) and Suzanne Schwarz *"A Just and Honourable Commerce:" Abolitionist Experimentation in Sierra Leone in the Late Eighteenth and Early Nineteenth Centuries,* The Hakluyt Society Annual Lecture 2013 (London: The Hakluyt Society, 2014). s.schwarz@worc.ac.uk

Gillian Weiss is an Associate Professor of History at Case Western Reserve University. A scholar of France and the Mediterranean world during the sixteenth, seventeenth and eighteenth centuries, she is the author of *Captives and Corsairs: France and Slavery in the Early Modern Mediterranean* (Stanford University Press, 2011), translated into French (Editions Anacharsis, 2014). She recently co-edited a special issue of *French History* with Megan Armstrong on "France and the Early Modern Mediterranean" and is currently writing a book about North African slaves in France during the reign of Louis XIV entitled *Slavery and the Sun King.* glw@case.edu

Awet T. Weldemichael is the Queen's National Scholar in African History at Queen's University, Kingston where he teaches history. He is currently researching the political economy of conflict in the greater Horn of Africa with a focus on Somalia and its adjoining waters in the western Indian Ocean region. awet.weldemichael@queensu.ca

Index

A

B

C

D

E

F

G

H

I

J

K

L

M

N

O

P

R

S

T